Phishing for Phools

Phishing for Phools

THE ECONOMICS OF
MANIPULATION AND DECEPTION

GEORGE A. AKERLOF

AND

ROBERT J. SHILLER

Princeton University Press • PRINCETON AND OXFORD

ISBN 978-0-691-16831-9

British Library Cataloging-in-Publication Data is available

This book has been composed in Adobe Galliard and Formata by Princeton Editorial Associates Inc., Scottsdale, Arizona

Printed on acid-free paper. ∞
Printed in the United States of America

10 9 8 7 6 5 4 3 2

CONTENTS

PREFACE   vii

INTRODUCTION   Expect to Be Manipulated: Phishing Equilibrium   1

PART ONE   *Unpaid Bills and Financial Crash*

CHAPTER ONE   Temptation Strews Our Path   15
CHAPTER TWO   Reputation Mining and Financial Crisis   23

PART TWO   *Phishing in Many Contexts*

CHAPTER THREE   Advertisers Discover How to Zoom In on Our Weak
   Spots   45
CHAPTER FOUR   Rip-offs Regarding Cars, Houses, and Credit Cards   60
CHAPTER FIVE   Phishing in Politics   72
CHAPTER SIX   Phood, Pharma, and Phishing   84
CHAPTER SEVEN   Innovation: The Good, the Bad, and the Ugly   96
CHAPTER EIGHT   Tobacco and Alcohol   103
CHAPTER NINE   Bankruptcy for Profit   117
CHAPTER TEN   Michael Milken Phishes with Junk Bonds as Bait   124
CHAPTER ELEVEN   The Resistance and Its Heroes   136

PART THREE   *Conclusion and Afterword*

CONCLUSION: EXAMPLES AND GENERAL LESSONS   New Story in America
   and Its Consequences   149
AFTERWORD   The Significance of Phishing Equilibrium   163

ACKNOWLEDGMENTS   175
NOTES   181
BIBLIOGRAPHY   233
INDEX   257

PREFACE

I t's "the economy, stupid!" said James Carville, campaign advisor to
presidential candidate Bill Clinton in 1992. He wanted to stick it to
President George H. W. Bush for an array of economic problems that
were tied to the economic recession that started during the Bush presidency. Well, we have a different, broader interpretation of Carville's
statement: that many of our problems come from the nature of the
economic system itself. If business people behave in the purely selfish
and self-serving way that economic theory assumes, our free-market
system tends to spawn manipulation and deception. The problem is
not that there are a lot of evil people. Most people play by the rules and
are just trying to make a good living. But, inevitably, the competitive
pressures for businessmen to practice deception and manipulation in
free markets lead us to buy, and to pay too much for, products that we
do not need; to work at jobs that give us little sense of purpose; and to
wonder why our lives have gone amiss.

We wrote this book as admirers of the free-market system, but hop-
ing to help people better find their way in it. The economic system is
filled with trickery, and everyone needs to know that. We all have to
navigate this system in order to maintain our dignity and integrity, and
we all have to find inspiration to go on despite craziness all around us.
We wrote this book for consumers, who need to be vigilant against a
multitude of tricks played on them. We wrote it for businesspeople,
who feel depressed at the cynicism of some of their colleagues and
trapped into following suit out of economic necessity. We wrote it for
government officials, who undertake the usually thankless task of regulating business. We wrote it for the volunteers, the philanthropists,
the opinion leaders, who work on the side of integrity. And we wrote
it for young people, looking ahead to a lifetime of work and wondering how they can find personal meaning in it. All these people will benefit from a study of phishing equilibrium—of economic forces that

build manipulation and deception into the system unless we take courageous steps to fight it. We also need stories of heroes, people who out of personal integrity (rather than for economic gain) have managed to keep deception in our economy down to livable levels. We will tell plenty of stories of these heroes.

Products of Free Markets

The late nineteenth century was a busy time for inventors: the automobile, the telephone, the bicycle, the electric light. But another invention of the time has received much less attention: the "slot machine." *Slot machine* in the beginning did not have its present-day connotation. The term referred to any sort of "vending machine": you deposited your coin in a slot; you got to open a box. By the 1890s slot machines were selling chewing gum, cigars and cigarettes, opera glasses, chocolate rolls in individual paper wrappers, even quick looks at the precursor-to-the-phone-book city directories—all manner of things. The basic innovation was a lock activated by the deposit of a coin.

But then a new use was discovered. It wasn't long before slot machines began to include gambling machines. A newspaper of the time dates the appearance of slot machines in this modern sense to 1893.[1] One of those early machines rewarded winners with fruit candy rather than money; it was not long before everybody ascribed special meaning to that rare coincidence: the appearance of three cherries.

Before the 1890s were over, a new kind of addiction, to gambling slot machines, had been born. In 1899 the *Los Angeles Times* reported, "In almost every saloon may be found from one to half a dozen of these machines, which are surrounded by a crowd of players from morning to night.... Once the habit is acquired it becomes almost a mania. Young men may be seen working these machines for hours at a time. They are sure to be the losers in the end."[2]

Then the regulators stepped in. Slot machines were ruining so many people's lives they had to be outlawed, or at least regulated, along with gambling more generally. They disappeared from public life, relegated almost entirely to the fringe: to special places designated as casinos, and to loosely regulated Nevada, where slot machines are widely to be found in supermarkets, gas stations, and airports; the average adult spends 4 percent of income on gambling, nine times the US national average.[3] But even in Nevada there are some limits: in 2010 the Nevada Gaming Control Board rejected a proposal to allow convenience store customers to take credit on a slot machine, rather than their usual change.[4]

With computerization, the slot machine has entered a new career. Following the title of the 2012 book by MIT's Natasha Schüll, the new machines are addictive by design.[5] Mollie, whom Schüll met at Gamblers Anonymous in Las Vegas, demonstrates the human side of this addiction. Mollie drew for Schüll a map that represents how she sees herself.[6] It shows her as a lonely stick figure, standing by a slot machine, surrounded—entrapped—by a circular road. That road connects six of the most important places in her life: the MGM Grand, where she works as a reservationist; three spots where she gambles[7]; the site of Gamblers Anonymous, where she tries to cure her gambling; and, finally, the site where she picks up medicine to fight her anxiety disorder. Mollie is fully aware of her problem: she does not go to the slots with an expectation of winning.[8] She knows she will lose. Rather, she is drawn by a compulsion. And when she gets there on her binges, she is solitary; the action is rapid and continuous. Mollie goes into what she calls "the zone." Press the red button. The lights and the show come on. She wins or loses. Press the red button one more time. And one more time. And one more time. Again. And again. And again … until the money is all gone. Mollie is not some outlier in Vegas. Ten years ago deaths due to cardiac arrest were an especially serious problem in the casinos. The emergency crews could not get through. Finally, the casinos created their own specially trained defibrillation teams. One surveillance video shows why such special training was necessary. In the video, as a squad from the casino defibrillates the heart arrest of a fellow player, the surrounding players play on, their trance unperturbed, even though the victim is literally at their feet.[9]

What Markets Do for Us

The history of the slot-machine-good/slot-machine-bad from the 1890s to the present illustrates our dual view of our market economy. Most fundamentally, we applaud markets. Free markets are products of peace and freedom, flourishing in stable times when people do not live in fear. But the same profit motive that produced those boxes that opened and gave us something we wanted has also produced slot machines with an addictive turn of the wheel that takes your money for the privilege. Almost all of this book will be figuratively about slot-machines-bad, rather than about slot-machines-good: because as reformers both of economic thought and of the economy we seek to change not what is right with the world, but rather what is wrong. But before we begin, we should reflect on what markets do for us.

To do so, it is useful to take a long perspective and return to that era of the late nineteenth/early twentieth century. In December 1900, in *The Ladies Home Journal* civil engineer John Elfreth Watkins Jr. participated in the sport of predicting what life would be like one hundred years hence. He predicted we would have "hot and cold air [coming] from spigots." We would have fast ships that would get us "to England in two days." "There will be airships," mainly used by the military, but sometimes for passengers and freight. "Grand opera will be telephoned to private homes and will sound as harmonious as though enjoyed from a theatre box."[10] The predictions go on.

Watkins described his predictions as seeming "strange, almost impossible"; but, remarkably, free markets, with their incentives to produce what people want, as long as a profit can be made, have made his predictions come true, and more.

However, free markets do not just deliver this cornucopia that people want. They also create an economic equilibrium that is highly suitable for economic enterprises that manipulate or distort our judgment, using business practices that are analogous to biological cancers that make their home in the normal equilibrium of the human body. The slot machine is a blunt example. It is no coincidence that before they were regulated and outlawed slot machines were so common that they were unavoidable. Insofar as we have any weakness in knowing what we really want, and also insofar as such a weakness can be profitably generated and primed, markets will seize the opportunity to take us in on those weaknesses. They will zoom in and take advantage of us. They will phish us for phools.

Of *Phish* and *Phool*

The word *phish*, according to the *Oxford English Dictionary*, was coined in 1996 as the Web was getting established. That dictionary defines *phish* as "To perpetrate a fraud on the Internet in order to glean personal information from individuals, esp. by impersonating a reputable company; to engage in online fraud by deceptively 'angling' for personal information."[11] We are creating a new, broader meaning for the word *phish* here. We take the computer definition as a metaphor. Rather than viewing phishing as illegal, we present a definition for something that is much more general and goes much further back in history. It is about getting people to do things that are in the interest of the phisherman, but not in the interest of the target. It is about angling, about dropping an artificial lure into the water and sitting and waiting as wary fish swim by, make an error, and get caught. There are so many phishers and they are so ingenious in the variety of their lures that, by the laws of probability, we all get caught sooner or later, however wary we may try to be. No one is exempt.

By our definition, a *phool* is someone who, for whatever reason, is successfully phished. There are two kinds of phool: psychological and informational. Psychological phools, in turn, come in two types. In one case, the emotions of a psychological phool override the dictates of his common sense. In the other case, cognitive biases, which are like optical illusions,[12] lead him to misinterpret reality, and he acts on the basis of that misinterpretation. Mollie is an example of an emotional phool, but not a cognitive phool. She was remarkably self-aware of her situation at the slots, but she could not help herself.

Information phools act on information that is intentionally crafted to mislead them. Enron stockholders are an example. The rise of Enron was based on the adoption of misleading (and then later, fraudulent) accounting. Its extraordinary profits were the result of its "mark-to-market" accounting, whereby future expected profits from an investment could be booked when the investment was made.[13] The more usual practice is to wait until the profits are actually realized. From 1995 to 2000 *Fortune* named Enron the country's Most Innovative Company.[14] *Fortune* was right; its editors just failed to understand the nature of the innovations.

Whether or not businessmen have good (or bad) morals is not the subject of this book, although sometimes both of these sides will appear. Instead, we see the basic problem as pressures for less than scrupulous behavior that is incentivized in competitive markets. They are terrific at incentivizing and rewarding businessmen heroes with innovative new products for which there is real need. However, unregulated free markets rarely reward a different kind of heroism, of those who restrain themselves from taking advantage of customers' psychological or informational weaknesses. Because of competitive pressures, managers who restrain themselves in this way tend to be replaced by others with fewer moral qualms. Civil society and social norms do place some brakes on such phishing; but in the resulting market equilibrium, if there is an opportunity to phish, even firms guided by those with real moral integrity will usually have to do so in order to compete and survive.

How Could We Know?

We anticipate that this book will be unpopular (to say the least) with those who think that people all but invariably make the best decisions for themselves. Who are Bob and George, they will ask, to say that individual people are not themselves—*always* and *invariably*—the best arbiters of the decisions that affect them? Like a great deal of economics, this argument makes sense in the abstract. But when we examine this question as it describes real people making real decisions (as we shall do throughout this book), we find that to a remarkable extent they are phished for phools: and, in consequence, they are making decisions that, applying just a bit of their own common sense, they would know are not to their benefit.

We do not have to be presumptuous to see that people are making such decisions. We know because we see people making decisions that NO ONE COULD POSSIBLY WANT. Henry David Thoreau remarked that "the mass of men lead lives of quiet desperation."[15] Remarkably, a century and a half later, in the United States, almost the richest country the world has ever known, too many lives are still led in quiet desperation. Just think about poor Mollie in Vegas.

NO-ONE-COULD-POSSIBLY-WANTs

Four broad areas indicate how widespread are the NO-ONE-COULD-POSSIBLY-WANTs, regarding personal financial security; the stability of the macroeconomy (the economy as a whole); our health; and the quality of government. In each of these four areas we shall see that phishing for phools has significant impact on our lives.

Personal Financial Insecurity. A fundamental fact of economic life has never made it into the economics textbooks. Most adults, even in rich countries, go to bed at night worried about how to pay the bills. Economists think that it is easy for people to spend according to a budget. But they forget that even if we are careful 99 percent of the time, the remaining 1 percent, when we act as if "money does not matter," can undo all that prior rectitude. And businesses are keenly aware of those 1-percent moments. They target the events in our lives when love (or other motivations) trumps our budgetary caution. For some, this is an annual Christmas potlatch. For others, it occurs at rites of passage: such as weddings (where the wedding mags assure brides that the "average wedding" costs almost one half of annual per capita GDP)[16]; funerals (where the parlor director carefully lays out the caskets to induce the choice, for example, of the Monaco "with Sea Mist polished finish, interior richly lined in 600 Aqua Supreme velvet, magnificently quilted and shirred")[17]; or births (where Babies "R" Us will give a "personal registry advisor").[18]

But rites of passage are not the only life punctuations where sticking to budget is presented as being mean. It is thus no coincidence that, as rich as we are in the United States, for example, relative to all previous history, most adults still go to bed worried about their bills. Producers have been just as inventive in getting us to feel we need what is produced as they have been in filling the needs that we really have. No one wants to go to bed at night worried about the bills. Yet most people do.[19]

One source of our angst about those bills comes from rip-offs: as consumers we are especially prone to pay too much when we step outside of our comfort zone to make the rare, expensive purchase.[20] In some 30 percent of home sales to new buyers, total—buyer plus seller—transaction costs, remarkably, are more than half of the down payment that the buyer puts into the deal.[21] Auto salesmen, as we shall see, have developed their own elaborate techniques to sell us more car than we really want; and also to get us to pay too much. Nobody wants to be ripped off. Yet we are, even in the most carefully considered purchases of our lives.

Financial and Macroeconomic Instability. Phishing for phools in financial markets is the leading cause of the financial crises that lead to the deepest recessions. Regarding financial crises, the now-famous phrase "This time is different" is simultaneously both true and false.[22] In the boom that precedes the crash, phishers convince buyers of the assets they have to sell that "this time is different." It is, for example: Swedish matches in the 1920s (Ivar Kreuger of Kreuger and Toll); the dot-coms in the 1990s; subprime mortgages in the 2000s (Angelo Mozilo of Countrywide). Yes, every time it *is* different: the stories are different; the entrepreneurs are different; their offerings are different. But, also, every time it is the same. There are the phishermen; there are the phools. And when the built-up stock of undiscovered phishes (called "the bezzle" by economist John Kenneth Galbraith[23]) gets discovered, asset prices crash. The investment managers who purchased the packages with the bad mortgages in the buildup to the 2008 crash could not possibly have wanted them. And then, painfully, when the phish was revealed, terrible side effects occurred: confidence was lost throughout the economy; stock prices halved; employed lost their jobs; and the unemployed could not find them. Long-term unemployment reached levels not seen since the Great Depression.

Ill Health. Even regarding health, which is probably the strongest need for those of us who are already well fed, well clothed, and adequately housed, the purveyors of medicines phish us for phools. Back in the 1880s, when Daniel Pinkham, off in New York, noticed that women there were greatly worried about kidney problems, he wrote home that they should be added to the list of ailments for which the family's Pinkham Pills would be a remedy.[24] Advice taken. Today the Pharmaceuticals can no longer just add a disease to a list. In the United States, they must run two gauntlets. They must obtain the approval of the Food and Drug Administration, which requires randomized controlled testing; they must also convince the doctors to prescribe their pills. But they also have more than a century of learning how to get past these barriers. Some drugs that successfully run both gauntlets are no more than marginally beneficial. Worse, a few are genuinely harmful, such as Vioxx (an anti-inflammatory like Aleve) and hormone replacement therapy. In its five-year career, from 1999 to 2004, Vioxx is estimated to have caused 26,000 to 56,000 cardiovascular deaths in the United States[25]; failure to notify women of suspicions about hormone replacement therapy, by doctors and Pharma, is estimated to have caused some 94,000 cases of breast cancer.[26] No one wants bad medicine.

The effects on health go far beyond bad medicine. Consider phood and its consequences. About 69 percent of American adults are overweight; and more than half of them (36 percent of Americans) are, furthermore, obese.[27] A cohort study of more than 120,000 gives a surprisingly precise picture.[28] The interviewees, who were mainly registered nurses, were followed up at four-year intervals, from the late 1970s through 2006. The average four-year gain was 3.35 pounds (translating into a twenty-year gain of 16.75 pounds). Statistical analysis associates the 3.35-pound gain with 1.69 pounds for potato chips, 1.28 pounds for potatoes (mainly French fries), and 1 pound for sugar-sweetened beverages. Figuratively, those nurses could not stop noshing on their potato chips (salt and fat) and French fries (fat and salt) or slurping their colas (sugar). They made those choices voluntarily. But beyond the nurses, and more generally, we know that Big Phood commissions scientific laboratories to calculate consumers' "bliss points" that maximize their craving for sugar, salt, and fat.[29] Yet no one wants to be obese.

Tobacco and alcohol are other health-related phishes. But there is a remarkable difference between the two. No one now thinks that it is smart to smoke. As he is writing this paragraph, George works in a large office building in Washington, HQ 1 (Headquarters 1) of the International Monetary Fund. There is a ban on smoking inside. But as he arrives in the morning, he passes a scattering of smokers outside. The smokers all pointedly avoid his gaze. Without a word spoken, they know that he is thinking that they are risking their lives: for a pleasure hardly worth it. As a result of this censure and self-censure, the fraction of smokers in the United States has fallen by more than half since the bad old days when people who should have known better were arguing that smoking really was good for your health:[30] it helped you lose weight.[31]

There is another legal drug, besides tobacco, that is quite possibly yet more deleterious; but it provokes far less censure. David Nutt and colleagues in the United Kingdom, and Jan van Amsterdam and Willem van den Brink in the Netherlands, convoked groups of experts to evaluate the relative harms of drugs in their respective countries.[32] Taking account of harm to others—rather than just harm to self—Nutt and his colleagues judged alcohol the worst of all; van Amsterdam and his associates viewed it as second to crack, but only by a slim margin.[33] We shall see later (from lifelong studies) that alcohol abuse is quite possibly the single greatest downer in American lives. Yet the bars and the restaurants and the airlines and our friends at parties all push us to have a drink, and then sometimes another, and another, ... There is little consideration that having another drink is a choice that is already all too easy. No one wants to be an alcoholic. Yet rather than dissuasions, there are persuasions.

Bad Government. Just as free markets work at least tolerably well under ideal conditions, so does democracy. But voters are busy with their own lives; it is thus all but impossible for them to know when a politician deviates from their true wishes regarding much legislation. And also just because we are human, we are prone to vote for the person who makes us the most comfortable. As a result, politics is vulnerable to the simplest phish, whereby politicians silently gather money from the Interests, and use that money to show that they are "just one of the folks." Our later chapter "Phishing in Politics" will describe a 2004 election campaign of Charles Grassley of Iowa, who at the time was the chair of the Senate Finance Committee, and who had gathered a multimillion-dollar war chest and showered the state with TV ads, in which he is just "one of us," back home, on his tractor lawnmower. There was nothing terribly unusual about the role of money in this campaign. On the contrary, we have chosen it because it is so typical. But (almost) no one wants a democracy where elections are bought in this way.

The Aim of *Phishing for Phools*

The plan for this book is to give a number of cases of phishing for phools that will illustrate how much it affects our lives: our activities, our thoughts, our goals, and the frustration of our goals. Some of the cases will involve everyday life, such as our cars, our food, our medicine, and the houses we buy and sell and live in. Others will be more systematic and technical, like the financial markets. But, above all, the examples we shall explore will have grave implications for social policy, including the role of government as a complement rather than a hindrance to free markets—since, just as our computers need protection against malware, so too we need protection against phishing for phools more broadly defined.

Expect to Be Manipulated: Phishing Equilibrium

The psychologists have taught us over the course of more than a century—in voices ranging in style and content from Sigmund Freud to Daniel Kahneman—that people frequently make decisions that are not in their best interest. Put bluntly, they do not do what is really good for them; they do not choose what they really want. Such bad decisions make it possible for them to be phished for phools. This truth is so basic that it is critical to the first story of the Bible, where the serpent beguiles innocent Eve to make a phoolish decision that she will instantly, and forever, regret.[1]

The fundamental concept of economics is quite different: it is the notion of market equilibrium.[2] For our explanation, we adapt the example of the checkout lane at the supermarket.[3] When we arrive at the checkout at the supermarket, it usually takes at least a moment to decide which line to choose. This decision entails some difficulty because the lines are—as an equilibrium—of almost the same length. This equilibrium occurs for the simple and natural reason that the arrivals at checkout are sequentially choosing the shortest line.

The principle of equilibrium, which we see in the checkout lanes, applies to the economy much more generally. As businesspeople choose what line of business to undertake—as well as where they expand, or contract, their existing business—they (like customers approaching checkout) pick off the best opportunities. This too creates an equilibrium. Any opportunities for unusual profits are quickly taken off the table, leading to a situation where such opportunities are hard to find. This principle, with the concept of equilibrium it entails, lies at the heart of economics.

The principle also applies to phishing for phools. That means that if we have some weakness or other—some way in which we can be phished for phools for more than the usual profit—in the phishing equilibrium someone will take advantage of it. Among all those business persons figuratively arriving at the checkout counter, looking around, and deciding where to spend their investment dollars, some will look to see if there are unusual profits from phishing us for phools. And if they see such an opportunity for profits, that will (again figuratively) be the "checkout lane" they choose.

And economies will have a phishing equilibrium in which every chance for profit more than the ordinary will be taken up. To practice our understanding, we will now turn to three "finger exercises" in the application of the concept of phishing equilibria.

Finger Exercise One: Cinnabon®

Consider an example of what we are driving at. Back in 1985, father and son Rich and Greg Komen of Seattle founded Cinnabon® Inc. with a marketing strategy. They would open outlets that baked on their premises the "world's best cinnamon roll."[4] Cinnamon's smell is an attraction to customers as a pheromone is for moths. The story is told how "numerous trips to Indonesia" were made "to acquire fine Makara cinnamon."[5] A Cinnabon® is made with margarine; it has 880 calories; and it is slathered with frosting. "Life Needs Frosting®" is the Cinnabon® Inc. motto. They carefully placed the outlets, with placards and mottos, in the track of people who would be vulnerable to that smell and to the story of the best cinnamon roll, with a little time on their hands in airports and shopping malls. Of course, the information about calories is there, but it isn't easy to find. Cinnabon® has been an explosive success, reflecting not only the delicious bun but also the Komens' strategy, replicated again and again. There are now more than 750 Cinnabon® bakeries in more than thirty countries.[6] Most of us probably take it for granted that there just happens to be such an outlet right where we are waiting for our delayed flight. We fail to appreciate how much effort and expertise went into understanding our weak moments and developing a strategy to take advantage of them.

Nor do most of us think of the presence of Cinnabon®, which undermines our plans to eat healthily, as the natural result of a free-market equilibrium. But it is: if Rich and Greg Komen hadn't done it, sooner or later someone else would have had a similar—although almost surely not identical—idea. The free-market system exploits our weaknesses automatically.

Finger Exercise Two: Health Clubs

Back in the spring of 2000, Stefano DellaVigna and Ulrike Malmendier were both graduate students at Harvard.[7] They were taking a special reading class in Psychology and Economics, down the Charles River, at MIT. They decided to find an example of the bad economic decision making that was the topic of this then-new field. They alighted on one they could find in their neighborhood: health clubs. Our main interest in health clubs is as an example of phishing for phools. But they are also of some interest for their own sake. In 2012, health clubs were a $22 billion industry in the United States, with more than 50 million customers.[8]

DellaVigna and Malmendier constructed a dataset of more than 7,500 health club users in the Boston area.[9] As budding jocks, when the customers were first at the health club, they were overoptimistic about their exercise plans; and they signed into contracts for which they overpaid. Typically, they would choose among three different methods of payment: by the visit; a contract to pay by credit card with automatic monthly rollover, unless cancelled; or by annual contract. Most (nonsubsidized) customers chose the monthly contract. But 80 percent of them would have paid less by the visit. Furthermore, the losses from this wrong choice were significant: $600 per year, out of average payments of $1,400.[10] Additionally, to add insult to injury, the health clubs put roadblocks in the way of cancellation. Of the 83 clubs offering automatic monthly renewal in the DellaVigna-Malmendier sample, all accepted cancellation by personal appearance; but only 7 would accept cancellation by phone. Only 54 would accept a letter; and, of these, 25 required it to be notarized.[11]

Of course the health clubs' offerings of these contracts in which people were "paying not to go to the gym"[12] were no coincidence. Since customers were willing to sign into contracts that were more profitable to provide than pay-per-visit, in phishing equilibrium we would expect them to be there. Otherwise there would have been unused opportunity for profit.

Finger Exercise Three: Monkey-on-the-Shoulder Tastes

The problems with a pure free-market equilibrium can be imagined better if we consider a metaphor for such a phishing equilibrium. Economist Keith Chen and psychologists Venkat Lakshminarayanan and Laurie Santos have succeeded in teaching capuchin monkeys how to use money to trade.[13] In a remarkable beginning for a free-market economy, the monkeys developed an appreciation for prices and expected payoffs; and they even exchanged sex for money.[14]

But let's, in our mind's eye, go way beyond the experiments already done. Suppose we opened the monkeys up to trading with humans quite generally. We would give a large population of capuchins substantial incomes and let them be customers of for-profit businesses run by humans, without regulatory safeguards. You can easily imagine that the free-market system, with its taste for profits, would supply whatever the monkeys choose to buy. We could expect an economic equilibrium, with concoctions appealing to strange capuchin tastes. This cornucopia would give the monkeys their choices; but those choices would be very different from what makes them happy. We already know, from Chen, Lakshminarayanan, and Santos, that they love Marshmallow Fluff–filled Fruit Roll-Ups.[15] Capuchins have limited ability to resist temptations. We have every expectation that they would become anxious, malnourished, exhausted, addicted, quarrelsome, and sickened.

We now come to the point of this thought experiment; we will see what it has to say about humans. Our view of the monkeys has analyzed their behavior as if they have two types of what economists call "tastes." The first type of "tastes" are what the capuchins would exercise if they made the decisions that are good for them. The second type of "tastes"—their Fruit Roll-Up tastes—are those they actually exercise. Humans are, no doubt, smarter than monkeys. But we can view our behavior in the same terms. We can imagine us humans, like the capuchins, as also having two different types of tastes. The first concept of "tastes" describes what is really good for us. But, as in the case of the capuchins, that is not always the basis for all of our decisions. The second concept of "tastes" are the tastes that determine how we really, actually make our choices. And those choices may not, in fact, be "good for us."

The distinction between the two types of tastes and the example of the capuchins gives us an instructive image: we can think about our economy as if we all have monkeys on our shoulders when we go shopping or when we make economic decisions. Those monkeys on our shoulders are in the form of the weaknesses that have been exploited by marketers for ages. Because of those weaknesses, many of our choices differ from what we "really want," or, alternatively stated, they differ from what is good for us. We are not generally aware of that monkey on our shoulder. So, in the absence of some curbs on markets, we reach an economic equilibrium where the monkeys on the shoulder are substantially calling the shots.

The Alleged Optimality of a Free-Market Equilibrium

There is a perhaps surprising result that, indisputably, lies at the very heart of economics. Back in 1776, the father of the field, Adam Smith, in *The Wealth of Nations,* wrote that, with free markets, as if "by an invisible hand ... [each person] *pursuing his own interest*" also promotes the general good.[16]

It took a bit more than a century for Smith's statement to be precisely understood. According to the modern version, commonly taught even in introductory economics, a competitive free-market equilibrium is "Pareto optimal."[17] That means that once such an economy is in equilibrium, it is impossible to improve the economic welfare of everyone. Any interference will make *someone* worse off. For graduate students, this conclusion is presented as a mathematical theorem of some elegance—elevating the notion of free-market optimality into a high scientific achievement.[18]

The theory, of course, recognizes some factors that might blemish such an equilibrium of free markets. These factors include economic activities of one person that directly affect another (called "externalities"); they also include bad distributions of income. Thus it is common for economists to believe that, those two blemishes aside, only a fool would interfere with the workings of free markets.[19] And, of course, economists have also long recognized that firms that are large in size may keep markets from being wholly competitive.

But that conclusion ignores the considerations that are central to this book. When there are completely free markets, there is not only freedom to choose; there is also freedom to phish. It will still be true, following Adam Smith, that the equilibrium will be optimal. But it will be an equilibrium that is optimal, not in terms of what we really want; but an equilibrium that is optimal, instead, in terms of our monkey-on-our-shoulder tastes. And that, for ourselves, as for the monkeys, will lead to manifold problems.

Standard economics has ignored this difference because most economists have thought that, for the most part, people do know what they want. That means that there is nothing much to be gained from examining the differences between what we really want and what those monkeys on our shoulders are, instead, telling us. But that ignores the field of psychology, which is, largely, about the effects of those monkeys.

As exceptions, behavioral economists, especially for the past forty years, have been studying the relationship between psychology and economics. That means that they have brought the consequences of the monkeys to center stage. But, curiously, to the best of our knowledge, they have never interpreted their results in the context of Adam Smith's fundamental idea regarding the invisible hand. Perhaps it was just too obvious. Only a child, or an idiot, would make an observation like that and expect anyone to notice. But we will see that this observation, simple as it may be, has real consequences. Especially so, because, as Adam Smith might say, as if by an invisible hand, others out of their own self-interest will satisfy those monkey-on-the-shoulder tastes.

Thus we may be making only a small tweak to the usual economics (by noticing the difference between optimality in terms of our real tastes and optimality in terms of our monkey-on-the-shoulder tastes). But that small tweak for economics makes a great difference to our lives. It's a major reason why just letting people be *Free to Choose*—which Milton and Rose Friedman, for example, consider the sine qua non of good public policy—leads to serious economic problems.[20]

Psychology and Monkeys on the Shoulder

Not all of psychology concerns the reasons why people make "dysfunctional" decisions. Some of it describes the working of the healthy human mind. But a great deal of the subject concerns decisions that give people what they think they want rather than what they really want. We see this by going back to an application of psychology as it was taught in the mid-twentieth century. The psychology of those days was largely based on Freud with special emphasis on his now experimentally validated conclusion regarding the role of the subconscious in decision making. Vance Packard described ways in which marketers and advertisers are *Hidden Persuaders* (which was the title of his 1957 book). That is, they manipulate us through our subconscious. In one example, which George and Bob both remember from more than fifty years ago, the makers of cake mixes appealed to housewives' desire for creativity by unnecessarily requiring the addition of an egg. Or, in another example, insurance companies played on desires for immortality through advertising that, curiously, portrayed the deceased father in after-death family pictures.[21]

Social psychologist/marketer Robert Cialdini has written a book full of impressive evidence of psychological biases.[22] According to his "list," we are phishable because we want to reciprocate gifts and favors; because we want to be nice to people we like; because we do not want to disobey authority; because we tend to follow others in deciding how to behave; because we want our decisions to be internally consistent; and because we are averse to taking losses.[23] Following Cialdini, each of these respective biases is paired with common salesman's tricks. One such example concerns how his brother, Richard, paid his way through college. Every week, Richard would purchase two or three cars from the advertisements in the local newspapers. He would clean them up and offer them for sale again. Here, Richard put "loss aversion" to work. Richard did not, as most of us would do, schedule his prospective buyers to come at different times. Instead, intentionally, he scheduled them with overlap. Each buyer, whatever the merits of the prospective car, was then apprehensive that he might lose out: that other guy might get *his* car.[24]

Information Phools

A great deal of phishing comes from another source: from supplying us with misleading, or erroneous, information. The phishermen in this guise play on what their customers think they will get. There are two ways to make money. The first is the honest way: give customers something they value at $1; produce it for less. But another way is to give customers false information or induce them to reach a false conclusion: so they think that what they are getting for $1 is worth that; even though it is actually worth less.

This book will be filled with many such examples, especially in the realm of finance. The finance optimists think that complicated financial transactions are about benignly dividing up risk and expected returns in the best possible way among people with different tastes for them, just as children used to trade marbles or baseball cards. People are smart, especially in finance, the mantra goes; the best way to police financial markets is to let them police themselves. As a notable example of the application of this mantra to public policy, the Commodity Futures Modernization Act of 2000 enabled extraordinarily complicated financial products to trade with only minimal supervision. The markets, it was said, would police themselves.

But just because we can say the mantra does not make it true. Another way to make money in finance is not to sell people what they really want. Remember the magician's trick: he puts a coin underneath one of three jars, swirls them around, and then opens them all up.[25] The coin is gone. But where is it? Voilà: it is in the hand of the magician. And that is what can also happen in the world of complicated finance. Figuratively, we buy a security that entitles us to whatever coin will appear when the cups are uncovered. But then in the swirl of complicated finance, somehow the coin is transferred to the magician's hand, so that when the cups are turned over, we get nothing. Later in the book we will present three chapters on financial manipulations. Each of these chapters will show many such tricks that can be considered as taking the coin from the swirling cups. More concretely, they entail maneuvers such as clever financial accounting and overly optimistic ratings. In this case people know what they want; but the clever manipulation of information suggests that they are getting what they want, when they are, on the contrary, getting something far different. Finally, we note that as long as there are profits to be made from such magicians' tricks, the magicians will be there. That is the nature of the economic equilibrium. And that is the basic reason why financial markets especially are in need of careful oversight. But we are getting a bit ahead of our story.

Theory and Practice

So far we have given the theory of phishing equilibrium and a few examples to illustrate it. That theory suggests that in real-life economic equilibrium there will be a lot of phishing for phools. The equilibrium occurs for the same reason that the lines in the supermarket seldom differ much in length: because the sequential customers are choosing what they consider to be the shortest line. Similarly, in competitive markets opportunities to make profits by phishing us for phools will be taken. We will now turn to the rest of the book, which will give example after example of how this general principle plays significant roles in our lives.

Where We Go from Here: Outline of *Phishing for Phools*

The book is divided into this introduction and three parts.

Introduction: Phishing Equilibrium. The major role of this introductory chapter has been to explain the concept of phishing equilibrium and the consequent inevitability of phishing. Returning to Cinnabon®, that inevitability means that in the absence of the Komens, someone else, among the world's billions, would have taken their place. Of course, what is true regarding the Komens also holds in every phishing equilibrium: if one person does not take up the opportunity for profit, it will be taken by someone else.

Part One: Unpaid Bills and Financial Crash. It is one thing for us (Bob and George) to create images about monkeys on our shoulders; to put *ph*'s rather than *f*'s on the beginning of words; and to talk abstractly about economic equilibrium. It is another to show that those *ph*'s and those equilibria play significant roles in our lives. The next two chapters, which constitute part one, make a first stab at hammering this home. Chapter 1 shows why most consumers end the month, or the week, worrying about how to pay their bills, and quite frequently fail to do so. We are all capable of making mistakes, and many of those mistakes are aided and abetted by those who are trying "to sell us something." Chapter 2 shows the role of phishing for phools in the Financial Crisis of 2008, with its devastating worldwide consequences. A good part of this story is what we call reputation mining on the part of many firms and advisors: the more-or-less-deliberate drawing down for profit of hard-won reputation for integrity. As of this writing we have not yet fully recovered from this crisis; and the same forces that led to this financial crisis are elements of our economic equilibrium. Those forces are hard to tame, and we must understand them, both to decrease the likelihood the crises will come again, and to handle them, if and when they do happen.

Part Two: Phishing in Many Contexts. Part two takes a new tack. It concerns the role of phishing for phools in specific contexts: advertising and marketing; real estate, car sales, and credit cards; lobbying and politics; food and drugs; innovation and economic growth; alcohol and tobacco; and two specific financial markets. We will give a separate outline of this section when we come to it.

Part two further reinforces the significance of phishing for phools in our lives. But there are other important lessons. The many examples throughout this book serve as practice exercises in the perception and understanding of phishing for phools. Part two will present new examples of phishing equilibria, and thus of the inevitability of the phish, as a consequence, not of evil people, but instead of the natural working of our economic system. Additionally, and perhaps most importantly, the experience we gain from these exercises regarding phishing for phools in different contexts leads us to a new perspective on the where and how of its practice. Beginning with the chapter on advertisers and marketers, whose duty is to lead us to buy what they are commissioned to promote, we will offer a new, more general view (beyond Cialdini's list and beyond current behavioral economics) regarding what makes people manipulable. People largely think by situating themselves within a story. A leading strategy of manipulation is to lead phools to graft new stories (advantageous to the phishermen) onto the old ones. (We add, parenthetically, that a major role of psychologists—literally from Freud to Kahneman—has been to elicit those stories that people are telling themselves. The psychologists have technical terms for them: such as "mental frames" or "scripts.")[26]

Part Three: Conclusion and Afterword. That takes us to the "conclusion." Parts one and two will have visited phishing for phools in settings ranging from the very general, such as consumer spending and financial markets, to the quite particular, such as congressional elections or the ways in which Big Pharma parries its regulators and phishes the doctors who prescribe its medicines. From these disparate examples, and from our theory of phishing, we will describe our new characterization, which gives us—and we hope will also give you—a new sense about economics: with an awareness of phishing for phools, and where and when it occurs. In the conclusion, "New Story in America and Its Consequences," we will see how this new perspective applies to current economic and social policy in the United States, with examples from three different areas of economic policy.

The afterword follows. It is written especially with regard to our potential critics, who we know will be asking if there is anything new in *Phishing for Phools*. This afterword presents our view of what, where, and how this book makes a contribution to economics.

We intend *Phishing for Phools* to be a very serious book. But we also intend it to be fun. We hope that you will enjoy the stories and the insights on the journey to conclusion and afterword, above and beyond any capital-M "Messages" entailed in appropriate appreciation of "phishing for phools."

PART ONE

Unpaid Bills and Financial Crash

ONE

Temptation Strews Our Path

Almost every American recognizes Suze (pronounced "Susie") Orman. When George asked an economist friend about her, he had the expected reaction. He had watched her TV show for only ten seconds. Our economist friends cannot stand her mommy-knows-best/I-told-you-to-do-that voice. They find her investment advice simplistic. Furthermore, curiously for economists, who tend to care about such things, they find her advice to be too much about money.

But that is the opposite of the reaction we got from one of the wisest people we know, Teodora Villagra, who was a cashier in the International Monetary Fund cafeteria. A refugee from Daniel Ortega's Nicaragua, she bought her own home on Capitol Hill; her son had just graduated debtless from college, with a degree in electrical engineering; most remarkably, she carried on to-be-continued-next-time conversations with hundreds of daily customers, as she also added up what they owed and counted their change. "Suze Orman is not about the money, she is about the people," Teodora told us. She had purchased a copy of a Suze Orman financial advice book for herself; what's more, she had given one to a fellow cashier.

Listening to Teodora and to Suze Orman herself leads us to appreciate what had been previously a puzzle to us: why Orman's audiences lap up her every word. Fitting together the pieces of this puzzle then in turn elucidates a major economic problem that affects billions, worldwide.

Suze Orman vs. Basic Economics

Orman's most popular book (more than three million sold) is *The 9 Steps to Financial Freedom: Practical and Spiritual Steps So You Can Stop*

Worrying.[1] Her portrait of consumer spending, and saving, is in stark contradiction to how economists think of it (and how it is described in the economics textbooks). The typical introductory economics textbook has us think of a trip to the supermarket. We have budgeted an amount of money to spend—unimaginatively—on apples and oranges. At different prices, with this budget, we can purchase different combinations of them, and we will buy the combination that makes us happiest. That, we are told, determines how many apples and how many oranges we will buy at each price; these correspondences between the price and the quantity the consumer wants to buy—we are further informed—are their "demand for apples" and their "demand for oranges."[2]

This intentionally pallid story is in no way as innocent as it seems. It is not science. But it is powerful rhetoric. The college freshmen, who are the target audience for the textbook, are being given a pronouncement; it will later be implied that not just the purchase of apples and oranges, but *all* economic decisions are made in this way: the decision maker has a budget (as in the fruits example for apples and oranges); she makes different choices dependent on the prices; and she makes the choice that yields her most preferred outcome. It is powerful rhetoric, because in the context of the fruit section of the supermarket, it is hard to imagine that anyone would behave differently.

The story is convincing for another reason. The freshman reading the textbook is unlikely to put up resistance because she cannot imagine how this parable about apples and oranges will be used with little further question in many different contexts in the remaining pages of the textbook, in her later courses of economics, or—yet further—in her graduate program if she becomes a professional economist. But the textbook rhetoric has gotten her to swallow something whole: this is how people think, quite generally, when they are making decisions. But do they? Almost surely they do in some contexts, such as in the fruit section of Safeway. But the example would have been much less powerful if, instead, it had pictured, for instance, a bride on the pages of *Wedding Magazine,* where budget and price would seem like secondary concerns, in preparation for the Most Important Day of Her Life. And that takes us back to Suze Orman, and not only to why she has those adoring audiences, but also why those audiences are much more than a whimsical example.

Suze's Advisees

How could consumers do anything other than what the textbooks describe? Orman tells us that people have emotional hang-ups with regard to money, and with regard to spending it. They are not honest with themselves; and, as a consequence, they do not engage in rational budgeting. How could she know? She is a financial advisor, and she has a test. She asks her new clients to add up their expenditures; and, when they do, those expenditures all but invariably fall short of what a documented accounting, from the records, later turns up.[3] Figuratively, relative to that proverbial trip to the supermarket, it's as if her advisees spend too much in the fruit section; by the time they reach dairy products, there is nothing left over for the eggs and milk. In real life, such budgetary failure translates into having nothing left over for savings, at the end of the month, after payments for current purchases. Yet worse, especially in times of crisis, it means the piggy bank is empty. In modern times, most likely that takes the form of adding to the credit-card bills, with their interest rates even now, in the middle of our long slump, being almost 12 percent.[4] They were even higher a few years ago.

This failure to deal cognitively and emotionally with money, says Orman, leads to those unpaid bills. It is her mission to keep those bills down, so that her readers and her clients will no longer *worry* at night. That is the role of mommy, and also why those audiences excuse that mommy-knows-best voice. It is worth noting, more than parenthetically, that *worries,* as noted in Orman's subtitle, are central concerns of the financial advice books, but you will have to search hard to find such a word, relating, as it does, people's finances and their emotions, in any economics textbook.

The Statistical Story

We do not need to take Orman's word for it; we can put together a statistical story, which indicates that a very significant fraction of consumers are worried about how they are going to make ends meet. A direct observation comes from economists Annamaria Lusardi and Peter Tufano, and sociologist Daniel Schneider. They asked the survey question, *"How confident are you that you could come up with*

$2,000 if an unexpected need arose within the next month?"[5] Almost 50 percent of their respondents, in the United States, replied either that they *could not,* or they *probably could not* come up with the needed $2,000. In a recent conversation, Lusardi emphasized further that the respondents were given a whole month to raise the money; that could be enough time to take out an equity mortgage on the house; get a new credit card; rustle up something from the parents, a brother, sister, friend, or cousin.

Statistics on consumer finances suggest why so many of Lusardi and her colleagues' respondents find it so difficult to obtain that $2,000. A recent economics article on "hand-to-mouth consumption" shows that in 2010 the median US working-age family held less than one month's income in cash, or in checking, savings, or money-market accounts; in addition, but not surprisingly, the median direct holdings of stocks or bonds was exactly zero.[6] A study using British diaries of spending gives another indication that many are just juggling the bills; for monthly earners, expenditures are down a full 18 percent in the last week of the monthly pay period, relative to expenditures in the first week after payday.[7]

We also know that a significant fraction of households do not make it. Some 30 percent of households say they have resorted to super-high-interest "alternative forms of borrowing" at least once over the past five years; those methods include, for example, use of pawn shops, auto-title loans, or short-term payday loans.[8] In 2009 a full 2.5 percent of householders reported they had gone bankrupt in the past two years (most of which had been pre-Crash).[9] That 2.5 percent may seem like a small, relatively innocuous number; nevertheless, it suggests that a quite significant fraction of the population will go bankrupt over the course of their lifetimes. No one knows the rate of repeat bankruptcy; but if, for example, those with one bankruptcy have two more over the course of their fifty-odd years of adulthood, then slightly more than 20 percent of the US population will go bankrupt in their adult life.[10]

Eviction is another way to not make it. A painstaking review of the court records for the city of Milwaukee by sociologist Matthew Desmond revealed similarly high statistics; the annual eviction rate from 2003 to 2007—a period totally before the financial crash—was 2.7 percent.[11] Such numbers for bankruptcy and eviction are just the tip of the iceberg indicating a much larger, statistically hidden condition of free markets. Even in the current United States, where the vast majority of the population has a level of consumption unparalleled in human history, most people worry about how to make the ends meet. Some even go over the edge: into bankruptcy; or eviction.

Another Perspective

Another assay poses for us the Suze Orman puzzle in a different perspective. Most of us think that if our income went up more than fivefold we would be on easy street. Our financial problems would be over. Indeed, that is exactly what John Maynard Keynes, one of the most astute economists of all time, thought would be the case when he looked forward from 1930. In an essay, which was little noticed when published, Keynes projected what life would be like "for our grandchildren," in 2030: one hundred years thence.[12] In one respect he almost hit a bull's-eye. He "supposed" that the standard of living would be eight times higher. For the United States, as of 2010, real income per capita was 5.6 times higher.[13] With another twenty years to go on Keynes's stopwatch, and with annual growth in per capita income at its historic average between 1.5 percent and 2 percent, his supposition will be remarkably close to target.

But in another respect, Keynes was totally off the mark. As you might expect, Keynes did not say that the grandchildren would be going to bed worried about their next pound or their next shilling. Instead, he said they would be worrying about how to use their surfeit of leisure. The workweek would fall to fifteen hours.[14] Men and women alike, Keynes said, would "experience ... a nervous breakdown of the sort which is already common in England and the United States amongst the wives of the well-to-do classes, unfortunate women, many of them, who have been deprived by their wealth of their traditional tasks and occupations—who cannot find it sufficiently amusing, when deprived of the spur of economic necessity, to cook and clean and mend, yet are quite unable to find anything more amusing."[15] (We add parenthetically that this statement may now seem politically incorrect; but it also presaged the "problem without a name" that is the centerpiece of *The Feminine Mystique,* which jump-started the women's movement some thirty years later.) Such abundance of leisure—despite incomes that have so far risen more than fivefold in the United States—has hardly come to pass. On the contrary, the housewife of our experience, exhausted from the first and the second shift, was way outside Keynes's prediction.[16]

Keynes's prediction may be remarkable for its inaccuracy; but it reflects how almost all economists (but not Suze Orman) think about consumption and leisure. And there is another prediction that also comes from that way of thinking that is equally invalid. People would not just have more leisure; they would be laying away a significant fraction of those earnings into savings so that their bills could be paid easily at the end of the month. But as we have seen, that too has not come to pass.

The Reason

The reason for the exhausted housewife and the lack of savings comes from the central prediction of this book. Free markets do not just produce what we really want; they also produce what we want according to our monkey-on-the-shoulder tastes. Free markets are also about producing those wants, so we will buy what they have to sell. In the United States the goal of almost every business person (with the exception of some who sell stocks and bonds and bank accounts, which we will discuss later) is to get you to spend your money. Free markets produce continual temptation. Life is a proverbial trip to a parking lot in which you are constantly passing spaces left open for the disabled.

Just walk down a city street. The shop windows are literally there to entice you to come in and buy. Back in the old days, when both Bob and George were younger, neighborhood shopping streets would typically have a pet store, with squirming puppies in the window. There was even a well-known song about it, from a young woman who was passing by:

> How much is that doggie in the window? (arf, arf)
> The one with the waggley tail.
> How much is that doggie in the window? (arf, arf)
> I do hope that doggie's for sale.[17]

Those puppies were, of course, no coincidence. They were there to entice you to come in and buy. But, more generally, that "doggie in the window" is a metaphor for all of free-market activity. That "waggley tail" is everywhere we go. At the shopping mall; in the supermarket; at the auto dealer; when house-hunting: temptation is laid out for us. Just to give one example, the eggs and the milk are strategically in the back of the supermarket; they are the most common purchase; and, figuratively, you have to go through the whole store to get them, being reminded of the other needs that you might have forgotten.[18] And when you get back to the checkout counter—waiting there—it is no coincidence that the candy and the magazines are there for you (and the kids). In the old days that used to be the home of the cigarettes: a helpful reminder for those who smoked.

This is the phish for candy and cigarettes. There are thousands more phishes in the supermarket, embodied in all the different products on the shelves, each with its own team of marketing experts and advertising campaigns, each the product of experimentation with many other possible marketing forms. And the phishing goes on beyond the supermarket, to almost everything one buys. Elizabeth Warren has emphasized the credit card.[19] Credit cards are tempting, and we will devote part of a later chapter to that. We agree. But the idea of tempting the consumer to buy, to spend her money, is in the very nature of free markets themselves. It goes beyond the credit card. The salesman does not get paid to be his brother's keeper, or to see that the shopper's purchases of apples and oranges leave enough to pay the bills at the end of the month. And, as Suze Orman knows best, it takes a great deal of self-control—an inner voice saying constantly: do not do this; do not do that; you need to keep the budget within balance.

That gives good reason why Keynes's prediction has proved so wrong. We are five and a half times richer than we were back in 1930. But free markets have also invented many more "needs" for us, and, also, new ways to sell us on those "needs." All these enticements explain why it is so hard for consumers to make ends meet. Most of us have better sense than to go in and buy the doggie, at least on a whim. But not all of us can be so rational—all of the time—when the streets and the supermarket aisles, and the malls, and now the Internet, are full to the brim with temptations.

Some say that our predicament is a product of the consumerism of the modern world. They would say that we are too materialistic; we have gone to the devil spiritually. But to our minds, the central problem lies in the equilibrium. The free-market equilibrium generates a supply of phishes for any human weakness. Our real per capita GDP can go up five-and-a-half-fold again, and then do it again; we will still be in the same predicament.

TWO

Reputation Mining and Financial Crisis

The story of the 2008–9 world financial crisis has been written and rewritten hundreds, if not thousands, of times. Much of this reporting takes the form of books focusing on one firm or government agency—be it J. P. Morgan Chase, Goldman Sachs, Bear Stearns, Lehman Brothers, Bank of America, Merrill Lynch, the Federal Reserve, the Treasury, or Fannie Mae and Freddie Mac—with the implicit message that "my institution" was at the heart of the crisis.[1] A silver lining of the financial crisis is the golden age of financial journalism that it spawned. But rather than give the detail of what happened in the usual five hundred pages, this chapter has a different aim. We will put it in a nutshell: we will discuss the central role of a kind of phishing that we call Reputation Mining.

Mediocre (and Perhaps Rotten) Avocados

If I have a reputation for selling beautiful, ripe avocados, I have an opportunity. I can sell you a mediocre avocado at the price you would pay for the perfect ripe one. I will have mined my reputation. I will also have phished you for a phool.

Such a story—although about a lot more than the purchase of an avocado—lies at the heart of the continuing financial crisis that dominates the economics of our times. The reputation mining in question involved the reputations of a variety of our financial institutions, and, notably among them, the subversion of the system for rating fixed-income securities. The reputations of the great US credit ratings agencies had been built up over the course of almost a century in rating bonds. The public used these ratings as an indicator of the likelihood of default. In the late 1990s and early 2000s, the ratings agencies took on themselves a new task: not just of rating bonds, but also of rating more complex securities, the new (complex) financial derivatives. Going back to our analogy, these were a new form of avocado. Because they were new, and especially because they were complex, it was hard for buyers to know whether they were being rated correctly. But since the ratings agencies had proved trustworthy in the past with the old avocados (the simpler old securities), buyers saw no reason not to trust them further, regarding their ratings of the new complex securities.

But the avocado-buying (security-buying) public failed to understand phishing equilibrium. If they could not themselves tell apart the good avocados (securities) from the mediocre, and in some cases, truly rotten, the new-avocado growers (the financial producers of the new securities) had little incentive to produce good new avocados. They could, more cheaply, produce bad new avocados (complex derivative packages backed with securities with high chances of default), and take them to the ratings agencies, which would mine their reputations by rating them AAA. In parable, regarding avocados—and in reality, regarding mortgage-based asset-backed securities—that is what happened.

Not only did it happen, it is just what we would expect in a phishing equilibrium, in which a grower of delicious avocados would be unable to compete. He would have to sell *his* perfect avocados at the price of the overrated mediocre ones. If the costs for producing perfect ones were greater than the costs for producing mediocre ones, his orchard could be put to more profitable use. He could allow himself to be bought out by a mediocre-avocado producer; or he would go bankrupt. The economist Carl Shapiro described this kind of equilibrium in 1982, and argued that such an equilibrium makes relatively mediocre products ubiquitous in a free market.[2] And on rare occasions, as preceded the financial crisis, truly rotten products are sold.

We might ask why the growing and false-rating of the new avocados (the new overrated securities) would cause a general financial crisis. Again the answer is elementary. Large financial institutions—commercial banks, hedge funds, investment banks, and the like—borrowed: indeed, the investment banks typically were borrowing more than 95 percent of their total assets, some of which included the new avocados (the complex mortgage-based derivatives).[3] But then when it was discovered, as inevitably it would be, that some of the new avocados were really rotten on the inside, they fell massively in value. It also became clear that these financial institutions owed much more than the value of their assets. And that is exactly what happened from Frankfurt to London to New York, and even in tiny Reykjavik, in 2008 (except of course the fall was in the value of the derivative mortgage-based securities rather than avocados). Emergency loans by the Federal Reserve and by the European Central Bank, accompanied by massive fiscal support for "troubled assets" in the United States and Europe, averted worldwide financial collapse and reenactment of the Great Depression.[4]

Phishing for phools played a critical role in this financial bubble and bust. Without due suspicion, the tragedy of 2008 was inevitable; just as, if we were in denial regarding phishing on our computer, we would in due course suffer the consequences.

Seven Questions

We will now turn to the story of what happened in some detail. But our preamble tells us to look for the answers to seven questions.

1. Why, initially, back in the 1950s, 1960s, and 1970s, were the investment banks trustworthy in underwriting correctly rated securities ("avocados")?

2. Why were the ratings agencies, at that time, rating those "avocados" correctly?

3. How did incentives at the investment banks change, so that trust was no longer the foundation of their business?

4. How were the changed incentives passed down the line to the ratings agencies, so they gave false ratings?

5. Why was the reputation mining so profitable?

6. Why were the buyers of the rotten securities ("avocados") so gullible?

7. Why was the financial system so vulnerable to the discovery that the securities ("avocados") were rotten?

Why Were the Investment Banks Initially Trustworthy?

The institutions that produce securities, in the United States and in the world economy, changed between 1970 and 2005. If an investment banker had gone into a coma in 1970, and had miraculously revived in 2005, he would have been surprised. The system had changed. He would have seen the institution he worked for increase massively in size. If his investment bank had been Goldman Sachs—which we will use repeatedly as an example—its capital would have increased more than five-hundred-fold. In 1970 the Goldman partnership had $50 million[5]; in 2005, its capital was more than $28 billion (with total assets of more than $700 billion).[6] In contrast, GDP (in similar inflation-unadjusted dollars) over that same period increased only twelvefold.[7]

If we revisit that seemingly simpler time, we will see a different world—in which investment banking was different. It was an era in which the investment banks had strong incentives to see that securities were rated correctly. Back in 1970 the typical investment bank—Goldman Sachs, Lehman Brothers, whatever—would have been "The Banker" for large enterprises. Its role was to give advice to *its* companies. The representative at the Bank knew the ways of Wall Street and his job was to inform his customers about the financial facts of life. He was one's "Trusted Friend": figuratively, and sometimes even literally, the now-on-Wall-Street high school/college buddy of the corporate finance officer. He would give savvy advice, on matters of gravitas such as how to jigger finances to evade the Internal Revenue Service or how to circumvent the regulators.

For himself, Trusted Friend was patient but not wholly undemanding. As reward, he would expect to be named underwriter to initiate issuances of stocks or bonds. The initial public offering for Ford Motor Company by Goldman Sachs in 1956, after the death of Henry Ford, illustrates.[8] The IPO (Initial Public Offering) was a complex affair—for tax reasons, and also because of the need to broker the interests of the Ford family and the Ford Foundation. The family had all of the voting rights but few of the shares; the Foundation had none of the voting rights but most of the shares.[9] Goldman Sachs senior partner Sidney Weinberg devoted two years to working out the details for a stingy personal fee of $250,000.[10] But then Goldman-the-Partnership was generously rewarded: it landed the Ford IPO deal.

In the late 1970s, co–senior partner John Whitehead had a premonition that, as it grew, Goldman Sachs would lose its Trusted-Friend ethics. He coined the fourteen principles of the partnership, intended as a future guide. Principle 1 begins: "Our clients' interests always come first." It continues—explaining why there is "really" no conflict of interest: "[since] our experience shows that if we serve our clients well, our own success will follow."[11] The Ford IPO illustrates how such success would occur. Portentously, as Whitehead had feared, these principles now seem to be the symbols of a bygone world, rather than his desired road map for the future.

Reputation for an investment bank of the time was important to attract clients. It also played another role, in relationships with other investment banks. When a bond or a stock was initiated, its sale would be shared (or "syndicated") with other investment banks. Such cooperation was necessary, as the lead banks needed the retail networks of the other members of the syndicate.[12] As in the Trusted Friend–customer relation, this was again I-scratch-your-back/you-scratch-mine. This was the era of "relational banking," where trust was essential.

Why Were the Ratings Agencies, at That Time, Rating Those "Avocados" Correctly?

In this simpler era not only did the investment banks have an incentive to produce good securities, the ratings agencies also had incentives to rate them correctly. The ratings agencies—the history of Moody's is especially clear-cut—had historically avoided any conflict of interest. Moody's lived off its book sales and other small fees. It was poor but scrupulous.[13]

At the time, as we have seen, reputation was all-important to the large underwriters. An incident, again from Goldman Sachs, illustrates why this was so. In 1969 Goldman underwrote an $87-million issue of Penn Central bonds.[14] Within a year Penn Central went bust. All of the assets of the partnership were potentially threatened. Lawsuits claimed that Goldman's had inside information of the fragility of the railroad that it had not disclosed. But Goldman argued that they knew of the operating losses of the railroad itself, but they also thought that these losses could be more than amply covered by Penn Central's rich real estate holdings. Goldman got off relatively easy with payments of less than thirty million dollars; but, if a little less lucky, all partnership assets would have been swallowed up.[15] This episode was a reminder to every investment bank that its business had to be squeaky clean. And that included its relations with the ratings agencies.

How Did Incentives at the Investment Banks Change, So That Trust Was No Longer the Foundation of Their Business?

But then the system changed: for the investment banks, and, as we will see in the next section, also for the ratings agencies. This is what the Banker would have seen on his 2005 reawakening. Goldman again serves as an example. Back in 1970 all of the capital of the enterprise belonged to partners. In 1999 Goldman had gone public. No longer did most partners have to tremble at the thought of a lawsuit that would make them liable for most of their personal fortunes.[16] Whereas in the old days Goldman had been overwhelmingly about the underwriting, now it was into many, many different businesses, from trading on its own account (in a trading room the size of a football field), to managing hedge funds, to creating and packaging new complex derivative securities. It was no longer the firm centered in a cramped office building at 20 Broad Street notable for its turret trading desk with 1,920 private telephone lines to its traders.[17] It had expanded worldwide: not only to have offices in New York, London, and Tokyo; in due course it would include such financial hot spots as Bangalore, Doha, Shanghai, and even tiny Princeton, New Jersey.[18] All of this is symbolized by its "sleek" new headquarters, opened in 2009:[19] forty-three stories in height; two city blocks in length; and described by architecture critic Paul Goldberger as an "understated palazzo." Goldman Sachs has become an empire.[20]

Financially, Goldman's, like the other investment banks, is now a "shadow bank." A good share of its liabilities is rolled over every night. It takes in "deposits" from large investors with large amounts of liquid assets looking for a haven. Those investors might be commercial banks, money market funds, hedge funds, pension funds, insurance companies, or other large corporations. Every night they give (we might say "deposit") literally billions of dollars, with the investment banks' promise to repay the very next day. This arrangement is known as buying and selling "repos" (repurchase agreements). The depositor is doubly protected. Not only can it claim its money back the very next day, but if Goldman's should fail, it need hardly skip a heartbeat. Why? Because the repos are backed by collateral, which are designated assets worth approximately the value of the deposit. In the event of failure, if the investor cannot collect the deposit, it will simply pocket the collateral instead.

This new arrangement, common to the investment banks, takes place because the holders of large deposits are wary of depositing their money in a regular commercial bank. They are afraid of large losses in case the bank fails.[21] The IndyMac Bank of Pasadena, California, illustrates the reason for such fears. When it was shuttered in July 2008, depositors with less than the $100,000 Federal Deposit Insurance Corporation (FDIC) guarantee were made whole. But any excess above that $100,000 was at risk, with the FDIC initially promising only 50 percent.[22] Consequently, it is safer for large holders of liquid assets to leave their money overnight with large investment banks, knowing that in the event of failure they can just take possession of the collateral.

There is an additional reason for investment banks' taking in such overnight deposits. Again, the history of Goldman's illustrates. In the late 1970s it was just beginning to discover the large profits that could be made from borrowing money and then trading on its own account. An investment bank, like Goldman's, was a hub for the country's, and later the world's, financial dealings. The swirl of Wall Street gave it an advantage. Not only did it automatically harvest the information that was more or less publicly available; it also could interpret what that information meant. Nothing contrary to the Insider Trading Laws needed to be spoken for much to be understood. The savvy teenager has a sixth sense regarding when to offer, or to accept, that first kiss.

To continue with Goldman as example, in the late 1960s/early 1970s, Gus Levy, who would in due course succeed Sidney Weinberg as senior partner, saw that large profits could be made as intermediary in the trade of large blocks of stocks by institutional investors.[23] As "Banker" for many of them, Goldman could identify a potential trader of a large block on one side; with its connections, it could then hunt out another institution to trade in the opposite direction. It would temporarily hold these large asset blocks in anticipation of the later resale. In this way it was beginning to trade on its own account. But playing the middleman in this way also opened up a potential conflict of interest: as the middleman in such deals, how much should Goldman keep for itself? What price should the buyer pay, what price should the seller take, when the difference between the two would accrue to Goldman's?

It was precisely John Whitehead's unease with such potential conflict of interest that pushed him to enunciate those "principles." He was fearful that Goldman would lose the ethic of serving the customer that had, with a few exceptions, informed it ever since Marcus Goldman had first set out his shingle in 1869. Marcus would give money to Jewish jewelry and leather merchants in lower Manhattan, in return for promissory notes for repayment, with some interest added. He would place these notes in the brim of his hat, and trade them at a small profit to respectable bankers, who bought those notes knowing that they could trust him to watch out for their interest.[24]

But in the 2000s, the ethic of "placing the client's interest first" can no longer be taken for granted. William Cohan's *Money and Power* quotes a hedge fund manager's view of Goldman's current practice: "[Goldman's question would be] Door 1 or Door 2—which has the highest present value for me? You wouldn't want to be in the door with the lower dollar sign."[25] That does not describe the old Goldman as Trusted Friend, putting the client first, with financial advice given in return for the occasional award of an underwriting job.

How Were the Changed Incentives Passed Down the Line to the Ratings Agencies?

But not only have the investment banks changed since that previous time of Banker as Friend. So has the relationship between the investment banks and the ratings agencies. In the boom leading to the financial crisis the ratings agencies had incentives to give the rating that was desired by the respective issuer of each new security, which was not necessarily the rating that was justified. The change initially occurred back in the 1970s, when for the first time Moody's began charging the investment banks for doing the ratings.[26] This toe in the water was hardly noticeable at the time: back then, as we have seen, in that era of relational banking, Banker as Friend depended above all on his reputation; he wanted the ratings on his issues to be totally scrupulous.

But since that time the incentives have changed. With the current attitude toward customers now as "Door 1 or Door 2," those who come to have their securities issued now return the compliment. That's the way competitive markets work. And what do such customers want out of a deal? They especially want a high rating for their issues; those ratings, of course, determine the interest they will later have to pay. And such a high rating is then what the investment banks now have to provide; otherwise their "customers" will take their business elsewhere. In turn the banks put pressure on the ratings agencies. Again, in the spirit of that first kiss, little needs to be spoken— probably nothing at all—for the ratings agencies to understand the needs and desires of the investment banks, who pay their bills. They now know: give a low rating; there will be no more deals. (This of course is doubly true where the investment bank, as is now often the case, is itself both the creator *and* the issuer of the security.)[27]

Thus there has been a reversal of fortune. No longer are the investment banks the overseers of the ratings agencies, looking over the agencies' shoulders to see that they make their ratings with due diligence. On the contrary, those investment banks, deal by deal, are looking for the highest ratings possible for whatever issue they are currently pushing. And the ratings agencies know the consequences if they fail to oblige.

Why Was the Reputation Mining So Profitable?

Here we see a bit of the true magic of complex financial structures. Part of the magic is real; but part is deceptive, and aids in phishing. Before modern financial derivatives, corporations would typically slice up the returns to the firm between payments to the bondholders and the payments to stockholders (which might be kept in the firm as "retained earnings"). Bondholders were promised fixed payments; stockholders got the profits that were left over. But modern finance discovered that the returns, with the different risks, could be divided in many, many different ways. Such new divisions would be useful if they neatly divide the returns between those (like bondholders) who want low risk and those (like stockholders) who are willing to assume higher risk. But this slicing can also be abused, since it can also be used to confuse investors. Suppose that a bank or an investment bank, or whatever, could take a bunch of rotten assets and package them in such a complicated way that the ratings agency would mistakenly rate most of them highly. Then those rotten assets would be turned into gold. The magician's equipment would be the packaging. The ratings agencies' focus on the wrong thing at the wrong time would be the reason the magician could be so successful.

And that is exactly what we have seen. We saw it in spades in the subprime loan market. In the Banker's previous incarnation, mortgages had been mainly initiated by banks. Being the local experts who could evaluate them best, once the loans were made, they would eat what they had cooked: the mortgages would go into their own asset portfolio. But then it was discovered—correctly so—that the risks from holding loans in one area alone could be hedged. Mortgages could be pooled together into vast packages. And shares in this package could then be sold. The risks would then be spread more widely. The banks in Delaware would no longer hold only mortgages made at home in Delaware, just as the banks in Idaho would no longer hold only the mortgages made at home in Idaho; instead each could hold a package of mortgages divided between Idaho and Delaware (or more generally, all banks could hold packages made up of mortgages from all over). Now the banks that originated the loans would no longer hold them for themselves, but they would pocket the origination fees and sell them into mortgage packages. Those packages were the modern descendant of the brim of Marcus Goldman's hat, as he sold off the promissory notes he originated to others.

But the gains from risk sharing were only the beginning of the profits that could be made from such large mortgage packages. If the package could be wrapped up so neatly and so beautifully that the ratings agencies would not notice, then even the origination of mortgages taken out by a NINJA homeowner—No Income, No Job or Assets—could be profitable. How did the bankers make the package pretty? How did they hide the bad loans? They did a financial magic trick that allowed the ratings agencies to divert their eyes from where those bad loans might be. Instead of selling the packages of securities directly, they sold the packages in different slices. Buyers of different slices—or "tranches," as they were called—would get different parts of the earnings. Those slices might be very complicated; but to give a simple example, one tranche might be the interest payments of the package of mortgages; while another tranche might be the repayments of principal. But that example just gives the flavor of very complicated transactions. Just as a child with scissors can cut a colored paper into an infinite number of shapes and sizes, the payments from mortgage packages could similarly be cut in any number of ways. And those shapes and pieces could be sold off as separate packages themselves.

By this time, now many steps from the original mortgages, the securities—these so-called mortgage-backed tranches—were very difficult, if not impossible, to inspect. The mortgages were in vast packages; the returns from them had been sliced in complicated ways; and the payments to be received were also steps away from the monthly payments by the homeowners who had taken out the mortgages. These complications gave the ratings agencies excuse to forgo adequate inspection of the underlying mortgages.[28]

Modern statistical techniques, taught as standard fare in business schools, gave further excuse. Statistical estimates of default rates could be based on past mortgage defaults, based on the historical records. The high ratings on the mortgage-backed securities made mortgages much more available, and in turn this led to unprecedented increases in house prices. With such house price increases, and also with high overall employment, mortgage defaults were at record lows.[29]

It did not matter that the statistical data series used to estimate default risk only encompassed periods when house prices had been rising, so that mortgage default was a rarity. Nor did it matter that these "financial products," as they were called, had been manufactured to have the illusion of a low chance of default. Nor did it matter that, indeed, the false ratings, for a time, themselves were a major factor in the rise of house prices, because they contributed significantly to the demand for houses. It did not matter because the incentives for the ratings agencies were no longer mainly to produce the proper ratings. Those incentives were to produce ratings that the underwriters wanted to buy. The business was in mining their previous reputation. They were in the business of phishing for phools.

How do we know such ratings inflation occurred? One ratings agency alone, Moody's, gave 45,000 mortgage-related securities a triple-A rating (for the period 2000 to 2007); that generosity for the mortgage-backed securities contrasts with only six US companies that were similarly rated AAA (in the later year 2010).[30] The ratings inflation was also confirmed by a surprisingly candid statement from a managing director of Moody's. He was speaking after a "town-hall" meeting of his employees in the wake of the crisis. "Why didn't we envision that credit would tighten after being loose, and housing prices would fall after rising? ... Combined, these errors make us look either incompetent at credit analysis, or like we sold our soul to the devil for revenue, or a little bit of both."[31]

Why Were the Buyers of the Rotten Securities ("Avocados") So Gullible?

Americans, and also the wider world, blissfully, had no reason to be suspicious. They had been told of the wonders of free markets. They were unaware of phishing for phools and its consequences. Only later would it be realized that the derivative packages contained rotten avocados. But, as we have also emphasized, there was no incentive either for the magician creators of the packages or for the raters of the packages to see through the magic trick. There is a bias toward seeing what is in our interest; a bias against seeing what is against it. The originator of the packages, typically an investment bank, was rewarded by high ratings on its offerings. And the ratings agency, in turn, would be shunned if it did not give the investment bank what it wanted. It was in the interest of neither the investment banks nor the ratings agencies to go back and do that extremely difficult—and perhaps even impossible—task of opening up the packages and carefully examining their innards.

For those who did manage to disentangle what was really going on, such as the handful of extremely astute, but also extremely peculiar individuals who are the protagonists of Michael Lewis's *Big Short*, there were huge potential profits to be made by selling short on the mortgage-backed packages (that is, making financial bets that those packages would decline in value).[32] But what was inside the packages was being intentionally hidden from view. The tranche securities could thus be tied up with fancy ratings. Lewis's short sellers were outlier exceptions; they were not the rule.

Let's go back to Goldman's. Surprisingly late in the game, in the summer of 2006, a clever finance graduate in mortgage-securities trading, Josh Birnbaum, saw the magic trick and understood the vulnerability for Goldman Sachs.[33] He was early in perceiving the rising default rates, and he was also privy to models with the detail necessary for understanding the mortgage default risks. Birnbaum convinced his superiors, all the way to the very top, of the merit of his arguments; and Goldman remarkably quickly reversed its portfolio, going from long to short on mortgage-backed securities—saving it billions of dollars. By the end of October 2009, the profits by Birnbaum's market group, which was shorting the market, were $3.7 billion.[34] This more than offset the $2.4 billion of mortgage losses in the rest of the company. The next year, when Birnbaum received compensation reputedly of something like $10 million, he quit Goldman. "I guess it depends on your perspective of what's fair, right?" He explained: "If you're a steelworker you probably think I got paid pretty well. If you're a hedge fund–manager you probably don't."[35]

Why Was the Financial System So Vulnerable to the Discovery That the Securities ("Avocados") Were Rotten?

The financial system itself was, and remains, immensely vulnerable to such phishing for phools. It was vulnerable before the crash especially because investment banks, with trillions of dollars of assets, were literally refinancing a significant portion of their assets every single day. The investment banks had the problem that if their assets fell below the value of their liabilities, overnight, there would be a huge shortfall in their financing. They would be out of business.

The usual business, let's say a corporation, has long-term obligations. When, for example, United Airlines found that its assets had less value than its liabilities in the fall of 2002, it went to bankruptcy court. A Chapter 11 resolution followed. The airline in bankruptcy renegotiated with its labor unions for more than $3 billion annually in wage cuts; got unsecured creditors to settle for four to eight cents on the dollar; and sloughed off its defined-benefit pension plan to the United States Pension Guarantee Corporation, with great loss to pensioners. And everywhere it trimmed operating costs. Many were hurt, but most employees kept their jobs. Scheduled flights were not canceled; and now more than a decade later, *Rhapsody in Blue* still plays in the Friendly Skies.[36]

But investment banks cannot go into Chapter 11 like that and stay in business, because their financing is different. They fund large parts of their trillions of dollars of liabilities overnight. To recall, these overnight agreements also specify the collateral to be forked over, should the bank not pay the next day. If such borrowing is, let's say, $300 billion a day, and the bank's capital and assets can no longer cover it, it cannot live through an extended bankruptcy, like United Airlines. Why not? Because its short-term creditors have a much better option than to wait for the Bankruptcy Court to prescribe their share of the haircut. They can take their collateral and walk away. But then the bank will not open up the next morning because it will still be short of funds. No one will be foolish enough to give the loans necessary to keep it in business.

That tells us why the new financial system, so dependent on borrowing short term, was on the verge of total collapse when it was discovered that much of its assets had been too highly rated, and were rotten. The mortgage-backed securities may have been rated very highly; but they were largely backed by subprime loans with high chance of default. When it was discovered that these loans were worth a lot less than previously thought, the investment banks were bankrupt.

Before the crisis, economists thought that purchasers of large securities would protect themselves. They thought that those purchasers would have asked the question embodied in a memento that Sidney Weinberg himself kept in his office from a trip as a youth to Niagara Falls: a pebble he purchased for 50 cents in a small sack, from a con man who said that he alone knew how to get diamonds from beneath the falls.[37] But if that guy wants to sell me those diamonds from beneath the falls, should I buy them? An important aspect of phishing for phools is the fencing of such embarrassing questions. There was a myth of the new economy that the complex mortgage-backed securities were tailored in such a way that risk had disappeared. The high ratings offered by the ratings agencies fenced the myth. While the myth remained unpunctured, phishing for phools was as profitable as it ever gets.

Summary

And, as we have demonstrated, it was a phishing equilibrium. As long as a significant part of the bond-buying public was willing to swallow the myth whole, the investment bankers had an incentive to produce those rotten avocados, and to extract from the agencies the high ratings that would be the cover-up. Unfortunately, that is what happened.

In 2008 then–New York State Attorney General Andrew Cuomo (who is now the governor) investigated the ratings agencies and imposed on them forty-two-month agreements to publish due diligence and evaluation criteria for residential mortgage-backed security ratings. To discourage the "ratings shopping" for good ratings, the agreements also required that agencies be paid for their services even if their ratings were not used.[38] The Dodd-Frank Act of 2010 further made changes that increased the liability of credit ratings agencies for faulty ratings.[39] The Cuomo agreements have now expired, and it is not clear whether the credit ratings problems will reappear once the market for residential mortgage-backed securities recovers. The conflict of interest from ratings paid for by issuers of securities remains.

In part two we will return to phishing for phools in financial markets. There, we will see two further examples, from US financial history, of similar distortions. We will introduce the concept of financial "looting" of firms; how it can occur for profit; and, furthermore, how relatively small opportunities to loot for profit can bring huge risks into the financial system.

Appendix: The Credit Default Swap Sideshow

If you go to the circus, you and your children may find that your favorite exhibits—the best magic shows, and so on—are not in the big tent, but rather at the sideshows. Let's now go to the Credit Default Swap Tent.

In the Big Tent, which we have described, the banks had discovered that they had the ability to make mortgages, and then as a form of alchemy, with the help of the ratings agencies, they could turn these mortgages into gold: by creating assets that were sufficiently complicated that the ratings agencies could, out of real—or pretended—ignorance, rate them highly. If the overall value of the derivative assets was more than what the banks loaned out to make the collection of mortgages, there was money on the table.

The creation of this magic was boosted by the presence of a new form of derivative contract: credit default swaps (CDSs). Such a derivative can be devised for any asset with fixed payments, such as a bond or any mortgage-backed asset. In the event of a default, the owner of the swap is paid the face value of the asset; but then he surrenders it (i.e., he "swaps" it) to the seller. It's a form of insurance. It's as if in the case of a fire (analogous to a payment default), you got paid the insurance value of your house; but then gave what might be left of the house to the insurer.

One might have thought that selling CDSs was a tremendously risky business. The insurer can get stuck with an asset that could be almost worthless. One might think that very few people would take such a risk. But leading up to the Financial Crisis of 2008 people were happy to do so, and even for very low reward. In those euphoric times they viewed the likelihood of default as so low that they saw themselves as just getting easy money.

The sale of CDSs by AIG Financial Products in London illustrates. American International Group was a very big, reputable, global insurance company.[40] It had a subsidiary, the AIG Financial Products unit in London. The head of this subsidiary in the early 2000s, Joseph Cassano, saw that he could sell CDS insurance contracts while holding a very small risk pool against them. He commissioned an econometric model, which told him that for the top-rated (the so-called super-senior) tranches of mortgage-backed securities, even in a recession as bad as the worst of the whole postwar period, there would be no more than a 0.15 percent chance of losing any significant amount of money.[41] The AIG auditors went along with this finding, and also with Cassano's conclusion that AIG could safely sell CDSs on such assets with no loss set-aside whatsoever.[42] This meant that payments from the sale of such swaps could be seen as pure gravy. And so he aggressively sold them, even at premiums of only 0.12 percent.[43] By 2007, AIG had $533 billion of credit default liabilities on its books.[44]

Whether or not Cassano was a true believer, the real phools (since Cassano was paying himself more than $38 million annually from 2002 to 2007[45]) were the folks back home at AIG headquarters, who were loath to question the goose that was laying the golden eggs. Furthermore, those liabilities could bring the company down, in due course, even if Cassano was right about not having to make any payments for default whatsoever. Because those contracts, especially the ones issued to Goldman Sachs, had some fine print.[46] That fine print specified that when the swaps declined in value by more than a given amount, AIG was required to post collateral to show that they could meet their swap obligations. As long as times were rosy, this fine print had no bite: the undiluted value of the CDSs and also AIG's AAA credit rating were assurance enough. And corporate headquarters was gratefully booking the profits, as this fine print was unknown even to the chief risk officer.[47] But then, in the financial turmoil surrounding the failure of Lehman Brothers in September 2008, AIG could not raise the credit for the called-for collateral. Knowing that if AIG filed for bankruptcy, all those CDSs would be in legal limbo, Treasury and the Federal Reserve stepped in.[48] They shoveled $182 billion into AIG. Remarkably, since $205 billion was recovered, the taxpayers made a profit on the deal.[49] But that is the good end to a bad story: that intervention was needed as a crucial step in saving the world from the Great Depression of the Twenty-First Century.

The CDSs played several roles in the financial crisis. AIG's holdings, as large as they were, were still only 1 percent of the approximately $57 trillion in the entire market.[50] These enormous quantities of potential liabilities played a major role in the loss of confidence at the time of the crisis. After all, even a bank that was perfectly hedged—owing, for example, $1 trillion in the event of defaults, and owed that same trillion in turn—still had a trillion-dollar headache. Even if it made its payments in full, it might still have to petition the bankruptcy courts to retrieve what it was owed.[51]

But the CDSs played another role beyond generating such "counterparty risk." If you held a mortgage-backed security, and backed up its payments with a CDS, from AIG for example, then you would have converted a quite-possibly totally rotten security into one that was totally safe—as long as AIG itself was solvent. The willingness of AIG, and others, to issue CDSs on bargain-basement terms emboldened the buyers and originators of those mortgage-backed securities. With the appropriately attached bungee cord, it is safe to jump from the bridge. Cassano and many others were providing such bungee cords, at very low cost. And there were many jumpers.

Phishing in Many Contexts

Part two presents nine chapters, each describing phishing for phools in some specific context. We might consider this part as exploring the "microeconomics" of phishing for phools. These chapters describe a significant phishing downside to the otherwise quite rich lives of most people in modern developed countries. The phishing we will see in these chapters, in total, may lead to just as significant a disruption to our overall happiness as the more "macroeconomic" problems of insufficient savings and financial crash we have already described.

But the aggregate impact of the disruption is only one of the takeaways from this part. As both of us, George and Bob, have been writing this book for the past five years, we have been learning about phishing for phools. We have developed a subtler view of it than we had at the beginning. We think that from our work we have developed a sixth sense, as dogs have for smells and elephants for sounds, regarding phishing for phools. That sixth sense is much abetted by a perspective on human thinking regarding what makes us so susceptible to phoolishness. We will see that characterization first in the chapter on advertising and marketing, where we will discuss how advertisers and marketers get to us by manipulating our mental frames.

Chapter 3: Advertisers Discover How to Zoom In on Our Weak Spots. If there is any place to view phishing for phools in its purest form, it is in advertising and marketing. We will see that people tend to think in terms of stories, and that basis for our thought plays a major role in making us manipulable. If you can divert the story someone is telling himself, in your favor, but not in his, you have ripened him up to be phished for a phool. Such diversion, of course, is a major advertising/marketing technique. The chapter will also explore the modern use of scientific statistical methods in advertising and marketing, giving another example of phishing equilibrium. Such techniques have proved profitable: therefore they are there. It is no coincidence that the ads that pop up in your Google search appear to have read your mind.

Chapter 4: Rip-offs Regarding Cars, Houses, and Credit Cards. This chapter visits three sites of phishing—all chosen as especially good places to view the disparate techniques of the phishermen. Two of these sites concern the largest purchases consumers make in their lives: cars and houses; so they are not inconsequential. The third site concerns credit cards. They are a small convenience, which comes at a remarkably high price.

Chapter 5: Phishing in Politics. The theory of democratic politics parallels the theory of free competitive markets. That is no coincidence. In democracies, the politicians are competing for your vote, as in free markets the sellers are competing for your dollar. We will see how, in equilibrium, phishing for phools significantly subverts democracy.

Chapter 6: Phood, Pharma, and Phishing. The food industry makes money by getting people to eat what it has to sell; Pharma makes money by getting people to swallow the pills it manufactures. Those who survive in this business have many tricks up their sleeves. One response to phishing is regulation. This chapter will discuss how a consumer movement initially accomplished the enactment of food and drug regulation, back at the very beginning of the twentieth century. But it will also describe how, today, phishermen finesse these regulations, as they have evolved ways to phish the regulators—rather than the public—for phools.

Chapter 7: Innovation: The Good, the Bad, and the Ugly. Economists now all but universally believe that economic growth is mainly the result of technical change and innovation. In this regard, they are almost surely right. But, contrary to most economic thinking, new ideas and technical innovation do not invariably yield economic progress; some of them, instead, give new ways to phish for phools.

Chapter 8: Tobacco and Alcohol. The preface began with Mollie and her addictive gambling. Gambling and drugs, and especially tobacco and alcohol abuse, are huge threats to our well-being. For many, many people, those threats are realized.

Chapter 9: Bankruptcy for Profit, and Chapter 10: Michael Milken Phishes with Junk Bonds as Bait. We will revisit financial markets. We will see, from the US savings and loan crisis of the late 1980s, how seemingly small deviations from standard financial accounting (a form of information phish) can be remarkably consequential.

Chapter 11: The Resistance and Its Heroes. In the conclusion to part two, we come around to a question that may be nagging some readers: Why is life in a modern economy reasonably OK? If there is so much potential for phishing, why isn't the free-market equilibrium unlivable? Our answer is that the assumption that underlies most economic analysis, and our own theory of phishing—that there is no barrier to self-centered opportunists—has never been completely accurate. There are idealists who draw attention to phishing, start social movements, and set in motion corrective forces.

THREE

Advertisers Discover How to Zoom In on Our Weak Spots

We now turn to advertising. Much as lawyers are supposed to defend their clients, even if guilty, advertisers are supposed to enhance the sales of the companies that hire them, even if those sales reduce customers' well-being. This aspect of advertising makes it a good hunting ground for phishing for phools.

This chapter will sample evidence from the history of advertising to draw out two aspects of phishing for phools. First, we will see that advertisers—as well as marketers more generally—tap into an aspect of human thought that makes us immanently phishable. Second, we will see the discovery of systematic ways to take advantage of our vulnerabilities to phishing, as advertisers over the past century have developed scientific, statistical methods to measure their effectiveness. This means that, even if they have no deep insights into our reactions, they can still zoom in on our phishable weak spots. Just as Thomas Edison tested more than sixteen hundred materials for the filament for the light bulb,[1] advertisers systematically use trial and error to see what causes us to buy what they want to sell.

Narrative in Human Thinking and the Role of Advertising

The human mind naturally thinks in terms of narratives. Much of our thought follows a pattern similar to a conversation.[2] In a conversation, first one person (perhaps ourselves) speaks. Then naturally, others make their point, to which we, or others, may respond. The conversation naturally evolves; as it does, the topic may even change, perhaps abruptly. In our thoughts, as in our conversations, our minds may change. It's not just that we acquire new "information";

we change our point of view and we interpret information in new ways.[3] Importantly, these evolutions of our thoughts mean that our opinions, and the decisions that are based on them, may be quite inconsistent.

This description of human thinking as narrative, or like narrative—so that it will not naturally, inevitably, be consistent—gives a role for advertising. Going back to our analogy between our thinking and our conversations, most advertising can be viewed as grafting stories of its own onto the mental narratives in our minds.[4] The object of these grafts is to get us to buy the advertiser's product.

An earlier example—the song "How Much Is That Doggie in the Window"—illustrates how that occurs. As the singer (who was Patti Page in real life) approaches the pet shop, the doggie in the window catches her eye; as the later, less-known verses continue, she decides she is going to buy the doggie and to give it to her boyfriend; and then leave for California.[5] Our mental life, as in a story, is subject to wanderings. Others, like the pet-store proprietor who placed the doggie there in the window, intentionally intervene in this mental life. That's what advertisers and marketers do much more generally. When their twist of what we are thinking serves their needs, but not ours, we have been phished for phools.

In the rest of this book we will keep coming back to storytelling. If this is our mode of thinking—or if it is a metaphor for how we think—it is easy to comprehend why it is easy for others to get into our minds for their purposes. We will see the role of "stories" literally in election and lobbying campaigns; in sales of drugs by the Pharmaceuticals; in the sale of tobacco and the resistance against it; and in the sale of junk bonds. But, as every one of us knows, our mutual storytelling is far deeper than these examples. It is essential to our humanity. After all, following *Pride and Prejudice,* "For what do we live, but to make sport for our neighbors, and laugh at them in our turn?"[6]

Advertising as Storytelling

Our assay of the lessons from advertising will begin with the lives of three of the great advertisers of the twentieth century.[7] Through these lives we will see the development of advertising as the development of ways to tell stories. But then we will also see another aspect of advertising: its supplementation of the "stories" with modern statistical methods, every bit as "scientific" as the best use of statistics in medical testing and in economics.

Albert Lasker. Lasker's father, Morris, was a nineteenth-century German Jewish immigrant; he started out as an itinerant peddler, advanced into merchandising, and then made a fortune in wholesale groceries, flour mills, and real estate.[8] Albert was born on May 1, 1880. In high school, he worked his way into being a reporter for the local Galveston, Texas, newspaper. The autobiographical sketch he related to *American Heritage* shows how, as a teenager, he got a scoop for that newspaper.[9] Eugene Debs, the turn-of-the-century US socialist leader, came to the annual meeting of the Brotherhood of Local Firemen in Galveston. He was going to reply to accusations of dishonesty, and it would be national news. Lasker told how he donned a Western Union uniform and appeared at the house where Debs was staying. Let through to deliver his "telegram," he handed Debs a note: "I am not a messenger boy. I am a young newspaper reporter. You have to give a first interview to somebody. Why don't you give it to me? It will start me on my career." Debs agreed. This may be a nice story, but Lasker's biographers went back to the records. The original story in the *Galveston Times*—presumably by Lasker—gave an account of a short and uneventful encounter with Debs.[10] Lasker, appropriately perhaps for an advertiser, loved a great story.

One might think that this ingenuity and aggressiveness, whether imagined or real, would have made Lasker a star student. But he barely graduated from high school. Morris, luckily, figured out what to do with a boy like that. He made use of some connections in Chicago, and shipped young Albert off, at 18, to Chicago: to the Lord and Thomas advertising agency.[11]

One of Lasker's early campaigns shows us advertising in its infancy. The Wilson Ear Drum Company was in trouble. A glance at its advertisement indicates why that was the case. On the side is a picture of an ear (and also the device, which fits into the ear).[12] The

ad is headlined: "DEAFNESS AND HEAD NOISES RELIEVED BY USING WIL-
SON'S COMMON SENSE EAR DRUMS," followed, in very light print, by:
"New scientific invention, entirely different in construction from
all other devices." Lasker's revision was bolder: "DEAFNESS CURED.
Louisville Man Originates a Simple Little Device That Instantly
Restores the Hearing—Fits Perfectly, Comfortably, and Does Not
Show. 190-Page Free Book Tells All About It." The copy that follows is patterned after a newspaper article (remember Lasker as the
teenage reporter): "Since the discovery of a Louisville man," it says,
"it is no longer necessary for any deaf person to carry a trumpet,
a tube, or any such old-fashioned device, for it is now possible for
anyone to hear perfectly by a simple invention that fits in the ear
and cannot be detected. The honor belongs to Mr. George H. Wilson, of Louisville, who was himself deaf, and now hears as well as
anyone." The improved headline and copy were accompanied by a
drawing of a man cupping his ear, with the expression of "the deaf-
est man you ever saw."[13] The languishing Wilson Ear Drum Company was revived. Lasker's career was on its way. He was writing
advertising in a new form, copied from the format of news stories.
It addressed people's natural skepticism regarding advertisements
by showing the reason why they should be interested in the product. It is called "reason why" advertising. This kind of advertising
may sound as if it ought to be a good thing: telling people the reason why they ought to benefit from the product. But, of course,
such "reason why" advertising may not be appealing to their
real intellect, but rather to those monkeys on their shoulders: as
the case of Wilson Ear Drums illustrates especially well. In 1913,
the *Journal of the American Medical Association* pronounced that
"as a cure for deafness [a pair of Wilson Ear Drums was] not worth
5 cents."[14]

Claude Hopkins. Claude Hopkins, the second of our three "greats,"
considerably expanded the scope of "advertising" into modern-day
marketing. His father, a newspaper editor, had died when Claude was
10, in 1876.[15] Having worked his way through school, he got a start
to his career as a bookkeeper at Bissell Carpet Sweeping Company.
When a famous Philadelphia copywriter produced nothing better

than "A carpet sweeper, if you get the right one—you might as well go without matches,"[16] Hopkins's substitute ad was adopted instead. He next convinced Melville Bissell, his boss, to promote carpet sweepers as Christmas presents. Dealers were offered "Queen-of-Christmas-Presents" displays for free. Hopkins also sent five thousand letters offering carpet sweepers as Christmas presents; he got one thousand orders in response. And then he convinced Bissell to produce carpet sweepers of twelve different types of rich wood: from light maple to dark walnut. Two hundred fifty thousand of them sold out in three weeks.[17]

Such talent was too much for Bissell and Grand Rapids, Michigan, and, before long, Hopkins was off to the big city: to Chicago, to work for Swift and Company (the meatpackers). Although Louis Swift resisted spending *his* money on advertising, Hopkins managed one notable success. Cotosuet was a form of lard: neither better, nor worse, than its competitor, Cottolene. But Hopkins made it different. In the food department of Rothschild's Department Store[18] he assembled the world's largest cake, with Cotosuet.[19] Purchasers of a pail of Cotosuet would be eligible for prizes; they also received a sample of the historic cake. More than 105 thousand people traipsed up four flights of stairs to look at it. The promotion went national; and Cotosuet sales soared.

Going from job to job, with considerable success, in 1907 Hopkins was discovered, and hired by Lasker, who in a few short years had become the young star of Lord and Thomas. Lasker had been on a train, by chance opposite Cyrus Curtis, publisher of the *Ladies' Home Journal* and *The Saturday Evening Post.* Since Curtis barely drank, Lasker took notice when he left for the dining car, to get a beer. Curtis explained that he had been attracted by an advertisement: for Schlitz Beer, written by Hopkins.[20]

The ad is in Lasker's style of reason-why storytelling; but with a new twist. All its claims are undeniable. But, also, every one of Schlitz's major competitors did the same—such as the aging of the beer, its production under sterile conditions, and the careful choice of ingredients. Hopkins and Schlitz uniquely had the audacity of bragging about what the other brewers did automatically.[21] (We note, parenthetically, that perhaps the most nauseating ad of all time, for

Anacin, made a similar phish. Anacin contained "the pain reliever doctors recommend most." But so did the presumably inferior Brand X, also featured in the ad. Brand X was pure aspirin.)[22]

Based on the Schlitz ad, after some further investigation, Lasker decided to hire Hopkins. Although Hopkins was already well-off, Lasker played to his weakness. Hopkins's wife wanted an automobile, but he felt that it was too extravagant. Lasker offered to buy him the automobile if Hopkins would begin working for him. Perhaps Hopkins appreciated the automobile ploy as straight out of his own playbook. Soon thereafter he joined full-time.[23]

Together, Lasker and Hopkins took on campaigns, including the continuation of Schlitz. The B. J. Johnson Soap Company came to Lord and Thomas for help. One of its soaps, at the time with lagging sales, was a combination of palm oil and olive oil: Palmolive. Lasker and Hopkins decided that they could do something with that; they invented the "beauty soap," advertising Palmolive on the appealing, but also rather dubious, proposition that just the use of this soap would make women much more beautiful.

They began their campaign, but on a trial scale first. In Benton Harbor, Michigan, they distributed coupons exchangeable for a free bar of the soap. The retailers in the area were notified in advance of the offering. That meant that in short order customers would be asking for Palmolive, to redeem the coupons. The store was also being given ten cents for each coupon redeemed, which was more than its cost for the soap. Almost overnight, nearly every store in the area was stocked with Palmolive.[24]

But Palmolive also got another, subtler dividend from the coupons. By affixing coupons to their advertisements, Lasker and Hopkins could tell which ads worked; which ones didn't. Just count the coupons that were returned. This small test may have been ostensibly about the ads for Palmolive in Benton Harbor; but for the field of advertising as a whole this empirical method of Hopkins and Lasker was far more consequential. It demonstrated how to conduct a small-scale experiment (on the effectiveness of advertising), whose results could be extrapolated nationally.[25]

Let's consider also Lasker's Hopkins-influenced work for oranges, which involved further innovation into branding and marketing.

Lord and Thomas created the "Sunkist" orange, a trademark contraction of "Sun Kissed." But this branding was just the beginning of marketing campaigns that included items such as bannered railway cars; Orange Week in Iowa (to parallel a nonexistent Orange Week in California); and lectures on the health benefits of oranges. Prior to the 1910s orange juice was a rarity. Oranges were commonly cut in half and eaten with a small fruit spoon. Orange juice became a staple in the American diet when Lord and Thomas and the California Fruit Growers Exchange developed, and distributed, electric and hand-glass juicers; just send 16 cents in stamps to get a glass one, direct from Sunkist.[26] In another marketing campaign, 12 Sunkist wrappers and 12 cents for the postage could be exchanged for one of those fruit spoons; this campaign proved so popular that it was expanded, so that, in due course, the wrappers could be sent in for each of the 14 items in a Rogers silver-plated tableware set.

We chose this example of oranges purposely because of its dividend in showing that even regarding the purchase of a few oranges, consumers will be influenced by the story that they are "Sun Kissed," as they also partake in the narratives created more generally by marketing campaigns (save the wrappers, get the spoon; send the stamps, get the juicer).

Standard economics takes the textbook description of the purchase of oranges and apples (as described in chapter 1, "Temptation Strews Our Path") as exemplary of the nature of all economic decision making. But that description misses completely how even the purchase of a lowly orange depends on the narratives in our minds. Then, it further ignores how others influence those narratives, often for their own purposes. Those narratives even influence some of our most important decisions: whom to marry, where to go to school, and for Secretaries of State, even the decision between war and peace.

David Ogilvy. Let's get one more advertiser under our belt before venturing further generalizations, or before venturing into the modern era. A bit of biography, as with Lasker and Hopkins, puts David Ogilvy in context. He went to a rigorous Scottish preparatory school, Fettes College; but he subsequently did so little work in his first year at college, at Oxford, that he was "sent down."[27] After a year, in 1931, as a pastry sous-chef at the Hotel Majestic in Paris, he returned to Britain to sell high-end Aga cookers. The pamphlet he wrote about his sales techniques—still considered a marketing classic—won him a place at Mather and Crowther (advertisers) in London.[28] But after only a few years he went off to America, to work on polling for George Gallup. After the war, in 1948, on a shoestring, he started his own agency, Ogilvy and Mather.[29] At the time he dreamed of five clients: General Foods, Bristol-Myers, Campbell's Soup, Lever Brothers, and Shell. In due course he would bag them all.[30]

Two of his advertisements illustrate his trademark style of atmosphere and suggestion. His Rolls-Royce ad shows an elegant young mother in the driver's seat of a Silver Cloud. She is slightly turned toward two equally elegant children, heading for the car, just outside the doorway of a fashionable grocery store. The extensive copy is headlined: "At 60 miles an hour the loudest noise in this new Rolls-Royce comes from the electric clock."[31]

Ogilvy is best known for "the man in the Hathaway shirt" campaign from the 1950s to 1970s. A large, color picture shows a debonair man, in different settings, always with an eye patch.[32] Every week, for years, *The New Yorker* would feature the man with the eye patch in a different guise: conducting the Philharmonic, painting, playing the oboe, and so on. Subscribers developed a habit of turning to the Hathaway ad; enticed by the saga of eye-patch man, they were curious about what he had been up to in the last week.[33]

It is useful to note what Ogilvy himself said about the eye-patch ad. He did not know if it would work.[34] But when he tried it, the sale of Hathaway shirts soared. He had the same empirical bent as Hopkins: he tried things to see what worked.

Phishing for Phools

From the history of the three "greats"—Lasker, Hopkins, and Ogilvy—we get a picture, from the world of advertising, of how selling works in free markets more generally. The response to advertising also reveals both the motives, and the susceptibility, of the buyers. Consumers are naturally skeptical of advertisers: they know that those ads are self-interested attempts to get them to buy. Addressing that skepticism was the basis for reason-why advertising. But that did not mean that there were no tricks. With Lasker and Hopkins, oranges were "Sun Kissed"; Schlitz was brewed "at double the necessary cost." Advertisers in Ogilvy's generation created atmosphere that identified the customer with, for example, the young mother in the Rolls-Royce; the Marlboro man; or Volkswagen's "Think Small." In each and every case, more generally, the advertisements were successful because narratives from these ads were grafted onto the customer's own.

One constant is expressed in Hopkins's autobiography: "I consider business as a game, and I play it as a game. That is why I have been, and still am, so devoted to it."[35] But if it is a game, what are the rules? What are the goals of the advertisers? Regarding the first of these goals, David Ogilvy put it succinctly: "We sell—or else."[36] In competitive free markets the competition is fierce. In their biographies and autobiographies, the advertisers, with their ever-present fear of losing their clients, bear witness to that. The role of the advertiser is to fulfill the wishes of those clients. It is to use techniques of influence to engender sales.

But we see something else in advertising that relates further to phishing for phools. The *Hidden Persuaders* scare of the 1960s—that advertisers had discovered subliminal ways into our minds—turned out to be exaggerated. But advertisers have a much more direct, although much less scary, way to accomplish their aims. That is by trial and error. In Ogilvy's *Confessions of an Advertising Man,* he says that he himself found it difficult to predict what would work and what would not. For example, as we have seen, he may have had an inkling that the eye patch would sell shirts, but he did not know. (And just as even the most sophisticated advertisers cannot predict what will make you buy, as consumers we do not quite know what motivates ourselves.) But then the advertisers, by statistical tests, can also see what works and what does not. Ogilvy prided himself as much on his knowledge of the statistical testing that he learned from Gallup as on his beautiful advertising copy.[37]

There is an analogy with real fishing (not just phishing). Try a spot. Drop your hook. See if the fish bites. If that does not work, go up the stream, or paddle to another part of the lake. By this trial and error fish will be caught. Like the fisherman, the advertisers may only have a hunch where the fish may be today. Trial and error reveals what will work. In free markets we do not need to swim to the bait. By trial and error it will come to us. The example of the man with the eye patch again illustrates. When Ogilvy tried it, as he wrote later, it was on a whim. But then when the sales of Hathaway shirts boomed, he continued. Of course, this reflects the basic idea underlying phishing equilibrium. If there is a way to make a profit from our monkey-on-the-shoulder tastes, the phishermen will keep trying until they find it.

Evolution of Marketing:
The Selling of the President, Then and Now

Lasker, Hopkins, and Ogilvy give a good portrait of advertising and marketing then. Since that time advertisers have learned to target their ads with much greater precision. Indeed, when browsing your computer, you may think at times that the advertisers have discovered how to practically read your mind, as they do through their use of *big data.* The high point of these skills is seen in presidential political campaigns; they are an especially revealing source since, relative to commercial marketing, they are much more open. A comparison of the differences between the Harding campaign of 1920 and the Obama campaign of 2012—one then, one now—therefore gives a clear view of the changes in marketing and advertising more generally, delineating a trend from the phishing in Lasker's, Hopkins's, and Ogilvy's day to something yet more pervasive and powerful. We will see that modern statistical techniques now tell marketers and advertisers—both private and political—where and how to phish, just as modern techniques in geology tell the oil and gas companies where and how to drill.[38]

Our first point of comparison will be the Harding campaign for US President in 1920. There we will see the application of Lasker-Hopkins style marketing, especially so, since Lasker himself was Harding's campaign impresario. Harding was known to be a horrific on-the-stump campaigner. So Lasker developed another strategy for him. Keep him in small-town Marion, Ohio, literally in his big white house with its wide front porch. That porch would be the stage set to fit the Republican aim of playing on the public's exhaustion from Woodrow Wilson's foreign entanglements. A vote for Harding was to be a vote to "return to normalcy" after World War I and in the recession of 1920–21. Nothing could be more normal, at least in the national myth of the United States circa 1920, than a big, friendly man in a small Ohio town on his comfortable home porch.[39] And how to play it up? Have delegations come to visit, with Harding emerging onto the porch to emit carefully crafted reason-why statements against the Democrat brand, and in favor of the Republican brand, and to give a speech concluding with the words, "Let's be done with wiggle and wobble." Those words were taken as the campaign motto and plastered onto billboards across the country.[40]

Lasker spread the message through the media of the time. The press was camping out in Marion, dependent for copy on the occasional shows dealt out from the porch. The campaign directly supplied thousands of pictures of their own, as it also supplied photo ops. The new media of the time were also brought in, as Lasker sent film clips to movie houses. Using just a smidgeon of scientific technique, the campaign polled movie audiences regarding their voting inclinations after a showing. When films of Harding playing golf got negative reactions, Lasker came back with a quick response. He brought the Chicago Cubs to Marion for an exhibition game, where Harding threw the first three pitches. The hero really was a baseball fan. Henceforth only in secrecy was golf the sport of the man who wanted to do away with wiggling and wobbling.[41]

Let us consider what has come to be more recently. The Obama campaign of 2012 illustrates how advertising (in this case in the "selling of the President") has really come into its own. Statistical testing may have begun in Benton Harbor with the coupons for Palmolive, and may have been used subsequently in a primitive way in the movie-polling of 1920; but the Obama campaign of 2012 shows its use as a new art form. Campaigns have the intermediate goals of registering their supporters; converting swing voters; and getting their supporters out to vote. The traditional campaign techniques, up until Obama 2012, have had the problem of collateral damage: that "our" registration drive will also register "their" voters; "our" messages to the wrong targets will not only swing voters in "our" direction, it will also swing voters in "their" direction; our messages to vote, delivered to the wrong household, will get out "their" vote, not "ours." The old-style solutions to this problem worked only imperfectly: choose places (or venues) that are heavily weighted with "our" voters. But even there the collateral damage problem does not go away. For example, a neutral get-out-the-vote drive in a 60/40 Democrat precinct will net 20 percent of the increase for the Democrats.

But modern campaigns have found a way to minimize collateral damage by targeting their voters individual-by-individual. With perfect targeting, for example, in the 60/40 precinct, only the 60-percent Democrats would be targeted; and none of the 40-percent Republicans. With modern statistical techniques, a huge amount of data, and massive polling, the Obama campaign was able to do something close to that in 2012. The task began with giving more than one hundred million potential voters a unique identification number. Individual information was then affixed to voters' files.[42] That information came from many rich sources. It began with publicly available voter registrations (which, in some states, identify registrants by party) and also with records regarding who voted, by election. Usefully, such information also includes names, addresses, and voting precincts. The files were also affixed with as many as one thousand different additional entries available from commercial sources, such as drawn from credit information, magazine subscriptions, and club memberships. The second step of the process was to poll medium-sized samples to get a measure of the likelihood of being registered; of their support for Obama; and of their voting in the election. On this basis, with the detailed data in the Democratic National Committee files, with such rich and detailed information on potential voters, it was possible to make a quite accurate estimate of the likelihood of registration, candidate-support, and vote for everyone in the huge data file.[43] Obama 2012 then was no longer the world of "knock on every door" of the 60/40 precincts. Now it was knock on the door only of those likely to support. Not only did this save the expense of approaching the unlikely; it also avoided the damage that could come from mobilizing "their" people to support Romney, rather than Obama.[44]

An additional advantage went beyond targeting the favorable voters in the favorable precincts. In previous times campaigns have steered clear of place (and venue) where they did not have clear majorities. In Illinois, for example, the Democrats avoided whole areas downstate; just as in New York, they avoided upstate. But now the very significant minorities of voters in such places could be approached, because they were individually targeted. For Obama 2012 these voters in Democrat minority areas were no longer dark matter.

The world of advertising and marketing is still about getting the right message and creating the right story. It is still about the story of the Man in the Hathaway Shirt; and that Palmolive will make you beautiful. But the Obama campaign illustrates that it helps greatly to know where to target your message, and, when you do, to know which message will resonate favorably. But then we all know that it is important to target the right stories to the right people; every school-boy and every schoolgirl knows that they can get into a great deal of trouble by telling the wrong story to the wrong person. The advertisers, like the campaigners, have found modern methods of honing that schoolboy/schoolgirl wisdom.

Appendix: Malaysian Airlines Flight #370

There is a curious similarity between newscasting and advertising. Both of them are engaged in telling stories. The advertisers want you to add their story to yours, so you will buy what they want to sell; the TV news business wants to entice you to pay attention to their story, so you will be the audience for the advertisements that earn their keep. If you watch, but your more thoughtful self says this is a bad way to spend your time, then you are being phished for a phool. An example illustrates.

Back in the spring of 2013, as you almost surely recall, Malaysian Airlines Flight 370 took off from Kuala Lumpur en route to Beijing. It never made it. (This would be the first of three Malaysian flights that would make the news.) Flight 370 had disappeared. And then TV news ran this story, day after day, week after week: for months. Both of us (Bob and George) remember wondering why *this* inconsequential-in-the-grand-scheme-of-things happening was being given *so much* play.

We have a theory. In his book of advice for authors, *Twenty Master Plots: And How to Build Them,* Ronald Tobias argued that all literature is a variation on twenty basic, deeply affecting stories: present in all cultures. This story has Master Plot #7: The Riddle; otherwise known as The Mystery. In Tobias's words, "The challenge for the reader is to solve the mystery before the protagonist does, which makes the riddle a contest: If the protagonist figures out the riddle before you do, you lose; if you figure it [out] before the protagonist, you win."[45]

Curiously, we (Bob and George) were, like much of the American public, drawn in. We too went into solve-the-riddle mode. Bob even concocted a solution of his own: that the pilot had been distracted and misread some instruments; he turned off the communications, thereby causing the crash; just as twenty-eight years earlier, the manager of the Chernobyl nuclear station turned off the emergency core cooling system and the reactor blew up.

Our eventual interest notwithstanding, we still felt somewhat snookered by Flight-370-the-Story. In our (Bob's and George's) attempts to solve this "riddle" we were a bit like Mollie at the slots. One wise part of our psyche was telling us this was a waste of our time; but we got involved anyway. However, unlike Mollie, whose life was in disarray, the direct cost to us of giving in to our milder addiction was negligible. But that does not mean that people collectively do not pay a high price for the addiction of all of us to bad news: because stories that could have been run instead, or deeper coverage of other stories, broadcast to millions, could well have affected public opinion, with considerable influence.

The Malaysian Airlines story serves up a further lesson. When we listen to a news program (read the newspaper, etc.), we tend to take for granted that we are hearing (reading) the "news": whatever that might be. Someplace in the back of our minds we have the notion that editors have culled the stories that best represent "the news" according to the "real" interests of their viewers. They are acting as our "news fiduciaries." In many respects the news business in the United States does behave that way. There are strong ethical standards, and especially a norm of "just the facts, ma'am." But in a phishing equilibrium, the selection of stories, with competitive news media, will give us what we ask for, as long as some outlet can cover its costs in providing it.

The playing of the Malaysian Airlines story was only a diversion; but a different sort of news, such as hate news, is much more consequential. There is the possibility that many of its acolytes do not really have a taste for it; rather, they tune in only because of the urging of monkeys on their shoulders. But whatever their true selves may want, in the presence of those malignant monkeys, that hate news will be there in phishing equilibrium. And those with special skills at purveying it will earn their fortunes in its provision.

FOUR

Rip-offs Regarding Cars, Houses, and Credit Cards

Just as anthropologists know that African rift valleys are good places to dig for skeletons, we know that rip-offs will be fertile ground to find phishing for phools.[1] This chapter will explore rip-offs at the auto dealer, in home closings, and in the use of credit cards. In each case consumers are making large payments, with surprisingly little benefit. We will see that phishing for phools adds significantly to what we pay for cars and homes, which are the most expensive consumer purchases of our lives; and credit cards phish us to spend considerably more on a daily basis.

Phishing at the Showroom

All of us are at least a little bit nervous when we go to the auto showroom to buy a car. One summer, a long time ago, one of us (George) was hired for a summer job by a Johnson and Johnson heir, who told a story about his father. Johnson-Father went to the local Rolls-Royce dealer in "dungarees." When the salesman brushed him off, he bought two Rolls-Royces on the spot, and watched the salesman's manner change.

Most of us do not have the resources to spoil a salesman's snubbing in this way. Rather, when, and if, we go shopping for a new car, we worry about the price of the Toyota Camry or the Honda Accord. On average, car buyers purchase a new one every eight years, or a used one every three.[2] So our ability to negotiate at the auto dealers is a factor in our budget.

There are some good figures, from a surprising source, that tell us how much we get ripped off. Back in the 1990s, two lawyer-economists, Ian Ayres and Peter Siegelman, sought to find out whether there were systematic differences in prices of new cars, by the race and gender of the buyer.[3] They hired recent black and white, and male and female college graduates. In all other respects besides race and gender the testers were chosen to be as similar as possible: for example, in age (between 28 and 32); and in education (with 3 to 4 years of post-secondary education). They drove similar rental cars to the dealers; wore similar "yuppie" clothes; indicated no need for financing; and gave the same home address. Also, these young men and women were, no doubt, later delighted to be described as having been "subjectively chosen to have average attractiveness." These testers were given detailed instructions regarding how to elicit an initial price offer for a specific model car, and, then, how to bargain toward a final price. In the final negotiated offer, Ayres and Siegelman found that white women were given a quote of $246 (inflation-adjusted) more than the white men; black women, $773 more; and black men, $2,026 more.[4] The black women were being asked for 3.7 percent more relative to the price of the car; the black men, for 9 percent more.[5] Whether or not the laws against discrimination by race and gender were being violated, which was the concern of Ayres and Siegelman, wearing their lawyer hats, the obvious takeaway is of course of considerable importance. It suggests that, much more generally, beyond the auto showroom, black men and black women are likely to get bad deals. They may pay the same price at the supermarket, but in other deals that are much more important to their financial well-being they are not so lucky: such as in the purchase of a house; or, yet more life-determining, in getting and maintaining a job.

Why are blacks and women charged so much more? Ayres and Siegelman consider a couple of possibilities. One possibility is pure animus: racial hatred or gender bigotry. However, they found that black salesmen and white salesmen quoted the same high prices to blacks. Instead, they concluded, salespeople just have a sense, based on racial and sexual stereotypes, regarding who is less likely to walk away from a bad deal. For example, African Americans may be "less likely than whites to own a car at the time they are shopping for a new one (and therefore might have more difficulty traveling to multiple dealerships)."[6] In other words, the differentials exist because the salespeople pay attention to race and sex to better their opportunity for phishing.

But there is even more evidence of phishing in their results than Ayres and Siegelman acknowledged. In their focus on differentials by race and gender, they failed to notice another fact that also emerges from their tables. Even after taking account of the differences in quotes by race and gender, there was still a lot of leftover variation in the quoted prices. This variation is important because it indicates the extent to which people are paying "more" or "less" for a car. With a quite possibly realistic assumption,[7] we estimated the excess that car buyers were paying above the point at which the dealers themselves would walk away from the sale. By this estimate almost one-third of the testers were being quoted more than an extra $2,000 (inflation-adjusted) for their car. That of course is why a visit to the auto dealer gives almost everyone the sweats. Some fraction of us is going to be seriously phished for a phool. Confidences from auto dealers corroborate this interpretation; some of them told Ayres and Siegelman that they earned as much as half of their profits from only 10 percent of their customers.[8]

Our research assistant Diana Li investigated these findings one step further. She researched the leading "tricks" that auto salesmen use to phool their customers. It is not surprising that her attempts to interview auto salesmen on these points quickly led to resistance. They clammed up. But one interviewee was remarkably forthcoming. He explained three major tricks of the salesmen.

First, he noted that most customers go to the showroom with an ideal car in mind. They have been primed by the commercials: it's got "the four-wheel drive, the backup camera, this *gizmodo,* that *gizmodo.*" When the customer discovers that this fully gizmodoed car sells for $10,000 in excess of the model's manufactured suggested retail price, the salesman's job is to push back against the customer's reluctance. "You just have to sell them on the benefit of those things anyway and turn a blind eye to the high probability that they won't need these things later on."

Price of trade-in was a second target for phishing. Diana's informant recommended: "Don't, don't, don't mention that you have a trade-in until after you've negotiated a price. Because if you tell us that you have a trade-in, then we will start mentally trying to figure out how we can give the impression of giving you more on the trade-in to hold the line on a price on the new car."

A third phish revealed another area for profit: financing. Once again the salesman plays the magician's (and the pickpocket's) trick:

to divert the focus of his mark. For example, if the salesman is able to focus the buyer's attention on the *monthly payment,* then the buyer will fail to notice the length of the contract. But each month of extra payments is then a month of pure gravy to the dealer.

Diana also took up the suggestion by Ayres and Siegelman of 50 percent of profits from 10 percent of customers. She did so in a line of questioning that avoided the inevitable pushback she had received previously when inquiring about the tricks of the trade. She opened her interviews with questions that were totally innocuous: pure placebo. But embedded in her questions was what she was really after. How plausible was it that 50 percent of profits came from 10 percent of customers? Most of her subjects found it quite possible. But in their explanations they added another dimension of the dealer phish that had eluded her research on tricks of sale. The dealers have service units. And the profits from service (at much higher prices than outside the dealership), rather than from sales, give added reason why 50 percent of profits come from 10 percent of sales.

This finding of Diana has given both authors, Bob and George, a significant dealer-phish Ahem. We both have old Volvos. When we bought them new, we avoided the usual phishes. We came carefully armed with the manufacturer's suggested retail price. We purchased no extras. We had no trade-in. And we both paid cash, so there were no finance charges. But as the careful people we usually are, we have been taking our Volvos to the respective dealers for maintenance. Initially that guaranteed that the warranty would hold in full; later we have taken pride in the dutiful maintenance of our aging Volvos. But as we have done so, we have also been aware of sticker shock each time we have been presented with the bill for the five-thousand-mile inspections (whose reminders, we now strongly suspect, are not so innocently preprogrammed to pop up on our control panels). We have always thought we were automobile-purchase careful. But thanks to Diana's research, we now know that we are among the 10 percent elect: in this case, because we are so careful. Ahem.

Rip-off at the Home Closing

We now come to buying a home, which is most families' lifetime major purchase; so a lot of money and emotion is up for grabs.[9]

Contrary to myth, Americans are not constantly on the move. We settle down. By the time we are 60, more than 80 percent of us own our own home; and we will stay in those owned homes, on average, for a good long time.[10] For current homeowners, their total stay in their homes, from the day they move in to the day they will move out, will, on average, be about twenty-four years.[11] These two numbers mean that a significant majority of Americans buy at least one home in their lifetimes; they also mean that the purchase of a home, for most of us, is quite infrequent.

But it is not just inexperience that makes the homebuyer vulnerable. The TV show *House Hunters* makes a nightly soap opera out of real-life couples searching to buy or to rent a home. Their search invariably involves the compromise they must make between dream and budgetary reality. But also it involves a second drama, which concerns how the house-buying couple reaches agreement between their often quite disparate wishes.

Homebuyers, then, are vulnerable to buying the wrong house, but there is also another source of rip-off that is not shown on TV: the closing costs. Once an offer has been accepted, the deadline to arrange the necessary financing is short: the seller is waiting anxiously for verification that the buyer can come up with the money, as promised. This makes the homebuyer, who is inexperienced, and whose focus also has previously been elsewhere, especially vulnerable to rip-off.

Usually, when we think of the transaction costs for the transfer of a house, we think of the real estate fees. In one sample of home purchases (involving Federal Housing Administration mortgages), the standard 6 percent was still the modal fee: paid by 29 percent of sellers. Some 47 percent did pay less; but, remarkably, 24 percent somehow managed to pay more.[12]

Framed as 6 percent, these fees seem fairly small: it's like the sales tax on a bottle of Tylenol at the local CVS. But, framed differently, those fees are huge. It is common for buyers to think of the real estate dealer who helps them as free of charge: the fees are paid by the seller. But to an economist, it does not matter who pays: because according to the standard logic of supply-demand analysis, if the buyers (rather than the sellers) were paying the agent, the price of the house would be correspondingly lower.[13] This change of perspective then suggests a different gauge of the relative size of those payments to the real estate dealer. For a first-time homebuying couple with a fairly typical 10 percent down payment, that 6 percent is 60 percent of their contribution.[14] Are these payments justified? We can't say for sure, but note that these fees are much lower in other countries; and people there do not seem to be complaining about bad service.[15]

But those payments to the real estate dealer are not the end of the transaction fees. In a large sample of Federal Housing Administration loans, additional closing costs were on average approximately a further 4.4 percent of the value of the mortgage.[16] Put together with the payments to the real estate agent, that means that the transaction costs, for those 10-percent-down first-time homebuyers, are about as large as all the money that they themselves are bringing to the table.

Those additional fees for closing come in many different forms. The bulk of them are for two purposes: for exchange of title, and for initiating the mortgage. And here, in the charges for initiating the mortgage, a careful study shows a remarkable example of rip-off, which went on for years until it was, finally, outlawed in the Dodd-Frank Financial Reform Act of 2010.[17] We will look at this rip-off in some detail, because we have some remarkable information regarding just how large it had been.

The typical homebuying couple, on moving into a new home, find themselves strapped for cash. Not only do they have to put up that down payment; they typically also need ready money to buy some new furniture and to repaint that pink kitchen. There is a convenient arrangement that allows them to get such needed cash. It is standard practice for Lending Bank, which is giving Homebuying Couple their mortgage, to provide such money now: if Homebuying Couple also agree to pay an interest rate higher than "par" for the duration of their mortgage. But that payment typically is not made directly to Homebuyer, but, instead, to the Mortgage Broker, who is the intermediary in the transaction. It would seem fair that if Lending Bank paid Mortgage Broker $3,000 extra for a mortgage with, let's say, a 5.25 percent interest rate—rather than the par of 4.25 percent—this extra $3,000 would be passed on to Homebuyer.

But did that happen in practice? Economists Susan Woodward and Robert Hall obtained data regarding the fraction of those payments from Lending Bank to Mortgage Broker that were being passed on.[18] They looked at two samples, with almost nine thousand different mortgage closings in total. In one sample, only an average of 37 cents for each dollar was passed on. In the second sample, Homebuyer did yet worse: with only an extra 15 cents for every dollar received by the mortgage broker. Nor were these rip-offs uncommon in the Woodward-Hall samples: some 93 percent[19] of the homebuyers were opting for such interest-above-par mortgages.[20] We add, parenthetically, that this test for rip-off regarding mortgages parallels the Ayres-Siegelman test for it regarding automobiles: both tests are based on observation of different payments for, in some sense, the exact same thing.

On the other side, the homebuyer may also pay the mortgage broker for a loan with interest *less than par*. Those payments are known as *points*. Here too there is opportunity for scam. The mortgage broker/consumer advocate Carolyn Warren described her observation of a somewhat elderly couple at their home closing. The wife objected to the $19 flood certification fee. That, they were informed correctly, was required by state law. The couple blithely passed over the $395 processing fee, which was unnecessary. And then they skipped over the $2,000 fee for points, which Warren knew was also bogus. Their interest rate was par; they should have paid no points.[21] That takes George back to his memory of his own purchase of a house in Chevy Chase, Maryland, in 1994. His real estate agent had told him he had to make up his mind quickly about the purchase; a couple, she said, had just arrived from Alaska, and was about to make a bid. She was also ever so helpful in shopping the mortgage. She found the broker; George paid points on the mortgage. Perhaps there really was a couple coming from Alaska.[22] George had thought he owed those points. Now he wonders; this is time for another Ahem.

Rip-off at the Checkout Counter

The role of credit cards starts with some economics that is known to every shopkeeper, but is so simple that it eludes the economics textbooks. The typical store sells its wares at a markup over cost. It's like the taxi driver who rents his taxi and pays one hundred dollars per day as a rental fee. Only after he has covered that hundred dollars plus fuel costs does he make what he needs to feed his family. The markup over costs counts for the store in the same way. On the low end, the owners pay off the fixed costs of renting the store and paying the utilities and the clerks at the counters. On the high end, beyond the break-even point, every additional sale boosts the profits. If, magically, the stores could invent a pill that they could give to their customers that would get them to buy more, it would be invaluable to increasing profits.

Curiously, such a pill has been invented. And as we can imagine, the stores use it. And, in addition, the holders of the monopoly rights on the use of the invention have also found clever ways to tax the stores, and also everyone else. The name of this magic pill is the credit card. We swallow it into our wallets.

One of the bases of the credit card's magic is that most of us think that we buy only what we need (or want), and that we could not be influenced by minor cues, such as whether we will pay by credit card or cash. But almost surely we are mistaken. How do we know that credit cards influence our spending in this way? First, there is circumstantial evidence that people with credit cards spend more. Psychologist Richard Feinberg found that tips left by those paying by credit card were 13 percent larger than those who paid in cash.[23] Another study showed that possessors of credit cards purchased more on their visits to a department store in the northeastern United States.[24] But these differences of expenditure cannot be decisive in answering the question whether credit cards cause people to spend more. Credit cardholders and card nonholders are different, and we need to know that it is the credit card, and not those differences, that are the cause of their differential spending patterns.[25]

To resolve this question, Feinberg conducted two further experiments. Following his training as a psychologist, Feinberg used two experiments of the sort that is common in social psychology. In the first experiment he gave a credit-card cue to a subject group, and compared their willingness to spend to a control group, who were not cued. For the cue, he placed MasterCard signs and logos at the corner of the table where the subject group was working. It was explained that these signs were being used in another experiment. The subjects were then asked how much they would spend on seven different pictured items: two dresses, a tent, a man's sweater, a lamp, an electric typewriter (the experiment was conducted in the early 1980s), and a chess set.[26] Every item went for significantly more in the subject group than in the uncued control group. The differences ranged from

11 percent more for the tent to approximately 50 percent more for each of the two dresses. In a second experiment, subjects were again asked how much they would be willing to spend; they were shown the item on a screen, and they were timed in their response. In the presence of a credit card in the corner on the screen, again subjects were willing to spend more (much more—triple, for a toaster: $165.66 in inflation-adjusted dollars, rather than $52.90).[27] These large differences in willingness to spend would explain why stores are more than happy to accept your credit card, even if the credit-card companies tax them a significant fraction of the purchase, with what is known as an "interchange fee."

As surprising as Feinberg's results may be, an economist might think his evidence is leading, but not necessarily conclusive. They did not involve actual expenditures. Two economists, Drazen Prelec and Duncan Simester, conducted an experiment that dealt with that objection. They conducted an auction, among Harvard Business School MBA students, for three prizes. The prizes were, variously, tickets to a Celtics game, tickets to a Red Sox game, and, as a consolation, banners for both the Celtics and the Red Sox. Students were randomly assigned to whether they would pay by credit card or by cash. It was also arranged that payment in cash would involve minimal inconvenience, since an ATM was on the route to where the payment should be made. The Celtics tickets got more than double in the credit-card condition; the Red Sox tickets got more than 75 percent extra; the banners got a mere 60 percent extra. This experiment seems to bear out Feinberg's findings.[28] (Our research assistant Victoria Buhler commented on these results that *business students,* especially, "should have known better.")

These two studies do not just show that credit cards get you to spend more; rather they seem to indicate that, shockingly and surprisingly, they get us to spend quite a bit more. They are the desired magic pill. But that pill comes at a price.

The Price of the Pill

How do the stores get us to hold, and to pay, with credit cards? They do a remarkable trick. They make its use free. In the United States, this used to be mandated by a federal law.[29] The Truth in Lending

Act of 1968 mandated that merchants could not charge customers more if they paid by credit card than if they paid by cash. But that law expired in 1984, and Truth in Lending credit-card-style now has been reenacted, but in only ten states, with about 40 percent of the US population. Despite interchange fees that stores pay to Visa, Master-Card, and so on, they do not commonly charge their customers for credit-card use. Nor do they give cash discounts to those who pay by cash. The Feinberg/Prelec-Simester studies suggest why. If people are unknowingly spending more because they are paying by credit card, it would be ill-advised for Macy's, or even the local supermarket, to remind their customers that they might, well, get a discount for paying by cash.

In giving customers free use of the credit card, it's as if the stores are offering free puppies. The users of those credit cards may really want their groceries, but they also come home with something that will be less welcome. Sometime in the next month the bill for those groceries will land on the doorstep. That is fine for a good share of credit cardholders. Some 50 percent of Americans say they always pay their credit-card bills in full.[30] But a significant proportion of us are not so conscientious. And they are left with the debt, which comes at a high cost.

That cost of credit cards is remarkably high. We will take three cuts at how high those costs may be. First, there are the aggregate statistics. For 2012, we have an aggregate estimate of $150 billion as revenues for the credit-card industry.[31] That means that people are paying, for the use of credit cards—which most of us would view as a convenience, but a fairly minor one—a significant fraction of the bills for our major necessities. That $150 billion is more than one-third of what we pay in the aggregate for mortgage interest on our homes[32]; it is more than one-sixth of what we spend for our home food consumption; and more than one-third of what we spend for motor vehicles and parts.[33]

Let's take a second cut at the cost of credit cards. How is this cost divided among different types of payment? We have estimates of three components of costs. A rough division of these payments is that about one-half consists of interest paid on overdue accounts; about one-third is for the interchange fees; and another one-sixth is for miscellaneous penalties, especially including late fees.[34]

An enterprising blogger, Sean Harper, a former student of *Freako-nomics*'s Steven Levitt, has given us a third cut. He calculated the interchange fees that a merchant would pay if you handed her your Citicorp Visa Rewards Card.[35] For a $1.50 pack of gum purchased at a convenience store, the fee was 40 cents; for a $30 tank of gas, $1.15; for a $100 grocery purchase, $2.05. Harper's list goes on. One gauge of the size of those fees is to compare them to the merchants' profits. For convenience stores they were 2¼ times their annual profits. As another gauge, with a 2 percent charge in the supermarket, the credit-card companies are taking almost one-fifth of the typical average markup on groceries.[36]

Economist Michelle White of the University of California at San Diego has described yet a further dimension to the costs of credit cards: as a major cause of personal bankruptcy. The fairly common finding that those who go bankrupt have large credit-card debts is suggestive, but it does not definitively establish credit-card misuse as the cause of bankruptcy: because it is natural for those with financial problems other than credit-card misuse to run up their credit-card bills. But direct evidence points strongly to the credit card as a major culprit: as a cause both for the high level of bankruptcies; and also for the sevenfold increase in them that accompanied a dramatic increase in credit-card debt between 1980 and 2006. In a special survey, the Panel Study of Income Dynamics in 1996 asked respondents if they had ever gone bankrupt; and if so, why. Of those who had experienced bankruptcy, 33 percent named "high debt/misuse of credit" as the primary reason.[37] That was more than the 21 percent who named job loss, and it was also more than the 16 percent of those who named medical causes.[38] A later survey conducted in 2006 of debtors who had sought counseling yields a similar finding: a full two-thirds of these debtors in counseling named "poor money management/excessive spending" as the source of their problems.[39] The experiments by Feinberg and by Prelec and Simester tell us why the credit card could easily play a major role in that mismanagement. For some, it would appear, credit cards are a trap.

That takes us back to phishing for phools. If credit cards are not phishing for phools, the companies who purvey them should tell it to the judge. As we read it, every aspect of this endeavor is involved in phishing for phools. It begins with the fees charged to the merchants, whose payments are large. They buy their magic pills, but at only one-third of the total cost. Next come the consumers, blithely purchasing their groceries, footwear, and whatever else, with the credit card extracting high rates of interest from those with overoptimistic expectations regarding how they will pay the bill when it comes. And then insult is added to injury with the late fees and the nuisance fees. At each and every stage, the competitive drive for profits plays on our weaknesses.

FIVE

Phishing in Politics

All of us have an experience—with a past girlfriend or boyfriend, perhaps—where we can look back with the wisdom of a few more years, and can now articulate clearly what we sensed only vaguely at the time. One of us (George) had such an experience in the last week of October 2004. George found himself, by strange circumstance, in Iowa, as the helper, and occasionally the surrogate, for Art Small Jr., who was the Democratic candidate for the US Senate from Iowa. His son, Art Small III, a former student of George's at Berkeley, had asked him to be an "economic advisor" to his father. George had responded that he would come to Iowa and help for a week.[1]

Art the Candidate's career had spanned being professor of English, pharmacist, congressional aide, representative and then senator in the Iowa legislature (and chair of the Appropriations Committee), lawyer, and printer.[2] In Iowa he was renowned for his integrity and honesty. That was reflected in his campaign, with its slogan, "THINK BIG, vote Small," and campaign buttons and posters in modest black and white. Art took no contributions from PAC funds or from special interests—so that for at least one week of the campaign his contributions amounted to only $103. He had signed up for the Senate race at the last minute, when he knew that no one else would take on themselves the duty of representing the Democrats against incumbent Charles Grassley.[3] During the course of George's week in Iowa he learned that Art also had special reason for that reluctance. Being a candidate for Senate, even of a no-hope campaign, was immensely arduous, and Art was also taking care of his wheelchair-bound wife. That became clear one day when Art took George home, and served a scrambled-eggs dinner. They both did the dishes together.

The major issue in the campaign was the role Grassley had played as chair of the Senate Finance Committee, as shepherd of the George W. Bush tax cuts of 2001 and 2003. The Congressional Budget Office had calculated that those cuts would increase the federal deficit by some $1.7 trillion.[4] If that money had instead been saved for a rainy day, just a few years later, in 2008, expenditure of that money would have gone a long way in rescuing the United States from the Great Recession. By our calculation, it would have been sufficient for the United States to reduce unemployment from an average of 9 percent to 7 percent for the four years 2009 through 2012.[5]

Whatever Art's or Grassley's respective merits or deficiencies, the opposition to Art was overwhelming. Iowa exports bacon; Grassley brought it home—from Washington. Subsidies for ethanol were just one of his trademarks. But it was not only his direct contributions to Iowa that were counting this election season. Grassley had amassed a $7.6 million campaign war chest.[6] It took only a few minutes of watching KCCI, Channel 8, Des Moines, to see where that money was going. Grassley would appear in a campaign ad, riding his tractor lawn mower round and round, with two push lawnmowers ingeniously attached in tow, as concentrically narrowing ellipses of shortened grass emerged in his rich Iowa lawn. *Grass*-ley, the ad intones. Get it? "I sure love the work of the United States Senate, but sometimes you've got to get away from it. So," he says slowly in a homey tone of voice, "I like to mow my lawn on weekends."[7]

Art fought the fight to the very end. The election results: Grassley, 70.2 percent; Small, 27.9.[8] In the Bible, David beat Goliath. But more often than not, the giant wins.

Democracy, the Role of Money in Politics, and, Yet Again, Phishing for Phools

The Grassley-Small campaign, and the role of money in it, is a microcosm of US congressional elections more generally. Aggregate statistics give us an idea that this election was, except for Art's lack of money, in no way exceptional. For the US House elections of 2008, total campaign expenditures of all candidates were more than $2 million per race, with incumbents spending more than double their challengers. In human terms, a representative must raise roughly $1,800 per day in office (Saturdays, Sundays, and holidays included). Open races, with no incumbent, were more than doubly expensive, at $4.7 million. Senate races are yet more costly. In 2008, Senate elections cost almost $13 million per race. The average incumbent spent more than $8 million on his reelection—as with Grassley, outspending the challengers.[9]

Going back to Grassley (as our example), if you show the Iowa public a man on a lawnmower, they are more likely to vote for him. As we discussed in chapter 3, on advertising, the voters graft the stories from the ads onto their narratives about themselves, their friends, and their neighbors. The lawnmower ad grafts the story that Grassley is a friend and neighbor. Like us Iowans, he mows his own lawn; and he even returns from Washington to do so. It is worth noting that although he had done many positive things in the Senate (closing inappropriate personal income-tax loopholes, and battling sex slavery, for example) the ad itself conveys nothing about the candidate's policies, or even about his character. On the contrary, if anything, the ad should leave the voters asking the source of the money to pay for it; but, with a successful ad, the thought does not occur to them.

The effects of phishing in politics parallel the effects of phishing in economics. Basic economic theory says that, in the absence of phishing, economic competition generates a good equilibrium (which is "Pareto optimal," as we discussed in the introduction, on phishing equilibrium); similarly, basic political science says that competitive democratic elections generate good outcomes. This result is usually attributed to political scientist Anthony Downs.[10] If voters are fully informed and vote their preferences, which can be represented on a scale from left to right, the platforms of the two opposing candidates will reach an equilibrium. The platforms of both candidates will conform to the preference of the "median voter": where half of the voters' most preferred stance is "to the left"; and the other half is "to the right."[11] This equilibrium occurs for much the same reason that the supermarket lanes equalize in length. It occurs because, if one of the two candidates does not choose that platform, the other candidate can win by doing so.

This equilibrium describes an outcome that weights the arguments of both sides and reaches a compromise. That is what we would ideally like democracy to do. So it would be very nice if Downs's description of voter and candidate behavior described reality. But it differs considerably from it, because, unfortunately, voters are phishable in two major ways. First, they are not fully informed: they are information phools. Second, voters are also psychological phools: for example, because they respond to appeals such as lawnmower ads. These phishabilities change the political equilibrium. They pull candidates' platforms away from the preferences of the median voter.

The winning electoral strategy with phishable voters is threefold: 1. Publicly, proclaim policies that will appeal to the typical voter on issues that are salient to her, and where she will be well informed. 2. But on other issues, where the typical voter is ill informed, but where potential campaign donors are well informed, take the stance that appeals to donors. Publicize this stance to would-be contributors, without broadcasting it widely to the general public. 3. Use the contributions from these "special-interest groups" for campaigning that increases popularity among the regular run of voters, who are more likely to vote for someone who "mows their lawn on TV."[12] With such rational strategies for winning elections, we do not get the median voting theorem as describing political outcomes. Instead we have a political phishing equilibrium.

Informed vs. Uninformed Voters

Although there may be some issues where it is fairly easy to be an informed voter, it is also true that the public leaves a great deal of the business of Congress "up to them": where only the "experts" understand what is involved; and almost everyone else is an uninformed voter. An example demonstrates that even the most intrepid voter will find it impossible to be fully informed—even about matters of the utmost importance. Quite arguably, the most consequential US congressional legislation of our times is H.R. 1424 of the 110th Congress (the Emergency Economic Stabilization Act of 2008). It authorized Treasury to spend up to $700 billion to support troubled assets. It prevented the collapse of the US financial system, and almost surely prevented (or delayed at least until now) the advent of the Second Great Depression. But, important as it was, only someone with inside information, or a soothsayer, could have foreseen how it would be used in the six months after its passage to bail out a good share of the US banking system, and also General Motors and Chrysler.[13]

The preamble of a bill is to explain its purpose. The preamble for H.R. 1424 tells us that it "provide[s] authority ... to purchase and insure certain types of troubled assets."[14] That would hardly seem to justify the bailouts. Even though we had a copy of the act in our hands, to identify the spot in the bill that authorized the bailout of the banks and of the auto companies we had to call a friend, Phillip Swagel, who had been Assistant Secretary of the Treasury in the fall of 2008, and was one of its principal drafters.[15] The most dramatic event in the use of Troubled Asset Relief Program (TARP) funds occurred when Henry Paulson, the Treasury Secretary, on October 13, 2008, summoned the CEOs of nine of the country's largest banks and got them, liking it or not, to accept $125 billion from the Treasury in exchange for preferred stock.[16] Authority for such a transaction derives from the first part of the "definition" of troubled assets in Section 3, 9(A):

> residential or commercial mortgages and any securities, obligations, or other instruments that are based on or related to such mortgages, that in each case was originated or issued on or before March 14, 2008, the purchase of which the Secretary [of the Treasury] determines promotes financial market stability.[17]

As Swagel explained to us, because the banks themselves were the owners of such assets, the bank bailout was authorized under the act. The authority for the takeover of General Motors and Chrysler is equally opaque. It comes from the second part of the definition of troubled assets, in Section 3, 9(B), as

> any other financial instrument that the Secretary ... determines the purchase of which is necessary to promote financial market stability.[18]

H.R. 1424 then illustrates the general principle that figuring out what is really in legislation with a technical component can be an all but impossible game of *Where's Waldo.* In the children's books, Waldo wears his red-and-white-striped shirt, blue pants, and beanie hat. In contrast, in the congressional legislation, the clauses in favor of the Interests are in camouflage. Neither the public nor even the press can read and interpret complex technical legislation.

Our only defense is the goodwill of the people in Congress to do the best they can for us. But they too may not understand the issues. Furthermore, they need to be elected. And for that they need to get the cash that funds their TV lawn mowing. And if, like poor Art, that money is absent, they will never see a day in Congress to represent our interests (or to express their own views).

Lobbying and Money

That takes us to the question of how the congresspeople get the money for their campaigns, and also to the role of the lobbyists. Some remarkable statistics about lobbyists, congressmen, and campaign funds circumscribe our answers to this question. There are about 12,000 lobbyists, which is more than twenty for each member of Congress.[19] MIT's Stephen Ansolabehere, John de Figueiredo,[20] and James Snyder have calculated that contributions to congressional campaigning, including the funds raised by the candidates themselves, and also the significant amounts raised by both the parties and the PACs, are less than the expenditures on congressional lobbying over an election cycle.[21] So much lobbying suggests that campaign contributions would come mainly from the corporate interests that hire lobbyists; quite possibly directly from the lobbyists themselves. But, on the contrary, only about one-eighth of campaign contributions come from corporations, unions, and other associations; the great bulk of donations, instead, come from individual contributors.[22] And the lobbyists themselves kick in only a small amount of extra dollars, given as "friends" of the candidate and of the campaign.[23]

This statistical pattern narrows the possible description of the two-way street between Interests and Congress. It is not a simple case of "protection for sale," as if senators and representatives are directly trading clauses in legislation to a corporate interest for direct campaign contributions, with the lobbyists acting as broker. The congresspeople in this case would be seriously rooked by their lobbyist brokers, whose take is more than eight times the corporate and union campaign contributions. That takes us to two questions:

Who are the lobbyists? And what service are they rendering for the congresspeople for so much money?

It is useful to piece together the nature of that service. From George's experience in Washington, we have gleaned that a critical role of the politician is to implant in the minds of the public a story about themselves. Our campaign metaphor—riding lawnmowers on TV—gives a vivid picture both of the politician creating the story, and also his disseminating it. But that is just the open aspect of the politician's story. There is also a more clandestine side. Leslie Aspin, the former chair of the House Armed Services Committee, and later Clinton's first Secretary of Defense, was known for his remark, "If you give Congress a chance to vote on both sides of an issue, it will always do it."[24] Our previous description of the winning election strategy tells us why Aspin's fellow congressmen were so taken by this bit of cynical wisdom. That strategy tells us that the congressman has dual goals: to appeal to the voters, on the one hand; and to appeal to campaign donors, on the other hand. It is thus no coincidence that both Romney and Obama were prominently caught at private fundraisers giving opinions in private that were highly unpopular with common voters: Romney in 2012, regarding the 47 percent who would "vote for the President no matter what [because they] are dependent upon the government"[25]; Obama, despite his notable self-control, four years earlier in 2008 at a fundraiser, regarding "Pennsylvania [voters in] small towns [as] bitter [and therefore] cling[ing] to guns or religion or antipathy to people who are not like them."[26]

The dual mandate of the politicians flips us back to the question of where the lobbyists fit in. The lobbyist is in a special position to help the politician. The very nature of his occupation—that he is being paid by an interested party—gives him special knowledge regarding where to find money on the loose: because Interests' willingness to pay the lobbyist to promote their cause identifies who would be especially enthusiastic about a politician of like mind. (Thus lobbyists' mere existence and employment by a given industry serves as an indicator of potential funds—where there is smoke, there is fire.) In the tough world where congressmen must extract significant sums from the public to run their campaigns, the lobbyist can then be the beacon to the much-needed pot of gold.[27]

In addition, a good lobbyist has a further role to play. He can help the politician thread the needle: of sculpting the story with the best trade-off between extracting votes from the general public, and money from the Interests. There is a view in political science—which, as we will see later, is similarly expressed in the Supreme Court decision regarding Citizens United—that activities like lobbying involve transfers of "information."[28] That may be true, but lobbying passes this information through carefully sculpted narrative, which is intentionally colored with bias. Advising on the creation of that narrative requires an intuitive understanding of two faces—public and private—that the politician wants to present simultaneously. That is the sort of sympathetic understanding that we get from our best friends and confidants. It is thus no coincidence that lobbyists are most typically drawn from ex-staffers, who have held that role in the past, and also from former members of Congress themselves. In the class of congressional retirees for 2010, a full 50 percent of senators and 42 percent of representatives became lobbyists (up from 3 percent for both houses in the easier times of 1974, when the candidates had much less need of donations).[29] And just as lobbyist-as-friend serves the goals of the politician, friend-of-politician makes the lobbyist attractive to potential clients.

A story reveals the place of Aspin's aphorism in the working of the Congress. Through its standard procedures, the US Senate has even constructed the opportunity for senators to vote both ways on almost all funding. The rookie senator Ted Kaufman—the inheritor of Joseph Biden's seat when he became Vice President in 2009—learned this fact the hard way. Appalled by the financial fraud that led up to the 2008 financial crisis, Kaufman co-sponsored a bill to prosecute it (FERA—the Fraud Enforcement and Recovery Act).[30] One of its major provisions was authorization of $165 million to the Department of Justice to fight white-collar crime. These funds were especially needed in 2009, because, in the aftermath of 9/11, Justice had gutted its white-collar crime division. The resources were transferred to anti-terrorism.[31] FERA easily and enthusiastically passed both the House and the Senate; Kaufman was elated. But in short order he discovered that while his colleagues had *authorized* $165 million, they would subsequently *appropriate* no more than $30 million in the annual budget bill.[32] His colleagues would not push farther, since larger expenditures would endanger Wall Street contributions. Aspin's witticism—and the optimal strategy of one story for the voters, another for the donors—had literally come to life.

But Does It Bite?

We have described the qualitative ways in which campaign spending and lobbying affect government, and yield to the exercise of monkey-on-the-shoulder tastes. But are the effects significant? Are they small relative to total federal government spending, which, at almost $4 trillion, is more than a thousand times larger?[33] For this purpose, we will explore whether the distortionary multiplier—that is, the ratio between the changes in spending and regulation because of the lobbyists and the payments they receive—is large or small.

As much as loyalty and friendship, a commitment to secrecy is also a trait of the ideal lobbyist; this means that the data we seek, some measure of campaign/lobbying costs relative to tangible changes in government activity, are hard to come by. We must look for rare events to get such a glimpse, just as volcanologists, at the first sign of volcanic eruptions, rush off to view the flowing magma that reveals what lies beneath the earth's surface. For us, the odd desire of Washington lobbyist Gerry Cassidy for a "tell-all" biography provides two such situations[34]; the lobbying for a change in taxation of overseas earnings by US corporations gives us a third; and revelations emanating from the 1980s savings and loan crisis give us a fourth.

Seawolf. In his January 1992 State of the Union address, George Bush proposed the withdrawal of already-appropriated funds for the building of two new *Seawolf* nuclear submarines. The producer of these ships, General Dynamics, responded immediately: they retained Gerry Cassidy, at the cost of $120,000 per month, to mastermind a publicity and lobbying campaign.[35] The *Seawolf* was saved, as the $2.8 billion proposed rescission was aborted.[36] But the payments to the lobbyists, and the increase in the campaign contributions, were small change relative to their effects. For the years 1991–92, General Dynamics' congressional campaign contributions increased by only $198,000 over the 1989–90 election cycle.

Tax Savings. A study by Raquel Alexander, Stephen Mazza, and Susan Scholz[37] further suggests how high the returns to lobbying can be. Back in the early 2000s, foreign subsidiaries of US multinationals were allowed to retain their earnings untaxed, as long as they were not repatriated; a large balance of never-US-taxed earnings had accumulated abroad. The United States wanted to get them back. The Congress enacted the American Jobs Creation Act (the AJCA) with a one-year 85 percent deduction (Section 965) on untaxed earnings brought home. The standard tax rate on dividends for the repatriated funds at the time would have been 35 percent; after that 85 percent deduction it was only 5¼ percent. On this basis, thirty-nine companies that had joined a coalition to lobby for the bill had tax savings of $46 billion on what they brought home; the total lobbying expenditures for the coalition firms were, in total, $180 million. The tax savings from the amnesty were, then, at least 255 times the lobbying costs.[38]

Cranberry Juice. Similar spectacular returns are reported for Ocean Spray, regarding the labeling of cranberry juice. During the Reagan administration the Food and Drug Administration threatened to require cranberry juice to be labeled as 75 percent water.[39] Ocean Spray turned to Cassidy for advice. A handful of congressmen were given speaking engagements with honoraria of $2,000 and $4,000; $375,000 of PAC contributions were also distributed. Prohibition against any regulation requiring disclosure of fruit-juice content was, with no fanfare, slipped into an appropriations bill.[40] Mission accomplished. The gains to Ocean Spray were huge: by 2005, US sales of cranberry juice had topped $750 million.[41] The costs of lobbying, in contrast, were minuscule.[42]

Charles Keating and Lincoln Savings. In the savings and loan crisis of the 1980s (which will be discussed in much greater detail in chapters 9 and 10), the court case against Charles Keating, the owner of Lincoln Savings and Loan, revealed some estimates of the relationship between campaign contributions and taxpayer losses. As a partial return on Keating's $1.4 million of campaign donations, five US senators browbeat the regulators who had begun to investigate him.[43] Those senators met with the regulators; and they pointedly said they wanted to be sure that the Federal Home Loan Bank Board would not "injure a constituent."[44] This and similar roadblocks Keating tossed in the way of the investigations were responsible for an estimated $1 billion of the $2 billion to $3 billion total cost of resolving his bankrupt savings and loan.[45]

Specific instances are rare in which we can make a price comparison of the cost of the campaign-contribution *quids* to the value of the benefits to the Interests from the *quos*. But circumstantial evidence of the effects of that money in politics abounds. It is, for example, no coincidence that the House Financial Services Committee is especially unwieldy: it has almost 15 percent of all the members of the House, and is known as a "money committee." Both parties strategically place members there who are likely to be vulnerable in their next elections.[46] Nor is it likely that the disappearance of that extra $135 million to fight white-collar crime authorized in the FERA was an accident. And we do not view it as just coincidence that the IRS is so underbudgeted that it fails to collect hundreds of billions of owed taxes (estimated by the IRS itself at $385 billion for 2006).[47] The budgets of Justice, the IRS, the Securities and Exchange Commission (SEC), and many other regulators are greatly curtailed. Such evidence is less specific than would be admissible in a court of law; but at the same time it is also revealing that the influence of rich donors trumps economic policy that would be good for the rest of us. We will revisit the underfunding of the SEC at greater length in the conclusion.

Summary

In sum, the nexus between lobbying and campaign funds, the Congress, and the Interests is a breeding ground of phishing for phools. Just as phishing for phools is a major factor in making markets less attentive to people's real needs, so it plays a similar role in undermining democracy. Democracy may be the best form of government known to mankind; but it does not automatically protect us from the exercise of monkey-on-the-shoulder tastes. On the contrary, in many ways, as we have seen, where politicians need to raise money to pay for their campaigns, it systematically creates and spawns them.

Postscript. We might add many postscripts to this chapter regarding issues we have not covered; one topic stands out as especially necessary of mention. This chapter has mainly focused on lobbying of the Congress. Quite possibly of yet greater importance is the lobbying of the regulatory agencies, not to mention lobbying of state and local governments.

SIX

Phood, Pharma,
and Phishing

In 1906 the upstart novelist Upton Sinclair intruded on the public's peace of mind. He wrote a novel, *The Jungle,* based on the meat-packing houses of Chicago. His intent was to expose the immigrant wage slavery of the early twentieth century, as Harriet Beecher Stowe's *Uncle Tom's Cabin* a half century earlier had exposed African American slavery (and was a major precipitator of the Civil War).[1] But *The Jungle* created an uproar of an unexpected type, as it led to the discovery by middle-class housewives that the steak they were serving for dinner might come from tubercular cattle.[2] Or tidbits from poisoned rats could be in the sausage, or from human remains in their "Durham's Pure Leaf" lard.[3] The demand for the packers' meat fell by half and their minions in the Congress passed the Federal Meat Inspection Act of 1906,[4] whose provisions have made the problems reported by Sinclair pretty much a thing of the past.

Another significant movement, in the first decade of the twentieth century, placed considerable restriction on phishing, with the passage of the Pure Food and Drug Act, also in 1906.

Given the state of medical knowledge and public credulity at the time, nineteenth-century America was fertile ground for unscrupulous "confidence men" to sell quack remedies. William Swaim is an example from the early part of the century. He bottled a concoction he called Swaim's Panacea. The label on the bottle illustrated its magic: Hercules is battling a many-snake-headed hydra. The Panacea was a "*Recent Discovery for the Cure of Scrofula or King's Evil, Mercurial Disease, Deep-Seated Syphilis, Rheumatism, and All Disorders Arising from a Contaminated or Impure State of the Blood.*"[5] But a report by a New York committee of doctors gave a different opinion: they said it had caused numerous deaths. Medicine may have been ineffective at the time, but in this case the doctors were right. Among Panacea's ingredients was mercury. Swaim, unfazed, responded to the physicians' thirty-seven-page report with a fifty-two-page reply: "I have not passed through life," he wrote, "without [observing] that assertions, however broad and unfounded, if permitted to pass into the mind of the hearer, without contradiction, will frequently be received with the acquiescence due only to established truth."[6] Swaim was a pusher of killer medicine, but not without a sense of humor.

Another example comes from William Radam, a gardener from Austin, Texas. Merging his botanical knowledge with the emerging science of the time, Radam hypothesized that all those devilish microbes recently discovered in European labs would cause decay, within the human body. He had himself observed that after thunderstorms fungi would not grow. The lightning did something to the air. Radam reasoned that he could make a concoction with the same natural effect. He called his cure Microbe Killer. When two patients seemed to recover miraculously, it was off to the races. No two batches of the Killer, apparently, were the same, as analyzed by the Department of Agriculture. Its overwhelming bulk was water, with other ingredients such as wine and a strong, but probably sufficiently diluted, acid. Radam moved to a mansion overlooking Central Park.[7]

The chief chemist at the Department of Agriculture, Harvey Washington Wiley, a colorful Indianan born in a log cabin, who had graduated from Harvard, wanted to curb such nonsense. He felt that the public should be aware of impurities in food and drugs. A food labeling law would be enforceable, because the science of the time allowed assays of food ingredients. A turning point in the campaign came from an experiment he conducted. Twelve young men volunteered to take all their meals in a dining room at the Department of Agriculture, with a diet variously laced with food additives such as borax and formaldehyde.[8] Within short order they lost their appetites and suffered indigestion. In retrospect it seems quite possible that these gastrointestinal upsets were not caused by the additives themselves, but instead by what was said about these brave young men. The press had made them minor heroes, describing them as the "poison squad."[9] The passage of the Pure Food and Drug Act followed shortly thereafter.

Fast-Forward to the Twenty-First Century

Back in 2010, when we began this chapter on food and drugs, we intended it to be a "just so" story. We would go back to the nineteenth-century rotten meat and snake oil; we would tell of the passage of the Meat Inspection Act and the Pure Food and Drug Act, as we have done; then we would fast-forward to the twenty-first century. Our message would be "this time it's different": with-regulation now—in contrast to without-regulation then—food and drugs are safe. But when we undertook to describe modern times, we found a surprise. It's another case of "this time is different," but again with its ironic—rather than with its literal—meaning. The literal meaning just ain't so. Neither food nor drugs are now as safe as we had thought. Phishing goes on, avoiding the net of the regulators, now in more sophisticated ways.

Consider food. Instead of the steaks from tubercular cattle reported by Sinclair, we have the phood industry. It phishes us, massively, with its offerings: laden with sugar, salt, and fat. We now rarely go to the hospital with food poisoning. But we have food-induced coronary diseases and diabetes. Phood's appeal to our monkey-on-the-shoulder tastes has been so well documented elsewhere that we will say no more. But it is powerful evidence of our theory of phishing for phools.[10]

Regarding drugs, we had, similarly, thought that the Swaim's Panaceas and the Radam's Microbe Killers were gone with the past. We thought that Food and Drug Administration (FDA) requirements for drug effectiveness and safety now protect the unwary; we saw doctors' required intermediation between patient and pill as adding further protection. But we had underestimated the ingenuity of the Pharmaceuticals, as we had also underestimated the power of phishing for phools.

Vioxx

We will discuss at some length an example. It is extreme; but, as we will see, it uncovers what can go wrong much more generally. Merck—which, for six consecutive years, for 1985 through 1990, had been named *Fortune*'s Most Admired firm—brought out a new product in 1999. As George knows personally, the pain from arthritis is one of the misfortunes of old age. Non-steroidal anti-inflammatory drugs (NSAIDs), such as aspirin, ibuprofen, and naproxen, can provide relief from pain, but they also have adverse side effects. Such painkillers work by inhibiting two types of enzyme: COX-1 and COX-2. Inhibiting COX-2 reduces inflammation and pain. But COX-1 protects the lining of the stomach, and its inhibition causes ulcers.[11] Overdosage of NSAIDs is thus a leading cause of death among the elderly.[12] Merck had the bright idea (as did Searle) to create a drug targeted to block COX-2, but not COX-1.[13] Merck developed such a drug; named it Vioxx; and got it approved by the FDA. But that approval carried with it the further stipulation of a more rigorous randomized controlled trial than had been so far conducted.[14] Merck named that study VIGOR (the VIoxx Gastrointestinal Outcomes Research study). The events surrounding VIGOR will give us a feeling for why, despite our modern safeguards, we are still vulnerable to phishing by Pharma.

Like publishing houses bringing out a best-selling book, the Pharmaceuticals carefully orchestrate the rollout of a blockbuster drug. The principal audience for the rollout are the doctors, who are the intermediaries between patient and pill. In turn, scientific articles in refereed medical journals are a critical link between doctor and prescription. For this reason the Pharmaceuticals with a new drug take special care to midwife such articles. In selecting the authors, who will receive the data from the experiments, the drug companies are not shooting in the dark. Their many connections (including those from the research support given by the company) clue them in: both regarding who will be influential and who will be favorable. The selectees are given easy access to the randomized controlled trials required by the FDA. They are also typically given "editorial support"—less graciously known as "ghostwriting"—for the article.[15] It is thus no coincidence that a higher fraction of journal articles sponsored by pharmaceutical companies are favorable to the drugs reviewed than articles funded by other sources.[16] Part of drug marketing is not just about the content of the articles published; it is also about their number. The lengths to which these numbers can be pushed was revealed in a minor scandal a few years ago, when the journal publisher Elsevier admitted that articles in six of its publications only appeared to be peer reviewed; they were sponsored by Pharmaceuticals, without mention of sponsorship.[17]

A report on Vioxx, based on VIGOR, then, naturally came out in the *New England Journal of Medicine* in November 2000, with lead author Claire Bombardier of the University of Toronto.[18] The trial had been conducted from January to July 1999: with 4,047 subjects receiving Vioxx, and 4,029 controls receiving naproxen (brand name: Aleve).[19] It appeared that the new wonder drug worked as promised. Not only did it alleviate pain; it also produced many fewer upper gastrointestinal events than Aleve. All told, there were 177 of them for the whole sample, the naproxen-takers having 2.2 times as many as the Vioxx-takers. The really serious gastrointestinal "complicated" events were also pretty much in the same ratio: 37 to 16.[20]

But then, there was a disturbing shadow, reported matter-of-factly by Bombardier and her coauthors. The Vioxx-takers had 17 heart attacks; the naproxen-takers 4. The ratio between these numbers was large; but 17 and 4 are sufficiently small so that the differences could just have occurred as a result of randomness.[21] Bombardier and her coauthors further suggest that, insofar as a difference between Vioxx and naproxen might exist, it was not due to the deficiencies of our boy, Vioxx.[22] Rather, it was probably because naproxen was cardiovascularly protective. These statistics and claims were presented in much the same voice as the side-effect mantras of the TV drug ads. And then the paper had another omission: that the Vioxx subjects had 47 confirmed serious thromboembolic events (that is, blocking of a blood vessel by a particle that has broken away from a blood clot) versus only 20 for the naproxen-takers.[23] Lest one think that 47 out of 4,047 is only a small number, it must be remembered that Vioxx had been developed for long-term use (especially, to relieve osteoarthritic pain). Over the course of, let us say, 5 years, at this rate of 1.16 percent for every six months, a user of Vioxx would have a quite significant chance of a "serious thromboembolic event."

We can well imagine how the authors of the paper would have felt. Their colleagues at Merck had developed a new wonder drug. It was being heralded as "super aspirin." The reduction in gastrointestinal complication resulted from the design of the drug itself. So the observed benefit there was to be expected. Anyone would be reluctant to rain on the parade. But recent research work had predicted that a COX-2 inhibitor such as Vioxx would also cause the observed cardiovascular side effects. This research (by the University of Pennsylvania's Garret FitzGerald with various coauthors) found that the suppression of COX-2 alone would interfere with the balance between two important lipids: prostaglandin and thromboxane. Jointly, they control the lining and width of blood vessels, and also the formation of blood clots. Inhibition of COX-2 alone would upset the balance between the two, and therefore be likely to lead to abnormal blood flow and/or clotting.[24] Merck was aware of this research, especially since it had funded it[25]; it had also been described in a press release in January 1999 from the University of Pennsylvania Health System.[26]

The statistics from VIGOR (and also from other studies conducted by Merck but not made public) should have been a red flag for caution, but Merck had its special reason to forge ahead. Vioxx was in competition with the alternative coxib painkiller Celebrex, which had passed through merger to archrival Pfizer.[27] Merck's marketing department was thus doing its part in the rollout. In the summer of 1998 as a pre-kickoff prior to Vioxx's introduction, Merck, jointly with Pfizer, Roche, Johnson and Johnson, and Searle, sponsored a lavish conference at the Kapalua (Maui) Ritz-Carlton. Sixty leading lights of the painkiller research world were brought in to hear praises sung of the new super aspirins.[28] On another front, Dorothy Hamill, the Olympic figure skater, was recruited to do talk shows and advertisements. Charmingly and cloyingly, she told a story everyone could relate to: not only had Vioxx relieved her crippling neck and back pain; she was back dancing joyfully on the ice.[29] And three thousand drug reps (overall there is one drug rep for every six physicians in the United States[30]) were sent into the field.[31] They did not go unarmed. After the publication of the Bombardier et al. article, the drug reps were instructed how to respond to doctors' concerns regarding cardiovascular side effects. They were to hold up cards with three panels; one of the panels read:[32]

Overall Mortality and Cardiovascular
Mortality Events per Patient-Years

	Vioxx $N = 3,595$	NSAIDs $N = 1,565$	Placebo $N = 783$
Total mortality	0.1	1.1	0.0
Cardiovascular mortality	0.1	0.8	0.0

These data ignored the data from VIGOR. Nor is it clear where they came from, if anywhere at all. A memorandum to the Democratic members of the House Committee on Government Reform has said that these figures "appear to have little or no scientific validity."[33] Additionally, as described in the *New England Journal of Medicine* by cardiologist Eric Topol, Merck's attempts to whitewash doctors' concerns were "relentless"; he describes med-ed symposia at national meetings with that purpose; and also journal articles by Merck employees and Merck consultants.[34] Regarding med-ed, Merck had developed a team of 560 doctor-speakers even before the launch.[35]

And so Vioxx was rolled out and defended. By 2004 annual sales had reached $2.5 billion.[36] But the shadow was looming ever larger. The statistical findings indicated that the possibility that Vioxx could cause heart attacks was a reality. Tellingly, the associate director of the FDA division for safety, David Graham, who had suspicions from the beginning, teamed up with the health maintenance organization Kaiser Permanente. They compared the incidence of myocardial infarction (heart attack) in 26,748 patients who had been given Vioxx to the incidence in matched patients with different treatment.[37] Again it showed a statistically significant increase in patients given Vioxx. With the evidence mounting, Merck took a peek at preliminary outcomes of APPROVe, a randomized trial aimed at showing that Vioxx suppressed (cancer-causing) colon polyps.[38] Of the subjects, all of whom had been prescreened for absence of cardiovascular problems, 3.5 percent had myocardial infarction or stroke.[39] This, finally, was too much: Merck removed Vioxx from the market on September 30, 2004. The toll in the United States, as estimated by David Graham, was 88,000 to 139,000 heart attacks, with deaths conservatively estimated in excess of 26,000.[40]

Gaming Approval

The Vioxx affair is not just an example of a Pharmaceutical doing a cover-up, run morally amok. It was also an accident that was waiting to happen: as the rules regarding safety, effectiveness, and prescriptions of drugs made Pharma a playing field for phishermen. Now we turn to phishing in Pharma for getting drugs prescribed: first, in obtaining FDA approval; and, afterward, in marketing them. We will comment on both of these, reflecting on the lessons from Vioxx. An appendix to this chapter will describe how Big Pharma also phishes for the prices they receive.

Obtaining FDA Approval

The public and the doctors, and possibly also the FDA, were taken by surprise largely because of their overconfidence in the "scientific method" of randomized trials. Just as Radam sold Microbe Killer on the basis of the science of the late nineteenth century, Vioxx was sold with the confidence that it represented the best from modern science, with checks on its validity by trials such as VIGOR.

But an important concept in statistics shows why randomized controlled testing will often fail, and especially why it failed with VIGOR. In the case of Vioxx, a great deal of data was necessary to show that the heart attacks that were showing up were not just occurring by chance. So much data was needed for a simple reason: thankfully, heart attacks, as serious as they are, do not occur often. In the language of statistical testing, the infrequency of heart attacks meant that the six-month VIGOR trial would have "low statistical power" in showing that Vioxx, taken over the longer term, would greatly increase the chances of hospitalization and of death. In contrast, the short-term (six-month) duration of VIGOR was only a small impediment to testing its much more immediate impact, which included the relief of pain and the reduction of gastrointestinal complications. This short-term/long-term problem is not just peculiar to Vioxx. Much more generally, the FDA standards for drug approval privilege drugs with short-term (but possibly quite small) benefits; while those standards allow drugs with long-term (but possibly quite serious) side effects to slip through.

But the FDA's difficulties of banning drugs with serious long-term risks went considerably beyond the problems of statistical power: because the FDA gave the drug companies at least five degrees of freedom regarding how to conduct and present their tests. These freedoms made it possible for drugs that were on the margin of effectiveness or of safety to pass the bar of approval.

First, the Pharmaceutical typically only needed to present two trials that demonstrated the effectiveness of the drug; but, of course, they might not show other trials that had shown negative results.[41] (In the case of Vioxx, studies with negative side effects were released to the medical community only after protracted delay.)[42]

Second, the Pharmaceutical had some choice regarding the length of the trial. (For example, in VIGOR, three heart attacks and a stroke were excluded because they had occurred beyond the "pre-specified date" for the end of the trial. Curiously, Merck chose the "pre-specified" date regarding cardiovascular events one month earlier than its cutoff for adverse gastrointestinal occurrences.)[43]

Third, the trial could select the target population, which might be chosen strategically so that the effectiveness of the drug would show up; or, alternatively, so that the side effects would not. (We see the spirit of such selection in Bombardier et al. They argue that cardiological failures in the Vioxx group significantly exceeded those for the naproxen subjects only for the 4 percent who should have been taking supplemental aspirin. The implication is: no worry; this small group should have been excluded from the VIGOR trial.)[44]

Fourth, there was some choice in the placebo-control.[45] (We now know that Merck purposely chose naproxen as the control in VIGOR because it was a non-steroidal "known to produce more severe gastrointestinal effects than many other non-selective NSAIDs."[46] If you want to win a race, choose the slowest runner as your competitor.)

Fifth, the Pharmaceutical could also choose the test population and where the test was conducted. Less than half of trials by GlaxoSmithKline are now conducted in the United States, and the growth rate of trials in less developed countries (China, for example, at 47 percent) is huge.[47] We wonder about the willingness of companies that test drugs in poorer countries, where regulation is less stringent, to mine their reputations to obtain contracts.

Marketing the Drugs

Beyond approval of a drug, there is further scope for the Pharmaceuticals to game the system. This time they are not gaming the FDA; they are gaming the doctors. Here, as we have discussed regarding the article by Bombardier and her coauthors, the medical journals are the first line of attack. The drug reps, bearing not only pens and product samples, but also reprints of the journal articles, are the second. And then the Pharmaceuticals have a third line: through medical education. Most states require some continuing education for licensed physicians. The drug companies make this convenient: they sponsor symposia for doctors, regarding the current state of medicine. They hire and pay the speakers. This affords another golden opportunity. If the Pharmaceuticals arrange the meetings, they can choose those who are favorable to their drugs (information they know from the prescription records of the pharmacies).[48] It is not just that the doctors will relax their suspicions if the drug companies are footing the bills for the educational outings; the drug companies also influence what will be taught by doctors to doctors.

We have seen all of this before in a different context, in chapter 5 on politics. The "marketing campaign," as it is called, is like a political campaign. The purpose of the journal articles, the sales rep visits, the med-ed, the plush rollout conferences, and the public ads on TV is to create the story of the new wonder drug. It is to put the doctors in the mental frame that their patients may have *this disease* for which *this drug* has been specially targeted. The goal of the campaign is to change doctors' mental frames: from focus on the side effects down the road *if the drug is prescribed,* to focus instead on the loss of benefits *if the drug is not prescribed.* The campaign reaches true success (like winning The Election for a politician) when the medical associations incorporate the drug into guidelines for treatment.

With the lack of power of tests for long-term side effects, and with the power of modern marketing, it should not be surprising that Vioxx is not the only drug with deleterious side effects that has been on the market in modern times. Hormone replacement therapy (HRT) for women in menopause began in 1942 with the introduction of estrogen supplements. They were made from pregnant mares' urine (hence the name of the drug Premarin—PREgnant MAres' uRINe). In 2003, Britain's Million Woman Health Study concluded that HRT, especially in the form of combined estrogen-progestagen supplement, had caused 20,000 extra cases of breast cancer in Britain in the preceding decade. This number extrapolates (on the basis of population) to 94,000 extra cases in the United States.[49] And consider a contemporary example. It is now estimated that one out of every nine school-aged children and adolescents in the United States has been diagnosed with attention-deficit hyperactivity disorder (ADHD). Ritalin, the drug that is most commonly prescribed, is powerful—its long-term side effects unknown. But we also know that many diagnoses are almost surely wrong, one way or the other, since the diagnosis rate for Kentucky (15 percent) is more than three times that for Nevada (4 percent); and among populous states, the diagnosis rate for Texas (9 percent) is half again as big as that for California (6 percent).[50]

Final Word

This chapter has focused on phishing of food and of drugs. In 1906, with considerable modification afterward, food and drugs were nationally regulated for the first time in the United States. The packers were no longer allowed to sell meat, for example, that was unsafe. But phishing has migrated elsewhere. As mentioned in the preface, the nurses are now getting fat on potato chips. They know what they are buying. The chips come in bags that are correctly labeled, even with the number of calories; but the companies are phishing their customers in another way. The potato chips are now scientifically designed, with the optimal amounts of fat and salt, to maximize their sales. Phishing for phools has taken a new form, within the new boundaries set by regulation. It is exhausting the opportunities for profit. That is the equilibrium. Phood is still served.

Regarding drugs, the Vioxx case yields a similar lesson. The Pharmaceuticals now must obtain FDA approval in order to market new drugs. Those drugs must also be prescribed by doctors. But the Pharmaceuticals have found creative ways to phish the FDA, and to phish the doctors. Regulation has not eliminated phishing—again in this case, as in the case of phood. It has just changed the focus of activity.

Appendix: Pills and Prices

So far we have focused on drug effectiveness and safety. But Big Pharma also phishes in another way: to obtain advantageous prices for its pills. When Merck was threatened by lawsuits for Vioxx-related damages, its lawyers went to town. But Pharma's lawyers also go to town in another way. Pharmaceuticals are one of the biggest sources of congressional lobbying. According to its industry-classification, the Center for Responsive Politics (a Washington think tank that keeps tabs on such things) says that the pharmaceuticals/health products industry spent more on lobbying from 1998 to 2014 than any other industry. For the full period, that was almost 50 percent more than the second on the list, which was insurance.[51] It would appear the payoff to Pharmaceuticals has been high. To give just one example, in the bill that added Part-D drug coverage to Medicare (the Medicare Modernization Act of 2006) Big Pharma got a special deal. The bill specified that the government could not engage in competitive bargaining to obtain lower prices for pills on behalf of the beneficiaries.[52]

But their lobbying prowess is not the only major advantage of the Pharmaceuticals in getting high prices for their drugs. Most businesses have to deal with the inconvenience that if the price is too high, customers will take their business elsewhere. But that tendency is greatly modulated for the Pharmaceuticals for two reasons. First, those who typically choose the drug—the doctors—do not pay the tab for their prescriptions. Compounding this problem of bad incentives, patients with insurance (including Medicare) typically do not pay either. This absence of consequence for decisions means that the Pharmaceuticals can charge enormous prices. All college students and their parents are familiar with this phenomenon, but in a different context. The professors assign the textbooks, but it is the students (and their parents) who pay the tab. Just to give one example, the current list price of the latest edition of Gregory Mankiw's (excellent) textbook, *Principles of Economics,* is $361.95; but you can get it at a bargain, on Amazon, for only $315.15.[53]

SEVEN

Innovation:
The Good, the Bad, and the Ugly

I f current economics were written as music, it would be in C major. It sings praise for free markets, as churchgoers at Christmastime stand up and sing the Hallelujah Chorus. The purpose of this book is to make economics more subtle. Being aware of the benefits of free markets should not also blind us to their defects. We want an economics in a minor key, more New World Symphony than Hallelujah Chorus. In all the previous chapters we have given examples of how phishing pollutes otherwise good economic equilibria. Here we apply this in a new context: to economists' interpretations of economic growth. We will first describe briefly the current theory of economic growth; but then, also, why it too needs to take account of phishing for phools.

The Fundamentals of Economic Growth

According to standard economics, at any given time free markets give immense benefit by giving huge amounts of choice. Today, in the worldwide global economy, they allow most of the world's adults to trade—perhaps indirectly—with one another. That yields a lot of choice: with some 25,000,000,000,000,000,000,000,000 (25 quintillion) possible pairs of adult buyers and sellers.[1] But there is another, probably yet more important, dimension to free markets. New ideas, resulting in new products and new services, over time, increase people's range of choice further. In free markets such new products and services that can generate increased profits will be selectively sought out and adopted. Over the course of the past century, one idea once a month by all the world's adults would have yielded more than three trillion new ideas.[2] The implications are enormous: over the course of a lifetime, in a typical developed country, output per capita will increase sixfold.[3] Older retirees in the United States were born in a country poorer than present-day Mexico.[4]

This critical role of new ideas as the engine of economic growth had been chewed over for decades, but then it was definitively established in 1957 by a simple, clever calculation: a 32-year-old economist at MIT, Robert Solow, took a page out of Sherlock Holmes to get his answer. He eliminated the other leading suspect.

Before the Solow calculation, economists did not know how to apportion economic growth between two causes. Increases in labor productivity (that is, increases in output per man-hour) could be due to new inventions (called "technical change"); or they could be due to increases in "capital" (e.g., machines, buildings, etc.).[5] With the simple assumption that the earnings of capital represent its contributions to output, Solow was able to calculate the fraction of increases in productivity that was attributable to capital growth. He found (for the United States for the years 1909 to 1949) that it was only one-eighth. The remaining seven-eighths must be due to the other suspect, which was new ideas. Solow said that this "residual" was due to "technical change."[6]

With that small neat calculation, economists' views of economic progress changed forever. No longer were increased standards of living thought to be mainly the result of ever more, ever larger factories, employing workers under appalling conditions: like the Manchester textile factories of the nineteenth century, or like the Bangladeshi textile factories of today. This simple one-line calculation created a new image of the sources of economic growth. Back at the time of the calculation, in the 1950s, it would have been characterized by phrases such as "Better Things for Better Living ... through Chemistry," the motto of DuPont. To later generations it would be Silicon Valley, a name that would emerge some two and a half decades into the future. In this vision, free-market capitalism does not just give us our current abundance of goods and services from people trading according to their comparative advantage; it also gives us ever-increasing abundance through the application of new ideas.

The Solow Residual and Phishing for Phools

There is almost surely a great deal of truth to Solow's calculation, and to his conclusion. But it is also Hallelujah economics. It reflects the innocence of its 1950s origins. Since that time, outside of economics, Americans, and to a great extent the rest of the world, have developed a more skeptical view than Solow's vision of new ideas in giving us uninterrupted progress. American history has always had its darker side: especially, the treatment of Native Americans, African Americans, Hispanics, Asian Americans, women, and gays. We began this chapter with mention of the New World Symphony. Its composer, Antonín Dvořák, wove into it themes from Negro spirituals and Native American dance: intentionally so.[7] Standard American History is no longer an unremitting crescendo, ending as it did in the 1959 Nixon-Khrushchev debate, with the superiority of American, relative to Soviet, kitchens.

That takes us back, curiously, to a subtle but erroneous inference from the Solow calculation. That erroneous inference is not only that progress is mainly due to new ideas, but also that new ideas invariably lead to economic progress. That is a natural conclusion as long as ideas are conceived as only technological: they make it possible to produce more output with less labor. But not all ideas, just as not all of our thoughts, are about things. Many of our ideas—perhaps even the core of our thinking—are about our fellow human beings. The mentally healthy have subtle abilities to perceive the thoughts of others: they have a theory of mind. It is one of the most attractive features of humanity. It underlies our sympathy for one another.

But theory of mind also has its downside. It also means that we can figure out how to lure people into doing things that are in our interest, but not in theirs. As a result, many new ideas are not just technological. They are not ways to deliver good-for-you/good-for-me's. They are, instead, new uses of the theory of mind, regarding how to deliver good-for-me/bad-for-you's. Such new ideas have emerged in every chapter of this book. We have seen, for example, the addictive slot machines of Las Vegas; the ratings agencies' labeling rotten "avocados" (i.e., rotten derivatives) as triple-A; the selling of the man in the Hathaway shirt and of the senator on the lawnmower; the doggie strategically placed in the window. The list goes on.

This means that our sense of economic progress is not as unambiguous as it seems. The indicators of economic growth (such as per capita income) may correctly reflect economic change; but not all such change is necessarily for the good. It was just a tacit assumption, reflecting the habitual patterns of thought of the times, that Solow's residual reflected "technical progress." Now we must look at economic growth more carefully, from a broader perspective.

To emphasize the point that not all inventions that expand our choices are for the best, or that some inventions carry their good with the bad, we offer three examples.

Three Inventions

Facebook. One of the best things about an electric light is the switch; it allows you to turn it off. Facebook can always be turned off; but, according to students at Yale we interviewed, its users often lack the mental discipline to do so, even when they know it would make them happier.

All of our interviews pretty much followed the same course. The interviewees would state the ostensible reason for using Facebook. They said it was "just talking to friends." They got "information." But then, in crescendo, as in an Ibsen play, more intense emotions would emerge: revealing a love-hate relation with Facebook. Its primary use was not, as originally stated, just linking friends with friends; rather, it was also the vehicle into "a reassuring alternate universe." There our interviewees got a social validation that was eluding them elsewhere.

The life of Yale undergraduates is competitive. For example, an admissions officer told the incoming class of 2009 that the applicant pool was so rich in talent that two wholly different classes could have been assembled from the applicant pool: with no regret from Admissions. Thus even at this elite college, the intensity of competition still leaves a need for recognition. It is quite possibly a healthy adaptation to create an alternative virtual universe, with an alternative currency of respect: such as "likes" from friends on Facebook.

But that lies also at the heart of the love-hate relation with Facebook. It also underlies our interviewees' desires for "likes." One of them told us: "You can't post pictures of your dog all the time because that's boring. There became this obsession with either being funny or exciting or being really attractive." One of our interviewees expressed nostalgia for the "old days," one or two years ago, before "likes" had become the craze. She deplored the get-the-likes rat race.

We were also told about another side of Facebook, as it had been used before the days of likes. One of the Yale students told us that

Facebookers post only their best, most enviable moments. But those moments made validation difficult for her. "The other time I ... hate Facebook ... is times like now—when I'm in [wintery] New Haven and everybody [else is] in much sunnier locations.... I want to step away, but in reality I'll keep looking at people's beach pictures and live vicariously through them."

Such findings from our Yale interviews conform to the results from a survey of Humboldt University students, regarding "emotions of Facebook users." When asked why *others* might be "frustrated or exhausted" by use of Facebook, about three-fifths (of the 86 percent of respondents answering the question) mentioned social causes: such as "envy," "lack of likes," "social isolation," and "not being invited" to events. The 30-percent mention of envy especially contrasted with respondents' reticence regarding how they felt on *their own* last use of Facebook; only 1 percent had admitted it.[8]

Is Facebook good or bad? It only allows expressions of "likes"; but not of "dislikes." This means that only positive validations are possible. Curiously, none of our interviewees mentioned their pleasure at giving "likes" to friends. But every "like" on Facebook is an act of generosity; it gives dignity and respect both to the givers and to the receivers. Our interviewees also indicated that the virtual universe of Facebook also interacted, strongly and usually positively, with the real universe. Their Facebook friends were, more often than not, real friends. Indeed their need for real friendship was also a critical feature in Facebook's popularity. If all your friends are posting on Facebook, opting out is like not going to the party where everyone else will be.

But Facebook is not without its negative aspects (as expressed by our interviewees as well as seen in the Humboldt survey). Where those negative aspects dominate, there is yet another new innovation. Robert Morris and Daniel McDuff, two students at the MIT media lab, have developed what they call "The Pavlov Poke," whereby your computer can be programmed to give you an electric shock if your time on Facebook has exceeded some limit.[9]

Rankings Everywhere. For another example of innovation (an economist might call it a "technical change"), consider the method adopted by United Airlines for herding passengers onto airplanes. In the spirit of a nineteenth-century duchy, United has conjured up a slew of honors and statuses. On a large plane, the order for boarding does not just depend on one's class of seat (First Class, Business Class, Economy Plus, and Economy)[10]; it also depends on the "elite" status conferred by the airline: Global Services, 1K, Premier Platinum, Premier Gold, and Premier Silver. Since people are addictively attracted to rankings, both of themselves and of others, the airline has discovered a remarkable phish for phools. It needs only to sit back and watch its customers jump through hoops, such as piling on miles and taking out United Airlines Visa cards, to attain those "elite" rankings of its creation.

We see the boarding of the plane as a Roz Chast moment. To recall, Roz Chast is the *New Yorker* cartoonist who draws people with funny expressions, with word-filled bubbles reflecting what is really on their minds. We would like to see one of her cartoons in which those bubbles express the momentary feelings of those Global Service/First Classers about their fellow travelers who are filing by to get to the back of the Airbus. And vice versa, we would also like to see the bubble-thoughts of those non-elites. Indeed, some interviews we conducted (again with Yale students) confirmed our suspicions regarding the content of those would-be bubbles. Self-aware, one of our interviewees expressed it in a single word. "The times that I do fly business class, I feel *smug* about being able to board first," she told us.[11]

Of course the rankings that determine airline seating are inconsequential. But fifteen years ago, reporter Nicholas Lemann wrote a book about a set of rankings that are not: from the Scholastic Aptitude Test (SAT) of the Educational Testing Service (ETS).[12] Back in the 1930s and 1940s mere attendance at a prep school like Exeter or Groton, for example, and a home on Beacon Hill (Boston) were pretty much sufficient for entrance into Harvard. Reformers of the time, who founded the ETS and promoted the SAT, wanted admissions to be broader based; and also with more account paid to "intelligence," which they thought could be measured by such a test.[13] Their innovation took hold; (following Lemann) these rankings have replaced having parents in the Social Register, but not without problems of their own. A new "meritocracy" has filled the gap; and as it has, where one ends up, and even one's take-home pay, increasingly depend on a college degree. Without such a degree, the Abraham Lincolns, or the Harry Trumans, or the Sidney Weinbergs among us now rarely stand a chance. The SAT itself plays a significant role in establishing whether and where young people go to college. And now rankings in education are pervasive. They begin at a very young age, in what economists Garey Ramey and Valerie Ramey have called "The Rug Rat Race."[14] And beyond the SAT and high school, the rankings go on. The colleges themselves are ranked[15]; the students in them are ranked (especially if they are going for further study); the journals in which their professors publish are ranked[16]; and so are the professors themselves, by where and how frequently they publish.[17]

These rankings have their effects. There are huge incentives for the students to study to the test; for the teachers to teach to the test; and for the professors to research to the journal "requirements." But the problems with rankings lie yet deeper than those serious distortions. And that takes us back to the Roz Chast bubbles, if those high in the rankings look down on those below. We think we see a side effect of such "smugness." Both of us (Bob and George) remember that United Airlines used to let families with children board first. A new norm seems to have arisen regarding the courtesy owed fellow travelers; in April 2012, United changed its policy; and that custom fell by the wayside.[18]

As with Facebook, we have mixed feelings about the educational rankings. We think we prefer a society in which the ETS plays its role in separating the haves from the have-nots to one in which that separation was based mainly on having parents in the Social Register. But we also have our reservations about an educational establishment that ranks people, as a certified "elite," who disrespect those who are ranked "below." Our ambiguity here mirrors the ambiguity that is a major theme of this book. Do we like free markets? Yes. But.

The Cigarette-Rolling Machine. Bizet's opera *Carmen* is set in Seville, Spain, in the 1820s. The protagonist, Carmen herself, works in a cigarette factory.[19] If the story had been set some eighty years later, she would most likely have been pictured as having a different occupation: because in the 1880s a Virginian, James Bonsack, invented a mechanical cigarette-rolling machine that greatly reduced the labor needed to make cigarettes.[20] The next chapter, on tobacco and alcohol, will describe the negative effect of this invention on human welfare.

EIGHT

Tobacco and Alcohol

In the modern United States, if phishing for phools is important anywhere, it is in the four great addictions: tobacco, alcohol, drugs, and
gambling. An addict is someone whose real tastes have been taken
over by a special monkey on his shoulder: the more the addict con-
sumes of these, the more necessary the monkey finds that consumption to be.[1]

In this chapter we will discuss the disparate careers of tobacco
and alcohol. Regarding tobacco, it is now considered stupid to
smoke—even, it would appear, to most smokers, since 69 percent
of US adult smokers want to quit.[2] In contrast, alcohol—at least in
moderation—is said to be good for one's health. We will see how
smoking has fallen into such disrepute, while alcohol has main-
tained its reputation.

Smoking and Health

If we go back some time, let's say to the 1920s, 1930s, and 1940s,
smoking was considered sophisticated. It made you sexy; it made you
cool. A famous Chesterfields ad gives the picture: an elegant man and
a glamorous woman are seated romantically on a beach. He is lighting a cigarette. The caption is: "Blow some my way."[3]

But then something happened. Ever since its discovery by Euro-
peans in the New World in the 1500s, tobacco had been questioned
regarding its effect on health.[4] Yet it was not until the 1950s that
definitive statistical evidence showed up. The answer arrived so late
because of a new invention. Back in the nineteenth century, pipes
and cigars were not uncommon, but tobacco was mainly chewed
and then spit out. That's what "spittoons" were for. But then, in the

1880s the cigarette-rolling machine was invented. In 1900 the cigarette was no more than a dot in the tobacco industry landscape, with annual US per capita consumption of just 49. By 1930 that number had increased to 1,365; and by 1950 to 3,322.[5] This increase was coincidental with an epidemic of lung cancer. In 1930 there were fewer than 3,000 lung cancer deaths. By 1950 there were 18,000.[6]

In the late 1940s two teams of researchers—one in the United States, the other in England—found a simple test for the role of smoking in this epidemic. They compared the smoking histories of lung cancer patients to similar histories from a carefully matched control sample. In the United States, Evarts Graham and Ernst Wynder constructed a sample of 684 lung cancer patients and their matches in US hospitals. Graham, who was at Washington University Medical School in St. Louis, had performed the first successful surgical lung-removal of a cancer patient; Wynder was an eager young medical student.[7] Comparing the smoking habits of those with lung cancer to a matched sample of male hospital patients, they found that the noncancer matches were 7½ times as likely either not to smoke at all, or to be light smokers.[8] Graham had initially been dubious that cigarette smoking caused lung cancer (why, he asked, was it typically isolated to only one lung, whereas inhalation went into both?); he had underwritten the study only because of Wynder's persuasiveness.[9] On seeing the results, he quit smoking himself, a convert to the antismoking cause.[10]

Meanwhile, across the Atlantic, a similar old/young pair—A. Bradford Hill, the professor of medical statistics at the London School of Hygiene and Tropical Medicine, and Richard Doll, a neophyte researcher in epidemiology—obtained similarly definitive results in a matched sample from London hospitals. For those who smoked more, the chances of being in the lung cancer group (rather than in the matched sample) rose systematically.[11] Graham and Wynder published their results in the *Journal of the American Medical Association*; Hill and Doll in the *British Medical Journal.* The year was 1950.

Within short order, nonepidemiological evidence showed biological links. When Graham, Wynder, and their fellow researcher Adele Croninger painted cigarette tars on the backs of mice, 59 percent developed lesions; 44 percent had full-scale carcinomas.[12] None of the control mice were so affected. Oscar Auerbach and his coauthors autopsied the lungs of smokers and nonsmokers; the smokers had greater incidence of the preconditions of lung cancer.[13]

Hearing such bad news, the tobacco industry devised its response. Big Tobacco (which consisted of five major firms in the United States) were experts in creating images. Previously they had recruited the best in advertising to their cause. (Our two friends Lasker and Ogilvy were among them; but Lasker in the 1940s became a leading fighter against cancer[14]; and when the link between cancer and smoking became clear, Ogilvy rejected cigarette advertising.)[15] The leading tobacco companies turned to the public relations firm Hill and Knowlton.[16] Its job was to create a new story, to graft onto the public's growing awareness that leading medical journals were publishing strong evidence that cigarette smoking causes cancer.

The industry could not refute the findings that lung cancer patients were much more likely to smoke than matched controls; nor that scientific evidence showed a relationship between cigarette tars and cancer. They followed the advice of Hill and Knowlton to do the next best thing. They created doubt. Just as we will see in chapter 10 that financier Michael Milken realized that the public would have a difficult time differentiating between two types of "junk bonds," the tobacco industry saw that the public would, likewise, have a hard time differentiating one "scientist" from another. Graham, Wynder, Hill, Doll, Croninger, Auerbach, and others had produced telling evidence. But the tobacco companies knew they could find other "scientists" (especially among smokers) who would strongly voice the opinion that there was no "proven" link between smoking and cancer. They set up an independent research institute, run by the independent Tobacco Institute Research Committee (the TIRC), overseen by an independent scientific advisory board (the SAB).[17]

Big Tobacco did not just "luck out" when it chose the head of the SAB, who would also be the scientific director of the TIRC. It is useful to review the career and character of the man they carefully chose, Clarence Little, since it shows the tactics of the industry, more generally, in creating doubt. Little indeed was a famous scientist. As a graduate student in genetics, he had developed a strain of inbred mice. His interest in genetics developed from an early age, as his Boston-Brahmin father (who had retired early as a dry-goods commission merchant to breed dogs) passed on the art of breeding to his son—beginning with a gift of pigeons at the age of three.[18] Clarence brought this talent with him to college, where as a Harvard undergraduate he mated a brother and sister mouse. Going on to graduate school and the Harvard faculty, he gained fame as a producer of inbred mice. In Little's most important discovery, he found it possible to transplant tumors from inbred mice to hybrid mice; but not in the opposite direction.[19] When the Tobacco Industry discovered Clarence, they realized they had spotted a man who "knew" that cancer was genetic; whatever epidemiological evidence there might be, cancer *could not* be caused by smoking. It was the result of bad genes. These views regarding science were reinforced by Little's political and social activities. Little believed in eugenics ("misfits" should be sterilized); among other such affiliations, he had been president of the Race Betterment Congress, in 1928–29.[20]

Little, whose administrative talents had also made him president of the University of Maine and then of Michigan, was the perfect man for the Tobacco Industry. Here was a true believer. Whatever the evidence might be, he had no doubts that it had not been "proved" that cigarette smoking caused cancer.[21] He believed there was a need for more research, but grants by the Tobacco Institute on Little's watch would not touch on the relationship between cigarette tars and cancer. Little was also a barrel of energy, who would voice his opinions loudly, frequently, and memorably (for example, as president of the University of Michigan he had opined that "some of the most distinguished loafing in America is being done by ... [university] faculties").[22]

With such a spokesman, with Little and like-minded men on the SAB and the TIRC, Hill and Knowlton insinuated a new story into the relationship between smoking and health. There was a "scientific controversy" regarding whether, or not, cigarette smoking caused cancer. When CBS's star investigative reporter Edward R. Murrow presented two shows on the "controversy," Little was interviewed, as well as Wynder. However weighty the evidence for round earth (smoking causes cancer), it would make sprightly TV to juxtapose it with flat earth (smoking does not cause cancer), with Murrow characteristically smoking cigarettes throughout the shows.

The preceding history gives the background for a historic document: the Surgeon General's Report of 1964. That document addressed this ambiguity; it made clear that there was no debate.

On the contrary, the report made it the official position of the US government that, in schoolboy English, smoking was stupid. In officialese: The Surgeon General Has Determined That Cigarette Smoking Is Dangerous to Your Health.[23]

John Kennedy's Surgeon General, Luther Terry, had created an advisory committee on the relationship between smoking and health. The report really came from this committee, as reflected in its official title: *Smoking and Health: Report of the Advisory Committee to the Surgeon General.*[24] It not only reviewed the scientific evidence regarding the links between cancer and cigarette smoking; it went beyond any previous epidemiological studies, such as Graham-Wynder and Hill-Doll, in an impressive way.

It showed the results of combining seven separate studies—from the United States, Canada, and Britain—of morbidity and smoking. These studies had recorded the smoking habits of 1,123,000 respondents. In each of the seven studies, smokers had been matched with controls who did not smoke. The studies all followed up to discover how many smokers had died: 26,223 smokers in all; and also they obtained death certificates regarding death by cause. The committee computed how many smokers would have died if they had the same mortality rates by disease and by age as the matched nonsmokers. The expected value was much smaller: 15,654. In the terminology of the report, the smokers had an "excess mortality" rate of 68 percent.[25] The excess mortality did not just occur—as might be thought—for lung cancer, where the ratio of actual to expected deaths was 10.8, or for bronchitis and emphysema, where the ratio was 6.1. It was across the board by disease. For example, for coronary artery disease the ratio was 1.7. The gaps between the actual deaths of the smokers and their expected deaths in these combined seven studies were so large that—coupled with the further incriminating scientific findings—forever after it would be hard for a reasonable person to argue that cigarette smoking was not dangerous to one's health.

Since the report there has been a fifty-year struggle between Big Tobacco and subsequent Anti-Tobacco social movements. Big Tobacco has won its share of victories. In the United States, appealing to its free-speech rights, Big Tobacco has been able to stave off obtrusive labeling requirements; in contrast to the United States, Australia requires cigarette packages to show gruesome pictures: for example, of cancerous lungs.[26] Big Tobacco is also still allowed to advertise in print, although not on television or on radio.[27] In the settlement to the lawsuit brought by forty-six state governments, the tobacco companies agreed to pay $206 billion for expenses incurred by the states from smoking-caused health problems. But that was a bargain-basement price for what was also implicit in the package: exemption from further liability.[28]

Big Tobacco may have won its share of victories; but so has Anti-Tobacco. And in each of those victories, the authority of the Smoking-Causes-Cancer Story, especially emanating from the Surgeon General's Report, has been critical. The victories of Anti-Tobacco in turn have played a major role in spreading The Story further. In the first of these, a twenty-six-year-old lawyer, John Banzhaf, in New York, brought a complaint to the Federal Communications Commission (the FCC). According to the complaint, under the fair use doctrine in their licensing, insofar as TV stations advertised cigarettes, they had an obligation to provide equal time in the public interest to present the harms of tobacco. Remarkably, the FCC agreed, although granting one-third, rather than equal, time, as had been requested.[29] The antismoking ads, with their grizzly pictures and occasional macabre humor, were so effective that Big Tobacco ran for cover. It endorsed a ban on all television advertising of tobacco products.[30] Both the initial antismoking ads, and the subsequent television ban on Big Tobacco, affected the balance in the war between the two stories: smoking-is-stupid (Anti-Tobacco) and smoking-is-cool (Big Tobacco).

Anti-Tobacco won another surprising victory. In addition to creating scientific doubt, as a major part of its defense, especially against liability, Big Tobacco emphasized smokers' right to choose. But Anti-Tobacco turned this argument in its favor: if smokers have a right to choose, nonsmokers in indoor spaces are denied such a right. In this mutation of the Big Tobacco argument, *your* indoor smoking is dangerous to *my* health; as a smoker, *you* are violating *my* rights. Arizona, which is a haven for sufferers from respiratory problems, proved fertile ground for the secondary-smoke movement. In 1973 it banned smoking in public places.[31] Now, across America, we see office workers, outside, puffing on their cigarettes. Their guilty faces wordlessly spread the story that smoking is stupid; no one would want to be one of them.

After the Surgeon General's Report, cool gradually turned into stupid. And that's where we are now. 42 percent of US adults (53 percent of men; 31 percent of women) smoked then[32]; almost 18 percent do now (20.5 percent of men; 15.3 percent of women).[33] The fraction of smokers in the population has declined steadily by 0.5 percent per year for the past fifty years.[34] Not only does a smaller fraction of the population now smoke; those who do, smoke less. In 1965 smokers averaged 1⅜ packs per day; they average ⁹/₁₀ of a pack now.[35]

It is good that we have had this progress. But the glass is still half empty. The US Centers for Disease Control estimates that almost 20 percent of all US deaths from 2005 to 2009 were caused by smoking.[36] (Even entertaining the possibility that this huge number might be an overestimate, there can still be little doubt that smoking is highly hazardous to one's health.) And we all have sad memories. For us (George and Bob), it's Eva, Joe, John, Peter, Miguel, Margaret, Richard, Fischer, Anthony, ... and many others: our friends. For others— we hope not for you—it's worse: a father or mother, brother or sister, son or daughter. And as the economy has globalized, so has smoking, largely driven by American Tobacco, "blowing some their way."

Countering the phishing of Big Tobacco, Anti-Tobacco has had one continuing powerful asset: the story that smoking is stupid. The Surgeon General's Report of 1964 played a major role in the initial creation and in the further propagation of that asset.

It is useful to place our story of Big Tobacco in the larger context of this book: if ever there was a phishing equilibrium, this was it. Big Tobacco followed the strategies we have described because they were profitable. And they were lucky—but only a little bit lucky—to find Clarence Little to support their cause. He was a talented, but also an immensely stubborn, scientist who exaggerated the role of genetics as a cause of cancer, to the exclusion of environmental causes, including cigarettes. His recruitment to the cause of doubt was just one more aspect of the phishing equilibrium: absent Little, the Tobacco Companies would just have taken the next person on their list.

Alcohol

Whereas there is now consensus regarding the harms of smoking, the opposite is true regarding alcohol. Here the consensus story would be that alcoholism is a serious condition; but it is also fairly rare. That is a natural takeaway from standard statistics of the life-course of alcoholism from the National Institute of Alcohol Abuse and Alcoholism. According to the NESARC—that is, the National Epidemiologic Survey on Alcohol and Related Conditions—13 percent of male youths (the 18 to 29s) show indications of "alcohol dependence"; for the later middle-agers (the 45 to 64s) that fraction has dropped to less than 3 percent of the population. For women, the prevalence is much less: 6 percent for the 18 to 29s, and 1 percent for the 45 to 64s.[37] Statistics from the Centers for Disease Control sound a similar message. By their accounting, excessive alcohol consumption accounts for about 3½ percent of all deaths.[38] These statistics sum up what we believe to be the dominant picture of the harms of alcohol in US society. Alcohol has serious harms. They affect many people in total, but, beyond those youthful binges, their lifetime effects are concentrated in a relatively small fraction of the population. And at the same time, it is commonly felt that alcohol is a necessary ingredient for a party or celebration. The advertisers use this theme, picturing fun-loving, beautiful people, drink in hand. With images of this sort, bringing up the topic of the harms of alcohol is a bit like burping in public.

But we have decided, although not without considerable discussion between us, that yes, we ought to burp in public because, whatever the NESARC and other survey evidence may show, there is also evidence that suggests an alternative picture: that the harms of alcohol could be comparable to the harms from cigarettes, affecting not just 3 or 4 percent of the population, as a chronic life-downer, but, rather, affecting 15 to 30 percent; the higher number especially if we also include the alcoholics' most affected family members.

The leading evidence for this view comes from an unusual study. Back in the 1930s, the founder of a then-prosperous chain of variety stores (W. T. Grant) was convinced by the head of the Harvard health services to fund a continuing study of the life-course of Harvard students.[39] Those students would be especially chosen for their mental and physical health. The purpose was to discover the determinants of a happy life, as demonstrated by these young men whose privilege and accomplishment already gave them a huge leg up in that direction.[40] 268 students were chosen for the study, from the classes of 1939 to 1944[41]; and the study continued for seventy-five-plus years, passing in relay through four different directors. The third director, George Vaillant, has been the especial chronicler of the Harvard Grant Study, as it is now called.[42]

The leading finding of this study has been the role of alcohol in the lives of these otherwise privileged men. Twenty-three percent were diagnosed at some point in their lives as alcohol abusers.[43] Almost 7½ percent suffered from "alcohol dependence."[44] What's more, in Vaillant's view this dependence was, for them, not a passing problem of youth, but rather a chronic, debilitating physical and mental illness. Not only did they, on average, die at much younger ages than their nonalcoholic colleagues[45]; alcohol wrecked their ability to relate to others.

Surprisingly, Vaillant demonstrates that alcohol abuse negatively affects personality. Prior to the Harvard study it was common wisdom among psychiatrists that alcoholism was largely caused by bad childhoods. In this rather Freudian view it was the natural result of bad, cold mothers and bad, cold fathers. The psychiatrists had more than ample evidence for such opinions: they saw at first hand the kvetching on their couches (perhaps psychiatrist-induced) of their alcohol-abusing patients about their miserable, abusive childhoods. But data from the Harvard study provided a unique check on those complaints. At the beginning of the study, skilled interviewers had not only queried the students themselves about their childhoods; they had even visited their homes and interviewed the parents. These past interviews showed that the alcoholics were no different from their more sober peers. On the contrary, it seemed the alcoholism itself had changed their personalities, turning them into the kvetchers they had become.[46] Vaillant reaches a more general conclusion: the alcoholism was depriving its victims of their capacity for intimacy—the very capacity he saw as the basis for the happiness of their more sober college-mates. Furthermore, there was also a flip side of that harm, since the alcoholics were also hurting their wives and their children. These consequences appeared in the deep psychiatric interviews. But it could even be seen in the cold, hard statistics, in the high rates of divorce where either husband or wife was alcoholic.[47]

A taste of the ruined lives of the alcohol-dependent Harvard men comes from the story of "Francis Lowell."[48] He graduated magna cum laude; served in World War II, winning three battle stars for his role in the crossing of the Rhine and the Roer in the Allied advance into Germany; graduated in the top 10 percent of his class from Harvard Law School; and joined a prestigious New York law firm. His life should have been made. But as time passed, the weekend boozing that he had begun in college took over. The woman he met in his twenties, who would be the one intimacy of his life, turned down his proposal of marriage when he was age 30; she said he drank too much. Both of them continued to live with their mothers on weekends until the death of the girlfriend's mother twenty-three years later; shortly thereafter she married someone else. Poor Francis from that time forward had only one confidant: himself. His law practice continued; but he turned to the bottle after lunch on Friday and continued the weekend bender through Sunday, oft-times explaining away Monday absences.

We do not view Vaillant's point of view as proved. The evidence, necessarily, must be subjective. But another smidgeon of evidence yields a similar picture. In 2006, *Oakland Tribune* reporter Dave Newhouse went to the fiftieth reunion of his high school class at Menlo-Atherton High School. Back in 1956, before it had become the center of "Silicon Valley," Menlo Park/Atherton was *Leave It to Beaver* country: modest suburbia. For the reunion Newhouse interviewed twenty-eight classmates, publishing their reminiscences in a book titled *Old Bears*.[49] These old grads tell their tales of joys and sadness with what seems like remarkable honesty. At this point in their lives they seem to want to set the record straight.

For the bulk of the Old Bears, the focal point of their well-fulfilled lives came from their love for their husbands and wives. But for a significant minority a critical role was played, instead, by alcohol. For six out of the twenty-eight, at some time in their lives alcohol took center stage. The president of the class, who was also its football star, married his high school sweetheart; opened a law office in Palo Alto; became a father; but he ended up divorced and, in due course, sentenced to San Quentin prison, after repeated arrests for DUI (driving under the influence).[50] Another graduate married one of her English teachers at Stanford; but she found herself drinking so heavily that she blacked out. The alcoholism did not ruin her life; she got divorced, eventually dried out, and was granted tenure as a professor of French at Rutgers in Newark.[51] The first marriage of carpenter Bill Lawson ended after twenty-four years; his wife, Susan, said he drank too much. He claimed he didn't; walked out; and remained single for the next fourteen years (almost to the time of the reunion).[52] A fourth Old Bear endured twenty-two years of a second marriage to a drunk, before finally ending it.[53] And two others, including Newhouse himself, claimed permanent scars from their parents' alcoholism.[54] The stories of the Old Bears thus mirror, with a smaller sample and less precision, Vaillant's portrait of the somewhat older and somewhat more upscale Harvard grads.

This takes us then back to our basic question regarding alcohol and its effects. There is reason why the NESARC and other standard statistical measures of alcohol abuse can hide its effects. Vaillant sees the major symptom of alcoholism as victims' loss of capacity for intimacy. In our view, such psychological ailment, if Vaillant's observations are right, is truly destructive of well-being. The NESARC is based on the definitions of alcohol abuse and alcohol dependence of the Diagnostic and Statistical Manual of the American Psychiatric Association. "Alcohol abuse" is determined by a positive single response to a battery of questions such as: "[Did you] have job or school troubles because of your drinking or being sick from drinking?" The more serious condition of "alcohol dependence" depends on positive response to at least three questions such as: "[Have you had] a period when you kept on drinking for longer than you had meant to?"[55] The answers to the questionnaire in the NESARC are totally confidential, with special provision taken that they are not known even to the interviewers. But that does not mean the respondents tell the truth. Since, tellingly, Alcoholics Anonymous views the critical part of the cure as the admission that "I am an alcoholic," we could expect the alcoholic subjects to be working hard at denial. This supposition is in accord with a fact: the respondents to the NESARC report alcohol consumption that would conform to only 51 percent of total sales in the United States.[56] Just possibly, it may take skilled interviewers like Newhouse and Vaillant, and also just the right moment and venue, to worm out a true diagnosis of alcoholism; especially so if, following Vaillant, the true harms from alcohol are its subjective, hard-to-observe changes in personality.

Remarkably, our knowledge regarding alcoholism and its discontents then leaves us in about the same place we were with respect to tobacco in the late 1940s. Recall that even experienced lung surgeon Graham had been dubious regarding the role of smoking in causing lung cancer. Our lack of knowledge about the effects of alcohol is not a coincidence, however. A diagnosis of lung cancer is much easier to see than a diagnosis of loss of affect. But there is further reason why our knowledge of the magnitude of harms due to alcohol abuse is so much in doubt. The unequivocal results of the lung cancer studies empowered the Surgeon General to create a much more powerful story. In the absence of a similar story, alcohol studies remain largely underfunded. Compared to cancer research, alcohol epidemiology and alcohol research are backwaters.

But that takes us back to the yet bigger theme of this book, regarding phishing for phools. In the absence of the necessary research, we are especially prone to be phished for phools, since we cannot know whether we have the right story.

There are also lots of Interests that uphold doubts about the harms of alcohol: such as the producers of beer, wine, and liquor; the retailers; and the restaurants. We see their thumb in numerous locations. The leading one is their opposition to taxes. In nominal terms, the taxes on alcohol have barely changed since the end of Prohibition, when moderate taxes on alcohol (not too high, since that would encourage moonshining) were enacted as a method of control. Philip Cook of Duke University estimates econometrically that a doubling of the price of ethanol (that is, the type of alcohol in alcoholic beverages) will decrease its demand by 40 percent.[57] Although no one would swear on their children's lives that this is the "true" effect of raising prices (or taxes), encouragingly, different methods of estimation all seem to yield the same qualitative results: that as the tax on ethanol goes up, the quantity of ethanol sold goes down.[58] Equally encouraging, other indicators, such as the motor vehicle fatality rate, the fatality rate from falls, the suicide rate, and even cirrhosis mortality also suggest that tax increases will affect not just the light drinkers, but the heavy drinkers as well.[59]

But, discouragingly, the public has failed to take advantage of this method of alcohol control, which even has the advantage that the revenues can be used to keep down taxes elsewhere. This can be seen at both the federal and the state levels. In 2013 the federal tax on a can of beer was 5 cents; on a bottle of wine, 21 cents; and on an 80-proof bottle of liquor (whisky, vodka, or gin), $2.14.[60] State taxes are also gentle. As one example, in Massachusetts, the state excise tax on a can of beer is 1 cent; the tax on a bottle of wine is 11 cents; and the tax on a bottle of liquor is 80 cents.[61]

We chose Massachusetts as our example because of a recent hullabaloo that illustrates the power of the liquor industry to phish us for phools in keeping the taxes low. In a rare display of moxie, the Massachusetts legislature, as part of an omnibus bill to reduce the state deficit, voted a 6.25 percent sales tax on liquor sales, earmarked for expenditure on treatment of alcohol and drug addiction. This legislation passed; but the tax was not in effect for long. The liquor dealers cried foul. Their sales, they said, were drastically cut as customers ran across the border to the state-run liquor stores in neighboring New Hampshire. The very next year, the liquor dealers put on the ballot a special referendum item to repeal the tax. A leading argument (which was stated in the referendum ballot summary itself) was that there were already state taxes on alcohol: "double taxation, a tax on a tax." Of course there was no mention that the excise tax (for example) was only one cent on a can of beer. This referendum and its success illustrates why and how the industry has been so successful in keeping those excise taxes so low (although we should also mention that the Massachusetts liquor dealers are especially lucky; most other states do not exempt liquor from the sales tax).[62]

There has been some success in moderating alcohol abuse. MADD (Mothers against Drunk Driving) was begun in 1982 by Candace Lightner, whose 13-year-old daughter had been killed by a drunk driver. Gruesomely, he had fled the scene, with the body on the pavement. In most states in the 1970s, the minimum legal age for purchase of alcohol had fallen to 18, matching the national decline in the voting age. MADD successfully campaigned to raise the minimum drinking age to 21. They also lobbied for a low bar on blood alcohol level used to determine drunkenness and for random road stops with breathalyzer checks.[63] The movement has met with considerable success. Since 1982, fatalities per capita due to drunk driving have fallen by 72 percent. (Over the same period, driving fatalities per capita without alcohol involvement also fell, but by only 6 percent.)[64]

MADD emphasizes its educational mission, and especially its spread of the story of drunk driving. MADD mobilized the image of the drunk driver who kills the innocent victim. More than 82 percent of drunk-driving fatalities are either the driver himself (66 percent) or a fellow occupant (16 percent).[65] The MADD protagonists are almost always innocent bystanders; sometimes a passenger occupant, but never the driver himself.[66] It is useful to note that this story of innocent victimization, and its success, exactly parallels the story of secondhand smoke. Just as those smokers out on the porches, with their cigarettes as dunce caps, spread the image that smoking is stupid, those stories of drunk-driving victims have played a significant role in the moderation of alcohol intake. Since 1981, US ethanol consumption per capita has fallen by a not-insignificant 18 percent.[67]

But the most basic fact about tobacco and alcohol is that they are easily available with only moderate taxes. This easy availability of tobacco through the market, in and of itself, is the basic phish of the smokers; likewise, the easy availability of alcohol is the basic phish of those who end up drinking too much.

NINE

Bankruptcy for Profit

L et us turn, in this and the next chapter, to a financial crisis that is now mostly forgotten, the so-called savings and loan (S&L) crisis of 1986–95. It is worth going back to that crisis of several decades ago to obtain deeper understanding of the real nature of the mostly hard-to-see phishing that often takes place in the financial world.

Savings and loan associations are a form of banking institution that became popular in the United States in the early twentieth century. Modeled after the British building societies, these banking institutions have helped small savers accumulate some cash and also get a loan to buy a house or a car. That's a laudable objective. But in the 1980s a large number of S&Ls became tools for phishermen, which led to their bankruptcy. These bankruptcies were not minuscule in size. Their resolution cost the taxpayer approximately 230 billion inflation-adjusted dollars.[1] Yet more costly, the tightening of credit and drop in asset prices from the crisis was quite possibly a major trigger of the recession of 1990–91.[2]

The S&L crisis illustrates the problems of a phishing equilibrium, in comparatively recent times, but in a different institutional situation. Especially it took a form of phishing that economist Paul Romer, and one of us, George, have dubbed "bankruptcy for profit."[3] (We are grateful to Paul for allowing us to base this chapter and the next on that earlier joint work.) We will see a world where the usual economics, in which firms maximize their profits, is turned topsy-turvy; a world in which phishing, in the form of misleading (and sometimes fraudulent) accounting, leads to bankruptcy; but still it is the road to riches.

Looting

Only a child would ask. Why do the bankruptcy courts immediately take over companies when they go bankrupt? The answer is so obvious: if the company has only $125,000 and it owes $77,000 to Peter and $243,000 to Paul, someone must decide how that $125,000 should be divided. The court takes over to ensure that Peter is not unfairly (i.e., illegally) paid before Paul can get his share. That is the child's version of why the courts immediately take over, once a firm goes bankrupt.

But there is also a subtler answer (for adults, who understand the subtler facts of life). If the owners of a solvent firm pay themselves a dollar today out of the firm, they diminish the amount they can distribute to themselves tomorrow by that dollar plus its earnings. So the owners of a solvent firm have no special incentive to take money out of it today. In contrast, if the owners of a bankrupt firm take an extra dollar out of their firm, they will sacrifice literally nothing tomorrow. Why? Because the bankrupt firm is already exhausting all of its assets, paying all those Peters and Pauls. Since there will be nothing left over for the owners, they have the same economic incentives as Genghis Khan's army, as it marched across Asia: what they do not take today, they will never see tomorrow. Their incentive is to loot.

In this chapter we will see a situation in which S&Ls went economically bankrupt. Yet the supervisors did not move in. Instead, not wanting to "bail out" the S&Ls, they let them remain open. There were massive profits to be made by the unscrupulous. Take over an S&L that was under water. They could be purchased for a song. Borrow as much money as possible. And then, through the phish of clever (or fraudulent) accounting, find a way to tunnel that borrowed money out of the S&L, and then back to oneself.[4]

How It All Began

In the early 1980s inflation in the United States had risen to 13.5 percent.[5] Paul Volcker, the chair of the Federal Reserve, addressed the problem by squeezing the economy. He let interest rates soar; the rate on three-month US Treasury bills, the world's safest bonds, went to 14 percent in 1981.[6] In the fall of 1982 and the spring of 1983 the

unemployment rate rose above 10 percent.[7] In this war against inflation the country's S&Ls—quiet, nice banks where people kept their
savings, which also financed home purchases—were collateral damage. They had been giving out thirty-year fixed-rate mortgages at 5, 6,
7 percent.[8] They needed deposits to back those mortgages. And how
were they to meet the competition from the rapidly rising money
market funds, which were an alternative convenient place for consumers to store their savings dollars?[9] Any economist would say that
the S&Ls were bankrupt: not necessarily in the accounting sense—
that would depend on the accounting rules—but in the economic
sense. The money flowing in from the payments on the S&Ls' invest-
ments (almost entirely in the form of those fixed-rate mortgages)
could not meet the money needed to go out to attract the deposits
needed to fund those mortgages.[10]

As a complication, the FSLIC—the Federal Savings and Loan Insurance Corporation, which was the guarantor of the S&L accounts—did
not have enough in its trust fund to make up the difference between
what the S&Ls had and what they owed. The existing S&L deposits
could be paid off only with an infusion from the federal government.
But it would take until the George H. W. Bush administration before
such funds would be authorized. In the meantime such a use of funds
was unthinkable, and the can was kicked down the road.

Kicking the Can

With that kick of the can we discovered the answer to the child's
question: what really does happen when bankrupt institutions are
not taken over by the courts or closed by their supervisors? In short
order, a minor problem, which should have cost the taxpayers some
$33 billion to $49 billion (in today's money), ballooned into a problem that cost at least four and a half times as much.[11] Yet worse, the
indirect damage from the crisis was even more important. Real estate
markets in California and Texas boomed; and then went bust.[12] Arguably, too, as we will see in the next chapter, the economically bankrupt S&Ls jump-started a permanent change in American corporate
finance—but that is getting ahead of our story.

There were various ways for Washington to put off the day of
reckoning for the S&Ls. And they undertook a series of changes in

regulations, which, given that the S&Ls were seriously under water, were bound to fail. In the beginning, the regulators allowed the S&Ls to pay a slight differential over the limit that their competitors, the commercial banks, were allowed to pay on savings deposits. But when interest rates surged into the double digits in the early 1980s, banks were no longer the chief competitors of the S&Ls; instead, it was the money market funds, which were new at the time; and they had no ceiling. The policy failed. The S&L regulator, the Federal Home Loan Bank Board, also made minor changes in accounting that would allow S&Ls to be operated even while bankrupt.[13] This medicine too was not strong enough.

So the problem went to Congress. This was the age of deregulation. The idea was that the S&Ls, which were mildly bankrupt at the time because of the rise in the rate of interest, could emerge from bankruptcy if they were deregulated. What was forgotten, and probably also not understood at the time, is a lesson known by the parent of every toddler. If you let your 1-year-old out of the playpen (deregulate it), you need to watch it more carefully, not less so.

So the S&Ls were let out of the playpen. The Depository Institutions Deregulation and Monetary Control Act of 1980 eliminated the ceiling (at the time, a bit above 5½ percent) that the S&Ls could pay on deposits.[14] This gave the S&Ls an almost unlimited supply of funds, because large institutions such as banks and brokerage firms were quite happy to loan to them as long as the interest paid was high enough (and especially so since the FSLIC was also guaranteeing repayment, at least up to a limit).[15] The S&Ls had been limited to lending money for housing. Now that constraint too was relaxed. By the Garn–St. Germain Act of 1982 they were additionally permitted to lend up to 10 percent of their deposits to developers, and the S&L regulators treated this condition liberally.[16] S&Ls were not only allowed to charge an origination fee of 2.5 percent; in addition, the loan could include the interest payments that the developer was slated to pay while the project was under construction.[17]

Phishing for Phools to Do a Good Loot

And then there were many ways to do a good loot. But the basics were always of the same ilk: take over an S&L; increase its "deposit base" many-fold by taking in deposits from large institutions; loan to a "developer" who makes outlandish payments to friends of the owners of the S&L, with no intention to pay off the loan to the S&L as promised. The S&L can meanwhile show healthy profits, since the "developer" can pay out its interest payments from the money it has been loaned. The fraudulent accounting underlies the phish-loot.

This strategy was used hundreds of times over, by many S&Ls that quickly expanded to have billions of dollars' worth of assets. Empire Savings and Loan of Mesquite, Texas, illustrates the "Texas Strategy."[18] According to this strategy, initially a group of colluding developers would trade land back and forth at successively higher prices. The prices of those trades provided the basis for friendly valuations, to be used for a development loan. Then with loan in hand, the development became a source of generous fees for the developer and his friends. The developer would pay high interest on the loan to the S&L (including generous points at the very beginning); there was no need at any time for money to come out of the developers' own pockets since the initial loan could also, generously, include payments of interest for the understandably long time until the project's completion. In the easiest scheme (although not the exact one used at Empire), the developer, whose talents at building had been appreciated and supported by the S&L, might reciprocally appreciate the promise of the S&L—a promise that, under the current arrangements, would be signaled by the S&L's high current profits and expanding balance sheet.[19] So the developer and his friends could purchase a sizable bloc of stock in the S&L. The only effective limit on the returns from this strategy was the thrift's ability to find new individuals with reasonably clean criminal records and balance sheets who were willing to play the role of developer, because regulations still put a limit on how much a thrift could lend to any one person or firm. Eventually Empire offered finder's fees to anyone who brought in a new potential "developer." In *Inside Job,* their prize-winning book on the S&L crisis, Stephen Pizzo, Mary Fricker, and Paul Muolo describe the "vacant, crumbling condos [along] I-30 built with loans from Empire Savings and Loan near Dallas."[20] Some housing sites were filled with building materials rotting in the sun. But that was more than could be said of many others: empty slabs of concrete, which were later dubbed "Martian landing pads" by a US attorney with a flair for description.[21]

The Pass-on to Real Estate Markets

The immediate effects of the S&Ls stand out in the Dallas commercial real estate market at the time. The usual accompaniment of high vacancy rates is collapse of construction. That is what happened in nearby Houston. Construction fell immediately to 2 percent of its previous peak value when the vacancy rate reached 32 percent. But in Dallas, when the vacancy rate reached a similar 32 percent, construction continued.[22]

The local real estate magnates placed the blame on out-of-control S&Ls. As early as June 1982, Mark Pogue of Lincoln Properties was saying: "All of us need to be more cautious.... How will this market absorb these millions of square feet?"[23] A year later, in June 1983, Dallas ranked second nationally to Houston in vacant office space. But it was, paradoxically, first in office construction. In October 1983, McDonald Williams of respectable Trammell Crow warned about the overbuilding. He placed the blame on "the push that savings and loans are making into commercial real estate.... They are going to keep us overbuilt, I think."[24] A year later, with the *National Real Estate Investor News* reporting that "old timers in Dallas [were] amazed at the surge in construction," Dan Arnold of Swearingen Company provided this explanation: "Financial institutions and lenders have money that must be placed."[25] Still later, in June 1985, Wayne Swearingen remarked: "We have developers sitting there with empty buildings, and the lenders are giving them money to start another one. I have to blame the lenders. I want them to show me where these builders are going to get cash flow.... The laws of supply and demand are not governing market behavior. Continuing construction in the face of high vacancy seems related to the availability of financing for new buildings, rather than need."[26]

The laws of supply and demand actually were working: as phishing for phools, looting style. The owner of an S&L could get any amount of money he wanted through paying a high enough rate of interest, pass that money on to friends, who then, if they were sufficiently clever, could launder it back to him. It is no coincidence that the Mafia, which had developed special skills in the art of laundering, played a major role in the looting of the S&Ls.[27]

Lesson Ignored

It is worth noting that what happened with the S&Ls should have served as warning for what would transpire some twenty years later in the buildup to the Crash of 2008. Again we would see phishing daisy chains. They would not be daisy chains of inflated land-values, to be accounted Mesquite-style as collateral against loans. Instead, they would be daisy chains of mortgage valuations: the kite in the valuations fenced through overrated mortgage-backed securities.

The next chapter shows how the looting of the S&Ls metastasized into the market for junk bonds in the beginning of our new age of greed. Soon-to-be-bankrupt S&Ls played a significant role in the expansion of the market for junk bonds, which underlay hostile takeovers of even the largest firms—previously deemed impossible.

TEN

Michael Milken Phishes
with Junk Bonds as Bait

The work of one man, Michael Milken, in the 1970s and 1980s changed the face of US finance forever. No longer could corporate executives of large US corporations be confident that their companies were too big to be challenged by corporate raiders threatening hostile takeovers because now the raiders could acquire even very large companies without putting up much capital. What enabled them to do this was the leveraged buyout, in which a raider's company could amass cash by taking on enormous debt (through high-yield, or "junk," bonds developed by Milken) to acquire, often, a much larger company. The leveraged buyouts massively increased everything related to corporate mergers and acquisitions, notably risks and potential payoffs. Accompanying awareness of the potentially huge payoffs (and ignoring the potentially huge risks) were new views of what a CEO could earn: for example, in the leveraged buyout of RJR Nabisco, with the $45.7 million golden parachute given to Edward Horrigan, the CEO of the tobacco subsidiary[1]; and a reputedly yet more capacious takeaway for Ross Johnson, the CEO of the whole company.[2] Back in those days such money was not considered small change. And as we will see, Milken's payments were not small either, even by today's standards. According to compensation expert Graef Crystal, any moderately paid CEO could, in this new era, easily hire a consultant to point out to his board of directors that others, like him, were earning not hundreds of thousands of dollars, but millions, or even tens of millions.[3] The age of "excess" (Crystal's word) had begun. Many of the bonds that Milken initiated failed later, resulting in what is known as the junk bond crisis of the 1980s. But the cause of the crisis should not be understood as just due to the crimes of this one man, who went beyond the law. More deeply, it was the consequence of an economic equilibrium with an opportunity to phish for phools. It also serves as a further example of the role of misleading financial ratings.

Gold Rediscovered in Northern California

Gold has been discovered more than once in Northern California. In 1969, it was found in an especially strange place: in an obscure 1958 book in a University of California–Berkeley library. The discoverer, an undergraduate business major from the Los Angeles suburbs, was Michael Milken. The book was *Corporate Bond Quality and Investor Experience,* by W. Braddock Hickman. The 536-page table-filled book was a highly technical report on investors' experience with bonds of various rating levels. Table 1 of Hickman's book summarizes the revelation.[4] From 1900 to 1943, low-grade corporate bonds (those rated below investment grade, and therefore of limited eligibility for commercial bank or insurance company investment) performed remarkably well. After subtracting out their default losses, these bonds realized an average annual return of 8.6 percent; in contrast, high-grade investment bonds had realized average yields of only 5.1 percent. These high returns on the low-grade bonds suggested that the low-grade bonds had actually been rather safe. Even though 1900 to 1943 included the terrible years of the Great Depression, their default losses still were less than 1 percent per year.

But just as gold in the ground needs to be extracted before it has value, so it was with *Corporate Bond Quality and Investor Experience.* The book had been out for more than a decade; it had sold only 934 copies[5]; and the data reported were already fifteen years old at the time of publication. It took Milken, with his knack for salesmanship, to extract the gold. As he launched his career in the early to late 1970s, he would bring a copy of Hickman's maroon-covered book to meetings with investors. His salesmanship resulted in the popular name *junk bond* for the low-grade debt, although Milken himself avoided using it. By 1975 the *Wall Street Journal* published an approving front-page article about Milken: "One Man's Junk Is Another's Bonanza." Bond trading, it said, had become "the fastest game in town."[6] Milken had become a superstar. And he was only five years out of graduate school.

People commonly make the fallacy, in the words of John Locke, of "taking words for things."[7] In this case, the mistake could be assuming that junk bonds from one decade are the same as junk bonds from another. They have the same name, *junk bonds,* and so phoolish investors can be expected to react the same to them, even if this time they are underwritten by institutions whose reputations are being mined. Maybe junk bonds would have remained the same thing as they had been before 1943, absent Michael Milken. But that was not the case.

The cognitive mistake exploited by Milken is described in Gary Smith's 2014 book *Standard Deviations: Flawed Assumptions, Tortured Data, and Other Ways to Lie with Statistics.*[8] The chapter "Apples and Prunes" describes the opportunities for deception from making convenient but unstated assumptions that equate dissimilar things under one name. Milken would equate two different kinds of junk bonds without telling any lies. *Apples* would be the "fallen angels" issued by once-successful companies down on their luck; those were the kind of junk bonds studied by Hickman. The *prunes* would be the new kind of junk bonds, which Milken would make happen. The fallen-angel junk bonds had indeed done surprisingly well up to 1943. The challenge for Milken as phisherman was to find a way to profit from this error by creating another kind of junk bond: not a fallen-angel junk bond, but a newly issued junk bond, with himself as the broker of the new issue.

The Milken story unfolds as he takes his first job after graduation from Berkeley and an MBA at the Wharton School of Business. He is employed at a somewhat down-at-the-heels Philadelphia investment bank, Drexel Harriman Ripley, which, through a series of mergers, evolved with considerable additional capital into Drexel Burnham Lambert. Only two years after starting that job, Milken convinced his new boss, Tubby Burnham, to allocate $2 million of that additional capital to open a trading desk in low-grade bonds. In no time flat he was making a 100 percent profit. This was the "pre-Milken" era, when such a gain was big money.[9]

But that $2 million was just the beginning of the opportunities for the middleman at the hub of the market for junk bonds. Whenever there is a gap between supply and demand at current prices, the middleman can capture some of the difference between the price buyers are willing to pay and the price sellers are willing to take. And young Milken was now in the position of being the dominant middleman in a market that could be huge indeed, if marketed right.

There was unquestioning demand for those junk bonds, after the Milken sales pitch. The gospel according to Braddock Hickman seemed to say that Milken could deliver higher returns by a full 3.5 percent.[10] All he needed to do was attract portfolio managers at banks, pension funds, and insurance companies with his story. Such big-money managers are known to scramble for returns that are higher by even a few basis points—that is, by a few hundredths of 1 percent.

But not only was there a huge demand for these bonds at the prevailing interest rates, there was also, potentially, a huge supply of them. As far as the eye could see, going back to the beginning of the nineteenth century, the returns on stocks had been enormous. So large is the gap between the return on stocks and the return on bonds that this difference has earned a name: the equity premium. The equity premium was so large that, for example, a $100,000 trust fund initiated in 1925 and invested in treasuries would have been worth only $1.3 million seventy years later, in 1995; but the same trust fund invested and reinvested in stocks would have been worth more than $80 million.[11] If you were so lucky as to have had a mildly rich great-grandmother who invested in a stock trust fund like this, you would not be poor.

The men around Milken who were thinking about junk bonds in the early 1980s saw that there could be very large returns from taking over a corporation by paying off the existing stockholders at the existing stock prices, with the proceeds from selling junk bonds. Pick the average firm, and the returns on equities were so high that they were likely to pay off the interest payments on the junk bonds. But one could do yet better by taking over a firm where the cost of labor could be much reduced: for example, by reducing wages, by firing unnecessary workers, or by delving into a pension fund with more than the legally required capital. Or one could also beat the average by taking over a firm whose management was incompetent, and replacing it. For Michael Milken and his propaganda machine and trading desk, the bonds issued in such raids could be a huge source of supply of bonds.

There might be some obstacles in getting at the gold, but every miner knows that the ore must be mined, and then refined, no matter how pure it may be. There is always some trouble. And so it was with the raids. Business is called "busy-ness" because it always involves complications. There were three leading obstacles for the raiders, and for Milken, in getting their hands on the returns from the underpriced stocks. But his operation was peculiarly positioned to deal with all three.

The first obstacle involved timing. If the targets of a hostile takeover had warning enough, they could mount a defense. They could raise the funds themselves for a management buyout, or they could seek a preferred partner for the takeover—a so-called white knight. But Milken had an answer to this. As he expanded his operations, an increasing number of his previous clients owed their prosperity to him. Allegedly, particularly useful in this regard were those who had taken over S&Ls; they could use the assets of those S&Ls to respond to Milken's suggestions. In a later lawsuit against Milken by the Federal Deposit Insurance Corporation (FDIC) and the Resolution Trust Corporation, especially prominent among the S&L owners were Thomas Spiegel of Columbia Savings and Loan, Charles Keating of Lincoln Savings and Loan, and David Paul of CenTrust.[12] Fred Carr's First Executive Life Insurance, likewise, allegedly furnished Milken another pot of billions of other people's money.[13] For the S&Ls, the lax enforcement of federal deposit insurance laws gave them a huge boost in what they could contribute. And those same lax regulations allowed the S&Ls to pay high enough rates of interest in deposits that they could have money to spare. So when Milken called with a new opportunity, the hint was taken seriously. By 1985 he could be so certain of closing a deal of eye-popping size that Drexel only needed to issue a letter saying that it was "highly confident" that it could do the financing. As demonstrated in Carl Icahn's run on Phillips Petroleum, Milken was able to raise $1.5 billion in forty-eight hours.[14] With such extraordinary powers, Milken and his men could take a targeted management by surprise. The raider could make his offer so quickly that the target had only hours for defense.

It is worth remarking, more than parenthetically, that Milken also had additional ways, beyond junk-bond financing, to reward those who helped him with his deals. Page after page of the lawsuit *FDIC v. Milken* alleges ways in which Milken tunneled money out to his friends. For example, according to the Complaint, Thomas Spiegel was given the opportunity to buy into a partnership holding warrants (a special form of stock option) in the Storer Communications takeover—a deal that had been largely financed through his Columbia Savings and Loan; Spiegel paid $134,596 for his share of the partnership; in short order that investment netted a profit in excess of $7 million.[15] The Complaint also alleges that on November 30, 1987, Charles Keating's Lincoln Savings and Loan and a subsidiary bought more than $34 million of junk bonds in the buyout of Beatrice International Food Company; that same day, he purchased 234,383 shares of equity in the takeover company.[16]

Fred Carr was allegedly dealt in in a different fashion: takeovers that he helped finance would subsequently invest the pension funds of their workers in his First Executive Life, which later went bankrupt.[17] This evidence suggests that while Milken's friends were getting rich, they all had good reason for buying what he had to sell.[18]

There was, however, a second obstacle to the raiders: the so-called holdup problem.[19] Typically a raider would have to pay a considerable premium above the current market price. For example, in the Milken-abetted takeover of Revlon by Ronald Perelman's Pantry Pride in 1985, Pantry Pride was forced to raise the initial bid of $47.50 a share to $58.00. But the increase could have been prohibitive if Pantry Pride had been too respectable. In that case, the current stockholders might have decided that they would rather remain as minority shareholders than offer up their stock. After all, if Warren Buffett wanted to take over a company in which you own stock, you might think twice before you offered to sell or—using the more technical term—before you "tendered" your shares. Wouldn't it be good to own the shares of a company controlled by this good guy, famous as he is for his impeccable financial judgment? But, in contrast, Pantry Pride and Perelman in 1985 were all but unknowns. Pantry Pride had net worth of $145 million (compared to Revlon's $1 billion); it was a supermarket chain that had recently emerged, in 1981, from Chapter 11 bankruptcy. Furthermore, Perelman was a "raider," to whom the existing Revlon management was obdurately opposed. This meant that the existing shareholders had a pretty easy choice: between offering their shares at a price with that "considerable premium," or staying in and seeing what happened next. Holdup problem solved.[20]

The "confidence letters" and reputations of the raiders thus helped solve two problems in carrying out the raids that would generate the huge supply of junk bonds. But then Milken had yet a third obstacle, this time on the demand side. The new-issue junk bonds and the bonds whose yields and default rates had been evaluated by Hickman might both be low-grade bonds, which made them similar in one respect, but in another respect they were totally different. The old bonds whose default rates had been calculated were bonds of firms that had been initially issued a high grade, but then had fallen on hard times. Think the Pennsylvania Railroad: when it went under, its bonds were fallen angels. But Milken's bonds were different: they were junk from the very beginning. If we were looking for a pet, it would be a mistake to choose a pit bull because studies showed that another type of "dog," Labradors, were family friendly. Similarly, it might be a mistake to stuff one's portfolio with Drexel Burnham Lambert new issues because Braddock Hickman, and later observers, had given high marks to fallen angels.

Milken was then faced with the following nightmare. If it were noticed that newly issued junk and fallen angels were different, that could undo his whole enterprise. The statistics available masked this in one way. NYU finance professor Edward Altman and his former student Scott Nammacher had found average default rates of 1.5 percent.[21] This figure is misleading since junk bonds have higher default rates as they age, and the market was growing very rapidly. Taking a simple average, like this, of default rates, was thus like inferring mortality rates from a population with one grandfather and one hundred 10-year-olds.

In due course the bias was perceived, but at least for a time Milken had a way to distract the dogs that might bark, and keep them silent. When junk bonds were about to default, there was a legal procedure—called an exchange offer (under Section 3(a)(9) of the Securities Act of 1933)—whereby they could be restructured and not count as a default.[22] Milken could rejigger things so that those whose bonds were about to go under would be offered at least a slightly better deal with a Drexel-choreographed exchange, aided and abetted by some other sweetheart deal. In a distinguished paper, Paul Asquith of

MIT, and David Mullins and Eric Wolff of Harvard Business School, showed that almost 30 percent of the new junk bonds issued in 1977 through 1980[23] had defaulted by the end of 1988; this included 10 percent that were involved in exchanges, but then had subsequently defaulted.[24]

In the early to mid-1980s the Milken scheme was developing epidemically. In March every year, Drexel would throw Milken's annual High-Yield Bond Conference. By 1985 this gala had earned the name Predators' Ball; it attracted 1,500 comers to the Beverly Hilton and nearby Beverly Hotel.[25] Those financiers had the potential of trillions of dollars—their own and junk-financed—to throw into hostile takeovers. The junk-bond business was thriving so well that, for 1986, Drexel gave Milken's trading group—which had moved from New York to Los Angeles in 1978—$700 million in bonuses. Milken, in charge of divvying it up, gave $550 million to himself.[26] That may have been greedy. But he was the impresario of the junk-bond market; his activities were affecting all of American business; in the calculus of finance, maybe he deserved it. Nothing like this had ever been paid before to a US executive in a single year.[27]

Much of what Milken did was perfectly legal. Phishing is legal unless it oversteps bounds of what good lawyers are hired to explain to people like Milken. Not only is the phishing legal; Milken's brand of it had even been described as, in some dimensions, heroic. Harvard Business School's Michael Jensen was arguing that takeovers such as those engineered by Milken would make our society richer. In his description, a takeover movement would oust entrenched incompetent management, and thereby raise prosperity for all.[28] But this argument misses the other side of the coin: the hostile takeovers could equally well uproot faithful managers; the profits from the raid could come, instead, from breaching the trust of employees, regarding their expectations of pay, benefits, work conditions, and pensions.[29]

The end of the Milken story is unusual. Usually the phishers never get caught. But Milken did land in prison. The FBI followed an insider-trading chain up to Ivan Boesky, a stock trader who had gained instant fame for his departure from the usual goo in a UC Berkeley commencement address, by saying: "I think greed is healthy."[30] When Boesky found himself threatened for his part in the chain, he saw the opportunity for another trade. He would do a plea bargain in return for evidence against Milken. Boesky had been only a minor figure in Milken's orbit, but, wired with a tape recorder, he obtained the evidence that would open up the investigation to Milken. To avoid a court trial on the initial 98 counts of his indictment, and also to get his brother off the hook, Milken pleaded guilty to six of them. One of those counts regarded his purchase of bonds from Boesky, with a promise to let Boesky buy them back. Such a deal was illegal by SEC regulations against "parking" of securities; it allowed Boesky to pay lower taxes, but at no risk to him.[31] This deal is indicative of Milken's disdain for the public interest; but it is also indicative of his generosity to most of the partners in his deals: he might gain, but so would the partners. Within months of the indictment, Milken's trading operation on Wilshire Boulevard in Los Angeles had closed, and, after that, the whole parent company, Drexel Burnham Lambert, went bankrupt.[32] The six counts to which Milken pleaded guilty, such as for "parking," would normally not send a man to prison. They would usually result in a fine. To our mind, the more serious offenses for the public interest were in the civil case we have cited, brought by the FDIC and the Resolution Trust Corporation. That case accused Milken, and other alleged "conspirators," of collusive use of other people's money.[33] The case was settled out of court; Milken's part of the settlement was $500 million.[34]

Six Observations

Six observations put the Milken fiasco in larger perspective.

Observation 1. Milken's junk-bonds operation demonstrates two types of information phish already seen in previous chapters. He combined distorted ratings (his junk bonds were insufficiently differentiated from Hickman's fallen angels) with wrong-minded accounting from the S&Ls, which were economically bankrupt. Allegedly, the S&Ls made purchases on his whim, and he tunneled the rewards.

Observation 2. In previous chapters we have introduced the theme of "stories." Regarding Milken, one story said he was a genius who had discovered new ways, all but literally, to mint money. Another story said that his junk bonds would have the same low default rates as Hickman's fallen angels.

Observation 3. Milken jump-started the new inequality. The 1980s saw sharp rises in the share of the top decile of income, the top 1 percent of income, and the top 1 percent of wages.[35] The indirect effect of Milken's operations on these changes will never be possible to quantify; we also think Milken, as clever as he was, was still only a few steps ahead of others in operations such as engineering takeovers that upset previous standards of executive compensation. Our theory of equilibrium in markets for phishing and also the founding of large private-equity funds in the takeover business suggests that takeovers like Milken's would almost surely have happened in his absence. But he was there—prominently—at the creation.

Observation 4. Milken's junk bonds illustrate another principle regarding phishing for phools in financial markets. Two previous chapters have demonstrated daisy chains between the phish and the financial markets. With the Milken junk bonds, as in the Crisis of 2008, the effects of the phish also traveled far from its initial site. His junk bonds played a significant role in the takeover wave of the early to mid-1980s: far distant from their S&L/insurance-company phishing home base.[36]

Observation 5. The operations of Michael Milken demonstrate the forces leading to phishing equilibrium. Using our previous analogy, when he reached the "checkout counter" after his graduation from Wharton, he noticed opportunities for profit. He would underwrite a new kind of junk bond, different from the fallen angels. The three "obstacles" he had to overcome (as described) show why those opportunities at the checkout counter had previously not been taken. Milken was the first to see how to overcome them.

Observation 6. This takes us to the most important practical observation of this book. Asset prices are highly volatile. The picture we have given shows the major reasons why that is so. A whole bestiary of phishes—such as reputation mining, looting, misleading accounting, extravagant stories in the news media, sales pitches of investor advisors and investment companies and real estate agents, and narratives of riches from nowhere—are largely responsible. The damage from that volatility is limited as long as the losers in the downturns are only those who themselves were duped. But a chain of additional losses occurs when the inflated assets have been purchased with borrowed money. In that case bankruptcies and fears of bankruptcies spawn an epidemic: of further bankruptcies, and of further fears of bankruptcy. And then credit dries up; and the economy tanks.

Epidemics, in economics and in medicine, call for immediate and drastic response. Two dramatic episodes in the past hundred years give us two contrasting experiments: regarding what happens when there is such a response; and when there isn't. The response to the Great Crash of 1929 was small and slow. And the world entered a mini Dark Age. It lasted fifteen years, through the Depression of the 1930s, and the Second World War. The 2008 collapse had portents similar to the Crash of 1929. But, in contrast, the world's fiscal authorities and the world's central banks intervened promptly; in coordination; and in appropriately high volume. The recovery has been weak; but, thank God, we have not entered the mini Dark Age of that earlier era.

There is now abroad in the land a view that the fiscal and the monetary authorities should not have responded either so quickly or so vigilantly in 2008–9. In this view, the expectation of intervention at the time of the crisis was its primary cause. (In economic-speak, it is said that the run-up in asset prices occurred because of "moral hazard.") But on the contrary, our view of finance, and the detailed facts that support our view, show that when run-ups in prices occur, they usually do so because of irrational exuberance, aided and abetted by phishes. The irrationally exuberant did not have on their minds the returns they would garner if the fiscal and monetary authorities intervened to maintain the economy and the flow of credit; or, in the extreme case, if their bank, or their enterprise, were "bailed out." Such considerations, insofar as they existed, were of only marginal consideration in the euphoria that preceded the Crash of 2008. The sellers at the inflated prices were making profits; and, on the other side of the deals, with their monkey-on-the-shoulder expectations, the buyers who were paying those inflated prices "knew" they were doing the right thing; even when they weren't. They were dancing while the music was playing.

The failure to see the necessity of quick and immediate intervention in financial crisis is based on an economics that fails to take account of such factors as looting, reputation mining, and irrational exuberance. It's based on a faulty logic that would also tell us to do away with fire departments, because there would then be no fires since people would be more careful.

We found out many years ago, to the world's great regret, what happens when there is no effective intervention at the time of financial collapse; when the epidemic is just allowed to run its course. Our analysis indicates not only that there are endemic and natural forces that make the financial system highly volatile; but it also indicates that in the face of financial collapse it is time to intervene. One mini Dark Age is one too many.

ELEVEN

The Resistance
and Its Heroes

The phishing equilibrium that we have described in this book is pervasive, but it is not comprehensive. And that is because we have individuals who step back from the profit incentive and who act as business leaders, government leaders, thought leaders, religious leaders. Standard economics (the "purely economic model") presumes no civil society, but in fact we live in a community of people who care about one another. We have mentioned a number of heroes throughout this book. Now we will focus on the nature of their heroism in resistance to phishing; the accomplishments of those heroes; and also what eludes them.

Really, to a remarkable extent it is these heroes who make the free-market system work as well as it does. It is not the unadulterated actions of markets that bring us the cornucopia we enjoy, for that same free-market system brings ever more sophisticated manipulations and deceptions.

Relative to all previous history, people in developed countries are doing remarkably well. Women in more than fifty countries, and men in eleven, have life expectancies of eighty years or more.[1] Modern cars may have their problems and their recalls, but they now always have seatbelts; with rare exception cars are no longer—as Ralph Nader opined 50 years ago—"unsafe at any speed."[2] Remarkably, as of February 2013, there had not been a single commercial airline fatality in the United States for four years.[3] Not only did the planes themselves have a perfect record; so too did the pilots and the mechanics who keep them in the air.

With such records for safety and product quality, the questions arise: Is it purely the market system that brought us this success? What is the role of our heroes? In this chapter we will venture at least a tentative answer to these questions. As we see it, when we can measure the qualities of the goods, services, and assets we buy—or when those qualities can be accurately graded, and we also understand those qualities and grades—then, for the most part, we get what we expect. The heroes of the chapter have reduced phishing by isolating information phishing to an outback of the hard-to-measure/hard-to-evaluate. (Chapter 2, on the financial crisis, illustrated one such example of that outback. The default risks of mortgage-backed securities were hard to rate; the buyers thought they were buying good avocados. But they were mistaken. And those mistakes triggered the Great Recession.) But these heroes, as the next chapter (the conclusion) will discuss, are much less effective against psychological phishing. If I have an urge to trash my budget or my diet, there are few protections against my doing so.

Standard Bearers

The first of our heroes are those who measure and enforce measurement of quality standards.

Since the beginning of the twentieth century there has been remarkable progress in our ability to measure the qualities of products, and also to grade them. This progress has allowed standardization. We got a glimpse of this with Harvey Washington Wiley and the founding of the Food and Drug Administration. Our hero Wiley was a chemist. And, as we saw earlier, the new chemistry—largely emanating from Germany, where Wiley had worked in the Imperial Food Laboratory[4]—allowed for testing of the contents of both food and drugs, so that mislabeling of ingredients could be detectable.

Throughout most of the nineteenth century, the US government's constitutional responsibility to "fix the standard of weights and measures" was run out of a small office in the Treasury; but then in 1901 it was transferred to the new National Bureau of Standards. In short order this agency was being used to test federal purchases governmentwide. With a budget of only $2 million, it was said to be saving $100 million a year, on purchases of $300 million.[5]

In 1927, Stuart Chase and Frederick Schlink, two of our heroes, wrote a best-selling book, *Your Money's Worth*. (Chase is credited, later, with coining the phrase "The New Deal.")[6] They described not only the work of the National Bureau, but also standardization, grading, and certification in many different industries—as accomplished by a remarkable mixture of government, private, and nonprofit endeavor. For the most part this activity goes unnoticed and taken for granted: the product of unsung heroes. Two examples illustrate: the grading of wheat, and the certification of electrical appliances.

In economics textbooks and economics articles, wheat is the archetypal pure simple commodity, bought and sold on competitive markets. Yet wheat in the flesh rather than in the textbook comes in many different varieties, with many different grades, and many possible imperfections. There is a system for classifying it and grading it, so it can be easily sold as a commodity by the trainload. The Grain Inspection, Packing, and Stockyard Administration of the US Department of Agriculture—the GIPSA—has an official classification of wheat by grade: eight different basic classes (such as durum wheat, hard red spring wheat); grades from 1 to 5 (according to weight per bushel; presence of damaged kernels and of foreign material, of wheat of other classes; and the count of animal filth, castor beans, crotalaria seeds, glass, stones, other foreign substances, and insect-damaged kernels); and further grading for other conditions (content of ergot, garlic, or smut, and improper treatment).[7]

Companies licensed by the GIPSA inspect approximately half of the grain grown in the United States.[8] But other arrangements are commonplace.[9] The grain elevators often do their own inspection, or they contract it out. Grain-warehousing laws regarding inspection, charges, and conditions of storage also add further protection; grain elevators can take out a federal or a state license, with the obligation of abiding by its respective restrictions.[10] As a result wheat is easily traded; and the buyer knows what she is purchasing.

The market for electrical appliances gives another model for the setting of standards. Home appliances such as electric lighting and fire extinguishers are commonly tested by Underwriters Laboratories; founded in 1894 as a nonprofit, it is the organization behind those certification marks with the letters UL at an angle inside a bold circle that appear on American electrical appliances. The manufacturers pay UL to test their products, and also to certify them.[11] The standards for electrical equipment in the United States, in turn, are commonly set by a different organization, the American National

Standards Institute, originally co-sponsored (under a different name) in 1918 by five engineering societies (including the American Institute of Electrical Engineering and the American Society of Mechanical Engineers) and three US departments (War, Navy, and Commerce).[12] Not only do these standards ensure safety; they also promote uniformity. Think of the usefulness of standard electrical sockets and connections, by country; of standard sizes for automobile tires; and of standard railway gauges and car-couplings.

In *Your Money's Worth,* Chase and Schlink went beyond the recommendation that products have standards. They urged that consumers have access to the same type of product evaluation that the government was using so successfully in its purchases. A few short years after the publication of their book, they started an organization to do just that.[13] In due course, after a complicated history in which the unionized employees rebelled and took over the show, this enterprise morphed into today's Consumers Union, which produces *Consumer Reports.*[14] It has a circulation of 7.3 million, and it rates all kinds of things from refrigerators to cars to air conditioners to video games.[15] The ratings benefit not just the consumers who are directly aware of them; they also benefit everyone else, because the producers run a competitive race against one another to get positive ratings. Consumers Union may be the most venerable of consumer activist organizations, but it is one of many. The umbrella organization for consumer activists, Consumer Federation of America, has more than 250 organization members, which in turn engage in research, education, consumer advocacy, and service.[16] But that number probably gives a very conservative picture of overall activity. It appears that we are getting by with more than a little help from our friends.

There is also another side to consumer activism—beyond standards/grading/evaluation. This other facet of consumer activism is partly concerned with value and product safety, but only as a by-product of a deeper commitment: that people's consumption is an act of citizenship; and citizenship entails moral obligations. Such civic-based, civil-society movements in the United States date back at least to the American colonists' nonimportation of British goods in the 1760s and 1770s (as most famously celebrated by the "Tea Party" that unloaded cargo of the British East India Company into Boston Harbor); in the next century, pre–Civil War abolitionists similarly boycotted slave-produced goods.[17] A good example of moral commitments, in what might be considered the beginning of modern times, is the National Consumers League, founded by Florence Kelley in 1899.

Kelley was one of those grand American women, and the goals and operation of the League derive from her forceful character and social conscience. At the age of 33, after graduate education in Zurich, she was named chief factory inspector for the State of Illinois, a remarkable post for a woman at the time. The daughter of a Quaker, abolitionist Republican congressman, she chose to live among the poor at Jane Addams's settlement house in Chicago.[18] The League held that, as consumers, we are the indirect employers of the workers in the factories that produce what we buy; so that, like the factory owners who employ them directly, we too have moral responsibility for their welfare. The League inspected working conditions, as Kelley had been doing for the state of Illinois, and it awarded its "White Label" to the products that passed its inspections.[19] That label further vouched for the safety of the product itself. Buying White Label would thus kill two birds: commitment to civil society and safety for the buyer's family.

In chapter 6, we saw another example of this symbiosis between concerns for workers' conditions and for product safety. Recall that Upton Sinclair had set out in *The Jungle* to expose the wage-slave labor of the Chicago meatpacking houses. But the public was especially shocked by the book's exposé of what was going into their own stomachs. To this day, the "shopping for a better world" movement still underlies one wing of consumer activism. Think our Prius-buying friends; purchasers of free-range meat and poultry; and United Students against Sweat Shops. And in 2015 the National Consumers League is alive and well, continuing Kelley's vision: currently fighting, among other things, against child labor with nicotine abuse in the tobacco fields of the US South.[20]

Business Heroes

Businessmen of conscience with good products have both moral and economic reasons to out the phishermen. And they have developed some ways to do so. In 1776, in London, an organization was established called "The Guardians, or Society for the Protection of Trade against Swindlers and Sharpers."[21] They would accept consumers' complaints in writing; support legal actions on their behalf; expel members with unethical business practices; and provide printed certificates for members to display as testimonial of "good credit and reputation." The Guardians live on, in modern reincarnation in the United States, as Better Business Bureaus. The reliance of BBBs on consumer complaints seems so obvious that it is taken for granted. But it provides a surprisingly subtle way for the members to take action against shoddy competitors. If member-businesses originated complaints against them, there would be good reason for skepticism, because of potential conflict of interest; but since the customers themselves bring the complaints (which are also checked by the BBBs), they are credible.

Further protection against phishing comes from the norms of business communities. Nell Minow is a leading shareholder activist, who practices shaming as a remarkably effective deterrent to bad behavior.[22] She has said that directors of large US corporations are remarkably sensitive to their reputations: "the most reputationally sensitive people in the world."[23] Nor is it just the doctors (the Hippocratic oath) or the lawyers (the oath to the bar), but almost all business organizations that have their stated principles. One example is the National Association of Realtors, with its 16¼-page, single-spaced code of ethics[24]; or the Chambers of Commerce, present in almost every US community of any size, with their statements of ethics. More personally, in family lore, when George's great-grandfather went belly up, to the tune of something like a half million bucks, in Baltimore around 1900, his sons assumed their father's debts. In turn, the Baltimore business community set them up with a healthy franchise—for the local dealership of Studebaker cars—so they could meet those obligations: on both sides, an example of business ethics in practice.

Government Heroes

Resistance to phishing for phools has taken another course: in the evolution of legal standards that protect us. An early US Supreme Court case, *Laidlaw v. Organ,* established the joint principle of *caveat emptor/caveat venditor* (buyer beware/seller beware) as a foundation of US commercial law. As soon as possible after he learned in the very early morning of February 19, 1815, that the Treaty of Ghent ending the War of 1812 had been signed, New Orleans tobacco merchant Hector Organ hotfooted it (before the news had spread) to Laidlaw and Company; he bought 111 hogsheads of tobacco—120,715 pounds of it. Organ had foreseen that the British naval blockade would be lifted, and the price of tobacco would rise. In his purchase of those hogsheads, Organ may have been a bit tricky; he had parried the question whether he knew something special.[25] But the Chief Justice, John Marshall, ruled that, absent fraud, it would be too cumbersome for courts to adjudicate who should tell what to whom when.[26] Instead, *caveat emptor/caveat venditor.*

This legal principle may seem to be an open invitation to phishing for phools, but since that time a line of legal heroes have been whittling away at it, making the law more flexible (and more reasonable). Even back then, in the time of Marshall and of Organ, *caveat emptor* was not absolute: as we saw, there was some protection against fraud. Now we also have considerable protection against negligence.

In this regard a landmark case, *MacPherson v. Buick Motor Car Company,* illustrates. In May 1910, Donald MacPherson, a stonecutter of names on gravestones, bought a Buick from the local dealer in Schenectady, New York.[27] He used the car mainly to travel to his jobs about the countryside. But then, the following July, the left rear wheel collapsed; its spokes had been made of rotten wood. The car overturned and MacPherson was trapped under it; he suffered impairment of his eyesight in both eyes, and also serious injury to his right arm.[28] He sued Buick. Benjamin Cardozo, at the time on the Appeals Court of New York, and later a US Supreme Court justice, ruled that Buick was negligent. Even though MacPherson had bought the car from a dealer (rather than directly from Buick), and even though the wheel had been supplied to Buick by a reputable manufacturer, Buick still bore responsibility. It should have foreseen the possibility of future serious accident, and inspected the wheels, which it had not done.[29] (Cardozo and MacPherson are also on our list of heroes.)

American law provides further legal protection against phishing for phools in yet another way, beyond fraud and negligence. All US states have enacted some form of the Uniform Commercial Code.[30] The code aims to fill out missing provisions of contracts, so we are not taken by surprise.[31] It imposes an obligation of "good faith" in commercial contracts, and it also makes another distinction, between "consumers" and "merchants."[32] This distinction means that we typical Joe-and-Jane-consumers have less responsibility for inspection of the fine print than the presumably more sophisticated "merchants."

The protections we have cited are useful, but *caveat emptor* has not gone away. An example shows its ambiguity of application, especially among sophisticated buyers. Three outcomes from two lawsuits regarding ABACUS, an investment vehicle set up by Goldman Sachs at the behest of financier John Paulson, demonstrate that ambiguity. Goldman had set up this investment vehicle, which allowed investors to make bets on whether default on mortgage-backed securities would be commonplace, or not. The investor John Paulson had played an important role in setting it up; and he had chosen mortgage-backed securities with high likelihood of default as its basis.[33] Allegedly, investors had been misled regarding what side Paulson would take: they were, allegedly, led to believe that he was going long (betting that mortgage defaults would be rare); instead he went short (betting that defaults would be common).[34] Paulson made approximately a billion dollars; those on the other side of the bets lost about the same amount.[35] The SEC filed a complaint against Goldman Sachs and also against its executive Fabrice Tourré. The case against Goldman itself was resolved in a settlement, with a $550 million fine[36]; additionally, Goldman agreed to alter its business practices, although it did not admit guilt. But the case against the executive Tourré, who had set up and sold the scheme, went to court. Tourré would become famous for emails to his girlfriend such as "I've managed to sell a few Abacus bonds to widows and orphans that I ran into at the airport."[37] The jury was not sympathetic; he was found liable for fraud on six counts[38]; and fined more than $825,000.[39] But then there was a further lawsuit, brought by ACA Capital Management, which had lost $120 million in the deal. That case was dismissed. The judgment: as a "highly sophisticated commercial entity," ACA should have known better.[40]

If you buy a toaster you do not need to read the fine print. But if your retirement fund enters a contract with potential liabilities in the hundreds of millions, or the billions, it will not be given such tolerance. *Caveat emptor* is thus alive and well, especially in the world of financial markets and presumably sophisticated investors; and it gives license to phish.

Regulator Heroes and the Question of Regulatory Capture

We get governmental protection against phishing not just from the law of contracts, which allows us to sue if something goes wrong; there are also regulations. The first major regulatory agency in the United States was the Interstate Commerce Commission, founded in 1887, to protect locals from predatory pricing by the railroads, as well as other abuses.[41] Since that time a governmentful of agencies has sprung into being, a sample list of major regulators showing them running from the Consumer Product Safety Commission (CPSC) through the Federal Deposit Insurance Corporation (FDIC) to the Nuclear Regulatory Commission (NRC).[42] But the benefits from this alphabet soup of regulation in the economy are not without debate.

In the second half of the twentieth century a theory developed that, beyond corruption, government regulators are routinely captured by the regulated. In 1955 political scientist Marver Bernstein proposed the idea that regulatory agencies are set up when the public is incensed by some abuse, but it soon stops paying attention. The regulated then capture the regulators, offering them bribes or jobs for their friends and relatives, or campaign contributions to the politicians with presumed oversight. The regulated companies focus their attention on changing the regulations that affect them, while the general public is unaware of the capture, being confused by the plethora of regulations beyond their comprehension. The regulated companies, it is alleged, then turn the regulators into a police force for their own advantage, preventing competition by rigid enforcement of rules whose justification is spurious.[43] This argument should sound familiar (see chapter 5, on politics).

In even more sinister form, this theory asserts that the government creation of regulatory authorities is surreptitiously instigated by the regulated themselves. They are the primary advocates of regulations because they know that they can abuse them.[44] This has been called the "economic theory of regulation," based as it is on economists' standard premise that most of what happens in an economy derives in one way or another from pursuit of self-interest.[45]

But capture theory has its problems. The evidence used to support it has typically been biased, relying on man-bites-dog stories when regulators fail, and without searching for the perhaps much more common dog-bites-man stories, in which regulators work hard and perform their duties; the evidence used has also had low standards of causality.[46] Equally important, capture does not just come in black and white, all or none; but, instead, in varying shades of gray.[47] Studies in *Preventing Regulatory Capture,* edited by Daniel Carpenter and David Moss, demonstrate what they call weak capture: there is influence by the Interests, but regulation does impose constraints and, on balance, serves the public good.[48] We saw such a case in chapter 6, on food and drugs. Nobody would want to revert to the license of the nineteenth century, which allowed Swaim's Panacea and Radam's Microbe Killer. But then we saw how the purveyors of drugs have shifted to phishing the regulators. We described how the FDA leaves itself vulnerable to being phished by the companies it regulates by giving them five degrees of freedom in designing clinical trials and reporting the results. Merck's gaming of the FDA in the case of Vioxx illustrated. But acceptance of the logic that just because regulation has problems we would be better off with none of it would similarly imply that because spouses, children, and friends are often troublesome, we should never get married, never become parents, and have no friends.

And, to return to the major theme of this chapter—the role of heroes—George lives in Washington, and he knows many regulator heroes, who work long hours and weekends to protect our financial and personal safety. He knows many who during the financial crisis worked so hard that they suffered illness (such as heart attack). And he also knows some who have left for Wall Street, not because that is what they were angling for all along, but rather as relief from the twenty-four-hour, seven-day-a-week demands of government service. Yes, among the regulators there are also many heroes. We will not name them here, but we know them personally.

Summary

The common thread in the many different examples of heroism cited in this chapter has been an ethical and altruistic attitude among leaders, in business, government, or elsewhere, who convince the public to adopt standards and institutions. As Benjamin Cardozo said in an 1889 commencement address at Columbia University, we do not demand "absolute community" as under socialism, for that runs counter to the incentivization of economic action.[49] We would say there must be a moral community, and within that a free market of individual action. That moral community has been successful in pushing back against informational phish.

But we are still wholly vulnerable to psychological phish. Every child who has eaten too much ice cream knows the meaning of the phrase "you got what you wished for." The Greeks even had a story about it: remember Midas. We can limit information phish; psychological phish is yet more difficult; and that takes us to the next chapter.

PART THREE

Conclusion
and Afterword

New Story in America
and Its Consequences

We began this book in one place, but are now ending it in another. In the beginning, we introduced phishing for phools with examples from what is now traditional behavioral economics: this was Cialdini's list (in the introduction, on phishing equilibrium). To recall, Cialdini had a list of six specific psychological biases whereby people could be manipulated.

But as our book has progressed, a new emphasis has emerged. That emphasis has given a much more general characterization of the reasons why people are phished. Since the marketing and advertising chapter (chapter 3), we have been saying that people are phishable because the "stories" they tell themselves are an important input into their decisions. Why does this mode of decision making make us so manipulable? Because the typical story meanders; it branches out. Most phishing, in some way or other, consists of grafting new branches onto the old "stories" people are telling themselves; sometimes, it also involves supplanting the old story with a new one.

There is another, equivalent, way to express the same thought. One of the most fundamental human skills is our ability to focus: on some things; not on others. We could have called the "stories" that people tell themselves when they make their decisions their "focus." This notion makes it immediately obvious why people are phishable, as well as giving us a clue regarding how phishing is accomplished, since manipulation of focus is the basis for two professions. Pickpockets and magicians have special skills at diverting our attention; then they do their sleight of hand.

Before writing the previous paragraph, we reviewed our many examples, from Cinnabon® onward. This check demonstrated that in every one of them, the phish occurred because the phisherman took advantage of the phool's wrong focus. In some cases the phisherman, like the magician and the pickpocket, himself generated that wrong focus. We also checked Cialdini's list of psychological biases; each one of them could be considered to be the result of an errant focus by the phool.

Phishing for Phools Itself Is a Story

That takes us to the most fundamental message of *Phishing for Phools.* We have written this book to offset what we consider to be another wrong focus. There is a story regarding free markets that is widely believed in the United States, and is also influential abroad. This story is derived from an unsophisticated interpretation of standard economics. It says that free-market economies, subject to the caveats of income distribution and externalities, yield the best of all possible worlds. Just let everyone be "free to choose," says the mantra, and we will have an earthly paradise, as close to the Garden of Eden as our existing technology, our human capabilities, and the distribution of income will allow.

We (the authors) see the cornucopia that free markets have delivered. But just as every coin has two sides, so do free markets. The same human ingenuity that produces the cornucopia also goes into the art of the salesman. Free markets produce good-for-me/good-for-you's; but they also produce good-for-me/bad-for-you's. They do both, so long as a profit can be made. The free market may be humans' most powerful tool. But, like all very powerful tools, it is also a two-edged sword.

That means that we need protection against the problems. Everyone with a computer knows this. The computer opens us up to the world in many different ways. We all know that we must take precautions against the phish and against the virus. We all know that others send us emails asking us to do things that are not good for us, but are good for them. We all know that, reciprocally, we do the same. We all know that we can become addicted to the computer, with its enticements of games, Facebook, and who knows what other attractions.[1] We have opened ourselves up to these downsides, which are a form of free market, because of the advantages; but only a real fool would pretend that there are no disadvantages, or take no precautions against them.

In contrast, the prominent economic story in the United States (and quite possibly the dominant one) since the 1980s has been that free markets—subject to the aforementioned caveats, which are usually considered more in their breach than in their observance—are always good for us: just so long as we are free to choose.

The Age of Reform

There is a significant period in US history, from approximately 1890 to 1940, called the Age of Reform. Three separate movements are identified with this reform: the agrarian Populism of the 1890s, led by William Jennings Bryan; good-government Progressivism from 1900 to 1920, led by Theodore Roosevelt; and New Deal experimentalism, led by Franklin Delano Roosevelt. These movements, and their goals, were very different, but at the end of the period there had emerged a new, more expansive view of the role of government, at all levels— but especially at the federal level—than that of our forefathers back in 1890.[2]

If we look back to the post–World War II years, presumably after the great Age of Reform, there was a remarkable consensus: government could be a useful counterweight to the excesses of free markets. There was, of course, some disagreement between the Republicans and the Democrats but, in the practice of domestic US policy, the difference was of nuance, not of kind. Republican president Dwight Eisenhower—not intentionally so[3]—appointed a Republican chief justice who reversed US history, and also a previous Supreme Court decision, to make racial segregation in schools illegal; what's more, when the governor of Arkansas, Orval Faubus, challenged that decision in Little Rock, Eisenhower sent in federal troops. He also fathered the interstate highway system. Eisenhower was a Republican, but in both cases he was willing to use the government where it would serve the needs of the people.

With the Democratic presidencies of John F. Kennedy and Lyndon Johnson, the policies continued: Kennedy used Keynesian stimulus to "get the economy moving again"; he also proposed civil rights legislation, which Lyndon Johnson steamrollered through Congress after Kennedy's death. Johnson also started Medicare. When the presidency passed back to the Republicans, with Richard Nixon, the reforms did not abate. Nixon started the Environmental Protection Agency; he also oversaw massive increases in Social Security benefits.[4] Thus the US national story—both Democrat and Republican—saw many different roles for government. Of course it did not work perfectly: that is not our point. But, according to the dominant national story at that time, government could be of service in many different ways.[5]

New Story Legitimated

But then an alternative story achieved currency: "In this present crisis, government is not the solution to our problem; government is the problem." With these words—usually quoted without the phrase "in this present crisis"—in his First Inaugural Address Ronald Reagan gave his imprimatur to a new national story.[6] It is easy to believe that government is the problem (no qualification): if one thinks that markets work perfectly as long as people are free to choose. But with externalities, with an unfair distribution of income, and with phishing for phools, markets do not work perfectly. In that case, there is a potential role for government. The Age of Reform had shown that government, used effectively, can be genuinely beneficial. That had now become Old Story.

New Story is wrong: because its characterization of the economy is wrong. Its characterization of US history is also wrong. Over many years, those years of the Age of Reform, and beyond, we saw a great expansion of governmental activity. By careful trial and error, in response to painful experience, we had implemented government programs and laws that addressed real needs: Social Security, Medicare, securities supervision, deposit insurance, the interstate highway system, aid to the indigent, supervision of food and drugs, environmental protection, auto safety laws, laws against mortgage-gouging, civil rights, and gender equality. Just to name a few. A long, hard-fought history—of nearly a century at the time of Reagan's inauguration—had evolved a system of government that did serve the people.

New Story—that government is the problem—is itself a phish for phools. Its appeal then and now has a ring of truth: especially since stories about what goes right are a much tougher sell for reporters than stories about what goes wrong. Reporters with stories such as "SEC employees are excellent hard-working public servants" quickly lose their jobs. So the news about government is mainly about its faults. Furthermore, the public's dependence on those government programs' working well is further reason why the "news" is: when they don't.

Three Examples

Our method throughout this book has been to combine economic theory, which forms the basis of each chapter, with examples that illustrate its applications. This method suggests how we will conclude. We will give three examples that contrast Old-Story and New-Story economics. Each of these examples will show that casting aside the reforms that come by trial and error out of experience to abide by New-Story economics crucially ignores the role of phishing for phools.

Social Security and Its "Reform"

We have presented our ideas about phishing for phools to many different audiences. Most insistently we are asked: "What do you do about it?"—especially regarding Suze Orman–style overspending. There is one obvious answer. A large number of finance advice books urge people to make a budget and stick to it. Elizabeth Warren, the senator, and her daughter, Amelia Tyagi, propose a rule of thumb.[7] They say that people should divide their take-home pay into three parts: 50 percent should be allocated for "must-haves"; 30 percent for "wants"; and 20 percent for savings, for a rainy day and also for old age. This is sensible advice, especially since an easy way to overspend is to define needs (i.e., "must-haves") too expansively; it also allows for "wants," such as occasional flowers and the meal out, which gives life some frosting. Basically their advice coincides closely with Suze Orman's: keeping oneself from financial worries entails staying on budget.

Careful budgeting is the direct, front-door way to address the low-savings problem. But that front door often seems to be blocked off: since, as life happens, careful budgeting is psychologically difficult. Passage through this front door being so difficult, the US government has opened up a back door, to prevent the worst consequences of low saving. Our national system of Social Security greatly reduces the poverty of the aged. With Social Security, we do not need to wait for people, one by one, to learn, Warren-Tyagi style, to put away that ever-elusive 20 percent. We have found a neater solution. Social Security reduces people's income via a tax (of 6.2 percent of earned income, currently up to $118,500, against both employees and employers[8]); it uses the funds it collects to give people a significant income in old age. The effectiveness of this program is remarkable. When benefits were raised in the 1960s, the poverty rate of those over 65 declined dramatically, falling from 35.2 percent in 1959 to 15.3 percent by 1975.[9] For people over 65, Social Security is the dominant source of unearned income. Not counting earned income and other government transfers such as veterans benefits, it is 94 percent for those in the bottom 20 percent in the income distribution; 92 percent, in the twentieth to fortieth percentile; 82 percent, in the fortieth to the sixtieth percentile; and 57 percent, in the sixtieth to eightieth percentile. Only for the top 20 percent is Social Security less than half of unearned income. But even for this top category, skewed as it is by inclusion of the well-pensioned and the very rich, it is far from a do-without; it is still 31 percent.[10] Take away their Social Security income, and the poverty rate of Americans over 65 would rise from 9 percent to 44 percent.[11]

Social Security thus goes a considerable distance in offsetting phishing-for-phools overspending. Coupled with Medicare, and 80 percent homeownership by the age of 60,[12] older Americans can afford an occasional present to the grandchildren. Nor does this relief of the problem of low savings come intrusively through the front door of telling people what to spend. Government has been a great help. (We remark, further, that other government commitments relieve more immediate problems of low saving. Macroeconomic policies of full employment mean that most of those spells of unemployment will be short; unemployment insurance makes it easier to be looking for a job; and disability insurance makes it easier for those who cannot take one.)

Given the dependence of the vast majority of the population on Social Security, it is surprising that any politician would tamper with it. But the belief in New Story has been so great that there was a serious threat. In 2004, the George W. Bush Administration proposed to "privatize" a significant portion of the program. The modified program would give more freedom to choose. Employees would be allowed to withhold up to 4 percentage points of their own 6.2 percent Social Security contributions.[13] They could invest that money in an approved mutual fund of their choice. At retirement, the retiree would own the money in his fund; but he would also have to pay back, to the Social Security system, the money used to purchase it. That is reasonable: since the reduced payments into the Social Security system would be used to build up the fund. The proposal, inventively, said that the payback would occur by reduction of the Social Security checks, as if the retiree had taken out a loan; the rate of interest on that loan was to be 3 percent plus the rate of inflation.[14]

We confess considerable admiration for the plan's use of free-to-choose logic; but we also confess that we think it is, to be blunt, daffy. It is like giving the most vulnerable part of the population a loan to speculate in the stock market, or the bond market, with government money—with payback on this loan beginning, at quite a high rate of interest, at the date of retirement.

One of us, Bob, did some simulations, with returns on stocks and bonds drawn from 100 years of historical US data to see whether it made sense.[15] To be sure, there was a sweet condition under which the plan did quite well for the retirees. If the returns on stocks mirror their performance in the United States for the past 100 years, then an investor who put all his money into stocks would gain quite a bit. But this involves two extreme assumptions. Portfolio strategies with a more usual mix of stocks and bonds, even with these high rates of stock returns, resulted on average in only small gains. And they were risky: the baseline plan (for the median worker, based on life-cycle-adjusted shares of stocks and bonds) resulted in losses some 32 percent of the time. With the more probable assumption regarding stock returns, that they mirror those of other countries, rather than the extraordinary returns of the United States for the past century, the plan was not just risky; it resulted in losses 71 percent of the time for the baseline portfolio. The all-stock portfolio made losses 33 percent of the time, and the median gains were now small.

The Bush Administration made this proposal a key initiative at the beginning of its second term. It was aborted when it proved unpopular. Ten years later, it seems unlikely to worm its way back to the top of the New-Story reform agenda. But plans of both the left and of the right mutate; and the privatization of Social Security à la Bush has morphed into the privatization of Medicare à la Paul Ryan. The most significant provision of the Ryan Plan is to end Medicare for those who reach 65 after 2022. They would instead receive vouchers with which to purchase medical insurance on the private market. Budgetary savings occur in the Plan because the vouchers are indexed to consumer prices, rather than to the much more rapidly increasing costs of health care. But these savings are not achieved without a downside. The Congressional Budget Office has estimated that by the year 2030, the typical person over the age of 65 would be paying 68 percent of her health care costs out of pocket, rather than 25 percent with the continuation of Medicare.[16] This plan, and the Republican budget proposals that take their cue from it, are very much based on New Story. They get the government off the backs of the American people, 2010s style.

Securities Regulation

The newspapers are full of multifarious governmental budgetary crises: just to name a few, in K to 12; in public higher education; in "infrastructure"; in the justice system; in the Centers for Disease Control; in funding for scientific research and to stave off global warming. There should always be, in every area, a bit of a budget crisis, in the sense that resources should not be treated as free (so that taxpayer dollars are spent with due respect). But these multiple crises go beyond such rational budgeting. If, following New Story, government is viewed as a "problem," rather than a help, government agencies will have to scramble just to maintain their budgets, whatever real needs may be.

Securities regulation is one of the most essential government functions. Regulation of corporate accounting and of securities ratings plays a major role in keeping the public appropriately informed. Earlier, we introduced economist John Kenneth Galbraith's notion of the "bezzle," which is the cumulation of undiscovered financial impropriety. In chapter 2 (on the financial crisis) we saw how the puncture of the big bezzle of subprime and the subsequent freezing of asset markets triggered the Great Recession. Given the critical responsibility of the US Securities and Exchange Commission to dampen bezzles, it is especially important to know if its budget too has been affected by New Story.

Just a glance at the SEC budget suggests that it is highly likely that it is inadequate. In 2014, the Commission oversaw close to $50 *trillion* of assets, with a budget of $1.4 *billion*.[17] That is just a tad more than ¼ of ¹⁄₁₀₀ of a cent per dollar of assets under surveillance. Two comparisons bolster our intuition that such a sum is too small. The Bank of America, a single entity partially supervised by the SEC, spends considerably more on marketing alone than the SEC budget in its entirety[18]; mutual funds' expenses are on average 1.02 cents per dollar of assets held, or 400 times as much as the SEC per dollar of asset supervised.[19]

If the SEC expenditure is so low, there should be signs of it. In chapter 2, we saw the failure of the SEC to regulate derivatives, or to regulate the ratings agencies, when it really mattered. There are also direct indicators from inside the agency of insufficient funds. As one example, consider the statements of Judge Jed Rakoff of the United States District Court of the Southern District of New York, who controversially refused to ratify an SEC-agreed settlement with Citicorp that he considered too compromising.[20] Rakoff has asserted that since 2008, largely for lack of funds, with rare exception, the SEC has sued only corporations—not individuals—for wrongdoing.[21] Cost considerations play a major role in this decision: since it is easier, legally, to go after corporations than to go after individuals. But the deterrence effects of prosecuting whole corporations are far weaker: since penalties against organizations are spread across all their stakeholders; whereas penalties against individuals are targeted to those directly responsible.

The Madoff case gives a second, much more detailed glimpse into the workings of the SEC, and as we will see, possibly, into the consequences of budgetary deficiency. It is now common knowledge how the great phisher-for-phools Bernard Madoff duped wealthy investors into a Ponzi scheme. Every month the investors would receive a statement showing how their Madoff-held assets had grown in value: with remarkable regularity. An investment quant from Whitman, Massachusetts, Harry Markopolos, followed up on this and presented his suspicions to the SEC Boston regional office. He claimed that Madoff's high, and smooth, returns (between 1 and 2 percent per month) defied the laws of finance.[22] Madoff said that he accomplished the smoothing by an investment strategy called a "collar." He said he bought options to cut off extraordinary losses and balanced this with sales of options that cut off extraordinary gains.[23] While such a strategy would have smoothed earnings, Markopolos saw that it would be much too costly for Madoff to make the high returns he credited to his investors. A Ponzi scheme was further suggested, since to practice such a collar, it would be necessary for Madoff to make more options trades than on the entire US market.[24]

Despite their cogency, Markopolos's suspicions were met with resistance at the SEC. His first complaints to the SEC office in Boston in 2000 and 2001 quickly died.[25] But Markopolos persisted, and the New York regional office, with jurisdiction over Madoff, decided to conduct an investigation in November 2005. Meaghan Cheung, a branch chief in the office, and Simona Suh, a staff attorney, were assigned the case.[26] But they, along with Doria Bachenheimer, who had made the assignments, appeared to place more suspicion on Markopolos, the complainant, than on Madoff, its target. All three were worried that Markopolos was self-interested. Bachenheimer expressed it succinctly: that he was a "bounty" hunter.[27] But there was also a clear cultural difference between Markopolos, a quant, and the team dealing with the case. Again Bachenheimer expressed it: that his complaint was "theories." He did not meet a lawyer's views of a whistleblower, which would be someone with inside information of wrongdoing who could testify credibly in court.[28] Nor did it help that the already angry Markopolos had insulted Cheung in a telephone conversation by indicating his low opinion of the SEC.[29] And so, when Madoff in due course came to the SEC, and was interviewed by Cheung and Suh, they were already ripe to be phished—as it turned out, by one of the great masters of the art. No evidence of fraud was found; and in due course the case was closed.

For us, the interest here is not in the details of the Madoff case, but rather what it indicates about the sufficiency of SEC funding more generally. The errors made in the New York office notwithstanding, there is indication that the staff were dedicated government officials, who cared about the SEC and its mission.[30] However, the investigative team showed little understanding of Markopolos's complaints or motives. This misunderstanding could have been cleared up if it had included someone with a background in finance. Additionally, quite possibly, absent the demoralization accompanying New-Story denial of respect to regulators, with salaries and workloads to match, the Markopolos complaint and/or the Madoff defense would have been seen in a different light. We can never know whether more generous funding would have made a difference. But we do know that the investigation did not work out well, and that is consistent with the ancient expression: "You get what you pay for." One-quarter of 1/100th of a cent ain't all that much; and such penny-pinching toward government agencies has been encouraged, not just in the SEC, by the New-Story view that "government is the problem."

Citizens United

Our third example comes from the political realm of our book. In our chapter on politics (chapter 5), we saw that money coming from interested parties is used to phish for votes in US elections.

There is more than a century of federal campaign law aimed at muting these problems of influence. The Tillman Act of 1907 kept corporations from making direct contributions to political campaigns. The Federal Elections Campaign Act Amendments of 1974 established the Federal Election Commission; they also put limits on contributions to election campaigns and on campaign spending. It did not take long, however, before ways were discovered, through political "friends" such as political action committees, to circumvent these laws concerning direct contributions. Without any direct contributions the PACs could still be of assistance to political campaigns. This posed a vexing question: how to control the PACs and other interested "friends" without violating constitutional rights of free speech. After years of wrangling, in 2002 the Congress came up with a compromise: the Bipartisan Campaign Reform Act (popularly known as McCain-Feingold).[31] In one of its important provisions, corporations, unions, and nonprofits were prohibited from funding broadcast advertisements mentioning a candidate within thirty days before a primary or within sixty days before a general election.

In 2007, a right-wing nonprofit organization involved in political advocacy, Citizens United, decided to challenge this provision. It had developed a documentary, *Hillary: The Movie,* which it planned to distribute via cable TV. The film would be free to viewers, who would get it on demand, but Citizens United would pay $1.2 million to a cable company for this service. Citizens United sought a ruling from the Federal Election Commission on whether its distribution would conform to McCain-Feingold, during the upcoming 2008 primary season, in which Hillary Clinton would be a candidate. Receiving a negative ruling, it sued for an injunction;[32] denied in district court, it appealed to the Supreme Court.

Since *Hillary: The Movie* was not to be generally broadcast, the case could have been easily decided on narrow grounds. Instead the Supreme Court decided it on very general First Amendment grounds regarding rights of free speech.[33] The five-vote majority opinion gives an especially clear example of New-Story thinking, with its failure to consider phishing for phools. Our view of free speech closely mirrors our view of free markets. We view both as critical for economic prosperity; and free speech as especially critical for democracy. But just as phishing for phools yields a downside to free markets, similarly, it yields a downside to free speech. Like markets, free speech also requires rules to filter the functional from the dysfunctional. Anyone who has ever run a meeting knows that. Even the most democratic town meeting has its rules. By analogy, by trial and error, Congress had been trying since the Tillman Act to set a few such rules.

Justice Anthony Kennedy wrote the majority opinion, joined by John Roberts, Antonin Scalia, Clarence Thomas, and Samuel Alito. The opinion explicitly denied the distinction between free speech by individuals and free speech by corporations. Yet more basically it seemed to see no downside to free speech so that rules might be in order. A critical passage reveals the basis for the decision: "By taking the right to speak from some and giving it to others, the Government deprives the disadvantaged person or class of the right to use speech to strive to establish worth, standing, and respect for the speaker's voice. The Government may not by these means deprive the public of the right and privilege to determine for itself what speech and speakers are worthy of consideration. The First Amendment protects speech and speaker, and the ideas that flow from each."[34]

But phishing for phools tells us that Kennedy had the argument wrong: there can be no absolutes in the rules of letting people speak, just as no one would allow someone to play loud music at Speakers' Corner in Hyde Park (where by right all British people, no matter how kooky, can voice their views). Kennedy seems to treat speaking solely as conveyance of information, without consideration of its role of persuasion, inevitably with its phish for phools. In an earlier passage he says: "Speech is an essential mechanism of democracy, for it is the means to hold officials accountable to the people. The right of citizens to inquire, to hear, to speak, and to use information to reach consensus is a precondition to enlightened self-government and a necessary means to protect it."[35] Of course we agree. But what he does not say is equally important to the case at hand. Speech is also a way to convince other people to act in *our* interests. If people are phishable, it is also a way to convince them to behave in a way that is in our interest, but not necessarily in *theirs*.

It is common sense, as John Paul Stevens wrote in the dissent, to treat corporations differently from people. He lamented the majority opinion's apparent lack of appreciation of "electioneering." Phishing is just not part of New Story. Stevens reminded the Court that there is evidence that corporations (as well as labor unions) often ask a congressman for favors, and then contribute to negative ads against the congressman's opponents, so that the congressman need run only positive ads, and therefore appear "above the fray." The corporations or unions then quietly notify the congressman to be sure he knows what they have done for him. The congressman gives his thanks, behind the scenes.[36] Stevens asserts: "There are threats of corruption that are far more destructive to a democratic society than the odd bribe. Yet the majority's understanding of corruption would leave lawmakers impotent to address all but the most discrete abuses."[37]

Metaphorically, we must place some limits on those with the resources to unleash huge loudspeakers that can drown out the messages of less well-endowed others. Our previous example (in chapter 5, on politics) of the Grassley-Small senatorial race of 2004 indicates that the rules already give huge advantage to those with the resources to dominate the airwaves. The Citizens United decision is thus an example in the political realm of the dangers of replacing Old-Story with New-Story thinking. The New-Story-based verdict failed to appreciate the need for careful compromise to temper the problems of phishing for phools.

Harvard law professor Lawrence Lessig has offered a plan that is such a compromise. US citizens would be given a voucher by the federal government to donate as much as $50 in total to candidates of their choice. They could also give an extra $100 out of their own pockets to every candidate. In return, the candidates who accept such donations would have to abjure donations from other sources (including from PACs).[38] Lessig estimates the cost at $3 billion per year.[39] But given the distortions to democracy we saw earlier, this would be a real bargain: the real job of congressmen would no longer be dialing for dollars. They could revert to pursuit of the people's business.

Conclusion

Our three examples, from Social Security legislation, securities regulation, and campaign finance law, span a good share of our discussion in our whole book. They demonstrate the importance of having the national story right. New Story has pervaded US policy, as our three examples show, regarding the relationship between government and households (Social Security); the relationship between finance and its oversight (securities regulation); and the relationship between the legal system and the electorate (campaign finance law). More generally, in situation after situation, we have shown that New Story is only a half truth. Free markets make people free to choose. But they also make them free to phish, and free to be phished. Ignorance of those truths is a recipe for disaster.

Through an American lens, with mainly American examples, we have demonstrated that stories, and especially the national story, do matter. But phishing for phools is, of course, not just an American phenomenon; it occurs everywhere. A functional national story requires, among other things, a correct interpretation of how the economy and how politics really work. It must take into account not only the upsides of markets and of democracy, but also the downsides. And those downsides include, importantly, phishing for phools.

The Significance of
Phishing Equilibrium

We have been giving example after example of phishing for phools. But that has posed a question that must be on some readers' minds. What is new in this book, relative to current economics? Don't all economists already know about phishing for phools? Curiously, the answer to this question is "yes," in the sense that when we economists see a case of phishing for phools, we can identify it, and we understand its causes. But does the conventional wisdom about free markets give us an instinct for when and how it will occur? The answer to that is "no."[1]

Most countries have learned respect for free markets, and, for the most part, rightfully so. They bring high standards of living. We learn from economics that competitive markets will be "efficient" since, under relatively mild assumptions, it has been shown that in equilibrium the welfare of one person cannot be improved without a sacrifice for someone else. In summary, economics typically describes free competitive markets as working "well"—although there is also need for intervention to solve the added problems of "externalities" and "unfair" income distribution, as can be accomplished with minimal intervention through appropriate taxes and subsidies.

But we take a different—and also more general—view of people, and of markets. That view pervades this book. We do not argue with the economics textbooks about the merits of free markets: Our mind's eye can take a journey across the boundary from China into North Korea, and then again across the boundary into South Korea.

But let's not carry our praise of markets too far. They may work quite well (as the textbooks describe) if all the appropriate assumptions are truly aligned. But every man has his weak spot, and so every one of us is oftentimes less than fully informed; and oftentimes we have difficulty knowing what we really want. As a by-product of these human weaknesses, we can be tricked. That may be human nature, but it is contrary to the stick-men that populate our economics lectures. And if people are less than perfect, those competitive free markets will not just be the playing field for providing us with what we need and want. They will also be the playing field for phishing for phools. They will be caught in a phishing equilibrium.

An illustration of this difference in point of view can be seen in a long and heated conversation with a generous friend and colleague. He agreed to listen to a presentation of *Phishing for Phools.* He quickly zoomed in on the question of this chapter. Was there anything that Joe-Schmoe-economist would not already understand? We explained that *Phishing for Phools* examines the role of markets when people have weaknesses, so markets are not efficient; and those with the weaknesses can, potentially, be tricked and fooled. It was wrong, he said, to combine the "pathology" with the standard economics.

But, relative to current economics, that is one of the fundamental points of this book. We believe that it is wrong—as in the textbooks, and in the standard mental frame of almost every economist—only to picture the healthy (i.e., "efficient") working of markets, with economic pathologies depicted as due only to externalities and income distribution. We believe that economies are more complicated—and also more interesting—than this standard view. This division of thought (between healthy and pathological), we further believe, is not just sloppy and wrong-minded, but also highly consequential.

Why so? Because it means that modern economics inherently fails to grapple with deception and trickery. People's naïveté and susceptibility to deception have been swept under the rug. Economists now, in 2015, are looking back at the 2008 world financial crisis; and at least some of us are asking the question: Why? We are not just asking why the Crash itself occurred, which we now understand in general terms. But, additionally, we economists are looking at ourselves. We wonder why so few of us had predicted it. It is truly remarkable that so few economists foresaw what would happen.[2] There are about 2¼ million article and book listings regarding finance and economics on Google Scholar.[3] That may not indicate enough economist-monkeys to randomly type *Hamlet,* but it should have been enough to generate quite a few papers that would tell how Countrywide, WaMu,

IndyMac, Lehman, and many, many others would in short order flame out and crash. We should have known that their positions in mortgage-backed securities and credit default swaps were fragile. At the time we should have also foreseen the future vulnerabilities of the euro.

We believe this huge lacuna tells us that economists (including those in finance) systematically ignore or downplay the role of trickery and deception in the working of markets. We have already put our finger on a simple reason why they were so ignored: economists' understanding of markets systematically excludes them. The pathology, as our friend made clear, is viewed as mainly due to "externalities." But that fails to see that competitive markets by their very nature spawn deception and trickery, as a result of the same profit motives that give us our prosperity. Had we economists appropriately seen free markets as a two-edged sword, we would all but surely have delved into the ways in which financial derivatives and mortgage-backed securities, and also sovereign debt, would turn out badly. More than a handful of us would have sounded the alarm.

Failure of the War on Cancer

In *The Emperor of All Maladies,* cancer-researcher/physician Siddhartha Mukherjee describes a similar error in the analysis and treatment of cancer.[4] Using economists' language, in this analogy there are diseases that we might view as due to "externalities." These diseases are bacteriological or viral in origin; most of the time, they have fairly simple cures. We only need discover a drug or a vaccine that will kill the body's foreign invader. By our externality analogy, in economics the "disease" is the harm to those downwind; the cure is a tax on the smoke.

But cancer, says Mukherjee, is different. It is not caused by a foreign invader like a virus or a bacterium. It is, instead, caused by the exact same natural forces as our own healthy physiology. It develops as a mutation of our own cells. Just as our own healthy cells have powerful defenses against attack, the mutations likewise have their own defenses. The problem is not that the body's defenses do not work well enough; in the case of malignancies, these defenses work too well. The malignant cancer cells are too resistant to attack; they refuse to die. The nature of cancer lies in the extension of our own benign physiology in these mutations. There is an exact analogy with *phishing for phools.* It results from the extension of the benign working of markets where everyone is sophisticated, to the working of those markets where some of us are naïve.

In the 1970s, advocates of a War on Cancer successfully lobbied for a "national commitment for the conquest of cancer."[5] With passage of the National Cancer Act of 1971, greatly increased federal resources were devoted to cancer research. We might think that such increase in funding could do no harm. But, curiously, Mukherjee views this "war" as a mistake. Its search for a quick and easy cure trivialized the problem; a quick and easy cure would be found only if cancer had a simple root cause: for example, a virus.[6] But such simplistic views of the cause of cancer diverted attention from discovery of its fundamental nature. Serious reductions in mortality from cancer would be forthcoming only after it was understood better: when it had been shown to be the result of mutations, whose ability to defend themselves was an extension of the body's own healthy defenses.

We are claiming that economists' view of markets makes similar oversimplification. It may be standard economics to pretend that economic pathologies are only "externalities." But the ability of free markets to engender phishing for phools of many different varieties is not an externality. Rather, it is inherent in the workings of competitive markets. And the same motives for profit that give us a healthy benign economy if everyone is fully rational are the same motives that give us the economic pathologies of phishing for phools.

Previous Work on Phishing for Phools

There are, of course, precursors to *Phishing for Phools.* We will describe here a few articles that are representative of the (roughly estimated again via Google Scholar) 200,000 with the distinction between the "sophisticated" and the "naïve," or between the "informed" and the "uninformed." The typical such article, as in our examples, combines the sophisticated and the naïve in some special way. And then, it will perceive, sometimes as its point of focus, but usually as a sideshow, that, yes, in the special context described, the sophisticated/informed take advantage of the naïve/uninformed.

For the first example, recall from the introduction Stefano DellaVigna and Ulrike Malmendier on health clubs' toggle-bolt contracts: those contracts are easy to get into; hard to cancel. In their modeling DellaVigna and Malmendier described the health-club strategy as taking advantage of their customers' present bias.[7] The high weight put by the customers on the present causes them to put off what they could do today until "just tomorrow"; but then when that "just tomorrow" comes, it has become the present, and so they put it off, yet again.

Xavier Gabaix and David Laibson have produced another way in which sellers take advantage of buyers, in this case because some attributes of the product are hard to see.[8] In their terminology those attributes are "shrouded." Implicitly they ask: what rice would restaurants serve if their customers could not tell the difference between Basmati and Uncle Ben's? The profit motive says the restaurants will choose the cheaper.

Gabaix and Laibson's leading example of shrouded attributes concerns inkjet printers. The buyers focus on the price of the *printers*. But the subsequent cost of the ink cartridges is significant relative to the initial cost of the printer (on average something like two-thirds).[9] The relevant cost does not just come then from the initial layout for the printer: it is the total cost of printing a page. In a survey of the buyers of one Hewlett-Packard model, only 3 percent of respondents knew the cost of the ink at the time they purchased their printer.[10] Nor is this a coincidence. Following Gabaix and Laibson, to the buyer of a printer, its price speaks loud and clear. It is also easy to find on the web. But try to track down the cost of the needed ink. That information has been spread over several different websites; the printer manufacturers have intentionally shrouded this attribute.[11] And from the survey evidence, they have been successful at it.[12]

One of us (Bob) performed another test for the theory of shrouded attributes. He had been persuaded by the TV advertisements to purchase gourmet cat food for his cat Lightning. In the ads the cats go to their food bowls so perky and happy. But does gourmet cat food really taste good? Bob tasted it. The advertised flavors that sound attractive to humans—turkey, tuna, duck, and lamb—did not seem to be there at all. The Gabaix-Laibson prediction of the provision of this usually shrouded attribute was spot on. But we should be careful to admit this is not the definitive test. If only Lightning could have spoken, we could really know.[13]

The world of finance also gives good examples where the phools do badly at the hands of the more knowledgeable. The plain-vanilla economics of finance presents conclusions that simply are not true. The fundamental proposition is that stocks are priced at their "fundamental value." That means that the price of stocks is equal to the appropriately discounted expected future payouts (from sources such as dividends and stock buybacks). But this cannot be true. There is much too much volatility in stock prices for this to be so.[14] And then there are all kinds of other strange happenings in financial markets relative to the plain-vanilla story. Why is the volume of trade so high? Why do stock traders on average keep their stocks for such short times? The list goes on.

Most finance economists (but not all!) have acknowledged that the plain-vanilla model has serious failings. And so they have been moved to picture a stock market (and also other asset markets) with two types of people.[15] On the one hand, there are the "informed" traders. These are the people who really understand the stock market; they are the intrepid people who, according to the theory, would drive stock prices toward their "fundamental" value if they were dominant. But then, the story goes, there are "uninformed" traders, who do not understand those fundamentals. The finance professors call them "noise traders" because such stock-purchasers are said to be trading, not on the basis of fundamentals, but instead on random "noise." Perhaps a good image of them comes from the 1990s purchasers of dot-com stocks prior to the burst of the bubble.[16] The noise trading papers claim to explain many stock price "anomalies": including the high return on stocks relative to bonds and the high variation of stock prices relative to their fundamentals.[17]

Examination of noise trading has been a successful research paradigm. In the mathematical models, phishing for phools does occur, as sophisticated investors take advantage of the noise traders. Indeed, such models can even generate explicit formulas for the respective "welfare" of the informed and the uninformed traders.[18]

These examples from economics and finance illustrate the very large body of work that contrasts the naïves with the sophisticates; the informed with the uninformed. The sophisticated/informed almost always do better than the naïve/uninformed. Wherever that occurs there is phishing for phools.

The Difference

If so much has been written about the naïve and the uninformed in behavioral economics and finance, there remains the question regarding where we come in. Perhaps there is nothing new here. Even if that is the case, we hope that you have enjoyed this book, and its stories. But we are also hopeful we have added a new perspective. We will now describe three ways in which this book presents a perspective that is, quite possibly, novel relative to current economics.

The Role of Equilibrium in Competitive Markets

The first of these perspectives concerns the place of behavioral economics within economics. The fundamental thinking of economists, as we indicated back in the introduction, and also discussed at the beginning of this chapter, emanates from Adam Smith. The central vision of economists is in terms of Smith's famous butchers, brewers, and bakers; they competitively respond to consumers' demands, and decide how much to supply, based on what consumers are willing to pay. This system has an insistent equilibrium. If the economy is not in such an equilibrium, there is an opportunity for profit. If so, we would expect someone to take advantage of it. Just as nature is said to "abhor a vacuum," we expect economic systems to abhor such unused opportunities for profit. In terms of our images, if there were no stall selling Cinnabons®, or the like, at the airport or at the mall, one would open soon.

This general way of thinking, with its insistence of general equilibrium, has been the central nervous system for economic thinking for almost two and a half centuries. Yet behavioral economics (we will come to finance in short order) seems oddly divorced from it. Our two examples from behavioral economics, of DellaVigna-Malmendier and Gabaix-Laibson, illustrate. In the style required now for a journal article, their modeling and examples are very special. In the DellaVigna-Malmendier description of health clubs, the budding jocks all have the special weakness of present bias. Gabaix-Laibson's model of shrouded markets is also special: they provide an illustrative model of the demand and supply of a base good and an add-on; some consumers are sophisticated and others are myopic, and firms decide whether or not to shroud the price of the add-on.[19] In accord with the standards of economics journal articles, these articles prove that phishing for phools exists. They do so by giving models and examples, where that phishing is undeniable; but the journals' demand for such undeniability comes at a cost. It means that the generality of phishing for phools cannot be conveyed.

And that is where this book comes in. Casting phishing for phools in an Adam Smith–style general-equilibrium framework, which is the benchmark for thinking for all economists, suggests its generality. That generality cues us into the inevitability of phishing.

Returning to the question of why economists missed the financial crisis: if we had been thinking about phishing for phools as a general phenomenon that occurs insofar as people have informational or psychological weaknesses that can be profitably exploited—or insofar as those weaknesses can be profitably created—economists would have been cued, as we should have been, to look for the phishes that in short order led to the crash.

Revealed Preference Unchallenged

There is another reason why behavioral economics and behavioral finance, with their special depictions of biases and also of markets, have failed to appreciate the ubiquity of phishing for phools. A common precept of standard economics is that people only make the choices that maximize their welfare. This assumption even has a fancy name, "revealed preferences": that people reveal what makes them better off by their choices.[20] Such an assumption, of course, is exactly at odds with our concept of the difference between what people really want (what is good for them) and what they think they want (their monkey-on-the-shoulder tastes). The particularity of behavioral economics—both its basis on particular psychological biases (such as present bias) and the embedding of those biases in special market situations (such as monopolistic competition)—have reinforced the notion that differences between what people want and their monkey-on-the-shoulder tastes are not the norm.

They are to be considered, perhaps, on a case-by-case basis—but just as rare exceptions. This message is not intended, but the presentation of behavioral economics, perhaps unconsciously, yields this implication.

Most economists therefore feel they can be comfortable with thinking that people's choices do reflect what they really want, with the further view that the number and consequences of dysfunctional decisions is small. This view is consistent with the observation that at least in developed countries most people purposefully manage to obtain their basic needs. Such purposefulness may lead us to believe that the difference between Pareto optimality in our true welfare and Pareto optimality in our monkey-on-the-shoulder welfare is inconsequential. That difference may arise in our contract at a health club, or in our purchase of ink cartridges. But these are exceptions, and so revealed preference is right: most of the time.

But thinking about phishing generally, as we do, has cued us, on the contrary, to see that phishing for phools is not some occasional nuisance. It is all over the place. Not only does it affect many decisions; in some cases it has sizable effect on welfare. Our examples have been carefully chosen not just to show the possibility of phishing for phools, but also to show its ubiquity and its overall importance in our economic lives. They are meant to counter the intuition of traditional (non-behavioral) economics that such phishes make little difference, because, for the most part, we purposefully choose what is good for us.

Our embedding of phishing for phools into general equilibrium with monkey-on-the-shoulder tastes thus goes beyond current behavioral economics by pointing out a truth that is natural to anyone who thinks in terms of general equilibrium theory. That thinking regards the inevitability of phishing. Once again, let's turn to our "favorite example." In general equilibrium, if a Cinnabon® stall at the airport could make a profit—absent something like it—then it will be there. So if we have a weakness—if we have a way in which we are phishable—the phishermen will be there in waiting. Just as much as the baker and the brewer and the butcher will be there if we have the resources to pay what it takes them to supply the bread and the beer and the meat, so too the tricksters will be there to phish us for phools.

Story Grafting

Relative to behavioral economics, *Phishing for Phools* makes a further contribution. As currently written, behavioral economics mainly follows from experimental evidence produced by psychologists. In our imagery, people make dysfunctional decisions: according to their monkey-on-their-shoulder tastes, rather than according to their real tastes. The psychologists have their lists of these dysfunctional motivations.

We agree that people have the biases on these lists. But a major aim of this book, beyond its notion of phishing equilibrium, has been to view such biases much more generally. Just as economists (see chapter 1 regarding financial worries and Suze Orman) impose their assumptions regarding how consumers behave (assuming, for example, that they budget painstakingly), the psychologists, and the behavioral economists who follow their lead, assume that decision makers operate according to some mode, typically from Cialdini's list. Just as economists have injected a great deal of ingenuity into concocting the possible "constraints" that face decision makers, the psychologists have also compiled an impressive list of possible "non-rational" behaviors. But in our opinion, which is shared by most sociologists and anthropologists, such lists have a problem. It is all very well to view people as behaving according to some bias from the "list"; but maybe they don't. Economists, psychologists, and social scientists more generally should be more inclusive: we should be inclusive of whatever thinking, conscious or subconscious, is the basis for people's decisions.

In this regard, following sociologists and cultural anthropologists, we have found a very general way to describe the mental frames that underlie people's decisions. The latter half of *Phishing for Phools* has gradually cast off the old skin of the behavioral economists' lists of behavioral biases; at the same time we have also, in crescendo, recast our argument in terms of this new view. It is inclusive, on the one hand, of the lists of psychological biases underlying dysfunctional decisions; but it is much more general.

We have obtained this greater generality by ourselves giving a picture to the mental frames that inform people's decisions. We have called them "the stories people are telling themselves." This description has a further advantage for us. It enables us to see, entirely naturally, how most phishing for phools occurs. The phish is a way to get someone to make a decision that is to the benefit of the phisher, but not to the benefit of the phool. Since our decisions are usually based on the stories we are telling ourselves about our situation, this gives us a transparent characterization of motivation that allows us to understand how most phishing for phools happens.

It also brings into economics a new variable. That variable is the story that people are telling themselves. Furthermore, it makes natural the idea that people make decisions that can be quite far from maximizing their own welfare, and that these stories are quite manipulable. Just change people's focus and one can change the decisions they make.

Summary

In sum, there may be nothing in this book that could be considered "new economics." If we were very much to invent economics anew, we would be neither right nor convincing. But our aim has been something different. It is to show that phishing for phools leads us to quite different conclusions from the usual takeaways of the old economics. The modern economy with its quite-free markets brings those of us who live in developed countries a standard of living that would be the envy of all previous generations. But let us not fool ourselves. It also brings us phishing for phools. And that too is consequential for our well-being.

This book may be about manipulation and deception, but we must acknowledge that there is also a great deal, and we repeat for emphasis, *a great deal* of goodness in the world. It is full of the heroes that we described in chapter 11. A large number of such generous heroes underlie this book.

One of the great pleasures upon completing this book is to write these acknowledgments: to be able to thank the many people who have contributed to this project. This book has not come from just the two authors sitting in a room alone, stewing away, to see what sentence would come next. On the contrary, the ideas in this book, and the work underlying its development, are in large part a compilation of what we have learned from our friends, particularly in the economics community, and also from the extraordinary research assistants who have helped us.

Our first debts go to our colleagues whose basic and fundamental ideas inform this book.

First we want to thank Paul Romer, who was the joint author of a paper with George on "Looting: The Economic Underworld of Bankruptcy for Profit." Chapters 9 and 10 on the S&L crisis and on junk bonds are a rewrite, in the style of this book, of that article. We are grateful to Paul for allowing us to do so. Another theme of the book, on narrative, also is largely due to another coauthor of George's. In George's joint work with Rachel Kranton on *Identity Economics,* one theme is the stories that people tell themselves, regarding who they are and what they should or should not do; and how such stories underlie their motivations. In a meeting of minds, Bob had independently discovered the role of "stories," especially regarding financial crises, in his previous work on the *Irrational Exuberance* of asset markets. Thus the role of narratives, which is perhaps our book's most important takeaway, merges two strands of thinking. We are both immensely grateful to Rachel. We are also grateful to Hui Tong, who worked with George on a paper titled "Lemons with Naïveté," which described an information-based phishing equilibrium. This work was the basis for our seminars on *Phishing for Phools* for several years.

We have a different sort of debt to Maxim Boycko, a coauthor of Bob's whom he met at a joint US National Bureau of Economic Research and USSR *IMEMO* conference in Moscow in 1989. Bob continues to work with him today on public attitudes and relationships with markets, comparing countries so as to reveal the roles of social norms and attitudes in market functioning.

In the fall of 2012, the manuscript had progressed to the point that Bob thought that we should hire some research assistants to help us. He advertised the post, and received some eighty applications. The three Yale undergraduates who were offered and accepted this job have played a major, major role in this book. They have not only been our research assistants, but also, in addition to Peter Dougherty from Princeton University Press, they have been our editors. We have on more than one occasion given them the task of assigning grades to the book: to each chapter, to each section of each chapter, and to each paragraph in each chapter. The grades they gave us were not always the highest, especially with modern standards of grade inflation, and our research assistants have then patiently explained why those low grades were deserved, and in conversations have led us out of the hole we were in. Each of these three research assistants is truly exceptional.

Victoria Buhler, who accepted the job when she was a junior, was so exceptional that David Brooks wrote a *New York Times* column lauding her for an essay she wrote in a class at Yale. When Victoria graduated and went on to a graduate year at Cambridge, she continued work on *Phishing for Phools.* That was the year when Bob won the Nobel Prize, which for at least a few months is an all-absorbing state, and she played an especially important role in filling the vacuum. Her interest is international politics, and she is so talented that George confesses that he once wrote an email to her, which began, not *if,* but "*when* you are Secretary of State."

Diana Li is also one of the three original research assistants. We found that we could ask Diana any question, ask her to do any task, and she would do it. The constraint seemed to be always on our side.

We were always worried that we might be asking her too much. She is a star debater, covered City Hall for the *Yale Daily News,* and is an economics major. One day recently she told us that she was going off to the World Debating Championships in Malaysia. Diana was always doing something like that. Every reader of *Phishing for Phools* will benefit from what she brought to the table. She is a masterly interviewer, and we always had a good laugh about her plans to bring *Phishing for Phools* to life. At one point the magazine *Glamour* asked Diana to be a candidate for an award. We wrote a letter on her behalf, but she did not get it. Apparently they do not know what glamour really is: to our minds, Real Glamour is being Diana Li.

Jack Newsham was also one of the original three research assistants. He, like Diana and Victoria, made major contributions to the book. He did interviews for us; and also gave us his editorial opinions: they were always right. He played an especially important role in the chapter on advertising, as he brought to our attention the work on Harding's campaign, which, with Lasker as the campaign impresario, exactly fit into the book. At Yale Jack prepared to be a reporter, and he brought his reportorial skills to our enterprise. After graduation, he went on to the *Boston Globe,* with a much-coveted position, especially now that newspaper jobs are, unfortunately, such a rarity. We were privileged that Jack worked for us, on *Phishing for Phools,* for two years.

In the later stages of our work on *Phishing for Phools* Stephan Schneeberger gave us excellent editorial comments on the manuscript and fact-checked chapters 4 to 8. We are very grateful for his dedication to this task, as we are also grateful to Yijia Lu for his excellent fact-checking of the preface through chapter 3. And Deniz Dutz, in the very final stages, did yeomanlike work; he re-fact-checked everything. And for six weeks in May and June 2015, Madeleine Adams was the copy editor; almost everywhere, she added elegance and grace to the manuscript we had given her.

The ideas in this book are a collage of what we have learned, and what we have listened to, over the course of our lives as economists. In this regard we owe special thanks to four others. Daniel Kahneman, yes that one, some twenty-five or thirty years ago, told us that the distinctive feature of psychology is that it views people as imperfect machines. The job of the psychologist, he said, was to figure out how and when those machines would be dysfunctional. In contrast, the basic concept of economics is equilibrium. We think that this book brings together these observations. Richard Thaler, with whom Bob has been organizing behavioral economics workshops for twenty-five years, has also been an influence; he initially suggested more than twenty years ago that we two ought to work together. He was our matchmaker. We are hugely indebted to him. Mario Small and Michele Lamont cued us into thinking about how people's decisions depend largely on the subconscious rather than the conscious. We decided that makes people manipulable; that insight was a key step in our undertaking this book.

Peter Dougherty, of Princeton University Press, has not just been an editor for the book, and a great friend of ours throughout the process, but his constant good editorial judgment, with pointing us where we ought to go, and why, has made this book possible. The NO-ONE-COULD-POSSIBLY-WANTs of the preface, for example, emanate from a conversation with Peter.

There are many others who have contributed to this book, especially George's colleagues at the International Monetary Fund, where for four years he worked on the manuscript, from October 2010 to October 2014, and Bob's colleagues at Yale University. These colleagues and friends include Vivek Arora, Michael Ash, Larry Ball, Roland Benabou, Olivier Blanchard, Irene Bloemraad, Nyla Branscombe, Lucia Buono, John Campbell, Elie Canetti, Karl Case, Philip Cook, William Darity, Stefano DellaVigna, Rafael Di Tella, Avinash Dixit, Curt Eaton, Joshua Felman, Nicole Fortin, Pierre Fortin, Alexander Haslam, Catherine Haslam, John Helliwell, Robert Johnson, Anton Korinek, Larry Kotlikoff, Andrew Levin, Annamaria Lusardi, Ulrike Malmendier, Sendhil Mullainathan, Abhinay Muthoo, Philip Oreopoulos, Robert Oxoby, Ceyla Pazarbasioglu, Shelley Phipps, Adam Posen, Zoltan Poszar, Natasha Schüll, Eldar Shafir, Carl Shapiro, Dennis Snower, Michael Stepner, Joseph Stiglitz, Phillip Swagel, George Vaillant, Teodora Villagra, Jose Vinals, Justin Wolfers, and Peyton Young.

Together we have given presentations of our work at UMass Amherst, the University of California at Berkeley, Duke University, George Washington University, Georgetown University, Johns Hopkins University, the University of Maryland, Princeton University (as part of the Bendheim Lectures in Finance), and the University of Warwick, as well as at the Canadian Economic Association, the International Monetary Fund, the World Bank, the Institute for New Economic Thinking, the Peterson Institute, Union Theological Seminary, and the Social Interactions, Identity and Well-Being group of the Canadian Institute for Advanced Research.

Bob has incorporated this book into his Behavioral and Institutional Economics class at Yale University, a class that is cross-listed in the Graduate School, the Law School, and the School of Management. Feedback from students in that class, with their varied and youthful perspectives, has proved valuable.

George wishes to thank the International Monetary Fund for generously supporting him as a visiting scholar at the Fund from October 2010 to October 2014, and Georgetown University from November 2014. He also thanks the Canadian Institute for generous financial support to him and to the Social Interactions, Identity and Well-Being group, which provided major inspiration for this book.

Our families have been a boost for us, notably our economist sons Robby Akerlof, now at Warwick University, and Ben Shiller, now at Brandeis University, as well as Derek Shiller, who is a philosopher at the University of Nebraska, Omaha. Virginia Shiller has always supported our work, and for years has been asked for her judgment: this idea, up or down, as she has also generously contributed ideas of her own. And we also want to thank our administrative assistants Bonnie Blake, Carol Copeland, Shanti Karunaratne, and Patricia Medina, who helped us carve out time for our writing endeavors.

Preface

1. "A Nickel in the Slot," *Washington Post,* March 25, 1894, p. 20.

2. "A Crying Evil," *Los Angeles Times,* February 24, 1899, p. 8.

3. Bernard Malamud, "Nevada Gaming Tax: Estimating Resident Burden and Incidence" (University of Nevada, Las Vegas, April 2006), p. 1, last accessed May 5, 2015, https://faculty.unlv.edu/bmalamud/estimating .gaming.burden.incidence.doc.

4. Richard N. Velotta, "Gaming Commission Rejects Slot Machines at Cash Registers," *Las Vegas Sun,* March 18, 2010, last accessed May 12, 2015, http://lasvegassun.com/news/2010/mar/18/gaming-commission-rejects-slot -machines-cash-regis/?utm_source=twitterfeed&utm_medium=twitter. Senator Harry Reid is famous as chair of the Nevada Gambling Commission for his stand against Mafia influence. The movie *Casino* is said to be based on Reid's stance against Frank Rosenthal (see "Harry Reid," *Wikipedia,* accessed December 1, 2014, http://en.wikipedia.org/wiki/Harry_Reid).

5. Natasha Dow Schüll, *Addiction by Design: Machine Gambling in Las Vegas* (Princeton: Princeton University Press, 2012).

6. Ibid., pp. 24–25.

7. These include a gas station/convenience store and a supermarket where she sometimes gambles, and then, most significantly, the Palace Station casino.

8. Schüll, *Addiction by Design,* p. 2. Mollie tells Schüll, "I am not playing to win. [I play] to keep playing—to stay in that machine zone where nothing else matters." We are thankful to Natasha Schüll for a telephone conversation on February 13, 2014, in which she further described Mollie and her behavior to us.

9. Ibid., p. 33. Schüll describes one surveillance video of a defibrillation: "Despite the man lying quite literally at their feet, touching the bottoms of their chairs, the other gamblers kept playing."

10. John Elfreth Watkins Jr., "What May Happen in the Next Hundred Years," *Ladies Home Journal,* December 1900, p. 8, https://secure.flickr .com/photos/jonbrown17/2571144135/sizes/o/in/photostream/. See "Predictions of the Year 2000 from *The Ladies Home Journal* of December 1900," accessed December 1, 2014, http://yorktownhistory.org/wp-content/

archives/homepages/1900_predictions.htm, for confirmation that the issue was for December.

11. *Oxford English Dictionary,* s.v. "phish," accessed October 29, 2014, http://www.oed.com/view/Entry/264319?redirectedFrom=phish#eid.

12. It is no coincidence that early research of Daniel Kahneman and Amos Tversky, who were pioneers in the modern field of cognitive psychology, concerned optical illusion. Kahneman has told George that the distortions in thinking that underlie the field of behavioral economics can be seen as being like "optical illusion." (Private conversation, some twenty-five years ago.)

13. Kurt Eichenwald, *A Conspiracy of Fools: A True Story* (New York: Random House, 2005), and Bethany McLean and Peter Elkind, *The Smartest Guys in the Room: The Amazing Rise and Fall of Enron* (New York: Portfolio/Penguin Books, 2003).

14. Bethany McLean and Peter Elkind, "The Guiltiest Guys in the Room," *Fortune,* July 5, 2006, last accessed May 12, 2015, http://money.cnn.com/2006/05/29/news/enron_guiltyest/.

15. Henry David Thoreau, *Walden: Or, Life in the Woods* (New York: Houghton Mifflin, 1910), p. 8, https://books.google.com/books/about/Walden.html?id=HVlXAAAAYAAJ.

16. According to Rebecca Mead, Condé Nast conducts an annual American Wedding Study, which reports the average cost of the American wedding. For 2006, it was $27,852, which was 60 percent of per capita GDP. Mead, *One Perfect Day: The Selling of the American Wedding* (New York: Penguin Books, 2007), Kindle locations 384–92 out of 4013. Since the Great Recession that fraction has abated relative to US GDP per capita. The most recent estimate, for 2014, says that it is "over $28,000," which was about 51 percent of per capita GDP. "BRIDES Reveals Trends of Engaged American Couples with American Wedding Study," July 10, 2014, accessed December 1, 2014, http://www.marketwired.com/press-release/brides-reveals-trends-of-engaged-american-couples-with-american-wedding-study-1928460.htm.

17. Jessica Mitford, *The American Way of Death Revisited* (New York: Knopf, 1998), Kindle location 790–92 out of 5319.

18. "From your very first appointment until your baby arrives your PRA will provide you with personal guidance on everything you'll need for baby." Babies "R" Us, "Baby Registry: Personal Registry Advisor," accessed March 20, 2015, http://www.toysrus.com/shop/index.jsp?categoryId=11949069.

19. The view that people worry about their bills can also be seen in the annual survey on Stress in America conducted on behalf of the American Psychological Association. Stress about money is the number one reported stress in American lives. The report from the latest survey says (p. 2): "Stress about money and finances appears to have a significant impact on Americans' lives." Nearly three-quarters (72 percent) of adults report feeling stressed about money at least some of the time and nearly one-quarter say that they experience extreme stress about money (22 percent rate their stress about money during the past month as an 8, 9, or 10 on a 10-point scale). "In some cases, people are even putting their health care needs on hold because of financial concerns." Furthermore, stress about work, which

may also be about money but expressed differently, comes a close second in the poll. American Psychological Association, *Stress in America: Paying with Our Health,* February 4, 2015, last accessed March 29, 2015, http://www.apa .org/news/press/releases/stress/2014/stress-report.pdf.

20. We are using the term *rip-off* in the sense that people are paying a high price for the services they are getting. We are not referring, except in rare instances, to transactions that are illegal. The *Wikipedia* entry "Ripoff" describes this as one usage of the term: "a bad financial transaction. Usually it refers to an incident in which a person is overcharged for something." Accessed November 13, 2014, http://en.wikipedia.org/wiki/Ripoff.

21. According to Sheharyar Bokhari, Walter Torous, and William Wheaton, the loan-to-value ratios in the United States in the late 1990s and early 2000s, before the housing boom, were less than 80 percent for only 40 percent of home purchases with mortgages purchased by Fannie Mae. Taking the transaction costs as about 10 percent of the sale price (6 percent for real estate fees, 4 percent for closing costs), this means that for 60 percent of house closings, those costs were 50 percent or more of the buyer's down payment. Bokhari et al., "Why Did Household Mortgage Leverage Rise from the Mid-1980s until the Great Recession?" Massachusetts Institute of Technology, Center for Real Estate, January 2013, last accessed May 12, 2015, http://citeseerx.ist .psu.edu/viewdoc/download?doi=10.1.1.269.5704&rep=rep1&type=pdf.

22. See Carmen M. Reinhardt and Kenneth Rogoff, *This Time Is Different: Eight Centuries of Financial Folly* (Princeton: Princeton University Press, 2009).

23. John Kenneth Galbraith, *The Great Crash,* 50th anniversary ed. (New York: Houghton Mifflin, 1988), Kindle location 1943–45 out of 4151.

24. James Harvey Young, *The Toadstool Millionaires: A Social History of Patent Medicines in America before Federal Regulation* (Princeton: Princeton University Press, 1961), p. 248.

25. See testimony by David J. Graham for the Senate Finance Committee, November 18, 2004, http://www.finance.senate.gov/imo/media/ doc/111804dgtest.pdf. At the time of his testimony Graham was associate director for science and medicine in the Office of Safety at the Food and Drug Administration. We are using his estimates of 88,000 to 139,000 extra cases of heart attack or sudden cardiac arrest due to Vioxx, of which 30–40 percent resulted in death (p. 1). We shall return to David Graham in chapter 6, "Phood, Pharma, and Phishing."

26. John Abramson, *Overdosed America: The Broken Promise of American Medicine,* 3rd ed. (New York: Harper Perennial, 2008), p. 70. This estimate extrapolates the findings of Great Britain's Million Women Health Study on the basis of population. In an article in *The Lancet* in August 2003, that study concluded: "Use of HRT [hormone replacement therapy] by women aged 50–64 years in the UK over the past decade has resulted in an estimated 20,000 extra breast cancers, 15,000 associated with oestrogen-progestagen; the extra deaths cannot yet be reliably estimated." Valerie Beral, Emily Banks, Gillian Reeves, and Diana Bull, on behalf of the Million Women Study Collaborators, "Breast Cancer and Hormone-Replacement Therapy in

the Million Women Study," *Lancet* 362, no. 9382 (August 9, 2003): 419–27. The extrapolation is conservative, since hormone replacement therapy was more common in the United States than in Britain.

27. Centers for Disease Control and Prevention, *Health, United States, 2013: With Special Feature on Prescription Drugs*, p. 213, table 64, accessed December 1, 2014, http://www.cdc.gov/nchs/data/hus/hus13.pdf. Figures are for 2011–12 for adults age 20 and over. We note that there has been more than a 50 percent increase in this fraction from the 22 percent recorded as obese in 1988 to 1994.

28. Dariush Mozaffarian et al., "Changes in Diet and Lifestyle and Long-Term Weight Gain in Women and Men," *New England Journal of Medicine* 364, no. 25 (June 23, 2011): 2395–96, accessed October 30, 2014, http://www.nejm.org/doi/full/10.1056/NEJMoa1014296?query=TOC#t=articleTop.

29. Michael Moss, *Sugar, Salt and Fat* (New York: Random House, 2013), Kindle location 287–89 out of 7341.

30. Adult smoking rates decreased from 43 percent in 1965 to 18 percent in 2014. "Message from Howard Koh, Assistant Secretary of Health," in US Surgeon General, *The Health Consequences of Smoking—50 Years of Progress* (2014), accessed March 6, 2015, http://www.surgeongeneral.gov/library/reports/50-years-of-progress/full-report.pdf.

31. The most famous advertising campaign along these lines was "Reach for a Lucky Instead of a Sweet." The lengthy copy explaining the health and beauty enhancements of Luckies ends: "A reasonable proportion of sugar in the diet is recommended, but the authorities are overwhelming that too many fattening sweets are harmful and that too many such are eaten by the American people. So, for moderation's sake we say:—'REACH FOR A LUCKY INSTEAD OF A SWEET.'" A 1929 advertisement for Lucky Strike cigarettes, from Julian Lewis Watkins, *The 100 Greatest Advertisements, 1852–1958: Who Wrote Them and What They Did* (Chelmsford, MA: Courier, 2012), p. 66. Reproduced at https://beebo.org/smackerels/lucky-strike.html. Last accessed March 29, 2015.

32. David J. Nutt, Leslie A. King, and Lawrence D. Phillips, on behalf of the Independent Scientific Committee on Drugs, "Drug Harms in the UK: A Multicriteria Decision Analysis," *Lancet* 376, no. 9752 (November 6–12, 2010): 1558–65; Jan van Amsterdam, A. Opperhuizen, M. Koeter, and Willem van den Brink, "Ranking the Harm of Alcohol, Tobacco and Illicit Drugs for the Individual and the Population," *European Addiction Research* 16 (2010): 202–7, DOI:10.1159/000317249.

33. Nutt, King, and Phillips, "Drug Harms in the UK," p. 1561, fig. 2.

Introduction: Expect to Be Manipulated: Phishing Equilibrium

1. Regarding the story of Eve—and also the fundamental view of this chapter and this book—it is useful to think of the interchange between Eve and the serpent as an equilibrium outcome in which the serpent purposefully takes advantage of an opportunity. Furthermore, we imagine him as premeditatedly waiting for Eve—having rehearsed to himself the pitch

that he will use. Among the many animals in the garden, it was that terrible serpent—and not some more innocent animal, such as a rabbit or a giraffe—who "just happened" to be there at the apple tree. The phisherman was there by design. Following the central theme of this chapter, that was no coincidence. The encounter was just what we would expect in a phishing equilibrium. We note that a literal reading might alternatively see the Creation itself as "the first story of the Bible." A Google search revealed that our view of the eating of the apple as "the first story" is not unusual.

2. In a conversation with George some twenty-five to thirty years ago, Kahneman emphasized this difference between economics and psychology.

3. Paul Krugman and Robin Wells, *Microeconomics,* 2nd ed. (New York: Worth Publishers, 2009), pp. 12–13, use this example to explain the nature of equilibrium. Robert H. Frank and Ben Bernanke also refer to this image in *Principles of Macroeconomics* (New York: McGraw Hill, 2003).

4. See Cinnabon, Inc., "The Cinnabon Story," accessed October 31, 2014, http://www.cinnabon.com/about-us.aspx.

5. Ibid.

6. "Cinnabon," *Wikipedia,* accessed October 22, 2014, http://en.wikipedia.org/wiki/Cinnabon.

7. Email from Stefano DellaVigna to George Akerlof, October 25, 2014.

8. International Health, Racquet, and Sportsclub Association, "Industry Research," accessed October 22, 2014, http://www.ihrsa.org/industry-research/.

9. Stefano DellaVigna and Ulrike Malmendier, "Paying Not to Go to the Gym," *American Economic Review* 96, no. 3 (June 2006): 694–719. See also DellaVigna and Malmendier, "Contract Design and Self-Control: Theory and Evidence," *Quarterly Journal of Economics* 119, no. 2 (May 2004): 353–402.

10. DellaVigna and Malmendier, "Paying Not to Go to the Gym," p. 696.

11. DellaVigna and Malmendier, "Contract Design and Self-Control," p. 391, and p. 375, table 1.

12. The title of DellaVigna and Malmendier's article in the *American Economic Review.*

13. M. Keith Chen, Venkat Lakshminarayanan, and Laurie R. Santos, "How Basic Are Behavioral Biases? Evidence from Capuchin Monkey Trading Behavior," *Journal of Political Economy* 114, no. 3 (June 2006): 517–37.

14. Stephen J. Dubner and Steven D. Levitt, "Keith Chen's Monkey Research," *New York Times,* June 5, 2005.

15. Venkat Lakshminarayanan, M. Keith Chen, and Laurie R. Santos, "Endowment Effect in Capuchin Monkeys," *Philosophical Transactions of the Royal Society B: Biological Sciences* 363, no. 1511 (December 2008): 3837–44.

16. Adam Smith, *The Wealth of Nations* (New York: P. F. Collier, 1909; originally published 1776), p. 19. Emphasis added.

17. For a version of Pareto's original writings, see Vilfredo Pareto, *Manual of Political Economy: A Critical and Variorum Edition,* ed. Aldo Montesano et al. (Oxford: Oxford University Press, 2014). This edition derives from *Manuale di Economia,* published in Italy in 1906, and also a later edition in French.

18. In 1954, Kenneth Arrow and Gerard Debreu published a joint article that proved the existence of such an equilibrium under rather general conditions. In due course both of them would receive the Nobel Prize: Arrow in 1972, and Debreu in 1982, both of them especially cited for this contribution. The existence of the general equilibrium, even with the generality of their assumptions, does not appear to us to be of tremendous interest (especially since it occurs for what to us is the obvious mathematical reason). But it was only a short step from there to the real economic pay dirt: that such equilibria are "Pareto optimal" under the same general conditions. To us this seems like a remarkable result. It means that, for a wide range of fairly natural assumptions, the equilibrium of competitive markets has properties that are quite good. That will be the result we emphasize here; it confirms in a precise way Adam Smith's intuition. The famous paper is Kenneth J. Arrow and Gerard Debreu, "Existence of an Equilibrium for a Competitive Economy," *Econometrica* 22, no. 3 (July 1954): 265–90.

19. Of course, there are other possible "blemishes" to economies, such as monopoly and oligopoly, which have received a great deal of attention from economists. But these are not "blemishes of free markets." Instead they are departures from them.

20. Milton Friedman and Rose D. Friedman, *Free to Choose: A Personal Statement* (New York: Harcourt Brace Jovanovich, 1980).

21. Vance Packard, *The Hidden Persuaders: What Makes Us Buy, Believe— and Even Vote—the Way We Do* (Brooklyn: 1g Publishing, 2007; original ed., New York: McKay, 1957), pp. 90–91 (cake mixes); p. 94 (insurance).

22. Robert B. Cialdini, *Influence: The Psychology of Persuasion* (New York: HarperCollins, 2007).

23. These correspond to Cialdini's categories of "reciprocation," "liking," "authority: directed deference," "social proof," "commitment and consistency," and "scarcity." We have referred to "scarcity" as "loss aversion" since Cialdini emphasizes (ibid., p. 204) that "the way to love anything is to realize it might be lost [*sic*]." Behavioral economists would, we think, have a slightly different classification.

24. Ibid., pp. 229–30.

25. London School of Economics economist Eric Eyster told George that he witnessed this magic trick used in a con game on the Chicago subway. The tricksters boarded his subway car, set the cups up on the floor, and did their swirl, inviting passengers to guess where the coin would end up. After several practice rounds, in which the guesser had given the correct answer, the con men would then invite someone to bet $100 that he would identify where the coin had ended up in the next round. Again the tricksters did the swirl, but the coin turned up elsewhere. The con men collected their $100, and they quickly disappeared off the subway at the next stop. Private conversation, June 2011.

26. It is useful to give some examples to illustrate what we mean. In the case of Vance Packard, the cake-baking housewives are embedding themselves in a story in which they are creative; the insurance-purchasing men are embedding themselves in a story in which they are literally "in the pic-

ture." It is useful to look at Cialdini's list of behaviors, since they encompass most of the psychological biases that have formed the basis for behavioral economics. According to Cialdini, the purchasers of his brother Richard's cars are embedding themselves in a story in which they are thinking of the possibility that they will "lose" the car (they are what Kahneman has called loss averse); what we here call stories, he calls "mental frames." For the other five items on Cialdini's list we can again view people as making their decisions from the point of view of a "story." People want to reciprocate gifts and favors: to do so they must be taking part in a story in which someone gives a gift, and it would be wrong not to reciprocate. People want to be liked: to do so they must be taking part in a story in which they are liked, or not liked, by someone else. People have deference to authority: to have this emotion they must consider themselves part of a story in which someone has authority over them. For example, in the famous experiment by Stanley Milgram in which a "teacher" told subjects to deliver electric shocks to a "learner," the subjects were identifying with the "teacher" who was in "authority," and they strongly resisted their inclinations to disobey (Stanley Milgram, *Obedience to Authority: An Experimental View* (New York: Harper & Row, 1974)). People tend to follow others (social proof): in this case they must be telling themselves a story in which either those others have better judgment or information than they do (in the information explanation); or else they do not want to incur disapproval by failing to conform (in the social conformity explanation). People want their decisions to be consistent: to do so they must be taking part in a story about consistency among their disparate decisions. Of course Freudian psychology is full of the implicit stories that are consciously, or unconsciously, going through people's minds.

Chapter One: Temptation Strews Our Path

1. Suze Orman, *The 9 Steps to Financial Freedom: Practical and Spiritual Steps So You Can Stop Worrying*, 2nd paperback ed. (New York: Crown/Random House, 2006). More than three million sold is claimed on the Suze Orman website, last accessed November 4, 2014, http://www.suzeorman.com/books-kits/books/the-9-steps-to-financial-freedom/.

2. It is useful to look at such a textbook. N. Gregory Mankiw's *Principles of Economics* (New York: Harcourt, Brace, 1998) is an especially good introduction to current economics, and it therefore gives an excellent example, but we could have sampled many others instead. Mankiw's chapter 21, on "The Theory of Consumer Choice," illustrates. As in most modern textbooks, he does not choose the proverbial apples and oranges, but instead Pepsi and pizza. The "budget constraint" is said to be the consumer's income of $1,000. The consumer's "optimal choice" with a price for Pepsi of $2 and a price of pizza of $1 is pictured in a graph (p. 456). The end of the chapter concludes with a disclaimer: "Do people really think this way? At some point, however, you might be tempted to treat the theory of consumer choice with some kind of skepticism.... And you know that you do not decide by writing down budget constraints and indifference curves. Doesn't this knowledge about

your own decision making provide evidence against the theory? The answer is no. The theory of consumer choice does not try to present a literal account of how people make decisions. It is a model.... The test of the theory is in its applications," which in modern economics is also called "its predictions." This is good rhetoric, but you are not told that "the model" fails to predict Suze Orman's worried clients, and the billions like them. The model may be a good predictor for some things, but it does not tell you when it will not work. The economist Alan Blinder has explained the limitations of models. They are like maps: we do not use a map of our neighborhood to travel to Antarctica, just as we would not use a map of Antarctica to travel to the local grocery store. Mankiw also continues, correctly: in "more advanced courses in economics ... this theory provides the framework for much additional analysis." He fails to mention here that the "this-is-just-a-model" disclaimer will not be seen again (p. 471, in that original edition).

3. See Orman, *9 Steps to Financial Freedom,* "Step 3, Being Honest with Yourself," especially pp. 38 and 42. "Most of my clients are shocked at how much they had underestimated [their expenditures] and that's when they've guessed as honestly as they could," she tells us.

4. Board of Governors of the Federal Reserve, Current Release, Consumer Credit, table G-19, for August 2014, released on October 7, 2014, accessed November 5, 2014, http://www.federalreserve.gov/releases/g19/current/.

5. Annamaria Lusardi, Daniel Schneider, and Peter Tufano, "Financially Fragile Households: Evidence and Implications," *Brookings Papers on Economic Activity* (Spring 2011): 84.

6. Greg Kaplan, Giovanni Violante, and Justin Weidner, "The Wealthy Hand-to-Mouth," *Brookings Papers on Economic Activity* (Spring 2014): 98, table 2, "Household Income, Liquid Income, Liquid and Illiquid Wealth Holdings, and Portfolio Composition, Sample Countries." They report that, while median household income was $47,040, median household holdings of cash and checking, savings, and money market accounts was $2,640 (or about two-thirds of one month's income) according to the 2010 Survey of Consumer Finances.

7. David Huffman and Matias Barenstein, "A Monthly Struggle for Self-Control? Hyperbolic Discounting, Mental Accounting, and the Fall in Consumption between Paydays," *Institute for the Study of Labor (IZA) Discussion Paper* 1430 (December 2005): 3.

8. FINRA Investor Education Foundation, *Financial Capability in the United States: Report of Findings from the 2012 National Financial Capability Study,* p. 23, last accessed May 14, 2015, http://www.usfinancialcapability. org/downloads/NFCS_2012_Report_Natl_Findings.pdf.

9. Ibid., p. 26. By 2012, with the continued depressed economy that fraction had risen to 3.5 percent.

10. Over the fifty-year period, at 2.5 percent every two years, on average people will experience 0.625 bankruptcies over the course of their adult lifetimes. But if those who have one bankruptcy have three of them (two repeats), the fraction of the population experiencing one bankruptcy will be 20.83 percent; in this case, there will also be two others. We have been

unable to find a statistical source on repeat bankruptcies. Laws limit how frequently people may file for bankruptcy and receive complete discharge of debts.

11. Matthew Desmond, "Eviction and the Reproduction of Urban Poverty," *American Journal of Sociology* 118, no. 1 (July 2012): 88–133. Desmond reports that in the average year there were evictions of about 16,000 adults and children out of a population of about 600,000 (p. 91). The eviction rate for occupied rental housing in all neighborhoods was 3.5 percent; and 7.2 percent in high-poverty neighborhoods (p. 97). Desmond describes the difficulties of those who get evicted, with a court record that makes it difficult to rent again. Even if these numbers are too high for some unknown reason, they still make the point: many families get thrown out of their homes and it will be difficult for them to find another.

12. John Maynard Keynes, "Economic Possibilities for Our Grandchildren," in *Essays in Persuasion* (London: Macmillan, 1931), pp. 358–73.

13. Eight times: ibid., p. 365. For the growth of US per capita income we used Angus Maddison's calculations for 1930 to 2000 ("US Real Per Capita GDP from 1870–2001," September 24, 2012, accessed December 1, 2014, http://socialdemocracy21stcentury.blogspot.com/2012/09/us-real-per-capita -gdp-from-18702001.html). We used the Council of Economic Advisors' unchained weighted estimates of GDP from *Economic Report of the President 2013*, table B-2 for growth in income from 2000 to 2010, and table B-34 for growth in population (accessed December 1, 2014, http://www.whitehouse .gov/sites/default/files/docs/erp2013/full_2013_economic_report_of_the_ president.pdf). This calculation yielded a ratio of real per capita income between 2010 and 1930 of 5.6.

14. Keynes, "Economic Possibilities," p. 369.

15. Ibid., pp. 366–67.

16. For a documentation of the lack of leisure of the American housewife see Arlie Russell Hochschild, *The Second Shift: Working Parents and the Revolution at Home* (New York: Viking, 1989).

17. For the lyrics see http://www.oldielyrics.com/lyrics/patti_page/how _much_is_that_doggy_in_the_window.html. Last accessed November 5, 2014.

18. Paco Underhill, *Why We Buy: The Science of Shopping* (New York: Simon and Schuster, 1999), p. 85.

19. See, for example, Oren Bar-Gill and Elizabeth Warren, "Making Credit Safer," *University of Pennsylvania Law Review* 157, no. 1 (November 2008): 1–101. Bar-Gill and Warren give many examples of the types of phishing in the consumer credit market that pervade this book, regarding credit cards, but also other forms of credit.

Chapter Two: Reputation Mining and Financial Crisis

1. Alan S. Blinder, *After the Music Stopped: The Financial Crisis, the Response, and the Work Ahead* (New York: Penguin Press, 2013), on the macroeconomy; Roddy Boyd, *Fatal Risk: A Cautionary Tale of AIG's Corporate*

Suicide (Hoboken, NJ: Wiley, 2011); William D. Cohan, *Money and Power: How Goldman Sachs Came to Rule the World* (New York: Doubleday, 2011); Greg Farrell, *Crash of the Titans: Greed, Hubris, the Fall of Merrill Lynch, and the Near-Collapse of Bank of America* (New York: Crown Business, 2010); Kate Kelly, *Street Fighters: The Last 72 Hours of Bear Stearns, the Toughest Firm on Wall Street* (New York: Penguin, 2009); Michael Lewis, *Boomerang: Travels in the New Third World* (New York: W. W. Norton, 2011) and *The Big Short: Inside the Doomsday Machine* (New York: W. W. Norton, 2010), on financial speculation; Lawrence G. McDonald, with Patrick Robinson, *A Colossal Failure of Common Sense: The Inside Story of the Collapse of Lehman Brothers* (New York: Crown Business, 2009); Gretchen Morgenson and Joshua A. Rosner, *Reckless Endangerment: How Outsized Ambition, Greed, and Corruption Led to Economic Armageddon* (New York: Times Books/Henry Holt, 2011), on Fannie Mae and Freddie Mac; Henry M. Paulson, *On the Brink: Inside the Race to Stop the Collapse of the Global Financial System* (New York: Business Plus, 2010), on the US Treasury; Raghuram Rajan, *Fault Lines: How Hidden Fractures Still Threaten the World Economy* (Princeton: Princeton University Press, 2010), on the financial system; Robert J. Shiller, *Subprime Solution: How Today's Global Financial Crisis Happened and What to Do about It* (Princeton: Princeton University Press, 2008); Andrew Ross Sorkin, *Too Big to Fail: The Inside Story of How Wall Street and Washington Fought to Save the Financial System* (New York: Viking, 2009), on the US Treasury; Gillian Tett, *Fool's Gold: How the Bold Dream of a Small Tribe at J. P. Morgan Was Corrupted by Wall Street Greed* (New York: Free Press, 2009); and David Wessel, *In Fed We Trust: Ben Bernanke's War on the Great Panic* (New York: Crown Business, 2009). Especially useful was the remarkably clear and well-documented *Financial Crisis Inquiry Report: Final Report of the National Commission on the Causes of the Financial and Economic Crisis in the United States* (Washington, DC: Government Printing Office, 2011), http://www.gpo.gov/fdsys/pkg/GPO-FCIC/pdf/GPO-FCIC.pdf. All of these books served as important background for the interpretive story that we are telling in this chapter.

2. Carl Shapiro, "Consumer Information, Product Quality, and Seller Reputation," *Bell Journal of Economics* 13, no. 1 (1982): 20–35.

3. Tobias Adrian and Hyun Song Shin, "Liquidity and Leverage," *Journal of Financial Intermediation* 19, no. 3 (July 2010): 418–37. Adrian and Shin calculated average balance sheets from sometime in the 1990s (varying by the bank) to the first quarter of 2008 for the five leading investment banks: Bear Stearns, Goldman Sachs, Lehman Brothers, Merrill Lynch, and Morgan Stanley. They held total assets averaging $345 billion; had average liabilities of $331 billion, with average equity of $13.3 billion. See table 2, "Investment Bank Summary Statistics."

4. See Paulson, *On the Brink,* and Blinder, *After the Music Stopped,* among many others.

5. See Charles Ellis, *The Partnership: The Making of Goldman Sachs* (New York: Penguin Press, 2008), p. 97. We rely very much on Ellis's book for a remarkable, accurate, and detailed picture of what was happening inside a financial firm. Such accounts are rare because of the desire for anonymity.

6. Goldman Sachs, *Annual Report 2005,* p. 65, table on "Consolidated Statement of Financial Conditions," accessed December 6, 2014, http://www .goldmansachs.com/investor-relations/financials/archived/annual-reports/ 2005-annual-report.html. Goldman had equity of $28.002 billion, with total assets of $706.804 billion.

7. Council of Economic Advisors, *Economic Report of the President 2007,* table B-26, http://www.gpo.gov/fdsys/pkg/ERP-2007/pdf/ERP-2007.pdf. This number was later revised slightly upward to 12.2 in the 2013 report.

8. Described by Ellis in *The Partnership.* See chapter 4, "Ford: The Largest IPO," pp. 53–72.

9. There were tricky tax conditions, since the family was giving up their monopoly on voting rights, and the foundation would now be receiving dividends. Ibid., p. 55.

10. Ibid., pp. 60–61.

11. Ibid., p. 185.

12. See ibid., p. 347, which also tells us that "the rules that governed syndicate participation were more like those of a fraternity than those of a hard-nosed, pay-for-performance business."

13. Thus, at the time of the crash, Michael M. Thomas lamented the old days when the chief bond raters at Moody's, Albert Esokait and Dominic de Palma, were "scrupulous and incorruptible." Thomas, "Rated by Idiots," *Forbes,* September 16, 2008.

14. Ellis, *The Partnership,* p. 103.

15. Ibid., p. 114, both for the payout and also for the view that the firm's capital might have been exhausted; p. 103, for the view that all of the capital in the enterprise belonged to the partners.

16. Ellis, *The Partnership,* pp. 569–70, tells us that at the time Goldman went public, "Many Goldman Sachs people had over 85 percent of their total assets invested in the firm." So even though by that time it was a limited liability corporation, partners still had a great deal to lose in the event of bankruptcy.

17. "Today Is Moving Day for Goldman Sachs," *New York Times,* April 1, 1957.

18. Goldman Sachs, "Who We Are," "What We Do," and "Our Thinking," all accessed December 1, 2014, http://www.goldmansachs.com/index.html.

19. Source for opening date: "200 West Street," *Wikipedia,* accessed October 22, 2014, http://en.wikipedia.org/wiki/200_West_Street.

20. Paul Goldberger, "The Shadow Building: The House That Goldman Built," *New Yorker,* May 17, 2010, accessed October 22, 2014, http://www .newyorker.com/magazine/2010/05/17/shadow-building.

21. We are grateful to Zoltan Pozsar for sharing with us his insights regarding the dependence of banking arrangements on firms' worries regarding large haircuts on conventional deposits at commercial banks if the bank should default. Source: Private conversations with George Akerlof at the International Monetary Fund in 2010–11.

22. Catherine Clifford and Chris Isidore, "The Fall of IndyMac," Cable News Network, July 13, 2008, accessed December 1, 2014, http://money.cnn .com/2008/07/12/news/companies/indymac_fdic/.

23. See Ellis, *The Partnership*, p. 78.

24. Ibid., p. 5.

25. Cohan, *Money and Power,* p. 602.

26. See Moody's, "Moody's History: A Century of Market Leadership," accessed November 9, 2014, https://www.moodys.com/Pages/atc001.aspx. According to this source, "The rationale for this change was, and is, that issuers should pay for the substantial value objective ratings provide in terms of market access." The other members of the big three apparently did likewise. Christopher Alessi, Roya Wolverson, and Mohammed Aly Sergie, "The Credit Rating Controversy," Council on Foreign Relations, Backgrounder, updated October 22, 2013, accessed November 8, 2014, http://www.cfr.org/financial-crises/credit-rating-controversy/p22328.

27. Evidence from the US Senate hearings on "Wall Street and the Financial Crisis" indicates that the "pressure exerted by investment banks frequently impacted the ratings process, enabling the banks to obtain more favorable treatment than they otherwise would have received." US Senate, Committee on Homeland Security and Government Affairs, Permanent Subcommittee on Investigations, *Wall Street and the Financial Crisis: Anatomy of a Financial Collapse,* Majority and Minority Staff Report, April 13, 2011, p. 278, http://www.hsgac.senate.gov//imo/media/doc/Financial_Crisis/FinancialCrisisReport.pdf?attempt=2.

28. Thus, for example, the *Financial Crisis Inquiry Report* states (p. 126) that: "The rating agencies were not adequately regulated by the Securities and Exchange Commission or any other regulator to ensure the quality and accuracy of their ratings. Moody's, the Commission's case study in this area, relied on flawed and outdated models to issue erroneous ratings on mortgage-related securities, failed to perform meaningful due diligence on the assets underlying the securities, and continued to rely on those models even after it became obvious that the models were wrong."

29. Kristopher Gerardi, Andreas Lehnert, Shane M. Sherlund, and Paul Willen, "Making Sense of the Subprime Crisis," *Brookings Papers on Economic Activity* (Fall 2008): 69–139, emphasizes the failure to foresee the future declines in prices as the major factor for the overly high ratings. The large declines in house prices that subsequently occurred were considered to be "meltdowns," which were considered highly improbable (p. 142).

30. *Financial Crisis Inquiry Report,* p. xxv. Additionally, according to Charles W. Calomiris ("The Subprime Crisis: What's Old, What's New, and What's Next," paper prepared for the Federal Reserve Bank of St. Louis Economic Symposium, "Maintaining Stability in a Changing Financial System," Jackson Hole, WY, August 2008, p. 21), 80 percent of subprime mortgages were put into conduits rated AAA; 95 percent, rated A or higher. The *Financial Crisis Inquiry Report* (p. xxv) states further that: "You will also read about the forces at work behind the breakdowns at Moody's, including the flawed computer models, the pressure from financial firms that paid for the ratings, the relentless drive for market share, the lack of resources to do the job despite record profits, and the absence of meaningful oversight."

31. US Senate, Committee on Homeland Security and Government Affairs, Permanent Subcommittee on Investigations, *Wall Street and the Financial Crisis,* p. 245.

32. Lewis, *The Big Short.*

33. He was alerted to it by the large trades by John Paulson in shorting the mortgage market, but then he did investigations through a model of his own. Cohan, *Money and Power,* pp. 493–95.

34. Ibid., p. 567.

35. Ibid., p. 595.

36. Associated Press, "Timeline of United Airlines' Bankruptcy," *USA Today,* February 1, 2006, accessed November 9, 2014, http://usatoday30 .usatoday.com/travel/flights/2006-02-01-united-timeline_x.htm; Bloomberg News, "United Airlines Financial Plan Gains Approval from Creditors," *New York Times,* December 31, 2005; and Micheline Maynard, "United Air Wins Right to Default on Its Employee Pension Plans," *New York Times,* May 11, 2005.

37. See Ellis, *The Partnership,* p. 2, footnote.

38. Bloomberg News, "Cuomo Announces Reform Agreements with 3 Credit Rating Agencies," June 2, 2008, http://www.bloomberg.com/apps/ news?pid=newsarchive&sid=a1N1TUVbL2bQ. For the forty-two-month length of agreement, see Michael Virtanen, "NY Attorney General Looks at Ratings Agencies," Associated Press, February 8, 2013, accessed March 21, 2014. http://bigstory.ap.org/article/ny-attorney-general-looks -ratings-agencies-0.

39. Danielle Carbone, "The Impact of the Dodd-Frank Act's Credit-Rating Agency Reform on Public Companies," *Corporate and Securities Law Advisor* 24, no. 9 (September 2010): 1–7, http://www.shearman.com/ ~/media/Files/NewsInsights/Publications/2010/09/The-Impact-of-the -DoddFrank-Acts-Credit-Rating-A__/Files/View-full-article-The-Impact-of -the-DoddFrank-Ac__/FileAttachment/CM022211InsightsCarbone.pdf.

40. Boyd, *Fatal Risk.*

41. *Financial Crisis Inquiry Report,* pp. 141 and 267.

42. Ibid., p. 267.

43. Ibid., p. 141.

44. Ibid.

45. Ibid.

46. Boyd, *Fatal Risk,* p. 196.

47. Ibid., p. 182.

48. *Financial Crisis Inquiry Report,* pp. 347–50.

49. US Department of the Treasury, "Investment in AIG," accessed March 11, 2015, http://www.treasury.gov/initiatives/financial-stability/TARP -Programs/aig/Pages/status.aspx.

50. Figure given by René M. Stulz, "Credit Default Swaps and the Credit Crisis," *Journal of Economic Perspectives* 24, no. 1 (Winter 2010): 80, for June 30, 2008.

51. Ibid., p. 82.

Chapter Three:
Advertisers Discover How to Zoom In on Our Weak Spots

1. Lemelson Center, "Edison Invents!" Copy in authors' files. Originally available at: http://invention.smithsonian.org/centerpieces/edison/000_story_02.asp.

2. See Roger C. Schank and Robert P. Abelson, *Scripts, Plans, Goals, and Understanding: An Inquiry into Human Knowledge Structures* (Hillsdale, NJ: L. Erlbaum Associates, 1977).

3. Our point of view corresponds to Jerome Bruner's interpretation of narrative psychology: "action is based on belief, desire, and moral commitment." "To understand man you must understand how his experiences and his acts are shaped by his intentional states." Bruner, *Acts of Meaning: Four Lectures on Mind and Culture* (Cambridge, MA: Harvard University Press, 1990), pp. 23 and 33. Thus what Bruner describes as "the rough and perpetually changing draft of our autobiography that we carry in our minds" (p. 33) is a major determinant of our actions. We call this "autobiography in our minds" the "stories" that people are telling themselves that play a major role in their decisions. Bruner emphasizes the role of "culture" in determining these stories, whereas we would consider culture as just one of their many determinants. For reviews of "narrative psychology," also see, for example, Michele L. Crossley, "Introducing Narrative Psychology," in *Narrative, Memory and Life Transitions,* ed. Christine Horrocks, Kate Milnes, Brian Roberts, and David Robinson (Huddersfield: University of Huddersfield Press, 2002), pp. 1–13.

This role of stories also has precedent in economics. One of us (Bob) explored the importance of epidemically spreading stories in the propagation of speculative bubbles; see Robert J. Shiller, *Irrational Exuberance* (Princeton: Princeton University Press, 2000), for example, pp. 161 and 163. This same theme was also an important topic in our joint book *Animal Spirits: How Human Psychology Drives the Economy, and Why It Matters for Global Capitalism* (Princeton: Princeton University Press, 2009). Stories also are related to identity economics, as described by George with Rachel Kranton in "Economics and Identity," *Quarterly Journal of Economics* 115, no. 3 (August 2000): 715–53, and *Identity Economics: How Our Identities Shape Our Work, Wages, and Well-Being* (Princeton: Princeton University Press, 2010). Relative to identity economics, what Bruner calls "the autobiography in our minds" would include persons' "social category," which is "who they are," and also the norms that affect them. And, of course, both the social category and the norms affect their intentions. In this way, consistent with Bruner's description of narrative psychology, the "stories" people are telling themselves affect their actions. Because people's views of their social category and the norms that affect them can change, perhaps quite rapidly, identity economics thus further captures what Bruner calls the changes that occur in these stories—changes that we emphasize in this book. There are also recent contributions to the use of narrative psychology in identity economics. Steven Bosworth, Tania Singer, and Dennis J. Snower have described identity as pertaining not just to "life stories," but also to stories of much higher frequency ("personal adaptations that are contextualized in time, space, situation, and social role"); see their paper "Cooperation, Motivation and Social Balance" (presented at the American Economic Association Meeting, Boston, January 3, 2015). They thus emphasize the changing nature of identity. Paul Collier uses the term *narratives* in a narrower sense, being the specific stories themselves, but he is plowing the same ground, as he considers the interplay among "identities, narratives and norms" and especially emphasizes how all three are transmitted through social networks. See Collier, "The Cultural Foundations of Economic Failure: A Conceptual Toolkit" (mimeo, Oxford University, February 2015), p. 6. Collier emphasizes the extent to which "narratives" can be as important as "observation" (p. 5).

4. The leading textbook on marketing, *Principles of Marketing,* 14th ed. (Upper Saddle River, NJ: Prentice Hall, 2010), by Philip Kotler and Gary Armstrong, takes a view of advertising that reflects much of the view we take in this chapter. In their case study of OgilvyOne, they write: "The ultimate objective of advertising is not to win awards, or even to make people like an ad. It's to get people to think, feel, or act in some way after being exposed to an ad. Ultimately, no matter how entertaining or artistic an ad, it's not creative unless it sells" (p. 460). It is also noteworthy that advertising is only one aspect of the general field of marketing, as Kotler and Armstrong define it. Their chapter on advertising and public relations is only 28 pages out of 613 total in the book.

5. The second verse continues:

I must take a trip to California
And leave my poor sweetheart alone
If he has a dog he won't be lonesome
And the doggie will have a good home.

The song then goes on about the benefits to her "sweetheart" from the doggie, whose bark will scare away a robber. http://www.oldielyrics.com/lyrics/patti_page/how_much_is_that_doggy_in_the_window.html.

6. Jane Austen, *Pride and Prejudice* (New York: Modern Library, 1995), chap. 15 of volume 3, or chapter 57 of the whole book.

7. Some statistics give a feeling for the overall size of advertising in the economy and its distribution, although, as we will indicate, different datasets do differ in their estimates. According to the Coen Structured Advertising Expenditure Dataset (www.galbithink.org/cs-ad-dataset.xls), which gives a long-term historical series, total advertising expenditures in 1970 were $19.55 billion out of a $1,038.3 billion GDP, or about 1.9 percent. Total advertising expenditures in 2007 had grown to $279.612 billion out of a $14,028.7 billion GDP, or 2.0 percent. Thus the share of GDP in advertising expenditure had grown—but not dramatically—by about 5 percent.

But the division among different types of outlets had changed dramatically, especially against print. Using relevant sections of the dataset, we found the following. Newspapers plus magazines, which counted for 35.79 percent of expenditures in 1970, in 2007 accounted for only 20.00 percent, for a fall of almost 45 percent in their share. Radio plus TV, inclusive of both broadcast and cable in 2007, had increased its share significantly, from 25.1 percent to 32.2 percent. Meanwhile direct mail advertising had also increased in share, by more than 50 percent, from 14.1 percent to 21.5. (Later in the chapter we will see reasons for such an increase in direct mail advertising.) According to the dataset, the Internet in 2007 was still less than 4 percent of advertising revenue (at $10.5 billion), but since that time the change has been extremely rapid. The changes that we have noted, and some kind of aggregate estimate of the size of advertising relative to GDP, give what is probably a pretty good overall picture, but the exact numbers should be viewed with some skepticism. For example, an alternative source places Internet advertising at more than double that amount for 2007, at $21.2 billion. Interactive Advertising Bureau, *Internet Advertising Revenue Report: 2013 Full-Year Results,* conducted by PricewaterhouseCoopers (PwC), accessed March 7, 2015, http://www.iab.net/media/file/IAB_Internet_Advertising_Revenue_Report_FY_2013.pdf. Since that time, according to the same source, Internet advertising revenue has more than doubled, being $42.8 billion in 2013, which was larger than the figure for all newspaper advertising for 2007 ($42.1 billion), as reported in the Coen Structured Advertising Expenditure Dataset. For an alternative source for newspaper revenues, see Newspaper Association of America, "The American Newspaper Media Industry Revenue Profile 2012," April 8, 2013, accessed March 7, 2015, http://www.naa.org/trends-and-numbers/newspaper-revenue/newspaper-media-industry-revenue-profile-2012.aspx.

8. Jeffrey L. Cruikshank and Arthur W. Schultz, *The Man Who Sold America* (Boston: Harvard Business Review Press, 2010), p. 17.

9. "The Personal Reminiscences of Albert Lasker," *American Heritage* 6, no. 1 (December 1954), accessed May 21, 2015. http://www.americanheritage.com/content/personal-reminiscences-albert-lasker?page=2.

10. Cruikshank and Schultz, *The Man Who Sold America,* pp. 31–32.

11. Ibid., p. 33.

12. For later variant of ad, ibid., picture between pp. 152 and 153.

13. Ibid., p. 52.

14. "The Propaganda for Reform," *Journal of the American Medical Association* 61, no. 18 (November 1, 1913): 1648.

15. Claude Hopkins, *My Life in Advertising and Scientific Advertising: Two Works by Claude C. Hopkins* (New York: McGraw Hill, 1997), p. 20.

16. Ibid., pp. 43–44.

17. Ibid., pp. 46–47.

18. Ibid., p. 61.

19. Cruikshank and Schultz, *The Man Who Sold America,* p. 95.

20. Ibid., pp. 91–92.

21. Ibid., p. 97.

22. Stephen R. Fox, *The Mirror Makers: A History of American Advertising and Its Creators* (Urbana: University of Illinois Press, 1984), p. 192.

23. Cruikshank and Schultz, *The Man Who Sold America,* p. 100.

24. Ibid., p. 106.

25. In *Scientific Advertising,* Hopkins explains this use of coupons, and the use of scientific method more generally (*My Life in Advertising and Scientific Advertising,* pp. 215–16).

26. Cruikshank and Schultz, *The Man Who Sold America,* pp. 115–21.

27. David Ogilvy, *Confessions of an Advertising Man* (New York: Atheneum, 1988), p. 30.

28. Kenneth Roman, *The King of Madison Avenue: David Ogilvy and the Making of Modern Advertising* (New York: Macmillan, 2009), p. 44.

29. Ogilvy, *Confessions of an Advertising Man,* p. 51.

30. Ibid.

31. See David Ogilvy, *Ogilvy on Advertising* (New York: Random House/Vintage Books, 1985), p. 10.

32. Ibid., pp. 59 and 79.

33. Fox, *The Mirror Makers,* p. 231.

34. Ogilvy, *Confessions of an Advertising Man,* pp. 145–46. Note that Ogilvy talks about its "story appeal." "Harold Rudolph has called this magic element 'story appeal' and demonstrated that the more of it you inject into your photographs the more people will look at your advertisements" (p. 144).

35. Hopkins, *My Life in Advertising and Scientific Advertising,* p. 34.

36. Ogilvy, *Confessions of an Advertising Man,* p. 20.

37. This follows his dictum, "The most important word in the vocabulary of advertising is TEST." Ibid., p. 114.

38. Two recent papers, by Song Han, Benjamin Keys, and Geng Li, "Credit Supply to Bankruptcy Filers: Evidence from Credit Card Mailings" (U.S. Federal Reserve Board, Finance and Economics Discussion Paper Series Paper No. 2011-29, 2011), http://www.federalreserve.gov/pubs/feds/2011/201129/201129pap.pdf, and by Hong Ru and Antoinette Schoar, "Do Credit Card Companies Screen for Behavioral Biases?" (presented at the meetings of the American Finance Association, January 2014) illustrate how private business uses Big Data. The credit card companies target their offers to different consumers. For example, low teaser interest rates (featured prominently in the offers) with later increases in the rates (disclosed in the fine print) were systematically targeted to poorer and less educated consumers. Those consumers were less likely to figure out what they were signing up for. On another note, Ru and Schoar also report that in 2006, prior to the financial crash, credit card companies in the United States were sending out six hundred million credit card offerings a month. The average adult in the United States could get thirty-six new credit cards a year. This excessive offering supports our discussion, in the next chapter, of the overall expense of credit cards. If the companies were sending out those offerings, they had to be recovering the expense of the mailings from the rest of us.

39. See John A. Morello, *Selling the President, 1920: Albert D. Lasker, Advertising and the Election of Warren G. Harding* (Westport, CT: Praeger, 2001), Kindle locations 831–48 and following out of 1801.

40. Ibid., Kindle locations 1074–84.

41. Ibid., Kindle locations 942–90.

42. Sasha Issenberg, *The Victory Lab: The Secret Science of Winning Campaigns,* 1st paperback ed. (New York: Crown/Random House, 2012), pp. 244–46. Note that one hundred million voters is the number from the previous (2008) campaign; that expanded by the time 2012 rolled around.

43. Issenberg describes how the data were used. He says that the behavior of the voters who were not polled was "simulated." Ibid., p. 248.

44. Issenberg explains this technique. Ibid., pp. 129–30.

45. Ronald B. Tobias, *Twenty Master Plots: And How to Build Them,* 2nd paperback edition (Blue Ash, OH: F + W Media, 1993), p. 139.

Chapter Four: Rip-offs Regarding Cars, Houses, and Credit Cards

1. As mentioned previously (preface, n. 20), we are using *rip-off* in the sense that people are paying a high price for the services they receive.

2. Number of new cars (used cars) sold divided by number of households. New cars sold, 2013: 15.6 million (Zacks Equity Research, "Strong U.S. Auto Sales for 2013," January 6, 2014, accessed December 1, 2014, http://www.zacks.com/stock/news/118754/strong-us-auto-sales-for-2013). Used cars sold, 2013: 41.0 million (Keith Griffin, "Used Car Sales Figures from 2000 to 2014," accessed December 1, 2014, http://usedcars.about.com/od/research/a/Used-Car-Sales-Figures-From-2000-To-2014.htm). Number of US households (including single-family households), 2013: 122.5 million (US Census Bureau, "America's Families and Living Arrangements: 2013," table H1, accessed December 1, 2014, https://www.census.gov/hhes/families/data/cps2013.html).

3. Ian Ayres and Peter Siegelman, "Race and Gender Discrimination in Bargaining for a New Car," *American Economic Review* 85, no. 3 (June 1995): 304–21.

4. Ibid., p. 309, table 2. The current dollars are based on 1989 prices, adjusted to 2014. 1989 was our best estimate for the year when the study was conducted. We used the Bureau of Labor Statistics CPI deflator: http://data.bls.gov/cgi-bin/cpicalc.pl?cost1=635.6&year1=1989&year2=2014. Last accessed March 25, 2014. We cite the fixed effects results of the final dollar profit figure.

5. Ayres and Siegelman, "Race and Gender Discrimination," table 2.

6. Ibid, p. 317.

7. We assumed that the distribution of final quoted prices was a truncated normal, with the mode exactly at the zero-profit point below which the dealer would walk away from the transaction.

8. Ian Ayres, "Fair Driving: Gender and Race Discrimination in Retail Car Negotiations," *Harvard Law Review* 104, no. 4 (February 1991): 854.

9. Once again, we reiterate that by *rip-off* we mean that people are paying a high price for the goods or services they are purchasing.

10. See US Census Bureau, *Statistical Abstracts of the United States,* 2012, Table 992, "Homeownership Rates by Age of Householder and Household Type: 1990 to 2010," last accessed May 22, 2015, https://www.census.gov/compendia/statab/2012/tables/12s0992.pdf. In 2010, 80.4 percent of householders aged 60 to 64 owned their own homes.

11. Twenty-four years may appear surprisingly large, because there is a quite different statistic that is much better known; misleadingly, it gives the impression that Americans are much more on the move. That number is not, as we have quoted, the time that *owners* will spend on average in their current house; instead it is the time that current *buyers* will stay in the houses they are buying. But the two measures are very different for a good reason: those who *buy* houses more frequently will have correspondingly greater weight in the average of *buyers'* length of stay. For example, persons who buy a house every two years will have twelve times the weight of those who buy one every twenty-four years, for the simple reason that they purchase a house twelve times as often. But to give a picture of how often people move, we do not want to know how long *buyers* will stay in the house they purchase; instead we want to know how long typical *people* (or typical owners) stay in the houses they occupy. For that, our measure of the average tenure of current occupants at the time they move out is appropriate.

We calculated the "more than twenty-four years" from the distribution of current tenure for owner-occupied housing reported by Peter Mateyka and Matthew Marlay, "Residential Duration by Race and Ethnicity: 2009" (paper presented at the Annual Meeting of the American Sociological Association, Las Vegas, 2011), p. 29, table 3. The calculation is made by doubling the mean value of tenure of current occupants, given the reported distribution. That doubling gives a good approximation for their tenure when they move out: because in steady state, homeowners will, on average, be sampled one-half way through their stay. (That approximation underestimates the expected length of stay, since it omits the growth in homeownership; but that underestimation will be small, since homeownership grows slowly.)

The length of time that buyers will stay in the single-family home they have just purchased is estimated by a different method. We estimated that at about 13.1 years. We made this estimate by dividing the stock of single-family homes for the year 2000 (76.313 million; source: US Census Bureau, "Historical Census of Housing Tables," October 31, 2011, accessed December 1, 2014, https://www.census.gov/hhes/www/housing/census/historic/units.html) by an estimate of single-family home sales, for that same year, of 5,840 million. Source: Obtained by adding existing home sales and new privately owned single-family home sales (US Census Bureau, *Statistical Abstracts of the United States, 2012,* accessed December 1, 2014, https://www.census.gov/prod/www/statistical_abstract.html, tables 979 and 974), and subtracting out sales of condos and apartments (table 980).

There is a yet further measure, regarding the length of stay of all movers, inclusive of renters. By this measure the average stay of movers in the US, in their newly rented, or newly purchased, home, is about 8.3 years. But again, this statistic is misleading regarding how often *people* move, since it too weights people proportionately to how often they do so. (We estimated it by dividing the total population by the number who move per year. Source for the national mover rate: US Census Bureau, "Census Bureau Reports

National Mover Rates Increases after a Record Low in 2011," December 10, 2012, accessed December 1, 2014, https://www.census.gov/newsroom/releases/archives/mobility_of_the_population/cb12-240.html.)

12. Susan E. Woodward, *A Study of Closing Costs for FHA Mortgages,* prepared for US Department of Housing and Urban Development, Office of Policy Development and Research, May 2008, http://www.urban.org/UploadedPDF/411682_fha_mortgages.pdf.

13. The logic is simple. Buyers and sellers will be indifferent between a sale of a house for $300,000 with a real estate fee of $18,000 paid by the buyer, and sale of the house for $318,000 with the real estate fee of $18,000 paid by the seller. In both cases the seller nets $300,000; the buyer pays $318,000. If the sale with the seller paying the fee is a deal both will agree to, so should the deal with the buyer paying the fee.

14. Even before the reduced credit constraints, average down payments of first-time homebuyers were pretty low. They averaged something like 15 percent in the early 1980s, and then gradually fell to an average that was less than 10 percent in 2007, before the crash. John V. Duca, John Muellbauer, and Anthony Murphy, "House Prices and Credit Constraints: Making Sense of the US Experience," *Economic Journal* 121 (May 2011): 534, fig. 1.

15. It has been a puzzle for economists why real estate brokerage fees in the United States are so high, where they are 1.5 percent to 2.5 percent above the average for other developed countries. Robert W. Hahn, Robert E. Litan, and Jesse Gurman, "Bringing More Competition to Real Estate Brokerage," *Real Estate Law Journal* 34 (Summer 2006): 89. It would appear that these fees remain high despite the possibility of competition through the Internet. Alex Tabarrok, "The Real Estate Commission Puzzle," April 12, 2013, accessed December 1, 2014, http://marginalrevolution.com/marginalrevolution/2013/04/the-real-estate-commission-puzzle.html.

16. Again from Woodward's sample from the late 1990s/early 2000s the mortgage origination fees averaged $3,400 (*A Study of Closing Costs for FHA Mortgages,* p. viii) and the title fees averaged $1,200 (p. xii). Since the mortgages taken out averaged $105,000, those fees were on average about 4.4 percent of the value of the mortgage (p. viii).

17. For the final ruling see US Bureau of Financial Protection, "Loan Originator Compensation Requirements under the Truth in Lending Act" (Regulation Z), 12 CFR Part 1026, Docket No. CFPB—2012-0037, RIN 3170-AA132, accessed November 11, 2014, http://files.consumerfinance.gov/f/201301_cfpb_final-rule_loan-originator-compensation.pdf. Critically, "to prevent incentives to 'up charge' consumers on their loans, the final rule generally prohibits loan originator compensation based upon the profitability of a transaction or a pool of transactions" (p. 4).

18. Susan E. Woodward and Robert E. Hall, "Consumer Confusion in the Mortgage Market: Evidence of Less Than a Perfectly Transparent and Competitive Market," *American Economic Review* 100, no. 2 (May 2010): 511–15.

19. Ibid., p. 513. The 93 percent is the weighted average of 88 percent in the single lender sample of 2,600 borrowers and 95 percent in the FHA sample of 6,300 borrowers (table 2).

20. The yield spread premium (YSP) is the name for what the bank pays to the mortgage broker if the loan pays more than par.

21. Carolyn Warren, *Mortgage Rip-offs and Money Savers: An Industry Insider Explains How to Save Thousands on Your Mortgage and Re-Finance* (Hoboken, NJ: Wiley, 2007), pp. xviii–xix.

22. Alaska has only one-quarter of 1 percent of the US population. It would be much more likely prospective buyers would come from nearby Pennsylvania or New York.

23. Richard A. Feinberg, "Credit Cards as Spending Facilitating Stimuli: A Conditioning Interpretation," *Journal of Consumer Research* 13, no. 3 (December 1986): p. 349, table 1. Overall, the tip averaged 16.95 percent of the check when paid with a credit card and only 14.95 percent when paid in cash.

24. Elizabeth C. Hirschman, "Differences in Consumer Purchase Behavior by Credit Card Payment System," *Journal of Consumer Research* 6, no. 1 (June 1979): 58–66. See especially results for Hypothesis 2a, p. 62.

25. Matias F. Barenstein found that average income for credit cardholders was $43,396, versus $25,155 for non–credit cardholders, in the Federal Reserve Consumer Expenditure Survey from 1988 to 1999. See Barenstein, "Credit Cards and Consumption: An Urge to Splurge?" in "Essays on Household Consumption" (PhD diss., University of California, Berkeley, 2004), p. 44, table A2.

26. It would appear that the experiment was undertaken in 1982 or perhaps a bit earlier, since Feinberg refers to presentations in that year. We use this year to calculate the current dollar values.

27. Feinberg, "Credit Cards as Spending Facilitating Stimuli," p. 352, table 1.

28. Drazen Prelec and Duncan Simester, "Always Leave Home without It: A Further Investigation," *Marketing Letters* 12, no. 1 (2001): 8.

29. See the answer to the question "Can the merchant charge credit card users more than cash customers for the same item?" "Making Purchases with Credit Cards—The Best Credit Cards to Use," August 26, 2014, accessed November 14, 2014, http://www.creditinfocenter.com/cards/crcd_buy.shtml #Question6.

30. FINRA Investor Education Foundation, *Financial Capability in the United States: Report of Findings from the 2012 National Financial Capability Study,* May 2013, p. 21, last accessed May 14, 2015, http://www.usfinancial capability.org/downloads/NFCS_2012_Report_Natl_Findings.pdf.

31. Robin Sidel, "Credit Card Issuers Are Charging Higher," *Wall Street Journal,* October 12, 2014.

32. Mortgage interest paid on owner- and tenant-occupied residential housing was $421 billion in 2012. Bureau of Economic Analysis, "Mortgage Interest Paid, Owner- and Tenant-Occupied Residential Housing," accessed October 29, 2014, https://www.google.com/#q=BEA+mortgage+interest +payments+2010.

33. In 2012 expenditure on food and beverages for off-premises consumption was $855 billion; personal consumption expenditures for motor vehicles and parts were $395 billion. Bureau of Economic Analysis, "National Income

and Product Accounts," table 2.3.5, "Personal Consumption Expenditures by Major Type of Product," for 2012, accessed November 15, 2014, http://www.bea.gov/iTable/iTable.cfm?ReqID=9&step=1#reqid=9&step=3&isuri=1&904=2010&903=65&906=a&905=2011&910=x&911=0.

34. We arrive at this rough breakdown from a collage of sources. For the year 2010, we get a rough estimate of total credit-card expenditures on interest from US Census Bureau, *Statistical Abstracts of the United States, 2012.* Total credit-card debt was 774 billion in 2009 for Visa, MasterCard, Discover, and American Express in table 1188. The rate on revolving credit is 0.1340 in *Statistical Abstracts,* table 1190. This yields $103.7 billion in interest expense. For 2009, the *New York Times* has reported penalty fees of $20.5 billion (Ron Lieber and Andrew Martin, "Overspending on Debit Cards Is a Boon for Banks," *New York Times,* September 8, 2009, accessed May 2, 2015, http://www.nytimes.com/2009/09/09/your-money/credit-and-debit-cards/09debit.html?pagewanted=all&_r=0). We get a figure of "$48 billion a year" for interchange fees from John Tozzi, "Merchants Seek Lower Credit Card Interchange Fees," *Businessweek Archives,* October 6, 2009, accessed May 2, 2015, http://www.bloomberg.com/bw/stories/2009-10-06/merchants-seek-lower-credit-card-interchange-fees. These three numbers add up to $171 billion, which is in the ballpark, relative to the aggregate estimate for 2009 of $167 billion for that year from Robin Sidel, "Credit Card Issuers Are Charging Higher." Viewing the late fees and the interchange fees as roughly constant, but the interest fees as variable, we get our characterization of the division (of the 2012 $150 billion of revenues).

35. http://truecostofcredit.com/400926. This website has now closed. Harper later started a consulting firm (subsequently taken over) that advised merchants on how to minimize their exchange fees. From the high charges he documents, it would appear that this is quite a useful service. Harper's examples of these charges can still be found in scattered spots on the Internet. The authors also have a copy of his original blog in their files.

36. Industry research reports sourced from Integra Information Systems show average gross margins at grocery stores of 10.47 percent, so the markup over costs is less than 12 percent. See Tim Berry, "On Average, How Much Do Stores Mark Up Products?" December 2, 2008, accessed October 23, 2014, http://www.entrepreneur.com/answer/221767.

37. Michelle J. White, "Bankruptcy Reform and Credit Cards," *Journal of Economic Perspectives* 21, no. 4 (Fall 2007): 178.

38. Ibid., p. 177.

39. Ibid., p. 179.

Chapter Five: Phishing in Politics

1. Advising anyone who seriously seeks our advice and who is running for public office is part of our nonpartisan commitment to public service. That includes parents of former students.

2. Iowa Legislature, "Legislators," accessed December 1, 2014, https://www.legis.iowa.gov/legislators/legislator/legislatorAllYears?personID=116.

3. Sue Morris, "Small Runs for Senate," *Le Mars Daily Sentinel,* March 24, 2004.

4. For the estimated cost of the 2001 tax cuts, see Joint Committee on Taxation, "Estimated Budget Effects of the Conference Agreement for H.R. 1836," May 26, 2001, p. 8, accessed December 1, 2014, https://www.jct.gov/publications.html?func=startdown&id=2001; and for the estimated cost of the 2003 tax cuts, "Estimated Budget Effects of the Conference Agreement for H.R. 2, the 'Jobs and Growth Tax Relief Reconciliation Act of 2003,'" May 22, 2003, p. 2, accessed December 1, 2014, https://www.jct.gov/publications.html?func=startdown&id=1746. See also Glen Kessler, "Revisiting the Cost of the Bush Tax Cuts," *Washington Post,* May 10, 2011, http://www.washingtonpost.com/blogs/fact-checker/post/revisiting-the-cost-of-the-bush-tax-cuts/2011/05/09/AFxTFtbG_blog.html.

5. By our calculation, use of the Bush tax-cut money for the years 2009 to 2012 would have greatly moderated the effect of the Great Recession. The calculation proceeds as possible. Not all of that $1.7 trillion had been costed out for years prior to 2008. Some $600 billion of that cost was to occur after 2008. (Sources on the total costs and their timing are the two Joint Committee on Taxation publications cited in note 4.) As a rule of thumb, with a zero interest rate the government expenditure multiplier is about 2. (International Monetary Fund, *World Economic Outlook,* April 2012, accessed December 1, 2014, http://www.imf.org/external/pubs/ft/weo/2012/01/, chap. 1, part 3.) This makes sense since the tax multiplier can be considered to be about 1, and the balanced-budget multiplier with constant interest rates is also close to 1. That means that a $100 billion increase in government expenditures will increase GDP by about $200 billion. US Gross Domestic Product for 2008 was $14.3 trillion (Council of Economic Advisors, *Economic Report of the President 2013,* table B-1, accessed December 1, 2014, http://www.whitehouse.gov/sites/default/files/docs/erp2013/full_2013_economic_report_of_the_president.pdf, so that a $100 billion increase in government spending would then give about a 1.4 percent boost to GDP. The rule of thumb of Okun's Law, which seems to be still valid (see Laurence Ball, João Tovar Jalles, and Prakash Loungani, "Do Forecasters Believe in Okun's Law? An Assessment of Unemployment and Output Forecasts," *IMF Working Paper* 14/24 [February 2014]: 7, table 1), is that a 2 percent increase in GDP is associated with a 1 percent decrease in unemployment. That $1.1 trillion could have been used to decrease unemployment, which averaged just shy of 9.0 percent for the four years 2009 to 2012, to just a touch above 7 percent.

6. Center for Responsive Politics, "Sen. Chuck Grassley," accessed November 16, 2014, http://www.opensecrets.org/politicians/summatry.php?cycle=2004&type=I&cid=n00001758&newMem=N.

7. Jessica Miller, "Ads Prove Grassley's Greener on His Side of the Ballot," *Waterloo–Cedar Falls Courier,* October 25, 2004, accessed November 16, 2014, http://wcfcourier.com/news/metro/article_fdd73608-4f6d-54be-aa34-28f3417273e9.html.

8. For the vote see "Statistics of the Presidential and Congressional Election of November 2, 2004," June 7, 2005, accessed November 16, 2014, http://clerk.house.gov/member_info/electionInfo/2004election.pdf.

9. Calculations made with data from US Census Bureau, *Statistical Abstracts of the United States, 2012,* table 426, "Congressional Campaign Finances—Receipts and Disbursements," accessed December 1, 2014, https://www.census.gov/prod/www/statistical_abstract.html, and data on number of seats being contested.

10. Anthony Downs, "An Economic Theory of Political Action in a Democracy," *Journal of Political Economy* 65, no. 2 (April 1957): 135–50. The median voter theorem had also been previously discovered by Duncan Black, "On the Rationale of Group Decision-making," *Journal of Political Economy* 56, no. 1 (February 1948): 23–34.

11. This result also requires the assumption that the preferences are single peaked, which means that the further from the voters' most preferred outcome, respectively on the left and the right, the less satisfied they will be.

12. Lawrence Lessig, *Republic Lost: How Money Corrupts Congress—And a Plan to Stop It* (New York: Hachette Book Group, 2011), gives the closest picture we could find in the literature. Political scientists have emphasized uninformed voters. Arthur Lupia, "Busy Voters, Agenda Control, and the Power of Information," *American Political Science Review* 86, no. 2 (June 1992): 390–403, describes voters as having imperfect information and interests as disseminating information that is deceptive. Lupia's book with Mathew D. McCubbins, *The Democratic Dilemma: Can Citizens Learn What They Really Need to Know?* (New York: Cambridge University Press, 1998), also provides evidence for the difficulty of citizens in getting the information they really need to make the right decisions, and for deceptive practices as well, by those who need to make them. Gene M. Grossman and Elhanan Helpman, *Special Interest Politics* (Cambridge, MA: MIT Press, 2001), also present models of campaign contributions with voters who are less than fully informed.

13. James R. Healey, "Government Sells Last of Its GM Shares," *USA Today,* December 10, 2013.

14. Emergency Economic Stabilization Act of 2008, H.R. 1424, 110th US Congress, accessible at https://www.govtrack.us/congress/bills/110/hr1424/text. The full preamble reads: "To provide authority for the Federal Government to purchase and insure certain types of troubled assets for the purposes of providing stability to and preventing disruption in the economy and financial system and protecting taxpayers, to amend the Internal Revenue Code of 1986 to provide incentives for energy production and conservation, to extend certain expiring provisions, to provide individual income tax relief, and for other purposes."

15. We are indebted to Phillip Swagel for giving an exact interpretation of the different authorities, and how the bill was interpreted. Email to George Akerlof, April 2, 2012.

16. At the dramatic meeting at the Treasury Department, the CEOs of the nine big banks were told that they were on a list to receive an infusion of funds under the TARP. There was more than a veiled threat, as spoken by Treasury Secretary Henry Paulson, to Wells Fargo's CEO, Richard Kovacevich. If he did not sign up he would "get a call tomorrow [from his regulator] telling you that you're undercapitalized"; and Wells Fargo

wouldn't be able to raise money in the private markets. Alan S. Blinder, *After the Music Stopped: The Financial Crisis, the Response, and the Work Ahead* (New York: Penguin Press, 2013), p. 201. Citicorp, Wells Fargo, and JP Morgan Chase received $25 billion each; Bank of America, $15 billion; Goldman Sachs, Merrill Lynch, and Morgan Stanley, $10 billion each; Bank of New York Mellon, $3 billion; and State Street, $2 billion: for a grand total of $125 billion. Henry M. Paulson, *On the Brink: Inside the Race to Stop the Collapse of the Global Financial System* (New York: Business Plus, 2010), p. 364.

17. Emergency Economic Stabilization Act, H.R. 1424, p. 3, https://www.govtrack.us/congress/bills/110/hr1424/text.

18. Ibid.

19. Center for Responsive Politics, "Lobbying Database," accessed December 1, 2014, https://www.opensecrets.org/lobby/.

20. De Figueiredo has since moved to Duke University School of Law and Fuqua School of Business.

21. Center for Responsive Politics, "Lobbying Database." The figures we have come from the election cycle of 1999–2000 by Stephen Ansolabehere, John M. de Figueiredo, and James M. Snyder, "Why Is There So Little Money in U.S. Politics?" *Journal of Economic Perspectives* 17, no. 1 (Winter 2003): 105–30.

22. Ansolabehere, de Figueiredo, and Snyder, "Why Is There So Little Money in U.S. Politics?" p. 108. They find, critically, that $3 billion was spent on the 1999–2000 congressional plus presidential election cycle. Of that, only $380 million was paid by corporations, unions, and other associations.

23. Robert G. Kaiser, *So Damn Much Money: The Triumph of Lobbying and the Corrosion of American Government* (New York: Vintage Books/Random House, 2010).

24. Steven V. Roberts, "House Votes Funds Permitting Study on MX to Continue," *New York Times,* December 9, 1982. Aspin made this memorable remark in regard to a vote against funding the MX missile, after saying: "It was a significant vote, an important vote. But it doesn't mean the MX is dead."

25. MoJo News Team, "Full Transcript of the Mitt Romney Secret Video," *Mother Jones,* September 19, 2012, accessed December 1, 2014, http://www.motherjones.com/politics/2012/09/full-transcript-mitt-romney-secret-video.

26. Mayhill Fowler, "Obama: No Surprise That Hard-Pressed Pennsylvanians Turn Bitter," *Huffington Post,* November 17, 2008, last accessed April 30, 2015, http://www.huffingtonpost.com/mayhill-fowler/obama-no-surprise-that-ha_b_96188.html.

27. Marianne Bertrand, Matilde Bombardini, and Francesco Trebbi find that lobbying depends on whom you know more than on what you know: "Is It Whom You Know or What You Know? An Empirical Assessment of the Lobbying Process," *American Economic Review* 104, no. 12 (December 2014): 3885–3920. Similarly, Jordi Blanes i Vidal, Mirko Draca, and Christian Fons-Rosen report that lobbyists connected to US senators generate 24 percent less revenue when their connection leaves office (p. 3731): "Revolving Door Lobbyists," *American Economic Review* 102, no. 7 (December 2012): 3731–48.

28. See, in the conclusion, our discussion of the Supreme Court decision *Citizens United v. Federal Elections Commission.* In political science the view that voters may lack "information" is implicit in the common distinction made between *informed* and *uninformed* voters.

29. Elliot Gerson, "To Make America Great Again, We Need to Leave the Country," *Atlantic Monthly,* July 10, 2012, accessed May 22, 2015, http://www.theatlantic.com/national/archive/2012/07/to-make-america-great-again-we-need-to-leave-the-country/259653/.

30. Jeff Connaughton, *The Payoff: Why Wall Street Always Wins* (Westport, CT: Prospecta Press, 2012), Kindle locations 304–5, out of 2996.

31. Ibid., Kindle locations 343–45.

32. Ibid., Kindle locations 408–12.

33. Federal budget outlays for fiscal 2013 were approximately $3.8 trillion. Council of Economic Advisors, *Economic Report of the President 2013,* table B-78.

34. Kaiser, *So Damn Much Money.*

35. Ibid., p. 238.

36. Ibid., pp. 228 and 232.

37. Raquel Meyer Alexander, Stephen W. Mazza, and Susan Scholz, "Measuring Rates of Return for Lobbying Expenditures: An Empirical Case Study of Tax Breaks for Multinational Corporations," *Journal of Law and Politics* 25, no. 401 (2009): 401–57. For the 35 percent rate absent the amnesty, and the 5.25 percent, see p. 412.

38. Ibid., p. 427, table 1. Among other firms that lobbied, but did not join a coalition, the ratio of savings to lobbying costs was lower, but still 154 to 1. Jason Farrell of the Center for Competitive Politics has said that these figures "overstate" the returns. He said, perhaps rightly so, that there is no evidence that the lobbying money changed even a single vote in the Congress. And, of course, the firms that were repatriating the earnings might have received a rate other than the full 35 percent in the absence of any lobbying. Farrell, "Return on Lobbying Overstated by Report," August 23, 2011, accessed November 18, 2014, http://www.campaignfreedom.org/2011/08/23/return-on-lobbying-overstated-by-report/. But we do have plenty of evidence from elsewhere that lobbying does change votes. And if the lobbying did trip the wire on this giveaway, the returns could be yet higher than 255 to 1, since much of that $180 million was the total lobbying of the corporations in the coalition, so much of the spending would have been on lobbying projects other than for Section 965 of the AJCA.

39. Kaiser, *So Damn Much Money,* p. 227.

40. Ibid., p. 228.

41. Sonia Reyes, "Ocean Spray Rides Diet Wave," *Adweek,* February 6, 2006, accessed November 18, 2014, http://www.adweek.com/news/advertising/ocean-spray-rides-diet-wave-83901.

42. Cassidy and company pioneered lobbying for university earmarks. John de Figueiredo and Brian Silverman have made an econometric study of their returns. They use university contract overhead rates to instrument lobbying expenditures, and estimate that for universities represented by a

senator on the Senate Appropriations Committee, a $1.00 increase in lobbying yields a $5.24 increase in earmarks; for universities represented by a member on the House Appropriations Committee, a $1.00 increase in lobbying yields a $4.52 increase in earmarks. For other universities not so represented they estimate the return as $1.57, but in many specifications it is not significant. Figueiredo and Silverman, "Academic Earmarks and the Returns to Lobbying," *Journal of Law and Economics* 49, no. 2 (2006): 597–625.

43. Stephen Pizzo, Mary Fricker, and Paul Muolo, *Inside Job: The Looting of America's Savings and Loans* (New York: Harper Perennial, 1991), p. 410.

44. These were the introductory remarks of Senator Dennis DeConcini. Ibid., p. 416.

45. Nathaniel C. Nash, "Savings Institution Milked by Its Chief, Regulators Say," *New York Times,* November 1, 1989.

46. Jason Linkins, "Wall Street Cash Rules Everything around the House Financial Services Committee, Apparently," *Huffington Post,* July 22, 2013, accessed May 22, 2015, http://www.huffingtonpost.com/2013/07/22/wall -street-lobbyists_n_3635759.html.

47. US Internal Revenue Service, "Tax Gap for Tax Year 2006: Overview," Table 1, Net Tax Gap for Tax-Year 2006. January 6, 2012, accessed November 18, 2014, http://www.irs.gov/pub/irs-soi/06rastg12overvw.pdf.

Chapter Six: Phood, Pharma, and Phishing

1. Anthony Arthur, *Radical Innocent: Upton Sinclair* (New York: Random House, 2006), Kindle locations 883–86 out of 7719; also 912–16.

2. When Sinclair was threatened with a lawsuit by J. Ogden Armour, of the meatpacking firm, he replied with a letter to the *New York Times.* Sinclair wrote that he had seen:

> The selling for human food of the carcasses of cattle and swine which have been condemned for tuberculosis, actinomycosis, and gangrene; the converting of such carcasses into sausage and lard; the preserving of spoiled hams with boric and salicylic acid; the coloring of canned and potted meats with aniline dyes; the embalming and adulterating of sausages—all of these things mean the dealing out to hundreds and thousands of men, women, and children of a sudden, horrible and agonizing death.

Ever cheeky, Sinclair added: "One hundredth part of what I have charged ought, if it is true, to be enough to send the guilty man to the gallows. One hundredth part of what I have charged ought, if it is false, to be enough to send me to prison." *New York Times,* May 6, 1906.

3. Upton Sinclair, *The Jungle* (Mineola, NY: Dover Thrift Editions, 2001; originally published 1906), p. 112, for poisoned rats in sausage; p. 82, for the remains in the lard.

4. James Harvey Young, *The Toadstool Millionaires: A Social History of Patent Medicines in America before Federal Regulation* (Princeton: Princeton University Press, 1961), p. 239.

5. Ibid., p. 59.

6. Ibid., pp. 65–66.

7. Ibid., pp. 144–57.

8. The full list of six different types of additives includes: boric acid and borax; salicylic acid and salicylates; sulphurous acid and sulphites; benzoic acid and benzoates; formaldehyde; and sulphate of copper and saltpeter. Harvey W. Wiley, *An Autobiography* (Indianapolis: Bobbs-Merrill, 1930), p. 220.

9. Ibid., pp. 215–20.

10. As mentioned in the preface, we refer the reader especially to Michael Moss, *Sugar, Salt and Fat* (New York: Random House, 2013).

11. Garret A. FitzGerald, "How Super Are the 'Super Aspirins'? New COX-2 Inhibitors May Elevate Cardiovascular Risk," University of Pennsylvania Health System Press Release, January 14, 1999.

12. Gurkirpal Singh, "Recent Considerations in Nonsteroidal Anti-Inflammatory Drug Gastropathy," *American Journal of Medicine* 105, no. 1, supp. 2 (July 27, 1998): 31S–38S. Singh estimated that gastrointestinal complications of NSAIDs were conservatively causing 16,500 deaths per year, which, if separately tabulated, would make them the fifteenth leading cause of death in the United States.

13. John Abramson, *Overdosed America: The Broken Promise of American Medicine,* 3rd ed. (New York: Harper Perennial, 2008), p. 25. See also Tom Nesi, *Poison Pills: The Untold Story of the Vioxx Scandal* (New York: Thomas Dunne Books, 2008), pp. 25–28.

14. See Nesi, *Poison Pills,* p. 134.

15. Abramson, *Overdosed America,* p. 106.

16. Justin E. Bekelman, Yan Li, and Cary P. Gross, "Scope and Impact of Financial Conflicts of Interest in Biomedical Research: A Systematic Review," *Journal of the American Medical Association* 289, no. 4 (January 22, 2003): 454–65; Joel Lexchin, Lisa A. Bero, Benjamin Djulbegovic, and Otavio Clark, "Pharmaceutical Industry Sponsorship and Research Outcome and Quality: Systematic Review," *British Medical Journal* 326, no. 7400 (May 31, 2003): 1167. Bekelman, Li, and Gross also refer to two studies of "multiple reporting of studies with positive outcomes, further compounding publication bias."

17. Bob Grant, "Elsevier Published 6 Fake Journals," *The Scientist,* May 7, 2009, accessed November 24, 2014, http://classic.the-scientist.com/blog/display/55679/. See also Ben Goldacre, *Bad Pharma: How Drug Companies Mislead Doctors and Harm Patients* (New York: Faber and Faber/Farrar, Straus and Giroux, 2012), pp. 309–10.

18. Claire Bombardier et al., "Comparison of Upper Gastrointestinal Toxicity of Rofecoxib and Naproxen in Patients with Rheumatoid Arthritis," *New England Journal of Medicine* 343, no. 21 (November 23, 2000): 1520–28.

19. Ibid., p. 1522.

20. Ibid., p. 1525, table 4.

21. The figures 17 and 4 do not appear in the original article; instead they can only be approximately inferred from the ratios of those in the Vioxx group and the naproxen group with myocardial infarctions. The numbers 17 and 4

were later published in table 1 of the subsequent editorial comment in the *New England Journal of Medicine:* Gregory D. Curfman, Stephen Morrissey, and Jeffrey M. Drazen, "Expression of Concern: Bombardier et al., 'Comparison of Upper Gastrointestinal Toxicity of Rofecoxib and Naproxen in Patients with Rheumatoid Arthritis,' N Engl J Med 2000;343:1520–8," *New England Journal of Medicine* 353, no. 26 (December 29, 2005): 2813–14. A further ambiguity concerned three additional Vioxx-subject acute myocardial infarctions and a stroke from VIGOR. They were known by Merck at the time of publication, but were additional to the seventeen heart attacks that had been considered. The authors claimed, in reply, that those observations had occurred beyond the sample deadline, and were therefore left out.

22. Bombardier et al. ("Comparison of Upper Gastrointestinal Toxicity of Rofecoxib and Naproxen in Patients with Rheumatoid Arthritis," pp. 1527 and 1526) write that naproxen had effects similar to aspirin on heart attacks. This claim is surprising because it had never been advertised by the marketers of Aleve.

23. Gregory D. Curfman, Stephen Morrissey, and Jeffrey M. Drazen, "Expression of Concern Reaffirmed," *New England Journal of Medicine* 354, no. 11 (March 16, 2006): 1193, supplementary appendix 1, table 3, "Summary of Adjudicated Cardiovascular Serious Adverse Experience."

24. Nesi, *Poison Pills,* pp. 109–110.

25. Merck had funded FitzGerald and his coauthors' work, and was "delay[ing its] publication for years." Ibid., n. 19, p. 110.

26. FitzGerald, "How Super Are the 'Super Aspirins'?"

27. Nesi, *Poison Pills,* pp. 96–97. Searle developed Celebrex, but by the time VIGOR ended Searle had merged with Pfizer.

28. Ibid. Leading lights brought in: p. 35; sixty of them: p. 41; Kapalua Ritz-Carlton: p. 34.

29. Ibid., pp. 22–23.

30. Carolyn B. Sufrin and Joseph S. Ross, "Pharmaceutical Industry Marketing: Understanding Its Impact on Women's Health," *Obstetrical and Gynecological Survey* 63, no. 9 (2008): 585–96. This number may have decreased since the time of this article as physicians are relying more on the web for information.

31. US Congress, Representative Henry A. Waxman, Memorandum to Democratic Members of the Government Reform Committee Re: The Marketing of Vioxx to Physicians, May 5, 2005, with accompanying documents, p. 3, http://oversight-archive.waxman.house.gov/documents/20050505114932-41272.pdf.

32. Ibid., p. 17.

33. Ibid., p. 18.

34. Eric J. Topol, "Failing the Public Health—Rofecoxib, Merck, and the FDA," *New England Journal of Medicine* 351, no. 17 (October 21, 2004): 1707–9.

35. Nesi, *Poison Pills,* p. 155.

36. Topol, "Failing the Public Health," p. 1707.

37. David J. Graham et al., "Risk of Acute Myocardial Infarction and Sudden Cardiac Death in Patients Treated with Cyclo-oxygenase 2 Selective

and Non-selective Non-steroidal Anti-inflammatory Drugs: Nested Case-Control Study," *Lancet* 365, no. 9458 (February 5–11, 2005): 475–81. This study compared the outcomes of patients at Kaiser Permanente who were prescribed Vioxx with the outcomes of matched patients who were not. The ratio of myocardial infarction among Vioxx takers relative to their matches was significantly greater than one. Also, tellingly, the ratio increased greatly with the Vioxx dosage. Although the study was not published until February 2005, the data pertained to patients at Kaiser Permanente between January 1, 1999, and December 31, 2001. Since Graham was at the FDA, these results would have been known prior to this publication date, and thus before Merck's taking Vioxx off the market.

38. Nesi, *Poison Pills,* p. 11.

39. Topol, "Failing the Public Health," p. 1707.

40. See Graham's testimony for the Senate Finance Committee, November 18, 2004, http://www.finance.senate.gov/imo/media/doc/111804dgtest .pdf.

41. US Food and Drug Administration, Center for Drug Evaluation and Research (CDER), *Guidance for Industry Providing Clinical Evidence of Effectiveness for Human Drugs and Biological Products,* May 1998, accessed December 1, 2014, http://www.fda.gov/downloads/Drugs/.../Guidances/ ucm078749.pdf. It says "With regard to quantity, it has been FDA's position that Congress generally intended to require at least two adequate and well-controlled studies, each convincing on its own, to establish effectiveness" (p. 3). See also David Healy, *Pharmageddon* (Berkeley: University of California Press, 2012), p. 77.

42. Nesi, *Poison Pills,* p. 14.

43. Curfman, Morrissey, and Drazen, "Expression of Concern Reaffirmed," p. 1193. They write, disapprovingly: "This date, which the sponsor selected shortly before the trial ended, was one month earlier than the cutoff date for the reporting of adverse gastrointestinal events. This untenable feature of trial design, which inevitably skewed the results, was not disclosed to the editors or the academic authors of the study."

44. Bombardier et al., "Comparison of Upper Gastrointestinal Toxicity of Rofecoxib and Naproxen in Patients with Rheumatoid Arthritis," p. 1526.

45. Abramson, *Overdosed America,* p. 102, reports a study of the painkiller OxyContin against a placebo. Not surprisingly, OxyContin proved effective, since the patients receiving OxyContin experienced less pain than those who received no painkiller at all. But of course they could have been given something else.

46. Quotation from Nesi, *Poison Pills,* p. 163.

47. Goldacre, *Bad Pharma,* p. 113.

48. Adriane Fugh-Berman, "Prescription Tracking and Public Health," *Journal of General Internal Medicine* 23, no. 8 (August 2008): 1277–80, published online May 13, 2008, accessed May 24, 2015, http://www.ncbi.nlm.nih .gov/pmc/articles/PMC2517975/. This information is useful to the sales reps, who will have a heads-up regarding what doctors are prescribing; it is also useful in the arrangement of med-ed.

49. See preface, note 26.

50. Susanna N. Visser et al., "Trends in the Parent-Report of Health Care Provider–Diagnosed and Medicated Attention-Deficit/Hyperactivity Disorder: United States, 2003–2011," *Journal of the American Academy of Child and Adolescent Psychiatry* 53, no. 1 (January 2014): 34–46. See fig. 1 for state differences. The parent-reported medication rates are considerably lower than the parent-reported diagnoses, but there is high correlation between diagnosis and medication by state. See fig. 2.

51. Center for Responsive Politics, "Lobbying: Top Industries," last accessed April 30, 2014, https://www.opensecrets.org/lobby/top.php?showYear =1998&indexType=i. All years, 1998–2015. The total for health care was more than $3 billion.

52. Robert Pear, "Bill to Let Medicare Negotiate Drug Prices Is Blocked," *New York Times,* April 18, 2007, last accessed April 30, 2015, http://www .nytimes.com/2007/04/18/washington/18cnd-medicare.html?_r=0. Also, the drug coverage of 6.5 million people was transferred from Medicaid into Medicare, where the payments for drugs were considerably higher, for an additional Pharma windfall. See Milt Freudenheim, "Market Place: A Windfall from Shifts to Medicare," *New York Times,* July 18, 2006, accessed November 4, 2014, http://www.nytimes.com/2006/07/18/business/18place .html?_r=1&pagewanted=print.

53. http://www.amazon.com/Principles-Economics-N-Gregory-Mankiw/ dp/0538453052, last accessed April 30, 2015. (These numbers for prices charged are almost certain to change.) There is another similarity between textbooks and drugs. Just as textbooks are protected by copyright, drugs are protected by patents. Somewhat different, there is no market for already-swallowed pills as there is for used textbooks, but the Pharmaceuticals must deal with the problem that drug patents expire after twenty years. They deal with this problem in much the same way as the textbook editors deal with the used-book market. The drug companies bring out new editions with minor changes. The case of Prilosec/Nexium gives a clear example. Just before Prilosec went off patent to be producible as a generic, its producer, Astra Zeneca, brought out a new drug, Nexium. Some molecules have "chirality": they come in either right-handed or left-handed form. The only difference between Nexium and Prilosec lies in the chirality of some of their molecules. (See Goldacre, *Bad Pharma,* pp. 146–48.) The marketing division then was assigned its task: to convince the good doctor that he should prescribe the new, new thing, just as the good teacher conscientiously assigns the latest-edition textbook.

Chapter Seven: Innovation: The Good, the Bad, and the Ugly

1. The US Census estimated the world population of adults (those over the age of 20) at 4.725 billion in mid-2014. US Census Bureau, "World Population by Age and Sex," last accessed December 1, 2014, http://www.census .gov/cgi-bin/broker. (For our calculation of buyer/seller pairs we approximate this as five billion.)

2. Based on an average world adult population size of about 3 billion. Calculation based on a 1915 total population of 1.8 billion; and using the current fraction of adults to calculate the adult population, and a constant growth of population over the period.

3. This corresponds to a growth rate in per capita income only slightly higher than 2.2 percent, viewing 80 as current life expectancy in developed countries.

4. According to Angus Maddison, US GDP per capita as late as 1940 was $6,838 (in International Geary-Khamis 1990 dollars). By that same metric, per capita GDP in Mexico in 2008 was $7,919. Maddison, "Historical Statistics of the World Economy: Per Capita GDP," accessed November 26, 2014, http://www.google.com/url?sa=t&rct=j&q=&esrc=s&source=web&cd=6&ved=0CEIQFjAF&url=http%3A%2F%2Fwww.ggdc.net%2Fmaddison%2FHistorical_Statistics%2Fhorizontal-file_02-2010.xls&ei=4t11VJfsG4uZNoG9gGA&usg=AFQjCNFFKKZ1UysTOutlY4NsZF9qwdu2Hg&bvm=bv.80642063,d.eXY. From 2008 to 2013 Mexican per capita income in inflation-adjusted US dollars changed by very little. World Bank, "GDP Per Capita (Current US$)," accessed November 26, 2014, http://data.worldbank.org/indicator/NY.GDP.PCAP.CD.

5. Unfortunately, the word *capital* in economics has multiple meanings. Investopedia gives two definitions of capital: "1. Financial assets or the financial value of assets, such as cash. 2. The factories, machinery and equipment owned by a business and used in production." Investopedia, "Definition of Capital," accessed May 25, 2015, http://www.investopedia.com/terms/c/capital.asp. As is typical of economists going back hundreds of years, in contrast to financiers, here we mean definition 2, and refer to the total such capital of all the businesses in a country.

6. Robert M. Solow, "Technical Change and the Aggregate Production Function," *Review of Economics and Statistics* 39, no. 3 (August 1957): 312–20. Solow examined the period 1909 to 1949 in the United States. He had a way to estimate how much increases in capital had increased productivity. Capital per employed hour of labor input had increased by approximately 31 percent. The share of the earnings of capital in total output (that is, of dividends plus rents plus undistributed profits, etc.) was approximately 1/3. He made the crude assumption that this "share of capital" represented its contribution to output (as would be true if markets were truly competitive). Making a subtle calculation, he showed that, in the absence of the change in capital, output per man-hour would have changed by 80 percent. That 31 percent change in the capital stock per hour of employed labor then accounted for about a 10 percent change in output per man-hour, and therefore one-eighth of its total change over the period.

7. The role of Native American and African American music is a major theme in Joseph Horowitz, *Dvořák in America: In Search of the New World* (Chicago: Cricket Books, 2003).

8. Hanna Krasnova, Helena Wenninger, Thomas Widjaja, and Peter Buxmann, "Envy on Facebook: A Hidden Threat to Users' Life Satisfaction?" *Wirtschaftsinformatik Proceedings 2013*, Paper 92, p. 4, table 1, and p. 5, table 2, http://aisel.aisnet.org/wi2013/92. Respondents were allowed to list more

than one reason for "frustration." Table 2 lists the fractions of respondents who considered various "social causes" to be a "frustration." Unfortunately, the authors do not say how multiple responses were distributed among "social causes," but only for the whole table. Overall, 80.7 percent of respondents mentioned only one reason for "frustration"; 17.3 percent mentioned two, and 2.0 percent mentioned three. Using these fractions we estimated that approximately 60 percent listed one or more of the "social causes."

9. Steve Annear, "The 'Pavlov Poke' Shocks People Who Spend Too Much Time on Facebook: It's Meant to Condition Social Media 'Addicts' to Step Away from the Screen and Enjoy the Real World," *Boston Daily,* August 23, 2013, accessed November 26, 2014, http://www.bostonmagazine.com/news/blog/2013/08/23/pavlov-poke-shocks-people-who-spend-too-much-time-on-facebook/.

10. A United Airlines website describes the boarding process as follows:

Pre-boarding comes [after passengers with disabilities]. This group includes Global Services℠ members and uniformed military personnel.

After pre-boarding is complete, listen for your boarding group number to be called. To get an idea of what your group number will be, here's the list for aircraft with two cabins—organized by Premier Access℠ member level.

Group 1—Premier Access boarding
- Global Services℠ (for those customers who didn't board during the pre-boarding announcement)
- Premier 1K®
- Premier® Platinum
- Premium cabins, including United First®

Note: On aircraft with three cabins, United Business® members board in this group. (Also, for three-cabin aircraft, on certain international routes, United First is referred to as United Global First® and United Business® is referred to as United BusinessFirst®.)

Group 2—Premier Access boarding
- Premier® Gold
- Star Alliance™ Gold
- Premier® Silver
- MileagePlus® Club Card members
- Presidential Plus℠ Card members
- MileagePlus® Explorer Card members
- MileagePlus® Awards Card members

Groups 3, 4, 5—General boarding

Note: Families with infants or with children who are under the age of 4 may board the aircraft when their group number is called.

"Arriving at a Single Boarding Process," April 22, 2013, accessed November 26, 2014, https://hub.united.com/en-us/news/company-operations/pages/arriving-at-a-single-boarding-process.aspx.

11. We are further reminded of an experiment conducted by Jeffrey Butler for his Berkeley PhD. Butler examined whether he could induce feelings of status in an experimental laboratory. Subjects were randomly assigned to two groups, high status or low status, dependent on their draw of an orange or purple poker chip out of a bag. The high-status subjects were given chairs three to a row, while being provided nice refreshments; the low-status subjects, in contrast, were seated five to a row, with the boring task of alphabetizing a list of names. We should not be surprised that when these subjects subsequently played what are known as the "Trust Game" and the "Truth Game," such status-based assignments made a difference. Those who had been assigned high status were more likely to punish breaches of trust, both among themselves and among the low-status types. Jeffrey Vincent Butler, "Status and Confidence," in "Essays on Identity and Economics" (PhD diss., University of California, Berkeley, 2008).

12. Nicholas Lemann, *The Big Test: The Secret History of the American Meritocracy,* 1st rev. paperback ed. (New York: Farrar, Straus and Giroux, 2000).

13. Ibid., pp. 7–8.

14. Garey Ramey and Valerie A. Ramey, "The Rug Rat Race," *Brookings Papers on Economic Activity* (Spring 2010): 129–99. The name of the paper comes from a US animated television series, *Rugrats* (1991–2004), which depicts the antics of clever toddler-aged children, and from the phrase *rat race,* meaning an unending meaningless pursuit, like that of laboratory rats placed to run in a scientist's maze or treadmill, drawing those two images together in a commentary on the pressures modern society places on children to succeed.

15. The best known probably come from *US News and World Report.* See http://colleges.usnews.rankingsandreviews.com/best-colleges.

16. There is even a website where one can obtain journal rankings by five different criteria: by subject area; by subject category; by region or by country; by different criteria for the ordering; and according to the number of citations of the journal. SCImago Journal and Country Rank, "Journal Rankings," accessed November 26, 2014, http://www.scimagojr.com/journalrank.php?country=US.

17. For example, the "h-index" ranks professors according to their article citations.

18. Thom Patterson, "United Airlines Ends Coach Preboarding for Children," CNN, May 23, 2012, accessed April 30, 2015, http://www.cnn.com/2012/05/23/travel/united-children-preboarding/.

19. Prosper Mérimée, *Carmen and Other Stories* (Oxford: Oxford University Press, 1989).

20. Allan M. Brandt, *The Cigarette Century: The Rise, Fall, and Deadly Persistence of the Product That Defined America* (New York: Basic Books, 2007), p. 27.

Chapter Eight: Tobacco and Alcohol

1. This has been found in neurological evidence regarding addiction. For this point of view and review of the evidence for it, see B. Douglas Bernheim

and Antonio Rangel, "Addiction and Cue-Triggered Decision Processes," *American Economic Review* 94, no. 5 (December 2004): 1558–90. As they write, "Recent research on the neuroscience of addiction has identified specific features of the brain that appear to produce systematic errors with respect to decisions regarding the consumption of addictive substances" (p. 1562).

2. Centers for Disease Control and Prevention, "Smoking and Tobacco Use: Fast Facts," accessed December 9, 2014, http://www.cdc.gov/tobacco/data_statistics/fact_sheets/fast_facts/.

3. Allan M. Brandt, *The Cigarette Century: The Rise, Fall, and Deadly Persistence of the Product That Defined America* (New York: Basic Books, 2007), picture between pp. 184 and 185.

4. US Surgeon General, *Smoking and Health: Report of the Advisory Committee to the Surgeon General of the Public Health Service* (1964), p. 5, accessed November 28, 2014, http://www.surgeongeneral.gov/library/reports/.

5. Consumption per capita for those 15 years of age or older: ibid., chap. 5, p. 45, table 1.

6. Ibid., p. 25. By 1955 there were almost 27,000; by 1962, more than 41,000.

7. Brandt, *The Cigarette Century*, pp. 131–34.

8. Ernst L. Wynder and Evarts A. Graham, "Tobacco Smoking as a Possible Etiologic Factor in Bronchogenic Carcinoma Study of Six Hundred and Eighty-Four Proved Cases," *Journal of the American Medical Association* 143, no. 4 (May 27, 1950): 329–36. They found that only 3.5 percent of those with cancer were not "moderately heavy to chain smokers for many years." The comparable figure for matched male hospital patients was 26.3 percent (p. 336).

9. Brandt, *The Cigarette Century*, pp. 131–32.

10. Ibid., p. 157. But, sadly, Graham had smoked too long. He later died of lung cancer.

11. For men, for those who smoked 0 cigarettes, the ratio of those from the lung cancer sample to those in the matched sample was 0.075; for smokers of 1 to 4 cigarettes a day, 0.56; for 5 to 14 a day, 0.87; for 15 to 24 a day, 1.03; for 25 to 49, 1.91; for more than 50 a day, 2.5. Richard Doll and A. Bradford Hill, "Smoking and Carcinoma of the Lung: Preliminary Report," *British Medical Journal* 2, no. 4682 (September 30, 1950): 742, fig. 1. The results for women were similarly upward sloping, although the increase was a bit noisier, as might be expected since they were only 6 percent of the lung cancer patients. There were only forty-one women with lung cancer in the sample of 688 with lung cancer (p. 742, table 5).

12. Ernst L. Wynder, Evarts A. Graham, and Adele B. Croninger, "Experimental Production of Carcinoma with Cigarette Tar," *Cancer Research* 13, no. 12 (1953): 863.

13. Oscar Auerbach et al., "Changes in the Bronchial Epithelium in Relation to Smoking and Cancer of the Lung: A Report of Progress," *New England Journal of Medicine* 256, no. 3 (January 17, 1957): 97–104.

14. Jeffrey K. Cruikshank and Arthur W. Schultz, *The Man Who Sold America* (Boston: Harvard Business Review Press, 2010), pp. 354–56.

15. Kenneth Roman, *The King of Madison Avenue: David Ogilvy and the Making of Modern Advertising,* paperback ed. (New York: Macmillan, 2009), p. 223.

16. Brandt, *The Cigarette Century,* p. 165; Naomi Oreskes and Erik M. Conway, *Merchants of Doubt: How a Handful of Scientists Obscured the Truth on Issues from Tobacco Smoke to Global Warming* (New York: Bloomsbury, 2010), p. 15. Oreskes and Conway document the creation of doubt not only regarding the effects of smoking, but also regarding acid rain, the ozone hole, global warming, and DDT. They show how remarkably easy it was strategically to insert doubt into the public discourse in each of these areas.

17. Brandt, *The Cigarette Century,* pp. 171 and 175.

18. "Little, Clarence Cook, Sc.D. (CTR Scientific Director, 1954–1971)," accessed November 28, 2014, http://tobaccodocuments.org/profiles/little_clarence_cook.html. No longer available on the web. Copy in authors' files.

19. Ibid.; *Time Magazine,* "Clarence Cook Little": Cover Story, April 22, 1937; George D. Snell, "Clarence D. Little, 1888–1971: A Biographical Memoir by George D. Snell" (Washington, DC: National Academy of Sciences, 1971).

20. Brandt, *The Cigarette Century,* p. 176.

21. Ibid., p. 175.

22. Ibid., p. 177.

23. This, of course, is the public health warning mandated by the Public Health Cigarette Smoking Act of 1970 to be placed on every pack of cigarettes. "Public Health Cigarette Smoking Act," *Wikipedia,* accessed March 28, 2015, http://en.wikipedia.org/wiki/Public_Health_Cigarette_Smoking_Act.

24. US Surgeon General, *The Health Consequences of Smoking—50 Years of Progress* (2014), pp. 21–22, accessed March 6, 2015, http://www.surgeongeneral.gov/library/reports/50-years-of-progress/full-report.pdf.

25. US Surgeon General, *Smoking and Health* (1964), p. 102, table 19.

26. Jason Bardi, "Cigarette Pack Health Warning Labels in US Lag behind World: Internal Tobacco Company Documents Reveal Multinational Effort to Block Strong Warnings to Smokers," University of California at San Francisco, November 16, 2012, accessed December 8, 2014, http://www.ucsf.edu/news/2012/11/13151/cigarette-pack-health-warning-labels-us-lag-behind-world. For the United States, also see Mark Joseph Stern, "The FDA's New Cigarette Labels Go Up in Smoke," *Wall Street Journal,* September 9, 2012, accessed March 28, 2015, http://www.wsj.com/articles/SB100008723963904438194045777633580009556096; and US Food and Drug Administration, "Tobacco Products: Final Rule 'Required Warnings for Cigarette Packages and Advertisements,'" accessed March 28, 2015, http://www.fda.gov/TobaccoProducts/Labeling/Labeling/CigaretteWarningLabels/ucm259953.htm. For Australia, see Tobacco Labelling Resource Center, "Australia: Health Warnings, 2012 to Present," accessed March 28, 2015, http://www.tobaccolabels.ca/countries/australia/.

27. Television and radio advertising was banned in the Public Health Smoking Act of April 1970. Since that time that act has been amended. The further Tobacco Control Act of 2009 brings some additional restrictions. "Tobacco Advertising," *Wikipedia,* accessed December 8, 2014, http://en.wikipedia.org/wiki/Tobacco_advertising.

28. Brandt, *The Cigarette Century,* pp. 432–37. In addition to the settlement with forty-six states, there had been settlements with Mississippi, Florida, Texas, and Minnesota for an additional $40 billion.

29. Ibid., pp. 267–69.

30. Ibid., p. 271.

31. Ibid., p. 288.

32. US Surgeon General, *Smoking and Health: A Report of the Surgeon General* (1979), "Appendix: Cigarette Smoking in the United States, 1950–1978," p. A-10, table 2, accessed November 28, 2014, http://www.surgeongeneral.gov/library/reports/.

33. Figures for 2014, Centers for Disease Control and Prevention, "Cigarette Smoking in the United States: Current Cigarette Smoking among U.S. Adults 18 Years and Older," accessed March 28, 2015, http://www.cdc.gov/tobacco/campaign/tips/resources/data/cigarette-smoking-in-united-states.html.

34. Centers for Disease Control and Prevention, "Trends in Current Cigarette Smoking among High School Students and Adults, United States, 1965–2011," November 14, 2013, accessed December 9, 2014, http://www.cdc.gov/tobacco/data_statistics/tables/trends/cig_smoking/.

35. Using table 2 from http://www.lung.org/finding-cures/our-research/trend-reports/Tobacco-Trend-Report.pdf, cigarette consumption per capita (18 or older) in 1965 was 4,259, and 1,232 in 2011. Table 4 of http://www.lung.org/finding-cures/our-research/trend-reports/Tobacco-Trend-Report.pdf indicates that 42.4 percent of the adult population were current smokers in 1965, and 19.0 percent of the adult population were current smokers in 2011 (http://www.cdc.gov/tobacco/data_statistics/tables/trends/cig_smoking/). Hence, the average smoker smoked 27.52 cigarettes daily in 1965, and 17.76 daily in 2011, or 1.376 packs in 1965 and 0.89 packets in 2011. Following World Health Organization estimates for 2015, for example, in Brazil 15.2 percent of the population 15 years of age or older smoke; in China, 26.3 percent; in France, 24.7 percent; in Germany, 26.2 percent; in Russia, 37.3 percent.

36. Centers for Disease Control and Prevention, "Smoking and Tobacco Use: Tobacco-Related Mortality," accessed March 28, 2015, http://www.cdc.gov/tobacco/data_statistics/fact_sheets/health_effects/tobacco_related_mortality/. The estimates are for average annual deaths from cigarette smoking for 2005–2009. Total annual deaths due to smoking were estimated at 480,317. Smoking directly caused 127,700 from lung cancer; 113,100 from respiratory diseases; and 160,000 from cardiovascular and metabolic diseases. 41,300 deaths occurred because of secondhand smoke—7,300 of them being from lung cancer, and 34,000 from coronary heart disease.

37. Bridget F. Grant et al., "The 12-Month Prevalence and Trends in DSM-IV Alcohol Abuse and Dependence: United States, 1991–1992 and 2001–2002," *Drug and Alcohol Dependence* 74, no. 3 (2004): 228, table 2.

38. Mandy Stahre et al., "Contribution of Excessive Alcohol Consumption to Deaths and Years of Potential Life Lost in the United States," *Preventing Chronic Disease* 11 (2014), accessed March 28, 2014, http://www.cdc

.gov/pcd/issues/2014/13_0293.htm. We divided Stahre's estimates of alcohol-attributed deaths by total deaths for the comparable period.

39. George E. Vaillant, *Triumphs of Experience: The Men of the Harvard Grant Study* (Cambridge, MA: Harvard University Press, 2012), pp. 54–55.

40. Ibid., p. 67: these young men were chosen within the Harvard class as those who were "especially likely to lead 'successful' lives."

41. Ibid., p. 66.

42. Ibid., p. 54.

43. Ibid., p. 296.

44. Ibid., p. 298. The 23 percent lumps together both the abusers and the dependents. As the base for this percentage we are using the number of interviewees who continued in the program (242), rather than the initial interviews, 268.

45. Ibid., p. 301.

46. Ibid., pp. 303–7.

47. In 57 percent of the divorces of the Grant Study men, at least one of the spouses was alcoholic (ibid., p. 358). Given that alcoholism is considerably greater among men than among women (which we know, for example, from the NESARC) and that the fraction of alcohol abusers and dependents among the Harvard men was about 23 percent, this is an outsize number. See also Fred Arne Thorberg and Michael Lyvers, "Attachment, Fear of Intimacy and Differentiation of Self among Clients in Substance Disorder Treatment Facilities," *Addictive Behaviors* 31, no. 4 (April 2006): 732–37; and Frank P. Troise, "The Capacity for Experiencing Intimacy in Wives of Alcoholics or Codependents," *Alcohol Treatment Quarterly* 9, no. 3 (October 2008): 39–55.

48. Vaillant, *Triumphs of Experience*, pp. 321–26.

49. Dave Newhouse, *Old Bears: The Class of 1956 Reaches Its Fiftieth Reunion, Reflecting on the Happy Days and the Unhappy Days* (Berkeley: North Atlantic Books, 2007).

50. Ibid., pp. 17–31.

51. Ibid., pp. 33–39.

52. Ibid., pp. 290–91.

53. Ibid., pp. 127–28.

54. Ibid., pp. 57 and 316.

55. National Institutes of Health, National Institute on Alcohol Abuse and Alcoholism, *Alcohol Use and Alcohol Use Disorders in the United States: Main Findings from the 2001–2002 National Epidemiologic Survey on Alcohol and Related Conditions (NESARC)*, January 2006, "Exhibit 2, National Epidemiologic Survey on Alcohol and Related Conditions (Section 2B): DSM-IV Alcohol Abuse and Dependence Diagnostic Criteria and Associated Questionnaire Items," pp. 8–9, accessed November 12, 2014, http://pubs.niaaa.nih.gov/publications/NESARC_DRM/NESARCDRM.pdf.

56. Philip J. Cook, *Paying the Tab: The Costs and Benefits of Alcohol Control* (Princeton: Princeton University Press, 2007), p. 210, n. 14.

57. Ibid., p. 71.

58. Ibid., pp. 72–73.

59. Ibid., pp. 103–5 and tables 6.4 and 6.5.

60. US Department of the Treasury, Alcohol and Tobacco Tax and Trade Bureau, "Tax and Fee Rates," accessed April 30, 2015, www.ttb.govtax_audit/atftaxes.shtml.

61. Urban Institute and the Brookings Institution, Tax Policy Center, "State Alcohol Excise Tax Rates 2014," accessed December 13, 2014, http://www.taxpolicycenter.org/taxfacts/displayafact.cfm?Docid=349.

62. Jeanette DeForge, "Ballot Question to Revoke Sales Tax on Alcohol Approved by Massachusetts Voters," *Republican,* November 3, 2010, accessed December 13, 2014, http://www.masslive.com/news/index.ssf/2010/11/ballot_question_to_revoke_sale.html; and Dan Ring, "Massachusetts Senate Approves State Sales Tax Increase to 6.25 Percent as Part of $1 Billion Tax Hike," *Republican,* May 20, 2009, accessed December 13, 2014, http://www.masslive.com/news/index.ssf/2009/05/massachusetts_senate_approves.html.

63. See Mothers against Drunk Driving, "History and Mission Statement," accessed March 28, 2015, http://www.madd.org.

64. "Drunk Driving Statistics," accessed December 13, 2014, http://www.alcoholalert.com/drunk-driving-statistics.html. The comparison period taken is 1982 to 2011. The sober drivers were driving considerably more at the end of this period, since the total number of vehicle miles traveled had increased much faster than population. So this may not be a bad safety record for them, either. Statistics on population are from Council of Economic Advisors, Economic Report of the President 2013, p. 365, table B-34, accessed December 1, 2014, http://www.whitehouse.gov/sites/default/files/docs/erp2013/full_2013_economic_report_of_the_president.pdf.

65. US Department of Transportation, National Highway Traffic Safety Administration, "Traffic Safety Facts, 2011: Alcohol Impaired Driving," December 2012, accessed May 25, 2015, http://www-nrd.nhtsa.dot.gov/Pubs/811700.pdf.

66. See "Voices of Victims," on the official MADD website, accessed December 13, 2014, http://www.madd.org/drunk-driving/voices-of-victims/.

67. National Institutes of Health, National Institute on Alcohol Abuse and Alcoholism, *Surveillance Report #95 Apparent Per Capita Ethanol Consumption, United States, 1850–2010* (August 2012), table 1, http://pubs.niaaa.nih.gov/publications/Surveillance95/CONS10.htm.

Chapter Nine: Bankruptcy for Profit

1. George A. Akerlof and Paul M. Romer, "Looting: The Economic Underworld of Bankruptcy for Profit," *Brookings Papers on Economic Activity* 2 (1993): 36. An alternative estimate of the cost by the National Commission on Financial Institution Reform, Recovery and Enforcement was 7 to 11 percent higher.

2. James H. Stock and Mark W. Watson, "Forecasting Output and Inflation: The Role of Asset Prices," *Journal of Economic Literature* 41 (2003): 797. For business cycle dates, National Bureau of Economic Research, "U.S. Business Cycle Expansions and Contractions," accessed January 13, 2015, http://www.nber.org/cycles.html.

3. Akerlof and Romer, "Looting."

4. For use of the concept of "tunneling," see Simon Johnson, Rafael La Porta, Florencio López de Silanes, and Andrei Shleifer, "Tunneling," *American Economic Review* 90, no. 2 (May 2000): 22–27.

5. Council of Economic Advisors, *Economic Report of the President 2013*, table B-64, "Year-to-Year Inflation of the Consumer Price Index," accessed December 1, 2014, http://www.whitehouse.gov/sites/default/files/docs/erp2013/full_2013_economic_report_of_the_president.pdf.

6. Ibid., table B-73, "Bond Yields and Interest Rates, 1942–2012," column 1.

7. US Department of Labor, Bureau of Labor Statistics, Tables and Calculators by Subject; Unemployment Rates by Month, http://data.bls.gov/pdq/SurveyOutputServlet.

8. Council of Economic Advisors, *Economic Report of the President 2013*, table B-73, column 9.

9. The money market funds held almost zero assets in 1980. See graph in "The Future of Money Market Funds," September 24, 2012, http://www.winthropcm.com/TheFutureofMoneyMarketFunds.pdf. The numbers in this graph accord with data from the Investment Company Institute's 2014 Fact Book. The data do not include the years 1980 to 1984, but they do show that by 1990 money market fund assets had reached $498 billion. http://www.icifactbook.org/fb_data.html. Last accessed January 1, 2015.

10. Akerlof and Romer, "Looting," p. 23.

11. Ibid., p. 34, calculation of resolution cost of $20 billion to $30 billion in 1993 dollars, brought up to date.

12. For a description of the boom and bust in Dallas, Texas, see ibid., pp. 39–42.

13. Ibid., pp. 23–24.

14. R. Alton Gilbert, "Requiem for Regulation Q: What It Did and Why It Passed Away," *Federal Reserve Bank of St. Louis Review* (February 1986): 22–37. The interest rate ceilings for the savings and loans were a bit more than the regulation ceilings for savings deposits at banks. The ceiling for banks in 1980 was approximately 5½ percent. See p. 29, chart 3.

15. Akerlof and Romer, "Looting," p. 24.

16. For the 10 percent from Garn–St. Germain, see Carl Felsenfeld and David L. Glass, *Banking Regulation in the United States*, 3rd ed. (New York: Juris, 2011), pp. 424–25. For liberal interpretation of the 10 percent in whatever assets the S&Ls wanted to loan against, see "Top Ten U.S. Banking Laws of the 20th Century," accessed December 1, 2014, http://www.oswego.edu/~dighe/topten.htm.

17. Akerlof and Romer, "Looting," p. 27. As a nice dividend, the developer could charge a "developer's fee" (which could be 2.5 percent, for example) for originating the project.

18. James E. O'Shea, *The Daisy Chain: How Borrowed Billions Sank a Texas S & L* (New York: Pocket Books, 1991), especially pp. 29–34. In the example related there, the money was tunneled out in a different way from the purchase of stock.

19. In O'Shea's example the developers bought supplies at inflated prices from the owners of the S&L.

20. Stephen Pizzo, Mary Fricker, and Paul Muolo, *Inside Job: The Looting of America's Savings and Loans* (New York: Harper Perennial, 1991), p. 108.

21. Ibid., p. 14.

22. Akerlof and Romer, "Looting," p. 40, table 11.2. Of course, construction in Dallas did also taper, but much more slowly and much less dramatically than in Houston.

23. Steve Brown, "Office Market Outlook: Dallas," *National Real Estate Investor News,* June 1982, p. 46.

24. Steve Brown, "City Review: Dallas," *National Real Estate Investor News,* October 1983, p. 127.

25. Steve Brown, "City Review: Dallas," *National Real Estate Investor News,* October 1984, pp. 183 and 192.

26. Steve Brown, "City Review: Dallas," *National Real Estate Investor News,* June 1985, pp. 98–100.

27. Pizzo, Fricker, and Muolo, *Inside Job.*

Chapter Ten: Michael Milken Phishes with Junk Bonds as Bait

1. Bryan Burrough and John Helyar, *Barbarians at the Gate: The Fall of RJR Nabisco* (New York: Random House, 2010), Kindle locations 10069–72 out of 11172.

2. Johnson reputedly received more than $50 million from the takeover. Bryan Burrough, "RJR Nabisco: An Epilogue," *New York Times,* March 12, 1999, http://www.nytimes.com/1999/03/12/opinion/rjr-nabisco-an-epilogue .html.

3. Graef S. Crystal, *In Search of Excess: The Overcompensation of American Executives* (New York: W. W. Norton, 1991), especially pp. 46–47. Jenny Chu, Jonathan Faasse, and P. Raghavendra Rau have shown that management-retained consultants (in contrast to board-retained consultants) generate large increases in management pay: Chu, Faasse, and Rau, "Do Compensation Consultants Enable Higher CEO Pay? New Evidence from Recent Disclosure Rule Changes" (September 23, 2014), p. 23, accessed May 27, 2015, http://papers.ssrn.com/sol3/Papers.cfm?abstract_id=2500054.

4. W. Braddock Hickman, *Corporate Bond Quality and Investor Experience* (Princeton: National Bureau of Economic Research and Princeton University Press, 1958). Table 1 is on p. 10.

5. George Anders and Constance Mitchell, "Junk King's Legacy: Milken Sales Pitch on High-Yield Bonds Is Contradicted by Data," *Wall Street Journal,* November 20, 1990, p. A1.

6. Lindley B. Richert, "One Man's Junk Is Another's Bonanza in the Bond Market," *Wall Street Journal,* March 27, 1975.

7. John Locke, *An Essay Concerning Human Understanding,* 30th ed. (London: William Tegg, 1849): "I endeavour as much as I can, to deliver myself from those fallacies, which we are apt to put upon our selves, by taking words for things" (p. 104).

8. Gary Smith, *Standard Deviations: Flawed Assumptions, Tortured Data, and Other Ways to Lie with Statistics* (New York: Duckworth Overlook, 2014).

9. Jesse Kornbluth, *Highly Confident: The Crime and Punishment of Michael Milken* (New York: William Morrow, 1992), p. 45.

10. Hickman, *Corporate Bond Quality and Investor Experience,* p. 10.

11. Jeremy J. Siegel and Richard H. Thaler, "Anomalies: The Equity Premium Puzzle," *Journal of Economic Perspectives* 11, no. 1 (Winter 1997): 191.

12. United States Federal Deposit Insurance Corporation et al. v. Michael R. Milken et al. (1991), Southern District of New York (January 18), Amended Complaint Class Action, Civ. No. 91-0433 (MP), pp. 70–71.

13. See James B. Stewart, *Den of Thieves* (New York: Simon and Schuster, 1992), pp. 521–22; and Benjamin Stein, *A License to Steal: The Untold Story of Michael Milken and the Conspiracy to Bilk the Nation* (New York: Simon and Schuster, 1992).

14. Kornbluth, *Highly Confident,* p. 64. Later, Drexel was able to raise $5 billion in a few hours in the buyout of RJR Nabisco. Burrough and Helyar, *Barbarians at the Gate,* Kindle locations 10069–72.

15. FDIC v. Milken, pp. 146–47.

16. Ibid., pp. 149–50.

17. Stein, *License to Steal,* pp. 89–92.

18. The criminal case against Keating was overturned on appeal, after he had served four and a half years of time and confessed to other crimes. Robert D. McFadden, "Charles Keating, 90, Key Figure in '80s Savings and Loan Crisis, Dies," *New York Times,* April 2, 2014, accessed May 27, 2015, http://www.nytimes.com/2014/04/02/business/charles-keating-key-figure-in-the-1980s-savings-and-loan-crisis-dies-at-90.html?_r=0. Spiegel was indicted on many counts, but went free after a seven-week trial. Thomas S. Mulligan, "Spiegel Found Not Guilty of Looting S & L," *Los Angeles Times,* December 13, 1994, accessed May 1, 2015, http://articles.latimes.com/1994-12-13/news/mn-8437_1_thomas-spiegel. Carr was investigated, but never charged. Scot J. Paltrow, "Executive Life Seizure: The Costly Comeuppance of Fred Carr," *Los Angeles Times,* April 12, 1991, accessed May 1, 2015, http://articles.latimes.com/1991-04-12/business/fi-342_1_executive-life.

19. This problem has been described in Sanford J. Grossman and Oliver D. Hart, "Takeover Bids, the Free-Rider Problem, and the Theory of the Corporation," *Bell Journal of Economics* 11, no. 1 (1980): 42–64.

20. Connie Bruck, *The Predators' Ball: The Inside Story of Drexel Burnham and the Rise of the Junk Bond Raiders* (New York: Penguin Books, 1989), pp. 193–240; Robert J. Cole, "Pantry Pride Revlon Bid Raised by $1.75 a Share," *New York Times,* October 19, 1985, accessed March 17, 2015, http://www.nytimes.com/1985/10/19/business/pantry-pride-revlon-bid-raised-by-1.75-a-share.html.

21. Paul Asquith, David W. Mullins Jr., and Eric D. Wolff, "Original Issue High Yield Bonds: Aging Analyses of Defaults, Exchanges and Calls," *Journal of Finance* 44, no. 4 (1989): 924.

22. Bruck, *The Predators' Ball,* p. 76.

23. Asquith, Mullins, and Wolff, "Original Issue High Yield Bonds," p. 929, table 2: weighted average of first four numbers in right-hand column.

24. Ibid. Number of successful exchanges that have defaulted (16, in table 7, p. 935) on new issuances from 1977 to 1980 divided by new issuances from 1977 to 1980 (155, in table 1, p. 928).

25. Bruck, *The Predators' Ball*, p. 10.

26. Stewart, *Den of Thieves*, p. 243.

27. Kurt Eichenwald, "Wages Even Wall St. Can't Stomach," *New York Times*, April 3, 1989, asserted that Milken had the highest one-year pay in US history.

28. See, for example, Michael C. Jensen, "Takeovers: Their Causes and Consequences," *Journal of Economic Perspectives* 2, no. 1 (Winter 1988): 21–48.

29. This opposite side of the coin has been argued in Andrei Shleifer and Lawrence H. Summers, "Breach of Trust in Hostile Takeovers," in *Corporate Takeovers: Causes and Consequences*, ed. Alan J. Auerbach (Chicago: University of Chicago Press, 1988), pp. 33–68.

30. Brian Hindo and Moira Herbst, "Personal Best Timeline, 1986: 'Greed Is Good,'" *BusinessWeek*, http://www.bloomberg.com/ss/06/08/personalbest _timeline/source/7.htm.

31. Bruck, *The Predators' Ball*, p. 320.

32. Bruck, *The Predators' Ball*.

33. FDIC v. Milken, pp. 70–71.

34. Alison Leigh Cowan, "F.D.I.C. Backs Deal by Milken," *New York Times*, March 10, 1992.

35. See Thomas Piketty, *Capital in the Twenty-First Century* (Cambridge, MA: Harvard University Press, 2014), p. 291, fig. 8.5, and p. 292, fig. 8.6.

36. Andrei Shleifer and Robert W. Vishny, "The Takeover Wave of the 1980s," *Science* 249, no. 4970 (1990): 745–49.

Chapter Eleven: The Resistance and Its Heroes

1. For 2013. World Bank, "Life Expectancy at Birth, Male (Years)" and "Life Expectancy at Birth, Female (Years)," accessed March 29, 2015, http://data .worldbank.org/indicator/SP.DYN.LE00.MA.IN/countries and http://data .worldbank.org/indicator/SP.DYN.LE00.FE.IN/countries.

2. Ralph Nader, *Unsafe at Any Speed: The Designed-In Dangers of the American Automobile* (New York: Grossman, 1965).

3. Jad Mouawad and Christopher Drew, "Airline Industry at Its Safest since the Dawn of the Jet Age," *New York Times*, February 11, 2013, http://www .nytimes.com/2013/02/12/business/2012-was-the-safest-year-for-airlines -globally-since-1945.html?pagewanted=all&_r=0.

4. US Food and Drug Administration, "About FDA: Commissioner's Page. Harvey Washington Wiley, MD," http://www.fda.gov/AboutFDA/ CommissionersPage/ucm113692.htm. Wiley called it the Imperial Health Laboratory in his autobiography: Harvey W. Wiley, *An Autobiography* (Indianapolis: Bobbs-Merrill, 1930), p. 150.

5. Stuart Chase and Frederick J. Schlink, *Your Money's Worth: A Study of the Waste of the Consumer's Dollar* (New York: Macmillan, 1927), pp. 4–5.

6. Ibid.

7. US Department of Agriculture, Grain Inspection, Packing, and Stockyard Administration, "Subpart M—United States Standards for Wheat," accessed May 1, 2015, http://www.gipsa.usda.gov/fgis/standards/810wheat.pdf.

8. Interview with Anthony Goodeman of the GIPSA, January 2015; US Department of Agriculture, Grain Inspection, Packing, and Stockyards Administration, "Explanatory Notes," table 5, "Inspection and Weighing Program Overview," pp. 20–33, accessed May 1, 2015, http://www.obpa.usda.gov/exnotes/FY2014/20gipsa2014notes.pdf. There is some ambiguity in the table regarding how much grain is inspected, since some of it, especially that for export, may be inspected twice.

9. Interview with Anthony Goodeman of the GIPSA.

10. US Department of Agriculture, Farm Service Administration, "Commodity Operations: United States Warehouse Act," accessed March 14, 2015, http://www.fsa.usda.gov/FSA/webapp?area=home&subject=coop&topic=was-ua; *Kansas Statutes Annotated* (2009), chap. 34, "Grain and Forage," article 2, "Inspecting, Sampling, Storing, Weighing and Grading Grain; Terminal and Local Warehouses, 34-228: Warehouseman's License; Application; Financial Statement; Waiver; Qualifications; License Fee; Examination of Warehouse," accessed May 1, 2015, http://law.justia.com/codes/kansas/2011/Chapter34/Article2/34-228.html.

11. Underwriters Laboratories, "Our History" and "What We Do," accessed March 3, 2015, http://ul.com/aboutul/history/ and http://ul.com/aboutul/what-we-do/.

12. American National Standards Institute, "About ANSI" and "ANSI: Historical Overview," accessed March 14, 2015, http://www.ansi.org/about_ansi/overview/overview.aspx?menuid=1 and http://www.ansi.org/about_ansi/introduction/history.aspx?menuid=1.

13. Lawrence B. Glickman, *Buying Power: A History of Consumer Activism in America* (Chicago: University of Chicago Press, 2009), p. 195.

14. Ibid., p. 212.

15. Gwendolyn Bounds, "Meet the Sticklers: New Demands Test Consumer Reports," *Wall Street Journal,* May 5, 2010, accessed March 14, 2015, http://www.wsj.com/articles/SB10001424052748703866704575224093017379202#mod=todays_us_personal_journal. That 7.3 million includes electronic subscriptions.

16. Consumer Federation of America, "Membership," accessed March 14, 2015, http://www.consumerfed.org/about-cfa/membership.

17. Glickman, *Buying Power,* pp. 31–32 and following, and p. 69 and following.

18. Florence Kelley, *Notes of Sixty Years: The Autobiography of Florence Kelley,* ed. Kathryn Kish Sklar (Chicago: Illinois Labor History Society, 1986).

19. Glickman, *Buying Power.* pp. 182–83.

20. National Consumers League, "Our Issues: Outrage! End Child Labor in American Tobacco Fields," November 14, 2014, accessed March 15, 2015, http://www.nclnet.org/outrage_end_child_labor_in_american_tobacco_fields.

21. *The Guardians, or Society for the Protection of Trade against Swindlers and Sharpers* (probably London, 1776), https://library.villanova.edu/Find/Record/1027765.

22. David Owen, "The Pay Problem," *New Yorker,* October 12, 2009, accessed March 12, 2015, http://www.newyorker.com/magazine/2009/10/12/the-pay-problem; David A. Skeel Jr., "Shaming in Corporate Law," University of Pennsylvania Law Review 149, no. 6 (June 2001): 1811–68.

23. Skeel, "Shaming in Corporate Law," p. 1812.

24. National Association of Realtors, "Code of Ethics," accessed March 15, 2015, http://www.realtor.org/governance/governing. The 16¼ pages comes from printing as a Word document.

25. M. H. Hoeflich, "Laidlaw v. Organ, Gulian C. Verplanck, and the Shaping of Early Nineteenth Century Contract Law: A Tale of a Case and a Commentary," *University of Illinois Law Review* (Winter 1991): 55–66. Also see the case itself: Laidlaw v. Organ, 15 U.S. 178, 4 L. Ed. 214, 1817 U.S. LEXIS 396 (Supreme Court 1817).

26. This interpretation follows from Hoeflich's subtle view that Verplanck, an influential jurist at the time, "believed not that Marshall had failed to incorporate morality into the law, but rather that in the specific case, he had misunderstood the facts and the extent to which concealment constituted fraud as a matter of fact and law; 'The concealment was therefore dishonest and fraudulent; consequently, the bargain if the seller objected to its execution was void in conscience'" (Hoeflich, "Laidlaw v. Organ," p. 62). Fraud would have invalidated Organ's claim. The role of fraud in the wording of Marshall's decision can be seen in the phrase "each party must take care not to say anything tending to impose upon the other" (Laidlaw v. Organ).

27. Sally H. Clarke, "Unmanageable Risks: MacPherson v. Buick and the Emergence of a Mass Consumer Market," *Law and History Review* 23, no. 1 (2005): 1.

28. Ibid., p. 2.

29. MacPherson v. Buick Motor Co., New York Court of Appeals, accessed March 15, 2015, http://www.courts.state.ny.us/reporter/archives/macpherson_buick.htm.

30. US Legal Inc., "U.S. Commercial Code," accessed March 15, 2015, http://uniformcommercialcode.uslegal.com/.

31. Ibid.

32. LawInfo, "Legal Resource Library: What Is the U.C.C.?" accessed March 15, 2015, http://resources.lawinfo.com/business-law/uniform-commercial-code/does-article-2-treat-merchants-the-same-as-no.html.

33. DealBook, "Goldman Settles with S.E.C. for $550 Million," *New York Times,* July 15, 2010.

34. Knowledge@Wharton, "Goldman Sachs and Abacus 2007-AC1: A Look beyond the Numbers," April 28, 2010, accessed March 15, 2015, http://knowledge.wharton.upenn.edu/article/goldman-sachs-and-abacus-2007-ac1-a-look-beyond-the-numbers/.

35. Ibid.

36. US Securities and Exchange Commission, "Goldman Sachs to Pay Record $550 Million to Settle SEC Charges Related to Subprime Mortgage CDO," July 15, 2010, accessed March 15, 2015, http://www.sec.gov/news/press/2010/2010-123.htm.

37. Christine Harper, "Goldman's Tourre E-Mail Describes 'Frankenstein' Derivatives," Bloomberg Business, April 25, 2010, accessed March 15, 2015, http://www.bloomberg.com/news/articles/2010-04-24/-frankenstein-derivatives-described-in-e-mail-by-goldman-s-fabrice-tourre.

38. Justin Baer, Chad Bray, and Jean Eaglesham, "'Fab' Trader Liable in Fraud: Jury Finds Ex-Goldman Employee Tourre Misled Investors in Mortgage Security," *Wall Street Journal,* August 2, 2013, accessed March 15, 2015, http://www.wsj.com/articles/SB10001424127887323681904578641843284450004.

39. Nate Raymond and Jonathan Stempel, "Big Fine Imposed on Ex-Goldman Trader Tourre in SEC Case," Reuters, March 12, 2014, accessed March 15, 2015, http://www.reuters.com/article/2014/03/12/us-goldmansachs-sec-tourre-idUSBREA2B11220140312.

40. Karen Freifeld, "Fraud Claims Versus Goldman over Abacus CDO Are Dismissed," Reuters, May 14, 2013, accessed March 15, 2015. http://www.reuters.com/article/2013/05/14/us-goldman-abacus-idUSBRE94D10120130514.

41. Joshua Bernhardt, *Interstate Commerce Commission: Its History, Activities and Organization* (Baltimore: Johns Hopkins University Press, 1923).

42. Christine Bauer-Ramazani, BU113: Critical Thinking and Communication in Business, "Major U.S. Regulatory Agencies," accessed March 15, 2015, http://academics.smcvt.edu/cbauer-ramazani/BU113/fed_agencies.htm.

43. Marver H. Bernstein, *Regulating Business by Independent Commission* (Princeton: Princeton University Press, 1955).

44. George J. Stigler, "The Theory of Economic Regulation," *Bell Journal of Economics and Management Science* 2, no. 1 (1971): 3; Richard A. Posner, "Theories of Economic Regulation," *Bell Journal of Economics and Management Science* 5, no. 2 (1974): 335.

45. "A central thesis of this paper is that, as a rule, regulation is acquired by the industry and is designed and operated primarily for its benefit. There are regulations whose net effects upon the regulated industry are undeniably onerous; a simple example is the differentially heavy taxation of the industry's product (whiskey, playing cards). These onerous regulations, however, are exceptional and can be explained by the same theory that explains beneficial (we may call it 'acquired') regulation." Stigler, "The Theory of Economic Regulation," p. 3.

46. Daniel Carpenter and David A. Moss, "Introduction," pp. 5–8, and Carpenter, "Detecting and Measuring Capture," pp. 57–70, in Carpenter and Moss, eds., *Preventing Regulatory Capture: Special Interest Influence and How to Limit It* (New York: Cambridge University Press/The Tobin Project, 2014).

47. Carpenter and Moss, "Introduction," p. 9.

48. Ibid., p. 5. Carpenter and Moss write: "The critical question is whether capture, where it exists, can be mitigated or prevented. We believe the evidence strongly suggests the answer is yes." The various essays in the volume show examples of success in mitigating regulatory capture, without deregulation, in

a number of ways: "involvement of subnational officials in federal notice and comment, creation of consumer empowerment programs tied to regulators, cultivation of diverse and independent experts, institutionalization of devil's advocates within agencies, and expanded review by OIRA to include agency *inaction* as well as action" ("Conclusion," p. 453, in Carpenter and Moss, *Preventing Regulatory Capture*). (OIRA is the Office of Information and Regulatory Affairs, created by the US Congress in 1980 to be part of the Office of the President.) One of many examples examined in the book is the Texas Office of Public Insurance Counsel (OPIC), created in 1991 not as a regulator (it is fully independent of the Texas Department of Insurance) but as a representative of consumers in negotiations between the regulator and regulated. OPIC has had a number of apparent successes in preventing regulatory capture, such as its successful lobbying for prohibition of clauses that allow plan administrator discretion whether to pay a claim with only limited judicial review, and against some laws that require consumers to submit to binding arbitration. See Daniel Schwarcz, "Preventing Capture through Consumer Empowerment Programs: Some Evidence from Insurance Regulation," pp. 365–96, in Carpenter and Moss, *Preventing Regulatory Capture*.

49. Benjamin N. Cardozo, "The Altruist in Politics" (commencement address, Columbia University, 1889), https://www.gutenberg.org/files/1341/1341-h/1341-h.htm.

Conclusion: Examples and General Lessons: New Story in America and Its Consequences

1. The *American Journal of Psychiatry* has published an editorial saying that Internet addiction "merits inclusion" as a disorder in the Diagnostic and Statistical Manual of Mental Disorders. Jerald J. Block, "Issues for DSM-V: Internet Addiction," *American Journal of Psychiatry* 165, no. 3 (2008): 306–7. Internet addiction has been particularly studied in South Korea, where high school students spend an average of twenty-three hours a week at gaming. It is noteworthy that South Korea trained more than a thousand counselors in treatment of this addiction, involved hospitals and treatment centers, and brought preventive programs into schools. Estimates for China are that 13.7 percent of Chinese adolescent Internet users "meet Internet addiction diagnostic criteria."

2. For example, see Richard Hofstadter, *The Age of Reform: From Bryan to FDR* (New York: Random House, 1955); and, for the period of the New Deal, also see William E. Leuchtenburg, *Franklin D. Roosevelt and the New Deal* (New York: Harper and Row, 1963).

3. David E. Rosenbaum, "The Supreme Court: News Analysis; Presidents May Disagree, but Justices Are Generally Loyal to Them," *New York Times,* April 7, 1994. Eisenhower is reputed to have said that his appointment of Earl Warren (and William J. Brennan Jr.) was one of his "biggest mistakes."

4. Social Security Perspectives, "President #6: Richard M. Nixon (1969–1974)," May 8, 2011, http://socialsecurityperspectives.blogspot.com/2011/05/president-6-richard-m-nixon-1969-1974.html.

5. A fascinating recent book by Bruno Boccara describes the role of psychoanalytic forces in generating national stories, which in turn inhibit policy objectives. See Boccara, *Socio-Analytic Dialogue: Incorporating Psychosocial Dynamics into Public Policies* (Lanham, MD: Lexington Books, 2014).

6. According to James T. Patterson, in his volume of the Oxford History of the United States covering the years 1974 to 2001, Reagan "said again and again" that "government is not the solution, it's the problem." Patterson, *Restless Giant: The United States from Watergate to Bush v. Gore* (New York: Oxford University Press, 2005), p. 162. Perhaps our favorite quotation on this theme comes from a press conference in 1986: "The most terrifying words in the English language are: I'm from the government and I'm here to help." There are many other versions. Ray Hennessey, "The 15 Ronald Reagan Quotes Every Business Leader Must Know," accessed January 16, 2015, http://www.entrepreneur.com/article/234547.

7. Elizabeth Warren and Amelia Warren Tyagi, *All Your Worth: The Ultimate Lifetime Money Plan* (New York: Simon and Schuster, 2005), p. 26.

8. Stephen Miller, "Income Subject to FICA Payroll Tax Increases in 2015," Society for Human Resource Management, October 23, 2014, accessed January 16, 2015, http://www.shrm.org/hrdisciplines/compensation/articles/pages/fica-social-security-tax-2015.aspx.

9. US Census Bureau, "Historical Poverty Tables—People," table 3, "Poverty Status, by Age, Race, and Hispanic Origin: 1959 to 2013," accessed December 1, 2014, https://www.census.gov/hhes/www/poverty/data/historical/people.html.

10. Ke Bin Wu, "Sources of Income for Older Americans, 2012" (Washington, DC: AARP Public Policy Institute, December 2013), p. 4.

11. Ibid., p. 1.

12. See chapter 4, n. 10.

13. Robert J. Shiller, "Life-Cycle Personal Accounts Proposal for Social Security: An Evaluation of President Bush's Proposal," *Journal of Policy Modeling* 28, no. 4 (2006): 428.

14. Ibid., pp. 428–29.

15. Ibid. Simulation results are reported in table 2, p. 438 and following.

16. Congressional Budget Office, "Long Term Analysis of a Budget Proposal by Chairman Ryan," April 5, 2011, pp. 2–4, accessed December 1, 2014, http://www.cbo.gov/publication/22085. The Ryan Plan would also give Medicaid as block grants to states. Budget balance is achieved not only by the reduced spending on Medicare and Medicaid, but also by an increase in government revenues for unspecified reasons. It was unclear what changes in policy would cause this rather large revenue increase. On this last point, see Paul Krugman, "What's in the Ryan Plan?" *New York Times*, August 16, 2012; and "The Path to Prosperity," *Wikipedia*, accessed December 15, 2014, http://en.wikipedia.org/wiki/The_Path_to_Prosperity.

17. Fiscal year 2013 budget (continuing resolution) was $1,417,514 thousand. US Securities and Exchange Commission, *FY 2014 Congressional Budget Justification*, p. 16, http://www.sec.gov/about/reports/secfy14congbudgjust.pdf. Budget Request Tables: "FY 2014 Budget Request by Strategic Goal and

Program." In January 2013, the assets under management were estimated at $49.6 trillion (p. 93).

18. Halah Touryalai, "10 Wall Street Expenses That Make the SEC's Budget Look Pathetic," *Forbes,* February 17, 2011, accessed January 16, 2015, http://www.forbes.com/fdc/welcome_mjx.shtml. The same can be said of Citigroup's expenditures for marketing and advertising: larger than the whole SEC budget.

19. Vanguard, "See the Difference Low-Cost Mutual Funds Can Make," accessed January 7, 2015, https://investor.vanguard.com/mutual-funds/low-cost.

20. Edward Wyatt, "Judge Blocks Citigroup Settlement With S.E.C.," *New York Times,* November 28, 2011, accessed June 10, 2015, http://www.nytimes.com/2011/11/29/business/judge-rejects-sec-accord-with-citi.html?pagewanted=all.

21. Jed S. Rakoff, "The Financial Crisis: Why Have No High-Level Executives Been Prosecuted?" *New York Review of Books,* January 9, 2014.

22. Harry Markopolos, *No One Would Listen: A True Financial Thriller* (Hoboken, NJ: Wiley, 2010), Kindle location 587.

23. That involved cutting off losses by the purchase of (put) options (which allowed him to sell stocks when their price fell below the "strike price"); paying for those puts with the sale of (call) options (which allowed their purchasers to buy stocks from him when the price went above the "strike price").

24. Markopolos, *No One Would Listen,* Kindle locations 850–52.

25. David Kotz, *Investigation of Failure of the SEC to Uncover Bernard Madoff's Ponzi Scheme,* Report of Investigation Case No. OIG-509, United States Securities and Exchange Commission, Office of Inspector General (2011), pp. 61–77, accessed May 29, 2015, https://www.sec.gov/news/studies/2009/oig-509.pdf.

26. James B. Stewart, "How They Failed to Catch Madoff," *Fortune,* May 10, 2011. Accessed May 2, 2015. http://fortune.com/2011/05/10/how-they-failed-to-catch-madoff/.

27. Kotz, *Investigation of Failure of the SEC to Uncover Bernard Madoff's Ponzi Scheme,* p. 249.

28. Ibid., p. 247.

29. Ibid., p. 250. Markopolos gives a graphic account of the conversation from his perspective: *No One Would Listen,* Kindle location 2585 and following. See also Suh's testimony on this subject: Kotz, *Investigation of Failure of the SEC to Uncover Bernard Madoff's Ponzi Scheme,* p. 251.

30. Lorena Mongelli, "The SEC Watchdog Who Missed Madoff," *New York Post,* January 7, 2009.

31. Jeffrey Toobin, "Annals of Law: Money Unlimited: How Chief Justice John Roberts Orchestrated the Citizens United Decision," *New Yorker,* May 21, 2012.

32. Cornell University Law School, Legal Information Institute, "Citizens United v. Federal Election Commission (08-205)," accessed January 16, 2015, http://www.law.cornell.edu/supct/cert/08-205. See also Toobin, "Annals of Law."

33. Toobin, "Annals of Law"; Oyez, "Citizens United v. Federal Election Commission," accessed March 18, 2005, http://www.oyez.org/cases/2000-2009/2008/2008_08_205.

34. Citizens United v. Federal Election Comm'n, 130 S. Ct. 876, 558 U.S. 310, 175 L. Ed. 2d 753 (2010).

35. Ibid.

36. Legal Institute, "Citizens United v. Federal Election Comm'n (No. 08-205)," accessed June 10, 2015, https://www.law.cornell.edu/supct/html/08-205.ZX.html.

37. Ibid.

38. Lawrence Lessig, *Republic Lost: How Money Corrupts Congress—And a Plan to Stop It* (New York: Hachette Book Group, 2011), p. 266.

39. Ibid., p. 268.

Afterword: The Significance of Phishing Equilibrium

1. Of course there are also quite a few who have not accepted this "conventional wisdom." In this regard, two great classics are Thorstein Veblen, *The Theory of the Leisure Class: An Economic Study of the Evolution of Institutions* (New York: Macmillan, 1899), and John Kenneth Galbraith, *The Affluent Society* (Boston: Houghton Mifflin, 1958). Much more recently, in two companion articles, Jon Hanson and Douglas Kysar have documented how departures from economic rationality (especially as depicted in behavioral economics) are an invitation to "manipulation." They develop the implications for the law and describe the implications for the tobacco industry in special detail. Hanson and Kysar, "Taking Behavioralism Seriously: The Problem of Market Manipulation," *New York University Law Review* 74, no. 3 (June 1999): 630–749, and "Taking Behavioralism Seriously: Some Evidence of Market Manipulation," *Harvard Law Review* 112, no. 7 (May 1999): 1420–1572.

2. A list of people who appear to have predicted the 2008 financial crisis is in Dirk J. Bezemer, "'No One Saw This Coming': Understanding Financial Crisis through Accounting Models," *Munich Personal RePEc Archive Paper* 15892 (June 2009): 9, table 1, http://mpra.ub.uni-muenchen.de/15892/1/MPRA_paper_15892.pdf. Unfortunately, it is difficult to judge verbal and imprecise predictions, and the predictions varied widely in terms of reasons given and suggested time frames for the crisis. One of us wrote in 2005: "The bad outcome could be that eventual declines [in the postboom stock market and housing market] would result in a substantial increase in the rate of personal bankruptcies, which could lead to a secondary string of bankruptcies of financial institutions as well. Another long-run consequence could be a decline in consumer and business confidence, and another, possibly worldwide, recession." (p. xiii) "Also part of a boom is activity expressly designed to deceive people, deliberate attempts by many people to exploit thinking errors among general investors. Doing this effectively often requires breaking the law. But, given the slowness of our justice process, the perpetrators of such schemes may be able to get away with deception for many years. This

too is part of the process of a speculative bubble." (p. 76) Robert J. Shiller, *Irrational Exuberance,* 2nd ed. (Princeton: Princeton University Press, 2005).

3. Google Scholar no longer allows a division by field. But we were able to tabulate the number of articles that contained either the word "economics" or "finance." That was 2,270,000 on December 15, 2014, at 12:22 PM Eastern Standard Time. Of course among them there must be a lot of duplicates. This corresponds to the type of numbers George remembers when Google Scholar let one choose one's field of inquiry as economics and finance.

4. Siddhartha Mukherjee, *The Emperor of All Maladies: A Biography of Cancer* (New York: Simon and Schuster, 2011).

5. Quotation is from President Richard M. Nixon, "Remarks on Signing of the National Cancer Act of 1971," December 23, 1971, The American Presidency Project, accessed January 17, 2015, http://www.presidency.ucsb.edu/ws/?pid=3275.

6. Mukherjee, *Emperor of All Maladies,* pp. 173–77.

7. Stefano DellaVigna and Ulrike Malmendier, "Contract Design and Self-Control: Theory and Evidence," *Quarterly Journal of Economics* 119, no. 2 (May 2004), p. 354.

8. Xavier Gabaix and David Laibson, "Shrouded Attributes, Consumer Myopia, and Information Suppression in Competitive Markets," *Quarterly Journal of Economics* 121, no. 2 (May 2006): 505–40.

9. Robert E. Hall, "The Inkjet Aftermarket: An Economic Analysis" (prepared on behalf of Nu-kote International, Stanford University, August 8, 1997), p. 2. This fraction is the approximate ratio of the sales of ink cartridges to the sales of new printers.

10. Gabaix and Laibson, "Shrouded Attributes, Consumer Myopia, and Information Suppression in Competitive Markets," p. 506, citing Hall.

11. Hall, "The Inkjet Aftermarket," pp. 21–22; Gabaix and Laibson, "Shrouded Attributes, Consumer Myopia, and Information Suppression in Competitive Markets," p. 507.

12. A later paper by Gabaix and Laibson with Sumit Agarwal and John C. Driscoll examined people's differing financial abilities by age. Younger people, they found, have poor financial abilities: they are inexperienced. Older people have poor financial abilities: they are losing their competence. In between, there is the "age of reason." But that, of course, should not be the major takeaway of their paper. The major takeaway is that at all ages, although at some more than others, we can be prey to those who seek to take advantage of us. That is a general problem of competitive free markets, but, as they indicate, it is a special problem for older people. Agarwal, Driscoll, Gabaix, and Laibson, "The Age of Reason: Financial Decisions over the Life Cycle and Implications for Regulation," *Brookings Papers on Economic Activity* (Fall 2009): 51–101.

13. But, of course, if Lightning could speak, as the parent of every two-year-old well knows, the taste would no longer be shrouded.

14. See, for example, Robert J. Shiller, "Do Stock Prices Move Too Much to Be Justified by Subsequent Changes in Dividends?" *American Economic Review* 71, no. 3 (June 1981): 421–36; and John Y. Campbell and Robert J.

Shiller, "Cointegration and Tests of Present Value Models," *Journal of Political Economy* 95, no. 5 (October 1987): 1062–88.

15. J. Bradford De Long, Andrei Shleifer, Lawrence H. Summers, and Robert J. Waldmann, "Noise Trader Risk in Financial Markets," *Journal of Political Economy* 98, no. 4 (August 1990): 703–38.

16. In other versions of two-types-of-people-finance, uninformed traders are replaced by those who have an occasional urgent, unforeseen need for liquidity, which forces them to sell their stocks irrespective of the expected future returns. This solves the problem for those finance economists who cannot bring themselves to conceive that there may be uninformed or, worse, even irrational traders.

17. See De Long, Shleifer, Summers, and Waldmann, "Noise Trader Risk in Financial Markets."

18. See formulas 21 and 25 in J. Bradford De Long, Andrei Shleifer, Lawrence H. Summers, and Robert J. Waldmann, "The Size and Incidence of the Losses from Noise Trading," *Journal of Finance* 44, no. 3 (1989): 688 and 690.

19. Gabaix and Laibson, "Shrouded Attributes, Consumer Myopia, and Information Suppression in Competitive Markets," p. 514.

20. Paul Samuelson, the MIT professor who wrote the leading textbook and set the tone of most standard economics in the post–World War II period, viewed "revealed preferences" as being at the heart of the theory of consumption. Regarding a formula derived from them, he wrote: "The importance of this result can hardly be overemphasized [sic]. In this simple formula are contained almost all of the meaningful empirical implications of the whole pure theory of consumer's choice." Samuelson, *Foundations of Economic Analysis* (Cambridge, MA: Harvard University Press, 1947), p. 111. See also the journal article on which this assertion is based: Samuelson, "Consumption Theory in Terms of Revealed Preference," *Economica*, n.s., 15, no. 60 (November 1948): 243–53. Of course, it is consumers' monkey-on-the-shoulder tastes that are being "revealed."

"200 West Street." *Wikipedia.* Accessed October 22, 2014. http://en.wikipedia
.org/wiki/200_West_Street.

Abramson, John. *Overdosed America: The Broken Promise of American Medicine.* 3rd ed. New York: Harper Perennial, 2008.

Adrian, Tobias, and Hyun Song Shin. "Liquidity and Leverage." *Journal of
Financial Intermediation* 19, no. 3 (July 2010): 418–37.

Agarwal, Sumit, John C. Driscoll, Xavier Gabaix, and David Laibson. "The
Age of Reason: Financial Decisions over the Life Cycle and Implications
for Regulation." *Brookings Papers on Economic Activity* (Fall 2009): 51–101.

Akerlof, George A., and Rachel E. Kranton. "Economics and Identity." *Quarterly Journal of Economics* 115, no. 3 (August 2000): 715–53.

———. *Identity Economics: How Our Identities Shape Our Work, Wages, and
Well-Being.* Princeton: Princeton University Press, 2010.

Akerlof, George A., and Paul M. Romer. "Looting: The Economic Underworld of Bankruptcy for Profit." *Brookings Papers on Economic Activity* 2
(1993): 1–73.

Akerlof, George A., and Robert J. Shiller. *Animal Spirits: How Human Psychology Drives the Economy, and Why It Matters for Global Capitalism.* Princeton: Princeton University Press, 2009.

Alessi, Christopher, Roya Wolverson, and Mohammed Aly Sergie. "The
Credit Rating Controversy." Council on Foreign Relations, Backgrounder.
Updated October 22, 2013. Accessed November 8, 2014. http://www.cfr
.org/financial-crises/credit-rating-controversy/p22328.

Alexander, Raquel Meyer, Stephen W. Mazza, and Susan Scholz. "Measuring
Rates of Return for Lobbying Expenditures: An Empirical Case Study of
Tax Breaks for Multinational Corporations." *Journal of Law and Politics*
25, no. 401 (2009): 401–57.

American National Standards Institute. "About ANSI" and "ANSI: Historical
Overview." Accessed March 14, 2015. http://www.ansi.org/about_ansi/
overview/overview.aspx?menuid=1 and http://www.ansi.org/about_ansi/
introduction/history.aspx?menuid=1.

American Psychological Association. *Stress in America: Paying with Our Health.*
February 4, 2015. Last accessed March 29, 2015. http://www.apa.org/
news/press/releases/stress/2014/stress-report.pdf.

Anders, George, and Constance Mitchell. "Junk King's Legacy: Milken Sales
Pitch on High-Yield Bonds Is Contradicted by Data." *Wall Street Journal,*
November 20, 1990.

Annear, Steve. "The 'Pavlov Poke' Shocks People Who Spend Too Much Time on Facebook: It's Meant to Condition Social Media 'Addicts' to Step Away from the Screen and Enjoy the Real World." *Boston Daily,* August 23, 2013. Accessed November 26, 2014. http://www .bostonmagazine.com/news/blog/2013/08/23/pavlov-poke-shocks-people -who-spend-too-much-time-on-facebook/.

Ansolabehere, Stephen, John M. de Figueiredo, and James M. Snyder. "Why Is There So Little Money in U.S. Politics?" *Journal of Economic Perspectives* 17, no. 1 (Winter 2003): 105–30.

Arrow, Kenneth J., and Gerard Debreu. "Existence of an Equilibrium for a Competitive Economy." *Econometrica* 22, no. 3 (July 1954): 265–90.

Arthur, Anthony. *Radical Innocent: Upton Sinclair.* New York: Random House, 2006. Kindle.

Asquith, Paul, David W. Mullins Jr., and Eric D. Wolff. "Original Issue High Yield Bonds: Aging Analyses of Defaults, Exchanges and Calls." *Journal of Finance* 44, no. 4 (1989): 923–52.

Associated Press. "Timeline of United Airlines' Bankruptcy." *USA Today,* February 1, 2006. Accessed November 9, 2014. http://usatoday30.usatoday .com/travel/flights/2006-02-01-united-timeline_x.htm.

Auerbach, Oscar, et al. "Changes in the Bronchial Epithelium in Relation to Smoking and Cancer of the Lung: A Report of Progress." *New England Journal of Medicine* 256, no. 3 (January 17, 1957): 97–104.

Austen, Jane. *Pride and Prejudice.* New York: Modern Library, 1995.

Ayres, Ian. "Fair Driving: Gender and Race Discrimination in Retail Car Negotiations." *Harvard Law Review* 104, no. 4 (February 1991): 817–72.

Ayres, Ian, and Peter Siegelman. "Race and Gender Discrimination in Bargaining for a New Car." *American Economic Review* 85, no. 3 (June 1995): 304–21.

Babies "R" Us. "Baby Registry: Personal Registry Advisor." Accessed March 20, 2015. http://www.toysrus.com/shop/index.jsp?categoryId=11949069.

Baer, Justin, Chad Bray, and Jean Eaglesham. "'Fab' Trader Liable in Fraud: Jury Finds Ex-Goldman Employee Tourre Misled Investors in Mortgage Security." *Wall Street Journal,* August 2, 2013. Accessed March 15, 2015. http://www.wsj.com/articles/SB10001424127887323681904578641843284 450004.

Ball, Laurence, João Tovar Jalles, and Prakash Loungani. "Do Forecasters Believe in Okun's Law? An Assessment of Unemployment and Output Forecasts." *IMF Working Paper* 14/24 (February 2014).

Bardi, Jason. "Cigarette Pack Health Warning Labels in US Lag behind World: Internal Tobacco Company Documents Reveal Multinational Effort to Block Strong Warnings to Smokers." University of California at San Francisco, November 16, 2012. Accessed December 8, 2014. http://www.ucsf.edu/news/2012/11/13151/cigarette-pack-health-warning -labels-us-lag-behind-world.

Barenstein, Matias F. "Credit Cards and Consumption: An Urge to Splurge?" In "Essays on Household Consumption." PhD diss., University of California, Berkeley, 2004.

Bar-Gill, Oren, and Elizabeth Warren. "Making Credit Safer." *University of Pennsylvania Law Review* 157, no. 1 (November 2008): 1–101.

Barr, Donald R., and E. Todd Sherrill. "Mean and Variance of Truncated Normal Distributions." *American Statistician* 53, no. 4 (November 1999): 357–61.

Bauer-Ramazani, Christine. BU113: Critical Thinking and Communication in Business, "Major U.S. Regulatory Agencies." Accessed March 15, 2015. http://academics.smcvt.edu/cbauer-ramazani/BU113/fed_agencies.htm.

Bekelman, Justin E., Yan Li, and Cary P. Gross. "Scope and Impact of Financial Conflicts of Interest in Biomedical Research: A Systematic Review." *Journal of the American Medical Association* 289, no. 4 (January 22, 2003): 454–65.

Beral, Valerie, Emily Banks, Gillian Reeves, and Diana Bull, on behalf of the Million Women Study Collaborators. "Breast Cancer and Hormone-Replacement Therapy in the Million Women Study." *Lancet* 362, no. 9382 (August 9, 2003): 419–27.

Bernhardt, Joshua. *The Interstate Commerce Commission: Its History, Activities and Organization.* Baltimore: Johns Hopkins University Press, 1923.

Bernheim, B. Douglas, and Antonio Rangel. "Addiction and Cue-Triggered Decision Processes." *American Economic Review* 94, no. 5 (December 2004): 1558–90.

Bernstein, Marver H. *Regulating Business by Independent Commission.* Princeton: Princeton University Press, 1955.

Berry, Tim. "On Average, How Much Do Stores Mark Up Products?" December 2, 2008. Accessed October 23, 2014. http://www.entrepreneur.com/answer/221767.

Bertrand, Marianne, Matilde Bombardini, and Francesco Trebbi. "Is It Whom You Know or What You Know? An Empirical Assessment of the Lobbying Process." *American Economic Review* 104, no. 12 (December 2014): 3885–3920.

Bezemer, Dirk J. "'No One Saw This Coming': Understanding Financial Crisis through Accounting Models." *Munich Personal RePEc Archive Paper* 15892 (June 2009). http://mpra.ub.uni-muenchen.de/15892/1/MPRA_paper_15892.pdf.

Black, Duncan. "On the Rationale of Group Decision-making." *Journal of Political Economy* 56, no. 1 (February 1948): 23–34.

Blanes i Vidal, Jordi, Mirko Draca, and Christian Fons-Rosen. "Revolving Door Lobbyists." *American Economic Review* 102, no. 7 (December 2012): 3731–48.

Blinder, Alan S. *After the Music Stopped: The Financial Crisis, the Response, and the Work Ahead.* New York: Penguin Press, 2013.

Block, Jerald. "Issues for DSM-V: Internet Addiction." *American Journal of Psychiatry* 165, no. 3 (2008): 306–7.

Bloomberg News. "Cuomo Announces Reform Agreements with 3 Credit Rating Agencies." June 2, 2008. http://www.bloomberg.com/apps/news?pid=newsarchive&sid=a1N1TUVbL2bQ.

———. "United Airlines Financial Plan Gains Approval from Creditors." *New York Times,* December 31, 2005.

Board of Governors of the Federal Reserve. Current Release, Consumer Credit, table G-19, for August 2014, released on October 7, 2014. Accessed November 5, 2014. http://www.federalreserve.gov/releases/g19/current/.

Boccara, Bruno. *Socio-Analytic Dialogue: Incorporating Psychosocial Dynamics into Public Policies.* Lanham, MD: Lexington Books, 2014.

Bokhari, Sheharyar, Walter Torous, and William Wheaton. "Why Did Household Mortgage Leverage Rise from the Mid-1980s until the Great Recession?" Massachusetts Institute of Technology, Center for Real Estate, January 2013. Last accessed May 12, 2015. http://citeseerx.ist.psu.edu/viewdoc/download?doi=10.1.1.269.5704&rep=rep1&type=pdf.

Bombardier, Claire, et al. "Comparison of Upper Gastrointestinal Toxicity of Rofecoxib and Naproxen in Patients with Rheumatoid Arthritis." *New England Journal of Medicine* 343, no. 21 (November 23, 2000): 1520–28.

Bosworth, Steven, Tania Singer, and Dennis J. Snower. "Cooperation, Motivation and Social Balance." Paper presented at the American Economic Association Meeting, Boston, January 3, 2015.

Bounds, Gwendolyn. "Meet the Sticklers: New Demands Test Consumer Reports." *Wall Street Journal,* May 5, 2010. Accessed March 14, 2015. http://www.wsj.com/articles/SB10001424052748703866704575224093017379202#mod=todays_us_personal_journal.

Boyd, Roddy. *Fatal Risk: A Cautionary Tale of AIG's Corporate Suicide.* Hoboken, NJ: Wiley, 2011.

Brandt, Allan M. *The Cigarette Century: The Rise, Fall, and Deadly Persistence of the Product That Defined America.* New York: Basic Books, 2007.

"BRIDES Reveals Trends of Engaged American Couples with American Wedding Study." July 10, 2014. Accessed December 1, 2014. http://www.marketwired.com/press-release/brides-reveals-trends-of-engaged-american-couples-with-american-wedding-study-1928460.htm.

Brown, Steve. "Office Market Outlook: Dallas." *National Real Estate Investor News,* June 1982, p. 46.

———. "City Review: Dallas." *National Real Estate Investor News,* October 1983, p. 127.

———. "City Review: Dallas." *National Real Estate Investor News,* October 1984, pp. 183, 192.

———. "City Review: Dallas." *National Real Estate Investor News,* June 1985, pp. 98–100.

Bruck, Connie. *The Predators' Ball: The Inside Story of Drexel Burnham and the Rise of the Junk Bond Raiders.* New York: Penguin Books, 1989.

Bruner, Jerome. *Acts of Meaning: Four Lectures on Mind and Culture.* Cambridge, MA: Harvard University Press, 1990.

Bureau of Economic Analysis. "Mortgage Interest Paid, Owner- and Tenant-Occupied Residential Housing." Accessed October 29, 2014. https://www.google.com/#q=BEA+mortgage+interest+payments+2010.

———. "National Income and Product Accounts." Table 2.3.5, "Personal Consumption Expenditures by Major Type of Product." Accessed November 15, 2014. http://www.bea.gov/iTable/iTable.cfm?ReqID=9&step=1#reqid=9&step=3&isuri=1&904=2010&903=65&906=a&905=2011&910=x&911=0.

Burrough, Bryan. "RJR Nabisco: An Epilogue." *New York Times,* March 12, 1999. http://www.nytimes.com/1999/03/12/opinion/rjr-nabisco-an -epilogue.html.

Burrough, Bryan, and John Helyar. *Barbarians at the Gate: The Fall of RJR Nabisco.* New York: Random House, 2010. Kindle.

Butler, Jeffrey Vincent. "Status and Confidence." In "Essays on Identity and Economics." PhD diss., University of California, Berkeley, 2008.

Calomiris, Charles W. "The Subprime Crisis: What's Old, What's New, and What's Next." Paper prepared for the Federal Reserve Bank of St. Louis Economic Symposium, "Maintaining Stability in a Changing Financial System," Jackson Hole, WY, August 2008.

Campbell, John Y., and Robert J. Shiller. "Cointegration and Tests of Present Value Models." *Journal of Political Economy* 95, no. 5 (October 1987): 1062–88.

Carbone, Danielle. "The Impact of the Dodd-Frank Act's Credit-Rating Agency Reform on Public Companies." *Corporate and Securities Law Advisor* 24, no. 9 (September 2010): 1–7. http://www.shearman.com/ ~/media/Files/NewsInsights/Publications/2010/09/The-Impact-of-the -DoddFrank-Acts-Credit-Rating-A__/Files/View-full-article-The-Impact -of-the-DoddFrank-Ac__/FileAttachment/CM022211InsightsCarbone.pdf.

Cardozo, Benjamin N. "The Altruist in Politics." Commencement address, Columbia University, 1889. https://www.gutenberg.org/files/1341/1341-h/ 1341-h.htm.

Carpenter, Daniel, and David A. Moss, eds. *Preventing Regulatory Capture: Special Interest Influence and How to Limit It.* New York: Cambridge University Press/The Tobin Project, 2014.

Center for Responsive Politics. "Lobbying: Top Industries." Last accessed April 30, 2015. https://www.opensecrets.org/lobby/top.php?showYear=1998 &indexType=i.

———. "Lobbying Database." Accessed December 1, 2014. https://www .opensecrets.org/lobby/.

———. "Sen. Chuck Grassley." Accessed November 16, 2014. http://www .opensecrets.org/politicians/summary.php?cycle=2004&type=I&cid=n00 001758&newMem=N.

Center for Science in the Public Interest. "Alcohol Policies Project Fact Sheet: Federal Alcohol Tax Basics." Accessed December 13, 2014. http:// www.cspinet.org/booze/taxguide/Excisetaxbasics.pdf.

Centers for Disease Control and Prevention. "Cigarette Smoking in the United States: Current Cigarette Smoking among U.S. Adults 18 Years and Older." Accessed March 28, 2015. http://www.cdc .gov/tobacco/campaign/tips/resources/data/cigarette-smoking-in-united -states.html.

———. *Health, United States, 2013: With Special Feature on Prescription Drugs.* Accessed December 1, 2014. http://www.cdc.gov/nchs/data/hus/hus13 .pdf.

———. "Smoking and Tobacco Use: Fast Facts." Accessed December 9, 2014. http://www.cdc.gov/tobacco/data_statistics/fact_sheets/fast_facts/.

Centers for Disease Control and Prevention. "Smoking and Tobacco Use: Tobacco-Related Mortality." Accessed March 28, 2015. http://www.cdc.gov/tobacco/data_statistics/fact_sheets/health_effects/tobacco_related_mortality/.

———. "Trends in Current Cigarette Smoking among High School Students and Adults, United States, 1965–2011." November 14, 2013. Accessed December 9, 2014. http://www.cdc.gov/tobacco/data_statistics/tables/trends/cig_smoking/.

Chase, Stuart, and Frederick J. Schlink. *Your Money's Worth: A Study of the Waste of the Consumer's Dollar.* New York: Macmillan, 1927.

Chen, M. Keith, Venkat Lakshminarayanan, and Laurie R. Santos. "How Basic Are Behavioral Biases? Evidence from Capuchin Monkey Trading Behavior." *Journal of Political Economy* 114, no. 3 (June 2006): 517–37.

Chu, Jenny, Jonathan Faasse, and P. Raghavendra Rau. "Do Compensation Consultants Enable Higher CEO Pay? New Evidence from Recent Disclosure Rule Changes." September 23, 2014. Accessed May 27, 2015. http://papers.ssrn.com/sol3/Papers.cfm?abstract_id=2500054.

Cialdini, Robert B. *Influence: The Psychology of Persuasion.* New York: HarperCollins, 2007.

"Cinnabon." *Wikipedia.* Accessed October 22, 2014. http://en.wikipedia.org/wiki/Cinnabon.

Cinnabon, Inc. "The Cinnabon Story." Accessed October 31, 2014. http://www.cinnabon.com/about-us.aspx.

Clarke, Sally H. "Unmanageable Risks: MacPherson v. Buick and the Emergence of a Mass Consumer Market." *Law and History Review* 23, no. 1 (2005): 1–52.

Clifford, Catherine, and Chris Isidore. "The Fall of IndyMac." Cable News Network, July 13, 2008. Accessed December 1, 2014. http://money.cnn.com/2008/07/12/news/companies/indymac_fdic/.

Coen Structured Advertising Expenditure Dataset. www.galbithink.org/cs-ad-dataset.xls.

Cohan, William D. *Money and Power: How Goldman Sachs Came to Rule the World.* New York: Doubleday, 2011.

Cole, Robert J. "Pantry Pride Revlon Bid Raised by $1.75 a Share." *New York Times,* October 19, 1985. Accessed March 17, 2015. http://www.nytimes.com/1985/10/19/business/pantry-pride-revlon-bid-raised-by-1.75-a-share.html.

Collier, Paul. "The Cultural Foundations of Economic Failure: A Conceptual Toolkit." Mimeo. Oxford University, February 2015.

Congressional Budget Office. "Long Term Analysis of a Budget Proposal by Chairman Ryan." April 5, 2011. Accessed December 1, 2014. http://www.cbo.gov/publication/22085.

Connaughton, Jeff. *The Payoff: Why Wall Street Always Wins.* Westport, CT: Prospecta Press, 2012. Kindle.

Consumer Federation of America. "Membership." Accessed March 14, 2015. http://www.consumerfed.org/about-cfa/membership.

Cook, Philip J. *Paying the Tab: The Costs and Benefits of Alcohol Control.* Princeton: Princeton University Press, 2007.

Cornell University Law School, Legal Information Institute. "Citizens United v. Federal Election Commission (08-205)." Accessed January 16, 2015. http://www.law.cornell.edu/supct/cert/08-205.

Council of Economic Advisors. *Economic Report of the President 2007.* Accessed December 1, 2014. http://www.gpo.gov/fdsys/pkg/ERP-2007/pdf/ERP-2007.pdf.

———. *Economic Report of the President 2013.* Accessed December 1, 2014. http://www.whitehouse.gov/sites/default/files/docs/erp2013/full_2013_economic_report_of_the_president.pdf.

Cowan, Alison Leigh. "F.D.I.C. Backs Deal by Milken." *New York Times,* March 10, 1992.

Crossley, Michele L. "Introducing Narrative Psychology." In *Narrative, Memory and Life Transitions,* edited by Christine Horrocks, Kate Milnes, Brian Roberts, and Dave Robinson, pp. 1–13. Huddersfield: University of Huddersfield Press, 2002.

Cruikshank, Jeffrey K., and Arthur W. Schultz. *The Man Who Sold America.* Boston: Harvard Business Review Press, 2010.

"A Crying Evil." *Los Angeles Times,* February 24, 1899.

Crystal, Graef S. *In Search of Excess: The Overcompensation of American Executives.* New York: W. W. Norton, 1991.

Curfman, Gregory D., Stephen Morrissey, and Jeffrey M. Drazen. "Expression of Concern: Bombardier et al., 'Comparison of Upper Gastrointestinal Toxicity of Rofecoxib and Naproxen in Patients with Rheumatoid Arthritis,' N Engl J Med 2000;343:1520–8." *New England Journal of Medicine* 353, no. 26 (December 29, 2005): 2813–14.

———. "Expression of Concern Reaffirmed." *New England Journal of Medicine* 354, no. 11 (March 16, 2006): 1190–93.

DealBook. "Goldman Settles with S.E.C. for $550 Million." *New York Times,* July 15, 2010.

De Figueiredo, John M., and Brian S. Silverman. "Academic Earmarks and the Returns to Lobbying." *Journal of Law and Economics* 49, no. 2 (2006): 597–625.

DeForge, Jeanette. "Ballot Question to Revoke Sales Tax on Alcohol Approved by Massachusetts Voters." *Republican,* November 3, 2010. Accessed December 13, 2014. http://www.masslive.com/news/index.ssf/2010/11/ballot_question_to_revoke_sale.html.

DellaVigna, Stefano, and Ulrike Malmendier. "Contract Design and Self-Control: Theory and Evidence." *Quarterly Journal of Economics* 119, no. 2 (May 2004): 353–402.

———. "Paying Not to Go to the Gym." *American Economic Review* 96, no. 3 (June 2006): 694–719.

De Long, J. Bradford, Andrei Shleifer, Lawrence H. Summers, and Robert J. Waldmann. "Noise Trader Risk in Financial Markets." *Journal of Political Economy* 98, no. 4 (August 1990): 703–38.

———. "The Size and Incidence of the Losses from Noise Trading." *Journal of Finance* 44, no. 3 (1989): 681–96.

Desmond, Matthew. "Eviction and the Reproduction of Urban Poverty." *American Journal of Sociology* 118, no. 1 (July 2012): 88–133.

Doll, Richard, and A. Bradford Hill. "Smoking and Carcinoma of the Lung: Preliminary Report." *British Medical Journal* 2, no. 4682 (September 30, 1950): 739–48.

Downs, Anthony. "An Economic Theory of Political Action in a Democracy." *Journal of Political Economy* 65, no. 2 (April 1957): 135–50.

"Drunk Driving Statistics." Accessed December 13, 2014. http://www.alcoholalert.com/drunk-driving-statistics.html.

Dubner, Stephen J., and Steven D. Levitt. "Keith Chen's Monkey Research." *New York Times,* June 5, 2005.

Duca, John V., John Muellbauer, and Anthony Murphy. "House Prices and Credit Constraints: Making Sense of the US Experience." *Economic Journal* 121 (May 2011): 533–51.

Eichenwald, Kurt. *A Conspiracy of Fools: A True Story.* New York: Random House, 2005.

———. "Wages Even Wall St. Can't Stomach." *New York Times,* April 3, 1989.

Ellis, Charles. *The Partnership: The Making of Goldman Sachs.* New York: Penguin Press, 2008.

Emergency Economic Stabilization Act of 2008, H.R. 1424. 110th US Congress. Accessed December 1, 2014. https://www.govtrack.us/congress/bills/110/hr1424/text.

Farrell, Greg. *Crash of the Titans: Greed, Hubris, the Fall of Merrill Lynch, and the Near-Collapse of Bank of America.* New York: Crown Business, 2010.

Farrell, Jason. "Return on Lobbying Overstated by Report." August 23, 2011. Accessed November 18, 2014. http://www.campaignfreedom.org/2011/08/23/return-on-lobbying-overstated-by-report/.

Feinberg, Richard A. "Credit Cards as Spending Facilitating Stimuli: A Conditioning Interpretation." *Journal of Consumer Research* 13, no. 3 (December 1986): 348–56.

Felsenfeld, Carl, and David L. Glass. *Banking Regulation in the United States.* 3rd ed. New York: Juris, 2011.

The Financial Crisis Inquiry Report: Final Report of the National Commission on the Causes of the Financial and Economic Crisis in the United States. Washington, DC: Government Printing Office, 2011. http://www.gpo.gov/fdsys/pkg/GPO-FCIC/pdf/GPO-FCIC.pdf.

FINRA Investor Education Foundation. *Financial Capability in the United States: Report of Findings from the 2012 National Financial Capability Study.* May 2013. Last accessed May 14, 2015. http://www.usfinancialcapability.org/downloads/NFCS_2012_Report_Natl_Findings.pdf.

FitzGerald, Garret A. "How Super Are the 'Super Aspirins'? New COX-2 Inhibitors May Elevate Cardiovascular Risk." University of Pennsylvania Health System Press Release, January 14, 1999.

Fowler, Mayhill. "Obama: No Surprise That Hard-Pressed Pennsylvanians Turn Bitter." *Huffington Post,* November 17, 2008, last accessed April 30, 2015, http://www.huffingtonpost.com/mayhill-fowler/obama-no-surprise-that-ha_b_96188.html.

Fox, Stephen R. *The Mirror Makers: A History of American Advertising and Its Creators.* Urbana: University of Illinois Press, 1984.

Frank, Robert H., and Ben Bernanke. *Principles of Macroeconomics.* New York: McGraw Hill, 2003.

Freifeld, Karen. "Fraud Claims Versus Goldman over Abacus CDO Are Dismissed." Reuters, May 14, 2013. Accessed March 15, 2015. http://www .reuters.com/article/2013/05/14/us-goldman-abacus-idUSBRE94D101201 30514.

Freudenheim, Milt. "Market Place: A Windfall from Shifts to Medicare." *New York Times,* July 18, 2006. Accessed November 4, 2014. http://www.nytimes .com/2006/07/18/business/18place.html?_r=1&pagewanted=print.

Friedman, Milton, and Rose D. Friedman. *Free to Choose: A Personal Statement.* New York: Harcourt Brace Jovanovich, 1980.

Fugh-Berman, Adriane. "Prescription Tracking and Public Health." *Journal of General Internal Medicine* 23, no. 8 (August 2008): 1277–80. Published online May 13, 2008. Accessed May 24, 2015. http://www.ncbi.nlm.nih .gov/pmc/articles/PMC2517975/.

"The Future of Money Market Funds." September 24, 2012. http://www .winthropcm.com/TheFutureofMoneyMarketFunds.pdf.

Gabaix, Xavier, and David Laibson. "Shrouded Attributes, Consumer Myopia, and Information Suppression in Competitive Markets." *Quarterly Journal of Economics* 121, no. 2 (May 2006): 505–40.

Galbraith, John Kenneth. *The Affluent Society.* Boston: Houghton Mifflin, 1958.

———. *The Great Crash.* 50th anniversary ed. New York: Houghton Mifflin, 1988. Kindle.

Gerardi, Kristopher, Andreas Lehnert, Shane M. Sherlund, and Paul Willen. "Making Sense of the Subprime Crisis." *Brookings Papers on Economic Activity* (Fall 2008): 69–139.

Gerson, Elliot. "To Make America Great Again, We Need to Leave the Country." *Atlantic Monthly,* July 10, 2012. Accessed May 22, 2015. http://www.theatlantic.com/national/archive/2012/07/to-make-america -great-again-we-need-to-leave-the-country/259653/.

Gilbert, R. Alton. "Requiem for Regulation Q: What It Did and Why It Passed Away." *Federal Reserve Bank of St. Louis Review* (February 1986): 22–37.

Glickman, Lawrence B. *Buying Power: A History of Consumer Activism in America.* Chicago: University of Chicago Press, 2009.

Goldacre, Ben. *Bad Pharma: How Drug Companies Mislead Doctors and Harm Patients.* New York: Faber and Faber/Farrar, Straus and Giroux, 2012.

Goldberger, Paul. "The Shadow Building: The House That Goldman Built." *New Yorker,* May 17, 2010. Accessed October 22, 2014. http://www .newyorker.com/magazine/2010/05/17/shadow-building.

Goldman Sachs. *Annual Report 2005.* Accessed December 6, 2014. http:// www.goldmansachs.com/investor-relations/financials/archived/annual -reports/2005-annual-report.html.

———. "Who We Are," "What We Do," and "Our Thinking." All accessed December 1, 2014. http://www.goldmansachs.com/index.html.

Graham, David J. Testimony for the Senate Finance Committee, November 18, 2004. http://www.finance.senate.gov/imo/media/doc/111804dgtest.pdf.

Graham, David J., D. Campen, R. Hui, M. Spence, and C. Cheetham. "Risk of Acute Myocardial Infarction and Sudden Cardiac Death in Patients Treated with Cyclo-oxygenase 2 Selective and Non-selective Non-steroidal Anti-inflammatory Drugs: Nested Case-Control Study." *Lancet* 365, no. 9458 (February 5–11, 2005): 475–81.

Grant, Bob. "Elsevier Published 6 Fake Journals." *The Scientist,* May 7, 2009. Accessed November 24, 2014. http://classic.the-scientist.com/blog/display/55679/.

Grant, Bridget F., et al. "The 12-Month Prevalence and Trends in DSM-IV Alcohol Abuse and Dependence: United States, 1991–1992 and 2001–2002." *Drug and Alcohol Dependence* 74, no. 3 (2004): 223–34.

Griffin, Keith. "Used Car Sales Figures from 2000 to 2014." Accessed December 1, 2014. http://usedcars.about.com/od/research/a/Used-Car-Sales-Figures-From-2000-To-2014.htm.

Grossman, Gene M., and Elhanan Helpman. *Special Interest Politics.* Cambridge, MA: MIT Press, 2001.

Grossman, Sanford J., and Oliver D. Hart. "Takeover Bids, the Free-Rider Problem, and the Theory of the Corporation." *Bell Journal of Economics* 11, no. 1 (1980): 42–64.

The Guardians, or Society for the Protection of Trade against Swindlers and Sharpers. London, 1776. https://library.villanova.edu/Find/Record/1027765.

Hahn, Robert W., Robert E. Litan, and Jesse Gurman. "Bringing More Competition to Real Estate Brokerage." *Real Estate Law Journal* 34 (Summer 2006): 86–118.

Hall, Robert E. "The Inkjet Aftermarket: An Economic Analysis." Prepared on behalf of Nu-kote International. Stanford University, August 8, 1997.

Han, Song, Benjamin Keys, and Geng Li. "Credit Supply to Bankruptcy Filers: Evidence from Credit Card Mailings." U.S. Federal Reserve Board, Finance and Economics Discussion Paper Series Paper No. 2011-29, 2011.

Hanson, Jon D., and Douglas A. Kysar. "Taking Behavioralism Seriously: Some Evidence of Market Manipulation." *Harvard Law Review* 112, no. 7 (May 1999): 1420–1572.

———. "Taking Behavioralism Seriously: The Problem of Market Manipulation." *New York University Law Review* 74, no. 3 (June 1999): 630–749.

Harper, Christine. "Goldman's Tourre E-Mail Describes 'Frankenstein' Derivatives." Bloomberg Business, April 25, 2010. Accessed March 15, 2015. http://www.bloomberg.com/news/articles/2010-04-24/-frankenstein-derivatives-described-in-e-mail-by-goldman-s-fabrice-tourre.

Harper, Sean. http://truecostofcredit.com/400926. Website now closed.

"Harry Reid." *Wikipedia.* Accessed December 1, 2014. http://en.wikipedia.org/wiki/Harry_Reid.

Healey, James R. "Government Sells Last of Its GM Shares." *USA Today,* December 10, 2013.

Healy, David. *Pharmageddon.* Berkeley: University of California Press, 2012.

Hennessey, Ray. "The 15 Ronald Reagan Quotes Every Business Leader Must Know." Accessed January 16, 2015. http://www.entrepreneur.com/article/234547.

Hickman, W. Braddock. *Corporate Bond Quality and Investor Experience.* Princeton: National Bureau of Economic Research and Princeton University Press, 1958.

Hindo, Brian, and Moira Herbst. "Personal Best Timeline, 1986: 'Greed Is Good.'" *BusinessWeek.* http://www.bloomberg.com/ss/06/08/personalbest _timeline/source/7.htm.

Hirschman, Elizabeth C. "Differences in Consumer Purchase Behavior by Credit Card Payment System." *Journal of Consumer Research* 6, no. 1 (June 1979): 58–66.

"History in Review: What Really Happened to the Shah of Iran." Accessed December 1, 2014. http://www.iransara.info/Iran%20what%20happened %20to%20Shah.htm.

Hochschild, Arlie Russell. *The Second Shift: Working Parents and the Revolution at Home.* New York: Viking, 1989.

Hoeflich, M. H. "Laidlaw v. Organ, Gulian C. Verplanck, and the Shaping of Early Nineteenth Century Contract Law: A Tale of a Case and a Commentary." *University of Illinois Law Review* (Winter 1991): 55–66.

Hofstadter, Richard. *The Age of Reform: From Bryan to FDR.* New York: Random House, 1955.

Hopkins, Claude. *My Life in Advertising and Scientific Advertising: Two Works by Claude C. Hopkins.* New York: McGraw Hill, 1997.

Horowitz, Joseph. *Dvořák in America: In Search of the New World.* Chicago: Cricket Books, 2003.

Huffman, David, and Matias Barenstein. "A Monthly Struggle for Self-Control? Hyperbolic Discounting, Mental Accounting, and the Fall in Consumption between Paydays." *Institute for the Study of Labor (IZA) Discussion Paper* 1430 (December 2005).

Interactive Advertising Bureau. *Internet Advertising Revenue Report: 2013 Full-Year Results.* Conducted by PricewaterhouseCoopers (PwC). Accessed March 7, 2015. http://www.iab.net/media/file/IAB_Internet_Advertising _Revenue_Report_FY_2013.pdf.

International Health, Racquet, and Sportsclub Association. "Industry Research." Accessed October 22, 2014. http://www.ihrsa.org/industry -research/.

International Monetary Fund. *World Economic Outlook,* April 2012. Accessed December 1, 2014. http://www.imf.org/external/pubs/ft/weo/2012/01/.

Investment Company Institute. "2014 Investment Company Fact Book: Data Tables." Accessed January 1, 2015. http://www.icifactbook.org/fb_ data.html.

Investopedia. "Definition of Capital." Accessed May 25, 2015. http://www .investopedia.com/terms/c/capital.asp.

Iowa Legislature. "Legislators." Accessed December 1, 2014. https://www .legis.iowa.gov/legislators/legislator/legislatorAllYears?personID=116.

Issenberg, Sasha. *The Victory Lab: The Secret Science of Winning Campaigns.* 1st paperback ed. New York: Crown/Random House, 2012.

Jensen, Michael C. "Takeovers: Their Causes and Consequences." *Journal of Economic Perspectives* 2, no. 1 (Winter 1988): 21–48.

Johnson, Simon, Rafael La Porta, Florencio López de Silanes, and Andrei Shleifer. "Tunneling." *American Economic Review* 90, no. 2 (May 2000): 22–27.

Joint Committee on Taxation. "Estimated Budget Effects of the Conference Agreement for H.R. 1836." May 26, 2001. Accessed December 1, 2014. https://www.jct.gov/publications.html?func=startdown&id=2001.

———. "Estimated Budget Effects of the Conference Agreement for H.R. 2, the 'Jobs and Growth Tax Relief Reconciliation Act of 2003.'" May 22, 2003. Accessed December 1, 2014. https://www.jct.gov/publications.html?func=startdown&id=1746.

Kaiser, Robert G. *So Damn Much Money: The Triumph of Lobbying and the Corrosion of American Government.* New York: Vintage Books/Random House, 2010.

Kansas Statutes Annotated (2009), chap. 34, "Grain and Forage," article 2, "Inspecting, Sampling, Storing, Weighing and Grading Grain; Terminal and Local Warehouses, 34-228: Warehouseman's License; Application; Financial Statement; Waiver; Qualifications; License Fee; Examination of Warehouse." Accessed May 1, 2015. http://law.justia.com/codes/kansas/2011/Chapter34/Article2/34-228.html.

Kaplan, Greg, Giovanni Violante, and Justin Weidner. "The Wealthy Hand-to-Mouth." *Brookings Papers on Economic Activity* (Spring 2014): 77–138.

Kelley, Florence. *Notes of Sixty Years: The Autobiography of Florence Kelley.* Edited by Kathryn Kish Sklar. Chicago: Illinois Labor History Society, 1986.

Kelly, Kate. *Street Fighters: The Last 72 Hours of Bear Stearns, the Toughest Firm on Wall Street.* New York: Penguin, 2009.

Kessler, Glen. "Revisiting the Cost of the Bush Tax Cuts." *Washington Post,* May 10, 2011. http://www.washingtonpost.com/blogs/fact-checker/post/revisiting-the-cost-of-the-bush-tax-cuts/2011/05/09/AFxTFtbG_blog.html.

Keynes, John Maynard. "Economic Possibilities for Our Grandchildren." In *Essays in Persuasion,* pp. 358–73. London: Macmillan, 1931.

———. *The General Theory of Employment, Interest and Money.* New York: Harcourt Brace Jovanovich, 1964.

Knowledge@Wharton. "Goldman Sachs and Abacus 2007-AC1: A Look beyond the Numbers." April 28, 2010. Accessed March 15, 2015. http://knowledge.wharton.upenn.edu/article/goldman-sachs-and-abacus-2007-ac1-a-look-beyond-the-numbers/.

Kornbluth, Jesse. *Highly Confident: The Crime and Punishment of Michael Milken.* New York: William Morrow, 1992.

Kotler, Philip, and Gary Armstrong. *Principles of Marketing.* 14th ed. Upper Saddle River, NJ: Prentice Hall, 2010.

Kotz, David. *Investigation of Failure of the SEC to Uncover Bernard Madoff's Ponzi Scheme.* Report of Investigation Case No. OIG-509. US Securities and Exchange Commission, Office of Inspector General. 2011. Accessed May 29, 2015. https://www.sec.gov/news/studies/2009/oig-509.pdf.

Krasnova, Hanna, Helena Wenninger, Thomas Widjaja, and Peter Buxmann. "Envy on Facebook: A Hidden Threat to Users' Life Satisfaction?"

Wirtschaftsinformatik Proceedings 2013. Paper 92. http://aisel.aisnet.org/wi2013/92.

Krugman, Paul. "What's in the Ryan Plan?" *New York Times,* August 16, 2012.

Krugman, Paul, and Robin Wells. *Microeconomics.* 2nd ed. New York: Worth Publishers, 2009.

Lakshminarayanan, Venkat, M. Keith Chen, and Laurie R. Santos. "Endowment Effect in Capuchin Monkeys." *Philosophical Transactions of the Royal Society B: Biological Sciences* 363, no. 1511 (December 2008): 3837–44.

Lattman, Peter. "To Perelman's Failed Revlon Deal, Add Rebuke from S.E.C." *New York Times Dealbook,* June 13, 2013. Accessed December 1, 2014. http://dealbook.nytimes.com/2013/06/13/s-e-c-charges-and-fines-revlon-for-misleading-shareholders/?_php=true&_type=blogs&_r=0.

LawInfo. "Legal Resource Library: What Is the U.C.C.?" Accessed March 15, 2015. http://resources.lawinfo.com/business-law/uniform-commercial-code/does-article-2-treat-merchants-the-same-as-no.html.

Legal Institute. "Citizens United v. Federal Election Comm'n (No. 08-205)." Accessed June 10, 2015. https://www.law.cornell.edu/supct/html/08-205.ZX.html.

Lemann, Nicholas. *The Big Test: The Secret History of the American Meritocracy.* 1st rev. paperback ed. New York: Farrar, Straus and Giroux, 2000.

Lemelson Center. "Edison Invents!" Copy in authors' files. Originally available at http://invention.smithsonian.org/centerpieces/edison/000_story_02.asp.

Lessig, Lawrence. *Republic Lost: How Money Corrupts Congress—And a Plan to Stop It.* New York: Hachette Book Group, 2011.

Leuchtenburg, William E. *Franklin D. Roosevelt and the New Deal.* New York: Harper and Row, 1963.

Lewis, Michael. *The Big Short: Inside the Doomsday Machine.* New York: W. W. Norton, 2010.

———. *Boomerang: Travels in the New Third World.* New York: W. W. Norton, 2011.

Lexchin, Joel, Lisa A. Bero, Benjamin Djulbegovic, and Otavio Clark. "Pharmaceutical Industry Sponsorship and Research Outcome and Quality: Systematic Review." *British Medical Journal* 326, no. 7400 (May 31, 2003): 1167–70.

Lieber, Ron, and Andrew Martin. "Overspending on Debit Cards Is a Boon for Banks." *New York Times,* September 8, 2009. Accessed May 2, 2015. http://www.nytimes.com/2009/09/09/your-money/credit-and-debit-cards/09debit.html?pagewanted=all&_r=0.

Linkins, Jason. "Wall Street Cash Rules Everything around the House Financial Services Committee, Apparently." *Huffington Post,* July 22, 2013. Accessed May 22, 2015. http://www.huffingtonpost.com/2013/07/22/wall-street-lobbyists_n_3635759.html.

"Little, Clarence Cook, Sc.D. (CTR Scientific Director, 1954–1971)." Accessed November 28, 2014. http://tobaccodocuments.org/profiles/little_clarence_cook.html.

Locke, John. *An Essay Concerning Human Understanding.* 30th edition. London: William Tegg, 1849.

Lupia, Arthur. "Busy Voters, Agenda Control, and the Power of Information." *American Political Science Review* 86, no. 2 (June 1992): 390–403.

Lusardi, Annamaria, Daniel Schneider, and Peter Tufano. "Financially Fragile Households: Evidence and Implications." *Brookings Papers on Economic Activity* (Spring 2011): 83–150.

Maddison, Angus. "Historical Statistics of the World Economy: Per Capita GDP." Accessed November 26, 2014. http://www.google.com/url?sa=t&rct=j&q=&esrc=s&source=web&cd=6&ved=0CEIQFjAF&url=http%3A%2F%2Fwww.ggdc.net%2Fmaddison%2FHistorical_Statistics%2Fhorizontal-file_02-2010.xls&ei=4t11VJfsG4uZNoG9gGA&usg=AFQjCNFFKKZiUysTOutlY4NsZF9qwdu2Hg&bvm=bv.80642063,d.eXY.

———. "US Real Per Capita GDP from 1870–2001." September 24, 2012. Accessed December 1, 2014. http://socialdemocracy21stcentury.blogspot.com/2012/09/us-real-per-capita-gdp-from-18702001.html.

"Making Purchases with Credit Cards—The Best Credit Cards to Use." August 26, 2014. Accessed November 14, 2014. http://www.creditinfocenter.com/cards/crcd_buy.shtml#Question6.

Malamud, Bernard. "Nevada Gaming Tax: Estimating Resident Burden and Incidence." University of Nevada, Las Vegas, April 2006. Last accessed May 5, 2015. https://faculty.unlv.edu/bmalamud/estimating.gaming.burden.incidence.doc.

Mankiw, N. Gregory. *Principles of Economics.* New York: Harcourt, Brace, 1998.

Markopolos, Harry. *No One Would Listen: A True Financial Thriller.* Hoboken, NJ: Wiley, 2010. Kindle.

Mateyka, Peter, and Matthew Marlay. "Residential Duration by Race and Ethnicity: 2009." Paper presented at the Annual Meeting of the American Sociological Association, Las Vegas, 2011.

Maynard, Micheline. "United Air Wins Right to Default on Its Employee Pension Plans." *New York Times,* May 11, 2005.

McCubbins, Mathew D., and Arthur Lupia. *The Democratic Dilemma: Can Citizens Learn What They Really Need to Know?* New York: Cambridge University Press, 1998.

McDonald, Lawrence G., with Patrick Robinson. *A Colossal Failure of Common Sense: The Inside Story of the Collapse of Lehman Brothers.* New York: Crown Business, 2009.

McFadden, Robert D. "Charles Keating, 90, Key Figure in '80s Savings and Loan Crisis, Dies." *New York Times,* April 2, 2014. Accessed May 27, 2015. http://www.nytimes.com/2014/04/02/business/charles-keating-key-figure-in-the-1980s-savings-and-loan-crisis-dies-at-90.html?_r=0.

McLean, Bethany, and Peter Elkind. "The Guiltiest Guys in the Room." *Fortune,* July 5, 2006. Last accessed May 12, 2015. http://money.cnn.com/2006/05/29/news/enron_guiltyest/.

———. *The Smartest Guys in the Room: The Amazing Rise and Fall of Enron.* New York: Portfolio/Penguin Books, 2003.

Mead, Rebecca. *One Perfect Day: The Selling of the American Wedding.* New York: Penguin Books, 2007. Kindle.

Mérimée, Prosper. *Carmen and Other Stories.* Oxford: Oxford University Press, 1989.

Milgram, Stanley. *Obedience to Authority: An Experimental View.* New York: Harper & Row, 1974.

Miller, Jessica. "Ads Prove Grassley's Greener on His Side of the Ballot." *Waterloo–Cedar Falls Courier,* October 25, 2004. Accessed November 16, 2014. http://wcfcourier.com/news/metro/article_fdd73608-4f6d-54be-aa34 -28f3417273e9.html.

Miller, Stephen. "Income Subject to FICA Payroll Tax Increases in 2015." Society for Human Resource Management, October 23, 2014. Accessed January 16, 2015. http://www.shrm.org/hrdisciplines/compensation/ articles/pages/fica-social-security-tax-2015.aspx.

Mitford, Jessica. *The American Way of Death Revisited.* New York: Knopf, 1998. Kindle.

MoJo News Team. "Full Transcript of the Mitt Romney Secret Video." *Mother Jones,* September 19, 2012. Accessed December 1, 2014. http://www .motherjones.com/politics/2012/09/full-transcript-mitt-romney-secret -video.

Mongelli, Lorena. "The SEC Watchdog Who Missed Madoff." *New York Post,* January 7, 2009.

Moody's. "Moody's History: A Century of Market Leadership." Accessed November 9, 2014. https://www.moodys.com/Pages/atc001.aspx.

Morello, John A. *Selling the President, 1920: Albert D. Lasker, Advertising and the Election of Warren G. Harding.* Westport, CT: Praeger, 2001. Kindle.

Morgenson, Gretchen, and Joshua A. Rosner. *Reckless Endangerment: How Outsized Ambition, Greed, and Corruption Led to Economic Armageddon.* New York: Times Books/Henry Holt, 2011.

Morris, Sue. "Small Runs for Senate." *Le Mars Daily Sentinel,* March 24, 2004.

Moss, Michael. *Sugar, Salt and Fat.* New York: Random House, 2013. Kindle.

Mothers against Drunk Driving. "History and Mission Statement." Accessed March 28, 2015. http://www.madd.org.

———. "Voices of Victims." Accessed December 13, 2014. http://www.madd .org/drunk-driving/voices-of-victims/.

Mouawad, Jad, and Christopher Drew. "Airline Industry at Its Safest since the Dawn of the Jet Age." *New York Times,* February 11, 2013. http://www .nytimes.com/2013/02/12/business/2012-was-the-safest-year-for-airlines -globally-since-1945.html?pagewanted=all&_r=0.

Mozaffarian, Dariush, Tao Hao, Eric B. Rimm, Walter C. Willett, and Frank B. Hu. "Changes in Diet and Lifestyle and Long-Term Weight Gain in Women and Men." *New England Journal of Medicine* 364, no. 25 (June 23, 2011): 2392–2404. Accessed October 30, 2014. http://www.nejm.org/doi/ full/10.1056/NEJMoa1014296?query=TOC#t=articleTop.

Mukherjee, Siddhartha. *The Emperor of All Maladies: A Biography of Cancer.* New York: Simon and Schuster, 2011.

Mulligan, Thomas S. "Spiegel Found Not Guilty of Looting S & L." *Los Angeles Times,* December 13, 1994. Accessed May 1, 2015. http://articles.latimes .com/1994-12-13/news/mn-8437_1_thomas-spiegel.

Nader, Ralph. *Unsafe at Any Speed: The Designed-In Dangers of the American Automobile.* New York: Grossman, 1965.

Nash, Nathaniel C. "Savings Institution Milked by Its Chief, Regulators Say." *New York Times,* November 1, 1989.

National Association of Realtors. "Code of Ethics." Accessed March 15, 2015. http://www.realtor.org/governance/governing.

National Bureau of Economic Research. "U.S. Business Cycle Expansions and Contractions." Accessed January 13, 2015. http://www.nber.org/cycles.html.

National Consumers League. "Our Issues: Outrage! End Child Labor in American Tobacco Fields." November 14, 2014. Accessed March 15, 2015. http://www.nclnet.org/outrage_end_child_labor_in_american_tobacco_fields.

National Institutes of Health, National Institute on Alcohol Abuse and Alcoholism. *Alcohol Use and Alcohol Use Disorders in the United States: Main Findings from the 2001–2002 National Epidemiologic Survey on Alcohol and Related Conditions (NESARC).* January 2006. Accessed November 12, 2014. http://pubs.niaaa.nih.gov/publications/NESARC_DRM/NESARCDRM.pdf.

———. *Surveillance Report #95: Apparent Per Capita Ethanol Consumption, United States, 1850–2010.* August 2012. http://pubs.niaaa.nih.gov/publications/Surveillance95/CONS10.htm.

Nesi, Tom. *Poison Pills: The Untold Story of the Vioxx Scandal.* New York: Thomas Dunne Books, 2008.

Newhouse, Dave. *Old Bears: The Class of 1956 Reaches Its Fiftieth Reunion, Reflecting on the Happy Days and the Unhappy Days.* Berkeley: North Atlantic Books, 2007.

Newspaper Association of America. "The American Newspaper Media Industry Revenue Profile 2012." April 8, 2013. Accessed March 7, 2015. http://www.naa.org/trends-and-numbers/newspaper-revenue/newspaper-media-industry-revenue-profile-2012.aspx.

"A Nickel in the Slot." *Washington Post,* March 25, 1894.

"The 9 Steps to Financial Freedom." Accessed November 4, 2014. http://www.suzeorman.com/books-kits/books/the-9-steps-to-financial-freedom/.

Nixon, Richard M. "Remarks on Signing of the National Cancer Act of 1971." December 23, 1971. The American Presidency Project. Accessed January 17, 2015. http://www.presidency.ucsb.edu/ws/?pid=3275.

Nutt, David J., Leslie A. King, and Lawrence D. Phillips, on behalf of the Independent Scientific Committee on Drugs. "Drug Harms in the UK: A Multicriteria Decision Analysis." *Lancet* 376, no. 9752 (November 6–12, 2010): 1558–65.

Ogilvy, David. *Confessions of an Advertising Man.* New York: Atheneum, 1988.

———. *Ogilvy on Advertising.* New York: Random House/Vintage Books, 1985.

Oldie Lyrics. "Patti Page: How Much Is That Doggy in the Window?" Accessed November 5, 2014. http://www.oldielyrics.com/lyrics/patti_page/how_much_is_that_doggy_in_the_window.html.

Oreskes, Naomi, and Erik M. Conway. *Merchants of Doubt: How a Handful of Scientists Obscured the Truth on Issues from Tobacco Smoke to Global Warming.* New York: Bloomsbury, 2010.

Orman, Suze. *The 9 Steps to Financial Freedom: Practical and Spiritual Steps So You Can Stop Worrying.* 2nd paperback ed. New York: Crown/Random House, 2006.

O'Shea, James E. *The Daisy Chain: How Borrowed Billions Sank a Texas S & L.* New York: Pocket Books, 1991.

Owen, David. "The Pay Problem." *New Yorker,* October 12, 2009. Accessed March 12, 2015. http://www.newyorker.com/magazine/2009/10/12/the-pay-problem.

Oyez. "Citizens United v. Federal Election Commission." Accessed March 18, 2005. http://www.oyez.org/cases/2000-2009/2008/2008_08_205.

Packard, Vance. *The Hidden Persuaders: What Makes Us Buy, Believe—and Even Vote—the Way We Do.* Brooklyn: Ig Publishing, 2007. Original edition, New York: McKay, 1957.

Paltrow, Scot J. "Executive Life Seizure: The Costly Comeuppance of Fred Carr." *Los Angeles Times,* April 12, 1991. Accessed May 1, 2015. http://articles.latimes.com/1991-04-12/business/fi-342_1_executive-life.

Pareto, Vilfredo. *Manual of Political Economy: A Critical and Variorum Edition.* Edited by Aldo Montesano, Alberto Zanni, Luigino Bruni, John S. Chipman, and Michael McClure. Oxford: Oxford University Press, 2014.

"The Path to Prosperity." *Wikipedia.* Accessed December 15, 2014. http://en.wikipedia.org/wiki/The_Path_to_Prosperity.

Patterson, James T. *Restless Giant: The United States from Watergate to Bush v. Gore.* New York: Oxford University Press, 2005.

Patterson, Thom. "United Airlines Ends Coach Preboarding for Children." CNN, May 23, 2012. Accessed April 30, 2015. http://www.cnn.com/2012/05/23/travel/united-children-preboarding/.

Paulson, Henry M. *On the Brink: Inside the Race to Stop the Collapse of the Global Financial System.* New York: Business Plus, 2010.

Pear, Robert. "Bill to Let Medicare Negotiate Drug Prices Is Blocked." *New York Times,* April 18, 2007. Last accessed April 30, 2015. http://www.nytimes.com/2007/04/18/washington/18cnd-medicare.html?_r=0.

"The Personal Reminiscences of Albert Lasker." *American Heritage* 6, no. 1 (December 1954). Accessed May 21, 2015. http://www.americanheritage.com/content/personal-reminiscences-albert-lasker.

Piketty, Thomas. *Capital in the Twenty-First Century.* Cambridge, MA: Harvard University Press, 2014.

Pizzo, Stephen, Mary Fricker, and Paul Muolo. *Inside Job: The Looting of America's Savings and Loans.* New York: Harper Perennial, 1991.

"Poor Beer vs. Pure Beer." Advertisement reproduced in *Current Advertising* 12, no. 2 (August 1902): 31. Accessed June 13, 2015. https://books.google.com/books?id=Xo9RAAAAYAAJ&pg=RA1-PA31&lpg=RA1-PA31&dq=schlitz+beer+both+cost+you+alike,+yet+one+costs+the+maker+twice+as+much+as+the+other+one+is+good+and+good+for+you&source=bl&ots=5jCKe1yFqB&sig=-X5uwF5VqK6BicU4IzneHyNRMmU&hl=en&sa=X&ei

=1lp2VbPQEc6VyATjjoOYCA&ved=0CB4Q6AEwAA#v=onepage&q=schlitz
%20beer%20both%20cost%20you%20alike%2C%20yet%20one%20costs%
20the%20maker%20twice%20as%20much%20as%20the%20other%20one
%20is%20good%20and%20good%20for%20you&f=false.

Posner, Richard. "Theories of Economic Regulation." *Bell Journal of Economics and Management Science* 5, no. 2 (1974): 335–58.

"Predictions of the Year 2000 from *The Ladies Home Journal* of December 1900." Accessed December 1, 2014. yorktownhistory.org/wp-content/archives/homepages/1900_predictions.htm.

Prelec, Drazen, and Duncan Simester. "Always Leave Home without It: A Further Investigation." *Marketing Letters* 12, no. 1 (2001): 5–12.

"The Propaganda for Reform." *Journal of the American Medical Association* 61, no. 18 (November 1, 1913): 1648.

"Public Health Cigarette Smoking Act." *Wikipedia.* Accessed March 28, 2015. http://en.wikipedia.org/wiki/Public_Health_Cigarette_Smoking_Act.

Rajan, Raghuram. *Fault Lines: How Hidden Fractures Still Threaten the World Economy.* Princeton: Princeton University Press, 2010.

Rakoff, Jed S. "The Financial Crisis: Why Have No High-Level Executives Been Prosecuted?" *New York Review of Books,* January 9, 2014.

Ramey, Garey, and Valerie A. Ramey. "The Rug Rat Race." *Brookings Papers on Economic Activity* (Spring 2010): 129–99.

Raymond, Nate, and Jonathan Stempel. "Big Fine Imposed on Ex-Goldman Trader Tourre in SEC Case." Reuters, March 12, 2014. Accessed March 15, 2015. http://www.reuters.com/article/2014/03/12/us-goldmansachs -sec-tourre-idUSBREA2B11220140312.

Reinhardt, Carmen M., and Kenneth Rogoff. *This Time Is Different: Eight Centuries of Financial Folly.* Princeton: Princeton University Press, 2009.

Reyes, Sonia. "Ocean Spray Rides Diet Wave." *Adweek,* February 6, 2006. Accessed November 18, 2014. http://www.adweek.com/news/advertising/ocean-spray-rides-diet-wave-83901.

Richert, Lindley B. "One Man's Junk Is Another's Bonanza in the Bond Market." *Wall Street Journal,* March 27, 1975.

Ring, Dan. "Massachusetts Senate Approves State Sales Tax Increase to 6.25 Percent as Part of $1 Billion Tax Hike." *Republican,* May 20, 2009. Accessed December 13, 2014. http://www.masslive.com/news/index.ssf/2009/05/massachusetts_senate_approves.html.

"Ripoff." *Wikipedia.* Accessed November 13, 2014. http://en.wikipedia.org/wiki/Ripoff.

Roberts, Steven V. "House Votes Funds Permitting Study on MX to Continue." *New York Times,* December 9, 1982.

Roman, Kenneth. *The King of Madison Avenue: David Ogilvy and the Making of Modern Advertising.* New York: Macmillan, 2009.

Rosenbaum, David E. "The Supreme Court: News Analysis; Presidents May Disagree, but Justices Are Generally Loyal to Them." *New York Times,* April 7, 1994.

Ru, Hong, and Antoinette Schoar. "Do Credit Card Companies Screen for Behavioral Biases?" Working paper, National Bureau of Economic Research, 2015.

Samuelson, Paul A. "Consumption Theory in Terms of Revealed Preference." *Economica,* n.s., 15, no. 60 (November 1948): 243–53.

———. *Foundations of Economic Analysis.* Cambridge, MA: Harvard University Press, 1947.

Schank, Roger C., and Robert P. Abelson. *Scripts, Plans, Goals, and Understanding: An Inquiry into Human Knowledge Structures.* Hillsdale, NJ: L. Erlbaum Associates, 1977.

Schüll, Natasha Dow. *Addiction by Design: Machine Gambling in Las Vegas.* Princeton: Princeton University Press, 2012.

SCImago Journal and Country Rank. "Journal Rankings." Accessed November 26, 2014. http://www.scimagojr.com/journalrank.php?country=US.

Seelye, Katharine Q., and Jeff Zeleny. "On the Defensive, Obama Calls His Words Ill-Chosen." *New York Times,* April 13, 2008.

Shapiro, Carl. "Consumer Information, Product Quality, and Seller Reputation." *Bell Journal of Economics* 13, no. 1 (1982): 20–35.

Shiller, Robert J. "Do Stock Prices Move Too Much to Be Justified by Subsequent Changes in Dividends?" *American Economic Review* 71, no. 3 (June 1981): 421–36.

———. *Irrational Exuberance.* Princeton: Princeton University Press, 2000; 2nd ed., 2005; 3rd ed., 2015.

———. "Life-Cycle Personal Accounts Proposal for Social Security: An Evaluation of President Bush's Proposal." *Journal of Policy Modeling* 28, no. 4 (2006): 427–44.

———. *Subprime Solution: How Today's Global Financial Crisis Happened and What to Do about It.* Princeton: Princeton University Press, 2008.

Shleifer, Andrei, and Lawrence H. Summers. "Breach of Trust in Hostile Takeovers." In *Corporate Takeovers: Causes and Consequences,* edited by Alan J. Auerbach, pp. 33–68. Chicago: University of Chicago Press, 1988.

Shleifer, Andrei, and Robert W. Vishny. "The Takeover Wave of the 1980s." *Science* 249, no. 4970 (1990): 745–49.

Sidel, Robin. "Credit Card Issuers Are Charging Higher." *Wall Street Journal,* October 12, 2014.

Siegel, Jeremy J., and Richard H. Thaler. "Anomalies: The Equity Premium Puzzle." *Journal of Economic Perspectives* 11, no. 1 (Winter 1997): 191–200.

Sinclair, Upton. *The Jungle.* Mineola, NY: Dover Thrift Editions, 2001; originally published 1906.

———. Letter to the *New York Times.* May 6, 1906.

Singh, Gurkirpal. "Recent Considerations in Nonsteroidal Anti-Inflammatory Drug Gastropathy." *American Journal of Medicine* 105, no. 1, supp. 2 (July 27, 1998): 31S–38S.

Skeel, David A., Jr. "Shaming in Corporate Law." *University of Pennsylvania Law Review* 149, no. 6 (June 2001): 1811–68.

Smith, Adam. *The Wealth of Nations.* New York: P. F. Collier, 1909. Originally published 1776.

Smith, Gary. *Standard Deviations: Flawed Assumptions, Tortured Data, and Other Ways to Lie with Statistics.* New York: Duckworth Overlook, 2014.

Snell, George D. "Clarence D. Little, 1888–1971: A Biographical Memoir by George D. Snell." Washington, DC: National Academy of Sciences, 1971.

Social Security Perspectives. "President #6: Richard M. Nixon (1969–1974)." May 8, 2011. http://socialsecurityperspectives.blogspot.com/2011/05/president-6-richard-m-nixon-1969-1974.html.

Solow, Robert M. "Technical Change and the Aggregate Production Function." *Review of Economics and Statistics* 39, no. 3 (August 1957): 312–20.

Sorkin, Andrew Ross. *Too Big to Fail: The Inside Story of How Wall Street and Washington Fought to Save the Financial System.* New York: Viking, 2009.

Stahre, Mandy, Jim Roeber, Dafna Kanny, Robert D. Brewer, and Xingyou Zhang. "Contribution of Excessive Alcohol Consumption to Deaths and Years of Potential Life Lost in the United States." *Preventing Chronic Disease* 11 (2014). Accessed March 28, 2014. http://www.cdc.gov/pcd/issues/2014/13_0293.htm.

"Statistics of the Presidential and Congressional Election of November 2, 2004." June 7, 2005. Accessed November 16, 2014. http://clerk.house.gov/member_info/electionInfo/2004election.pdf.

Stein, Benjamin. *A License to Steal: The Untold Story of Michael Milken and the Conspiracy to Bilk the Nation.* New York: Simon and Schuster, 1992.

Stern, Mark Joseph. "The FDA's New Cigarette Labels Go Up in Smoke." *Wall Street Journal,* September 9, 2012. Accessed March 28, 2015. http://www.wsj.com/articles/SB10000872396390443819404577633580009556096.

Stewart, James B. *Den of Thieves.* New York: Simon and Schuster, 1992.

———. "How They Failed to Catch Madoff," *Fortune,* May 10, 2011. Accessed May 2, 2015. http://fortune.com/2011/05/10/how-they-failed-to-catch-madoff/.

Stigler, George J. "The Theory of Economic Regulation." *Bell Journal of Economics and Management Science* 2, no. 1 (1971): 3–21.

Stock, James H., and Mark W. Watson. "Forecasting Output and Inflation: The Role of Asset Prices." *Journal of Economic Literature* 41 (2003): 788–829.

Stulz, René M. "Credit Default Swaps and the Credit Crisis." *Journal of Economic Perspectives* 24, no. 1 (Winter 2010): 73–92.

Sufrin, Carolyn B., and Joseph S. Ross. "Pharmaceutical Industry Marketing: Understanding Its Impact on Women's Health." *Obstetrical and Gynecological Survey* 63, no. 9 (2008): 585–96.

Tabarrok, Alex. "The Real Estate Commission Puzzle." April 12, 2013. Accessed December 1, 2014. http://marginalrevolution.com/marginalrevolution/2013/04/the-real-estate-commission-puzzle.html.

Tett, Gillian. *Fool's Gold: How the Bold Dream of a Small Tribe at J. P. Morgan Was Corrupted by Wall Street Greed.* New York: Free Press, 2009.

Thomas, Michael M. "Rated by Idiots." *Forbes,* September 16, 2008.

Thorberg, Fred Arne, and Michael Lyvers. "Attachment, Fear of Intimacy and Differentiation of Self among Clients in Substance Disorder Treatment Facilities." *Addictive Behaviors* 31, no. 4 (April 2006): 732–37.

Thoreau, Henry David. *Walden: Or, Life in the Woods.* New York: Houghton Mifflin, 1910. https://books.google.com/books/about/Walden.html?id=HVIXAAAAYAAJ.

Time Magazine. "Clarence Cook Little": Cover Story, April 22, 1937.

"Tobacco Advertising." *Wikipedia.* Accessed December 8, 2014. http://en
.wikipedia.org/wiki/Tobacco_advertising.

Tobacco Labelling Resource Center. "Australia: Health Warnings, 2012 to
Present." Accessed March 28, 2015. http://www.tobaccolabels.ca/
countries/australia/.

Tobias, Ronald B. *Twenty Master Plots: And How to Build Them.* 2nd paperback ed. Blue Ash, OH: F + W Media, 1993.

"Today Is Moving Day for Goldman Sachs." *New York Times,* April 1, 1957.

Toobin, Jeffrey. "Annals of Law: Money Unlimited: How Chief Justice John Roberts Orchestrated the Citizens United Decision." *New Yorker,* May 21, 2012.

Topol, Eric J. "Failing the Public Health—Rofecoxib, Merck, and the FDA."
New England Journal of Medicine 351, no. 17 (October 21, 2004): 1707–9.

"Top Ten U.S. Banking Laws of the 20th Century." Accessed December 1,
2014. http://www.oswego.edu/~dighe/topten.htm.

Touryalai, Halah. "10 Wall Street Expenses That Make the SEC's Budget Look Pathetic." *Forbes,* February 17, 2011. Accessed January 16, 2015.
http://www.forbes.com/fdc/welcome_mjx.shtml.

Tozzi, John. "Merchants Seek Lower Credit Card Interchange Fees."
Businessweek Archives, October 6, 2009. Accessed May 2, 2015.
http://www.bloomberg.com/bw/stories/2009-10-06/merchants-seek-lower
-credit-card-interchange-fees.

Troise, Frank P. "The Capacity for Experiencing Intimacy in Wives of Alcoholics or Codependents." *Alcohol Treatment Quarterly* 9, no. 3 (October
2008): 39–55.

Underhill, Paco. *Why We Buy: The Science of Shopping.* New York: Simon and
Schuster, 1999.

Underwriters Laboratories. "Our History" and "What We Do." Accessed
March 3, 2015. http://ul.com/aboutul/history/ and http://ul.com/
aboutul/what-we-do/.

United Airlines. "Arriving at a Single Boarding Process." April 22, 2013.
Accessed November 26, 2014. https://hub.united.com/en-us/news/
company-operations/pages/arriving-at-a-single-boarding-process.aspx.

Urban Institute and the Brookings Institution, Tax Policy Center. "State
Alcohol Excise Tax Rates 2014." Accessed December 13, 2014. http://www
.taxpolicycenter.org/taxfacts/displayafact.cfm?Docid=349.

US Bureau of Financial Protection. "Loan Originator Compensation
Requirements under the Truth in Lending Act" (Regulation Z), 12 CFR
Part 1026, Docket No. CFPB—2012-0037, RIN 3170-AA132. Accessed
November 11, 2014. http://files.consumerfinance.gov/f/201301_cfpb_final
-rule_loan-originator-compensation.pdf.

US Census Bureau. "America's Families and Living Arrangements: 2013."
Accessed December 1, 2014. https://www.census.gov/hhes/families/data/
cps2013.html.

———. "Census Bureau Reports National Mover Rate Increases after a
Record Low in 2011." December 10, 2012. Accessed December 1, 2014.
https://www.census.gov/newsroom/releases/archives/mobility_of_the_
population/cb12-240.html.

US Census Bureau. "Historical Census of Housing Tables." October 31, 2011. Accessed December 1, 2014. https://www.census.gov/hhes/www/housing/census/historic/units.html.

———. "Historical Poverty Tables—People." Table 3, "Poverty Status, by Age, Race, and Hispanic Origin: 1959 to 2013." Accessed December 1, 2014. https://www.census.gov/hhes/www/poverty/data/historical/people.html.

———. "Housing Vacancies and Homeownership, 2005." Accessed December 1, 2014. http://www.census.gov/housing/hvs/data/ann05ind.html.

———. *Statistical Abstracts of the United States, 2012.* Accessed December 1, 2014. https://www.census.gov/prod/www/statistical_abstract.html.

———. "World Population by Age and Sex." Accessed December 1, 2014. http://www.census.gov/cgi-bin/broker.

US Congress, Representative Henry A. Waxman. Memorandum to Democratic Members of the Government Reform Committee Re: The Marketing of Vioxx to Physicians, May 5, 2005, with accompanying documents. http://oversight-archive.waxman.house.gov/documents/20050505114932-41272.pdf.

US Department of Agriculture, Farm Service Administration. "Commodity Operations: United States Warehouse Act." Accessed March 14, 2015. http://www.fsa.usda.gov/FSA/webapp?area=home&subject=coop&topic=was-ua.

US Department of Agriculture, Grain Inspection, Packing, and Stockyard Administration. "Explanatory Notes," table 5, "Inspection and Weighing Program Overview." Accessed May 1, 2015. http://www.obpa.usda.gov/exnotes/FY2014/20gipsa2014notes.pdf.

———. "Subpart M—United States Standards for Wheat." Accessed May 1, 2015. http://www.gipsa.usda.gov/fgis/standards/810wheat.pdf.

US Department of Transportation, National Highway Traffic Safety Administration. "Traffic Safety Facts, 2011: Alcohol Impaired Driving." December 2012. Accessed May 25, 2015. http://www-nrd.nhtsa.dot.gov/Pubs/811700.pdf.

US Department of the Treasury, Alcohol and Tobacco Tax and Trade Bureau, "Tax and Fee Rates." Accessed April 30, 2015. www.ttb.govtax_audit/atftaxes.shtml.

US Department of the Treasury. "Investment in AIG." Accessed March 11, 2015. http://www.treasury.gov/initiatives/financial-stability/TARP-Programs/aig/Pages/status.aspx.

US Food and Drug Administration. "About FDA: Commissioner's Page. Harvey Washington Wiley, MD." http://www.fda.gov/AboutFDA/CommissionersPage/ucm113692.htm.

———. "Tobacco Products: Final Rule 'Required Warnings for Cigarette Packages and Advertisements.'" Accessed March 28, 2015. http://www.fda.gov/TobaccoProducts/Labeling/Labeling/CigaretteWarningLabels/ucm259953.htm.

US Food and Drug Administration, Center for Drug Evaluation and Research (CDER). *Guidance for Industry Providing Clinical Evidence of Effectiveness for Human Drugs and Biological Products.* May 1998. Accessed December 1, 2014. http://www.fda.gov/downloads/Drugs/.../Guidances/ucm078749.pdf.

US Internal Revenue Service. "Tax Gap for Tax Year 2006: Overview." January 6, 2012. Accessed November 18, 2014. http://www.irs.gov/pub/irs-soi/06rastg12overvw.pdf.

US Legal Inc. "U.S. Commercial Code." Accessed March 15, 2015. http://uniformcommercialcode.uslegal.com/.

US News and World Report. "U.S. News College Rankings." http://colleges.usnews.rankingsandreviews.com/best-colleges.

US Securities and Exchange Commission. *FY 2014 Congressional Budget Justification.* http://www.sec.gov/about/reports/secfy14congbudgjust.pdf.

———."Goldman Sachs to Pay Record $550 Million to Settle SEC Charges Related to Subprime Mortgage CDO." July 15, 2010. Accessed March 15, 2015. http://www.sec.gov/news/press/2010/2010-123.htm.

US Senate, Committee on Homeland Security and Government Affairs, Permanent Subcommittee on Investigations. *Wall Street and the Financial Crisis: Anatomy of a Financial Collapse.* Majority and Minority Staff Report. April 13, 2011. http://www.hsgac.senate.gov//imo/media/doc/Financial_Crisis/FinancialCrisisReport.pdf?attempt=2.

US Surgeon General. *The Health Consequences of Smoking—50 Years of Progress.* 2014. Accessed March 6, 2015. http://www.surgeongeneral.gov/library/reports/50-years-of-progress/full-report.pdf.

———. *Smoking and Health: Report of the Advisory Committee to the Surgeon General of the Public Health Service.* 1964. Accessed November 28, 2014. http://www.surgeongeneral.gov/library/reports/.

———. *Smoking and Health: A Report of the Surgeon General.* 1979. Accessed November 28, 2014. http://www.surgeongeneral.gov/library/reports/.

Vaillant, George E. *Triumphs of Experience: The Men of the Harvard Grant Study.* Cambridge, MA: Harvard University Press, 2012.

van Amsterdam, Jan, A. Opperhuizen, M. Koeter, and Willem van den Brink. "Ranking the Harm of Alcohol, Tobacco and Illicit Drugs for the Individual and the Population." *European Addiction Research* 16 (2010): 202–7. DOI:10.1159/000317249.

Vanguard. "See the Difference Low-Cost Mutual Funds Can Make." Accessed January 7, 2015. https://investor.vanguard.com/mutual-funds/low-cost.

Veblen, Thorstein. *The Theory of the Leisure Class: An Economic Study of the Evolution of Institutions.* New York: Macmillan, 1899.

Velotta, Richard N. "Gaming Commission Rejects Slot Machines at Cash Registers." *Las Vegas Sun,* March 18, 2010. Last accessed May 12, 2015. http://lasvegassun.com/news/2010/mar/18/gaming-commission-rejects-slot-machines-cash-regis/?utm_source=twitterfeed&utm_medium=twitter.

Virtanen, Michael. "NY Attorney General Looks at Ratings Agencies." Associated Press, February 8, 2013. Accessed March 21, 2014. http://bigstory.ap.org/article/ny-attorney-general-looks-ratings-agencies-0.

Visser, Susanna N., Melissa L. Danielson, Rebecca H. Bitsko, Joseph R. Holbrook, Michael D. Kogan, Reem M. Ghandour, Ruth Perou, and Stephen J. Blumberg. "Trends in the Parent-Report of Health Care Provider-Diagnosed and Medicated Attention-Deficit/Hyperactivity Disorder: United States, 2003–2011." *Journal of the American Academy of Child and Adolescent Psychiatry* 53, no. 1 (January 2014): 34–46.

Warren, Carolyn. *Mortgage Rip-offs and Money Savers: An Industry Insider Explains How to Save Thousands on Your Mortgage and Re-Finance.* Hoboken, NJ: Wiley, 2007.

Warren, Elizabeth, and Amelia Warren Tyagi. *All Your Worth: The Ultimate Lifetime Money Plan.* New York: Simon and Schuster, 2005.

Watkins, John Elfreth, Jr. "What May Happen in the Next Hundred Years." *Ladies Home Journal,* December 1900. https://secure.flickr.com/photos/jonbrown17/2571144135/sizes/o/in/photostream/.

Watkins, Julian Lewis. *The 100 Greatest Advertisements, 1852–1958: Who Wrote Them and What They Did.* Chelmsford, MA: Courier, 2012.

Wessel, David. *In Fed We Trust: Ben Bernanke's War on the Great Panic.* New York: Crown Business, 2009.

White, Michelle J. "Bankruptcy Reform and Credit Cards." *Journal of Economic Perspectives* 21, no. 4 (Fall 2007): 175–200.

Wiley, Harvey W. *An Autobiography.* Indianapolis: Bobbs-Merrill, 1930.

Woodward, Susan E. *A Study of Closing Costs for FHA Mortgages.* Prepared for US Department of Housing and Urban Development, Office of Policy Development and Research, May 2008. http://www.urban.org/UploadedPDF/411682_fha_mortgages.pdf.

Woodward, Susan E., and Robert E. Hall. "Consumer Confusion in the Mortgage Market: Evidence of Less Than a Perfectly Transparent and Competitive Market." *American Economic Review* 100, no. 2 (May 2010): 511–15.

World Bank. "GDP Per Capita (Current US$)." Accessed November 26, 2014. http://data.worldbank.org/indicator/NY.GDP.PCAP.CD.

———. "Life Expectancy at Birth, Female (Years)." Accessed March 29, 2015. http://data.worldbank.org/indicator/SP.DYN.LE00.FE.IN/countries.

———. "Life Expectancy at Birth, Male (Years)." Accessed March 29, 2015. http://data.worldbank.org/indicator/SP.DYN.LE00.MA.IN/countries.

Wu, Ke Bin. "Sources of Income for Older Americans, 2012." Washington, DC: AARP Public Policy Institute, December 2013.

Wyatt, Edward. "Judge Blocks Citigroup Settlement With S.E.C." *New York Times,* November 28, 2011. Accessed June 10, 2015. http://www.nytimes.com/2011/11/29/business/judge-rejects-sec-accord-with-citi.html?pagewanted=all.

Wynder, Ernst L., and Evarts A. Graham. "Tobacco Smoking as a Possible Etiologic Factor in Bronchogenic Carcinoma Study of Six Hundred and Eighty-Four Proved Cases." *Journal of the American Medical Association* 143, no. 4 (May 27, 1950): 329–36.

Wynder, Ernst L., Evarts A. Graham, and Adele B. Croninger. "Experimental Production of Carcinoma with Cigarette Tar." *Cancer Research* 13, no. 12 (1953): 855–64.

Young, James Harvey. *The Toadstool Millionaires: A Social History of Patent Medicines in America before Federal Regulation.* Princeton: Princeton University Press, 1961.

Zacks Equity Research. "Strong U.S. Auto Sales for 2013." January 6, 2014. Accessed December 1, 2014. http://www.zacks.com/stock/news/118754/strong-us-auto-sales-for-2013.

Abramson, John, 183n26, 208n13, 208n15, 210n45
ACA Capital Management, 143
Addams, Jane, 140
addictions: gambling, ix; Internet, 150, 227n1. *See also* alcohol; tobacco
ADHD. *See* attention-deficit hyperactivity disorder
Adrian, Tobias, 190n3
advertising: alcohol, 110; anti-smoking, 108; cat food, 167–68; expenditures, 195–96n7; goals of, 53, 195n4; history of, 47–54; measuring effectiveness of, 51, 53–54; online, 54, 195–96n7; political, 54–57, 73, 74, 75; psychological manipulation in, 7; "reason why," 48, 49, 53; statistical methods in, 45, 53, 56–57; storytelling in, 46–48, 49–53, 74, 197n34; targeted, 54, 56–57; tobacco, 103, 105, 108, 184n31, 216n27; trial and error in, 52, 53–54. *See also* marketing
Agarwal, Sumit, 231n12
Age of Reform, 151–52
AIG Financial Products, 38–40
airlines: customer rankings of, 100–101, 102, 213n10; Malaysian Airlines Flight 370, 57–59; safety of, 136
AJCA. *See* American Jobs Creation Act
Akerlof, George A., 117, 194n3, 219n1, 220n3, 220nn10–13, 220n15, 220n17, 221n22

alcohol: abuse and dependence, xv–xvi, 109–10, 111–14; advertising, 110; consumption rates of, 116; driving under influence of, 112, 115–16; easy availability of, xvi, 116; effects on lives, 111–14; health risks of, xv–xvi, 109–11, 114; industry interests, 114, 115; legal drinking age, 115; moderate use of, 103; psychological effects of, 111, 113; research on, 114; taxes on, 114–15
Alessi, Christopher, 192n26
Aleve (naproxen), 86–87, 88, 92
Alexander, Raquel Meyer, 81, 206nn37–38
Alito, Samuel, 160
Altman, Edward, 130
American International Group (AIG), 38–40
American Jobs Creation Act (AJCA), 81
American National Standards Institute, 138–39
Anders, George, 221n5
Annear, Steve, 213n9
Ansolabehere, Stephen, 77, 205nn21–22
Armour, J. Ogden, 207n2
Armstrong, Gary, 195n4
Arnold, Dan, 122
Arrow, Kenneth J., 186n18
Arthur, Anthony, 207n1
Aspin, Leslie, 78, 79, 80, 205n24
Asquith, Paul, 130–31, 222n21, 222n23, 223n24

asset-backed securities, 24–25. *See also* mortgage-backed securities

asset prices: bubbles in, xiv, 134; fundamental values and, 168; irrational exuberance and, 134; volatility of, 133–34, 168. *See also* housing markets; stocks

Astra Zeneca, 211n53

attention-deficit hyperactivity disorder (ADHD), 93–94

Auerbach, Oscar, 104–5, 215n13

Austen, Jane, *Pride and Prejudice*, 46, 195n6

automobile dealers: financing by, 62–63; phishing by, 60–63; service profits of, 63

automobile industry, federal bailouts of, 75–76

automobiles: driving under the influence, 112, 115–16; safety of, 136, 142

avocados analogy, 23, 24–25, 34

Ayres, Ian, 60–62, 198nn3–6, 198n8

Bachenheimer, Doria, 158

Baer, Justin, 226n38

Bank of America, 157

bankruptcies: corporate, 27–28, 35–36; court roles in, 118; credit card debt and, 70; personal, 18–19, 70, 188–89n10; of savings and loans, 117, 119–20

banks: bailouts of, 75–76, 204–5n16; failures of, 29, 164–65; mortgage business of, 32. *See also* financial industry; investment banks

Banks, Emily, 183n26

Banzhaf, John, 108

Bardi, Jason, 216n26

Barenstein, Matias F., 188n7, 201n25

Bar-Gill, Oren, 189n19

Bauer-Ramazani, Christine, 226n42

BBBs. *See* Better Business Bureaus

Beatrice International Food Company, 129

behavioral economics, 6, 169–72

Bekelman, Justin E., 208n16

Bell, Laurence, 203n5

Beral, Valerie, 183n26

Bernanke, Ben, 185n3

Bernhardt, Joshua, 226n41

Bernheim, B. Douglas, 214–15n1

Bernstein, Marver H., 144, 226n43

Bero, Lisa A., 208n16

Berry, Tim, 202n36

Bertrand, Marianne, 205n27

Better Business Bureaus (BBBs), 141

Bezemer, Dirk J., 230n2

bezzles, xiv, 156–57

biases: cognitive, xi; general, 172; in lobbying, 79; psychological, 7, 149, 150, 167, 170, 186–87n26

Biden, Joseph, 79

Big Data, 54, 56–57, 197n38

Big Tobacco, 105–6, 107–8, 109. *See also* tobacco

Bipartisan Campaign Reform Act (McCain-Feingold), 159–60

Birnbaum, Josh, 35

Bissell, Melville, 49

Bissell Carpet Sweeping Company, 48–49

Bizet, Georges, *Carmen*, 102

B. J. Johnson Soap Company, 50

Black, Duncan, 204n10

Blanes i Vidal, Jordi, 205n27

Blinder, Alan S., 187–88n2, 189n1, 190n4, 204–5n16

Block, Jerald J., 227n1

Boccara, Bruno, 228n5

Boesky, Ivan, 131–32

Bokhari, Sheharyar, 183n21

Bombardier, Claire, 88, 89, 92, 208–9nn18–22, 210n44

Bombardini, Matilde, 205n27

bond ratings, 23–24, 27–28, 125. *See also* credit ratings agencies

bonds, junk. *See* junk bonds

Bonsack, James, 102

Bosworth, Steven, 194–95n3

Bounds, Gwendolyn, 224n15

Boyd, Roddy, 189–90n1, 193n40, 193nn46–47

Brandt, Allan M., 214n20, 215n3, 215n7, 215nn9-10, 216nn16-17, 216nn20-22, 217nn28-31
Bray, Chad, 226n38
Brennan, William J., Jr., 227n3
Britain: consumer spending in, 18; Guardians, 140-41; lung cancer research in, 104
British Medical Journal, 104
Brown, Steve, 221nn23-26
Bruck, Connie, 222n20, 222n22, 223n25, 223nn31-32
Bruner, Jerome, 194n3
Bryan, William Jennings, 151
Buffett, Warren, 129
Buhler, Victoria, 68
Buick, 142
Bull, Diana, 183n26
Burnham, Tubby, 126
Burrough, Bryan, 221nn1-2, 222n14
Bush, George H. W., vii, 80, 119
Bush, George W., 73, 155-56
businesses. *See* corporations
business heroes, xii, 140-41
Butler, Jeffrey Vincent, 214n11
Buxmann, Peter, 212-13n8

California Fruit Growers Exchange, 51
Calomiris, Charles W., 192n30
campaign contributions: in congressional elections, 72, 73-74, 77, 78; by corporations, 159-62; by lobbyists, 77; by political action committees, 72, 77, 81, 159; reform proposals, 162; regulation of, 159-60; by special interests, 75, 77, 78, 80-83. *See also* politics
Campbell, John Y., 231-32n14
cancer: breast, xiv, 93; genetic causes of, 106, 109, 165-66; lung, 104-5, 107-8; war on, 166
capital, 97, 212nn5-6
capuchin monkeys, 4-5
Carbone, Danielle, 193n39
Cardozo, Benjamin N., 142, 145-46, 227n49

Carmen (Bizet), 102
Carpenter, Daniel, 145, 226-27nn46-48
Carr, Fred, 128, 129, 222n18
Carville, James, vii
casinos. *See* gambling
Cassano, Joseph, 38-39, 40
Cassidy, Gerry, 80, 81, 206n42
cat food advertising, 167-68
caveat emptor/caveat venditor, 142, 143
CDSs. *See* credit default swaps
Celebrex, 89, 209n27
Center for Responsive Politics, 95
Centers for Disease Control, 109, 110, 156
CenTrust, 128
CEO compensation, 124, 133, 221n3
Chambers of Commerce, 141
Chase, Stuart, 137-38, 139, 223-24nn5-6
Chast, Roz, 101, 102
Chen, M. Keith, 4, 185n13, 185n15
Cheung, Meaghan, 158
Chrysler, 75-76
Chu, Jenny, 221n3
Cialdini, Robert B., 7, 149, 150, 172, 186nn22-24, 186-87n26
cigarette-rolling machines, 102, 103-4
cigarettes. *See* tobacco
Cinnabon Inc., 2-3, 9, 171
Citicorp, 157, 204-5n16, 229n18
Citizens United decision, 79, 160-62
Clark, Otavio, 208n16
Clarke, Sally H., 225nn27-28
Clifford, Catherine, 191n22
Clinton, Hillary, 160
cognitive biases, xi
Cohan, William D., 30, 189-90n1, 192n25, 193nn33-35
Cole, Robert J., 222n20
Collier, Paul, 194-95n3
Columbia Savings and Loan, 128, 129
commercial law, 141-43
Commodity Futures Modernization Act of 2000, 8

Congress: fundraising by members of, 73–74, 77, 78–79, 162; legislation, 75–77, 79–80; lobbying, 77–82, 81–82, 94–95, 206n38, 206–7n42; savings and loan crisis and, 120. *See also* House of Representatives; Senate

Congressional Budget Office, 73, 156

Connaughton, Jeff, 206nn30–32

Consumer Federation of America, 139

Consumer Reports, 139

consumers: activism of, 139–40; bankruptcies of, 18–19, 70, 188–89n10; complaints of, 140–41; financial worries of, xiii, 17–20, 182–83n19; organizations of, 139; savings of, 18, 20, 119, 153–54, 188n6. *See also* credit cards

consumer spending: advertising and, 52–53; budgeting, xiii, 153; with credit cards, 17, 21, 67–69; decisions on, xiii, 16–17, 52, 140, 172; economic theory of, xii, 16, 170–71, 187–88n2; emotions and, 17, 21; Orman on, 15–17, 21, 153; revealed preferences, 170–71, 232n20; shrouded attributes and, 167–68, 169–70; temptations in free markets, 20–22

Consumers Union, 139

contracts, 142–43

Conway, Erik M., 216n16

Cook, Philip J., 114, 218nn56–59

corporate takeovers. *See* leveraged buyouts

corporations: bankruptcies of, 27–28, 35–36; campaign contributions by, 159–62; CEO compensation, 124, 133, 221n3; free speech rights of, 160–61; multinational, 81; shareholder activists, 141

Cowan, Alison Leigh, 223n34

cranberry juice labeling, 81

credit cards: costs of, 69–71, 197n38, 202n34; interchange fees on, 68, 69–71; interest rates on, 17, 69, 71; as magic pills, 67–69; marketing of, 197n38; phishing and, 70–71; temptations to spend with, 17, 21, 67–69

credit default swaps (CDSs), 37–40, 165

credit ratings agencies: history of, 27; mortgage-backed securities and, 24–25, 32–35, 36–37, 192nn28–30; regulation of, 37, 192n28; relations with investment banks, 30–31, 32–34, 37, 192nn26–27; reputation mining by, 23–25. *See also* bond ratings

crime, white-collar, 79. *See also* fraud

Croninger, Adele B., 104, 105, 215n12

Crossley, Michele L., 194n3

Cruikshank, Jeffrey L., 196n8, 196nn10–13, 196nn19–21, 196nn23–24, 197n26, 215n14

Crystal, Graef S., 124, 221n3

Cuomo, Andrew, 37

Curfman, Gregory D., 208–9n21, 209n23, 210n43

Curtis, Cyrus, 49

Dallas real estate market, 121, 122, 221n22

Debreu, Gerald, 186n18

Debs, Eugene, 47

debt: alternative forms of, 18; auto loans, 62–63. *See also* credit cards; mortgages

DeConcini, Dennis, 207n44

de Figueiredo, John M., 77, 205nn20–22, 206–7n42

DeForge, Jeanette, 219n62

DellaVigna, Stefano, 3, 167, 169, 185n7, 185nn9–12, 231n7

De Long, J. Bradford, 232n15, 232nn17–18

democracy: competitive elections in, 74–75; informed vs. uninformed voters, xvi, 74–77; money in politics and, xvi, 73–74, 82–83

de Palma, Dominic, 191n13

Department of Agriculture, 85, 138

Department of Justice, 79, 82

Depository Institutions Deregulation and Monetary Control Act of 1980, 120

derivatives: credit default swaps, 37–40, 165; designing, 31–33; regulation of, 157. *See also* mortgage-backed securities

Desmond, Matthew, 18, 189n11

Djulbegovic, Benjamin, 208n16

doctors, 87, 90, 92–93, 95, 104

Dodd-Frank Act of 2010, 37, 65

Doll, Richard, 104, 105, 215n11

Downs, Anthony, 74, 75, 204n10

Draca, Mirko, 205n27

Drazen, Jeffrey M., 208–9n21, 209n23, 210n43

Drew, Christopher, 223n3

Drexel Burnham Lambert, 126–32, 222n14

Driscoll, John C., 231n12

drugs. *See* food and drug regulations; pharmaceutical industry

Dubner, Stephen J., 185n14

Duca, John V., 200n14

Dvořák, Antonín, New World Symphony, 96, 98

Eaglesham, Jean, 226n38

economic growth: innovation and, 96–99; standard theory of, 96–97

economics textbooks: consumer choice theory, 16, 187–88n2; prices of, 95

economic theory of regulation, 144

Edison, Thomas, 45

Educational Testing Service (ETS), 101–2

Eichenwald, Kurt, 182n13, 223n27

Eisenhower, Dwight D., 151, 227n3

elections. *See* campaign contributions; politics; voters

electrical appliances, 138–39

Elkind, Peter, 182nn13–14

Ellis, Charles, 190n5, 191nn8–12, 191nn14–16, 192nn23–24, 193n37

Elsevier, 87

Emergency Economic Stabilization Act of 2008, 75–76, 204n14

emotions, consumer spending and, 17, 21

The Emperor of All Maladies (Mukherjee), 165–66

Empire Savings and Loan, 121

Enron, xi

Environmental Protection Agency, 152

equilibrium. *See* markets; phishing equilibrium

equity premium, 127

Esokait, Albert, 191n13

ethics codes, 141

ETS. *See* Educational Testing Service

eugenics, 106

European Central Bank, 25

Eve, 1, 184–85n1

eviction rates, 18–19, 189n11

externalities, 5, 150, 163, 164, 165, 166

Eyster, Eric, 186n25

Faasse, Jonathan, 221n3

Facebook, 99–100, 150

Farrell, Greg, 189–90n1

Farrell, Jason, 206n38

Faubus, Orval, 151

FCC. *See* Federal Communications Commission

FDA. *See* Food and Drug Administration

FDIC. *See* Federal Deposit Insurance Corporation

Federal Communications Commission (FCC), 108

Federal Deposit Insurance Corporation (FDIC), 29, 128–29, 132, 144

Federal Election Commission, 159, 160. *See also* Citizens United decision

Federal Elections Campaign Act Amendments of 1974, 159

Federal Home Loan Bank Board, 82, 120

Federal Meat Inspection Act of 1906, 84

Federal Reserve, 25, 39, 118–19, 134

Federal Savings and Loan Insurance Corporation (FSLIC), 119, 120

Feinberg, Richard A., 67–68, 70, 201n23, 201nn26–27

Felsenfeld, Carl, 220n16

FERA. *See* Fraud Enforcement and Recovery Act

financial advisors, 153. *See also* Orman, Suze

financial crises: phishing as cause of, xiii–xiv; predicting, 165; responses to, 134–35; stories told in, xiii–xiv

Financial Crisis of 2008: asset price bubbles and, xiv, 33–34, 134; bank failures in, 29, 164–65; credit default swaps and, 39–40; economists' failure to predict, 164–65, 170, 230n2; fraud preceding, 79; government bailouts in, 25, 75–76, 134, 204–5n16; myths in, 36–37; reputation mining in, 23–25, 31–33; similarities to savings and loan crisis, 123

financial industry: complex products of, 8, 24–25, 31–33; deregulation of, 120; phishing in, 8; regulation of, 8, 81–82, 132, 156–59. *See also* banks; investment banks; savings and loan crisis

financial markets: informed vs. uninformed traders, 8, 168; Social Security privatization and, 155; stocks, 127, 134, 168; volatility in, 133–34, 168. *See also* asset prices; derivatives; junk bonds; securities regulation; stocks

First Amendment, 160

First Executive Life Insurance, 128, 129

FitzGerald, Garret A., 88–89, 208n11, 209nn25–26

focus, manipulation of, 32, 149–50

Fons-Rosen, Christian, 205n27

food: safety of, 84–86; unhealthy, xv, 86, 94. *See also* food and drug regulations; supermarkets

Food and Drug Administration (FDA): cranberry juice labeling, 81; drug regulation by, 86, 90, 94; drug trials, xiv, 87, 91–92, 145; founding of, 137

food and drug regulations: history of, 84–86, 145; labeling, 81; new drug trials, xiv, 87–88, 90, 91–92, 145; quality standards, 137–38

fools. *See* phools

Ford Motor Company, 26–27

Fortune, xi, 86

Fowler, Mayhill, 205n26

Fox, Stephen R., 196n22, 197n33

frames. *See* stories

Frank, Robert H., 185n3

fraud, xi, 79, 157–59. *See also* phishing

Fraud Enforcement and Recovery Act (FERA), 79–80, 82

free markets: benefits of, ix, x, xi–xii, 163; consumer temptations in, 20–22; conventional wisdom on, 150, 151, 163, 164, 166; innovation and, x, xi–xii; negative side of, ix–x, 150; New-Story thinking on, 152–53; pressures for phishing in, vii–viii, xi–xii; vulnerability to phishing in, x, 5–6, 9, 163–66. *See also* markets

free speech, 160–61

Freifeld, Karen, 226n40

Freud, Sigmund, 1, 7

Freudenheim, Milt, 211n52

Fricker, Mary, 121, 207n43, 221nn20–21, 221n27

Friedman, Milton, 6, 186n20

Friedman, Rose D., 6, 186n20

FSLIC. *See* Federal Savings and Loan Insurance Corporation

Fugh-Berman, Adriane, 210n48

Gabaix, Xavier, 167, 169–70, 231n8, 231nn10–12, 232n19

Galbraith, John Kenneth, xiv, 156–57, 183n23, 230n1

Gallup, George, 52, 53

Galveston Times, 47
gambling, viii–ix, x
Garn-St. Germain Act of 1982, 120
gender, of auto buyers, 60–61
General Dynamics, 80–81
General Motors, 75–76
Gerardi, Kristopher, 192n29
Gerson, Elliot, 206n29
Gilbert, R. Alton, 220n14
GIPSA. *See* Grain Inspection, Packing, and Stockyard Administration
Glass, David L., 220n16
GlaxoSmithKline, 92
Glickman, Lawrence B., 224nn13–14, 224n17, 224n19
Goldacre, Ben, 208n17, 210n47, 211n53
Goldberger, Paul, 28, 191n20
Goldman, Marcus, 30, 32
Goldman Sachs: ABACUS case, 143; capital of, 26; changes at, 28, 29–30; credit default swaps and, 39; headquarters of, 28; principles of, 27, 30; short sales of mortgage-backed securities by, 35; TARP funds received by, 204–5n16; underwriting by, 26–28
Goodeman, Anthony, 224nn8–9
government: heroes in, 141–45; Reagan on, 152, 228n6; roles in markets, 151–57, 163. *See also* Congress; politics; regulatory agencies; Supreme Court
Graham, David J., 90, 183n25, 209–10n37, 210n40
Graham, Evarts A., 104, 105, 215n8, 215n10, 215n12
Grain Inspection, Packing, and Stockyard Administration (GIPSA), 138
Grant, Bob, 208n17
Grant, Bridget F., 217n37
Grassley, Charles, xvi, 72–73, 74
Great Crash of 1929, 134
Great Depression, 134
Great Recession, xiv, 73, 134, 137, 203n5

Griffin, Keith, 198n2
Gross, Cary P., 208n16
Grossman, Gene M., 204n12
Grossman, Sanford J., 222n19
Guardians (Society for the Protection of Trade against Swindlers and Sharpers), 140–41
Gurman, Jesse, 200n15

Hahn, Robert W., 200n15
Hall, Robert E., 65–66, 200nn18–19, 231n9, 231n11
Hamill, Dorothy, 89
Han, Song, 197n38
Hanson, Jon, 230n1
Harding, Warren, 54–55
Harper, Christine, 226n37
Harper, Sean, 70, 202n35
Hart, Oliver D., 222n19
Harvard Grant Study, 110–12, 218n40, 218n47
Hathaway shirt ads, 52, 54
Healey, James R., 204n13
health care. *See* doctors; Medicaid; Medicare; pharmaceutical industry
health clubs, 3, 167, 169
health risks: of alcohol, xv–xvi, 109–11, 114; from quack remedies, 84–85; of tobacco, xv, 103–8, 109, 217n36; from unhealthy eating, xv, 94. *See also* cancer; food and drug regulations
Healy, David, 210n41
Helpman, Elhanan, 204n12
Helyar, John, 221n1, 222n14
Hennessey, Ray, 228n6
Herbst, Moira, 223n30
heroes: in business, xii, 140–41; consumer organizations, 139–40; in government, 141–45; quality standards enforcers, 137–39, 140; in regulatory agencies, 144–45, 226–27n48; resistance to phishing, viii, 136–37, 145–46; shareholder activists, 141
Hewlett-Packard printers, 167

Hickman, W. Braddock, *Corporate Bond Quality and Investor Experience*, 125, 126, 127, 130, 221n4, 222n10

Hidden Persuaders (Packard), 7, 53–54

high-yield bonds. *See* junk bonds

Hill, A. Bradford, 104, 105, 215n11

Hill and Knowlton, 105, 106

Hillary: The Movie, 160

Hindo, Brian, 223n30

Hirschman, Elizabeth C., 201n24

Hochschild, Arlie Russell, 189n16

Hoeflich, M. H., 225nn25–26

Hofstadter, Richard, 227n2

holdup problem, 129–30

Hopkins, Claude, 48–51, 53, 196nn15–18, 197n25, 197n35

hormone replacement therapy (HRT), xiv, 93, 183–84n26

Horowitz, Joseph, 212n7

Horrigan, Edward, 124

House Hunters, 64

House of Representatives: Appropriations Committee, 206–7n42; Committee on Government Reform, 90; Financial Services Committee, 82. *See also* Congress

house purchases: closing costs of, 64, 65, 183n21, 200n16; down payments on, 65, 200n14; phishing in, 64–66; real estate fees for, 64–65, 200n13, 200n15; stories of, 64; transaction costs of, xiii, 64–65, 183n21. *See also* mortgages

housing: developers of, 121; duration of stays in, 64, 199–200n11; eviction rates, 18–19, 189n11; homeownership rates, 64, 154

housing markets: bubbles in, 33–34; savings and loan crisis and, 119

Houston real estate market, 121

"How Much Is That Doggie in the Window," 20–21, 46, 195n5

HRT. *See* hormone replacement therapy

Huffman, David, 188n7

Humboldt University, 100

Icahn, Carl, 128

identity economics, 194–95n3

income distribution, 133, 150, 163, 164

incomes: growth of, 19–20, 21; from Social Security, 154

IndyMac Bank, 29

inflation, 118–19

information: informed vs. uninformed traders, 8, 168; informed vs. uninformed voters, xvi, 74–77; misleading, xi, 7–8; phishing, xi, 75, 137

innovation: economic growth and, 96–99; free markets and, x, xi–xii; predictions of, x; slot machines, viii

institutional investors, 29–30, 127, 143

interest rates: on credit cards, 17, 69, 71; Federal Reserve policy on, 118–19; on mortgages, 119; on savings deposits, 120, 220n14

Internal Revenue Service (IRS), 82

International Monetary Fund, xv

Internet: addiction to, 150, 227n1; advertising on, 54, 195–96n7; Facebook, 99–100, 150; phishing on, x–xi, 150

Interstate Commerce Commission, 144

investment banks: borrowing by, 24–25; changes in industry of, 26, 28–30; overnight financing by, 28–29, 35, 36; relations with ratings agencies, 30–31, 32–34, 37, 192nn26–27; reputation mining by, 31–33; reputations of, 27; syndicates of, 27; trustworthiness of, 26–28, 30. *See also* Goldman Sachs; junk bonds

Iowa Senate campaign, xvi, 72–73, 74

irrational exuberance, 134

IRS. *See* Internal Revenue Service

Isidore, Chris, 191n22

Issenberg, Sasha, 198nn42–44

Jensen, Michael C., 131, 223n28
Johnson, Lyndon B., 151
Johnson, Ross, 124, 221n2
Johnson, Simon, 220n4
Johnson and Johnson, 89
Journal of the American Medical Association, 48, 104
The Jungle (Sinclair), 84, 140, 207nn2–3
junk bonds: default rates of, 130–31; exchange offers, 130–31; fallen angels, 126, 130; market for, 126–27, 131; performance of, 125–26, 127; phishing using, 126, 128–31, 132–33; savings and loans and, 128, 129, 132; use in leveraged buyouts, 124, 127–29, 130, 131

Kahneman, Daniel, 1, 182n12, 185n2, 186–87n26
Kaiser, Robert G., 205n23, 206nn34–36, 206nn39–40
Kaiser Permanente, 90, 209–10n37
Kaplan, Greg, 188n6
Kaufman, Ted, 79–80
Keating, Charles, 81–82, 128, 129, 222n18
Kelley, Florence, 140, 224n18
Kelly, Kate, 189–90n1
Kennedy, Anthony, 160–61
Kennedy, John F., 107, 151
Kessler, Glen, 203n4
Keynes, John Maynard, 19–20, 21, 189nn12–15
Keys, Benjamin, 197n38
King, Leslie A., 184nn32–33
Koeter, M., 184n32
Komen, Greg, 2–3, 9
Komen, Rich, 2–3, 9
Kornbluth, Jesse, 222n9, 222n14
Kotler, Philip, 195n4
Kotz, David, 229n25, 229nn27–29
Kovacevich, Richard, 204–5n16
Kranton, Rachel, 194n3
Krasnova, Hanna, 212–13n8
Krugman, Paul, 185n3, 228n16
Kysar, Douglas, 230n1

Laibson, David, 167, 169–70, 231n8, 231nn10–12, 232n19
Laidlaw v. Organ, 141–42, 225n26
Lakshminarayanan, Venkat, 4, 185n13, 185n15
La Porta, Rafael, 220n4
Lasker, Albert, 47–48, 49–51, 53, 54–55, 105
Lasker, Morris, 47
Lehman Brothers, 39
Lehnert, Andreas, 192n29
leisure time, 19–20
Lemann, Nicholas, 101, 214nn12–13
Lessig, Lawrence, 162, 204n12, 230nn38–39
Leuchtenburg, William E., 227n2
leveraged buyouts, 124, 127–30, 131, 133
Levitt, Steven D., 70, 185n14
Levy, Gus, 29–30
Lewis, Michael, 34–35, 189–90n1, 193n32
Lexchin, Joel, 208n16
Li, Diana, 62–63
Li, Gong, 197n38
Li, Yan, 208n16
Lieber, Ron, 202n34
life expectancies, 136
Lightner, Candace, 115
Lincoln Savings and Loan, 81–82, 128, 129
Linkins, Jason, 207n46
liquor. *See* alcohol
Litan, Robert E., 200n15
Little, Clarence, 105–6, 109
loans, automobile, 62–63. *See also* debt; mortgages
lobbyists: former members of Congress as, 79; influence of, 80–82, 83, 206n38, 206–7n42; number of, 77; for pharmaceutical industry, 94–95; roles of, 77–80, 144
Locke, John, 126, 221n7
López de Silanes, Florencio, 220n4
Lord and Thomas, 47, 49–51
Los Angeles Times, viii
Loungani, Prakash, 203n5

lung cancer, 104–5, 107–8
Lupia, Arthur, 204n12
Lusardi, Annamaria, 17–18, 188n5
Lyvers, Michael, 218n47

MacPherson, Donald, 142
MacPherson v. Buick Motor Car Company, 142
MADD (Mothers against Drunk Driving), 115–16
Maddison, Angus, 189n13, 212n4
Madoff, Bernard, 157–59
Mafia, 122
magic tricks, 8, 149–50, 186n25
Malamud, Bernard, 181n3
Malaysian Airlines Flight 370, 57–59
Malmendier, Ulrike, 3, 167, 169, 185nn9–12, 231n7
Mankiw, N. Gregory, 95, 187–88n2
marketing: brands, 51; of credit cards, 197n38; by pharmaceutical industry, 87–90, 92–94, 211n53; promotions, 49, 51; storytelling in, 46. *See also* advertising
markets: equilibrium, x, 1, 5–6, 163, 169, 171, 186n18; government roles in, 151–57, 163. *See also* free markets
Markopolos, Harry, 157–59, 229n22, 229n24, 229n29
Marlay, Matthew, 199n11
Marshall, John, 142, 225n26
Martin, Andrew, 202n34
Massachusetts, alcohol taxes in, 115
Mateyka, Peter, 199n11
Mather and Crowther, 52
Maynard, Micheline, 193n36
Mazza, Stephen W., 81, 206nn37–38
McCain-Feingold Act, 159–60
McCubbins, Matthew D., 204n12
McDonald, Lawrence G., 189–90n1
McDuff, Daniel, 100
McFadden, Robert D., 222n18
McLean, Bethany, 182nn13–14
Mead, Rebecca, 182n16
media. *See* advertising; news media
Medicaid, 228n16
medical journals, 87–88, 92–93

Medicare: benefits of, 154; drug coverage in, 95, 211n52; establishment of, 151, 152; privatization proposal, 156, 228n16
medicine. *See* doctors; pharmaceutical industry
Menlo-Atherton High School graduates, 112–13
mental frames. *See* stories
Merck, 86, 87–90, 92, 94, 145, 209n25
Mérimée, Prosper, 214n19
Milgram, Stanley, 186–87n26
Milken, Michael: career of, 125, 126; compensation of, 131, 223n27; downfall of, 131–32; High-Yield Bond Conferences, 131; junk bond market and, 125–27, 130–31, 132–33; leveraged buyouts, 124, 127–30; phishing by, 126, 128–31, 132–33
Miller, Jessica, 203n7
Miller, Stephen, 228n8
Minow, Nell, 141
Mitchell, Constance, 221n5
Mitford, Jessica, 182n17
Mongelli, Lorena, 229n30
monkey-on-the-shoulder tastes, 4–5, 6, 20, 54, 59, 170–71, 172
Moody's, 27–28, 31, 34, 191n13, 192n28, 192n30. *See also* credit ratings agencies
moral community, 145–46
moral hazard, 134
Morello, John A., 197nn39–41
Morgenson, Gretchen, 189–90n1
Morris, Robert, 100
Morris, Sue, 203n3
Morrissey, Stephen, 208–9n21, 209n23, 210n43
mortgage-backed securities: in ABACUS, 143; credit default swaps and, 38–40; credit ratings of, 24–25, 32–35, 36–37, 192nn28–30; default risk of, 33, 35, 36–37, 38, 143, 165; development of, 32; short selling, 34–35, 143; subprime

loans in, xiv, 32–33, 36, 192n30;
    tranches of, 33
mortgage brokers, 65–66, 201n20
mortgages: fees of, 65, 200n16,
    201n20; interest payments on,
    201n32; interest rates on, 119;
    subprime, xiv, 32–33, 36, 192n30.
    See also house purchases
Moss, David A., 145, 226–27nn46–48
Moss, Michael, 184n29, 208n10
Mothers against Drunk Driving
    (MADD), 115–16
Mouawad, Jad, 223n3
Mozaffarian, Dariush, 184n28
Muellbauer, John, 200n14
Mukherjee, Siddhartha, *The
    Emperor of All Maladies*, 165–66,
    231n4, 231n6
Mulligan, Thomas S., 222n18
Mullins, David W., Jr., 131, 222n21,
    222n23, 223n24
Muolo, Paul, 121, 207n43, 221nn20–
    21, 221n27
Murphy, Anthony, 200n14
Murrow, Edward R., 106

Nader, Ralph, 136, 223n2
Nammacher, Scott, 130
naproxen (Aleve), 86–87, 88, 92
narrative psychology, 194–95n3
narratives. *See* stories
Nash, Nathaniel C., 207n45
National Association of Realtors, 141
National Bureau of Standards,
    137–38
National Cancer Act of 1971, 166
National Consumers League, 140
National Epidemiologic Survey on
    Alcohol and Related Conditions
    (NESARC), 110, 113
National Institute of Alcohol Abuse
    and Alcoholism, 110
National Real Estate Investor News,
    122
NESARC. *See* National Epidemi-
    ologic Survey on Alcohol and
    Related Conditions

Nesi, Tom, 208nn13–14, 209nn24–
    25, 209nn27–29, 209n35, 210n38,
    210n42, 210n46
Nevada, gambling in, viii–ix
New England Journal of Medicine,
    87–88, 90
Newhouse, Dave, *Old Bears*, 112–13,
    218nn49–54
news media: reporting on govern-
    ment, 152–53; storytelling in,
    57–59, 106
New-Story thinking, 152–53, 154–56,
    159, 160–62
New Yorker, 52, 101
Nexium, 211n53
Nixon, Richard M., 151–52, 231n5
noise traders, 168
NO-ONE-COULD-POSSIBLY-
    WANTs, xii–xvi
nuclear submarines, 80–81
Nutt, David J., xv, 184nn32–33

Obama, Barack, 55–57, 78
Ocean Spray, 81
Ogilvy, David, 51–52, 53, 54, 105,
    197n27, 197nn29–32, 197n34,
    197nn36–37
Ogilvy and Mather, 52
older people: Social Security, 152,
    153–56; vulnerability to phishing,
    231n12. *See also* Medicare
Old-Story economics, 151–52, 153–54
OPIC. *See* Texas Office of Public
    Insurance Counsel
Opperhuizen, A., 184n32
oranges, Sunkist, 51, 53
Oreskes, Naomi, 216n16
Organ, Hector, 141–42
Orman, Suze, 15–17, 21, 153, 187n1,
    188n3
O'Shea, James E., 220nn18–19
overweight individuals, xv, 94
Owen, David, 225n22
Oxford English Dictionary, x–xi
OxyContin, 210n45

Packard, Vance, *Hidden Persuaders*,
    7, 53–54, 186n21, 186n26

PACs. *See* political action committees

Palmolive soap, 50

Paltrow, Scott J., 222n18

Panel Study of Income Dynamics, 70

Pantry Pride, 129–30

Pareto, Vilfredo, 185n17

Pareto optimality, 5, 74, 171, 186n18

Patterson, James T., 228n6

Patterson, Thom, 214n18

Paul, David, 128

Paulson, Henry M., 76, 189–90n1, 190n4, 204–5n16

Paulson, John, 143, 193n33

Pavlov Poke, 100

Pear, Robert, 211n52

Penn Central, 27–28

Pennsylvania Railroad, 130

Perelman, Ronald, 129–30

personal financial insecurity, xiii, 17–20, 182–83n19

Pfizer, 89, 209n27

pharmaceutical industry: arthritis drugs, 86–90; drug prices, 94–95; lobbyists, 94–95; marketing by, 87–90, 92–94, 211n53; medical education, 90, 93; patents of, 211n53; phishing by, 87–95; quack remedies, xiv, 84–85. *See also* food and drug regulations; Vioxx

Phillips, Lawrence D., 184nn32–33

Phillips Petroleum, 128

phishing: asset price volatility and, 133–34; broader meaning of, xi; consequences of, xii–xvi; economic scholarship on, 164–65, 166–70; by focus manipulation, 32, 149–50; as general phenomenon, 170, 171, 173; information, xi, 75, 137; on Internet, x–xi, 150; legal protections, 141–43; psychological, 6–8, 146; resistance to, viii, xii, 136–37, 145–46; stories in, xiii–xiv, 10, 149, 162, 172–73; theory of mind used in, 98; trial and error in, 54; vulnerability to, x, 7, 163–66

phishing equilibrium: of Big Tobacco, 109; economic pressures for, vii–viii, xi–xii, 1–2; in economics, 163–73; in financial markets, 24, 37, 135; finger exercises, 2–5; in free markets, x, 5–6, 9; of news media, 58–59; in politics, xvi, 74, 75, 82–83, 159, 161–62; savings and loan crisis, 117–18

phood industry, 86, 94. *See also* food

phools: bad decisions by, 1, 6–7; definition of, xi; information, xi, 75; psychological, xi, 75; voters as, 75; vulnerability of, 7, 163–64

pickpockets, 149–50

Piketty, Thomas, 223n35

Pinkham, Daniel, xiv

Pizzo, Stephen, 121, 207n43, 221nn20–21, 221n27

Pogue, Mark, 122

political action committees (PACs), 72, 77, 81, 159

politics: advertising, 54–57, 73, 74, 75; costs of campaigns, 73–74, 205n22; equilibria in, 74–75; money's role in, xvi, 73–74, 78–82, 159–62; phishing in, xvi, 74, 75, 82–83, 159, 161–62; presidential campaigns, 54–57, 78; Senate campaigns, xvi, 72–73, 74; special-interest groups in, 75, 77; stories in, 74, 78, 79. *See also* campaign contributions

Ponzi schemes, 157–59

Posner, Richard A., 226n44

poverty rates, 154

Pozsar, Zoltan, 191n21

Predators' Ball, 131

Prelec, Drazen, 68, 70, 201n28

presidential campaigns, 54–57, 78. *See also* campaign contributions; politics

Pride and Prejudice (Austen), 46

Prilosec, 211n53

printers, inkjet, 167

product quality. *See* quality standards

psychological phishing, 6–8, 146

psychology: biases, 7, 149, 150, 167, 170, 186–87n26; causes of alcoholism, 111; decision making, 1, 6–7; mental frames, 10; of phools, xi, 75; theory of mind, 98
Pure Food and Drug Act of 1906, 84, 85, 94

quality standards, 137–39, 140

race, of auto buyers, 60–61
Race Betterment Congress, 106
Radam, William, 85
Rajan, Raghuram, 189–90n1
Rakoff, Jed S., 157, 229n21
Ramey, Garey, 102, 214n14
Ramey, Valerie A., 102, 214n14
Rangel, Antonio, 214–15n1
rankings, 100–102, 214n11, 214nn15–17
ratings agencies. See credit ratings agencies
Rau, P. Raghavendra, 221n3
Raymond, Nate, 226n39
Reagan, Ronald, 152, 228n6
real estate markets, savings and loan crisis and, 119, 121, 122. See also housing
Reeves, Gillian, 183n26
regulation: of campaign financing, 159–60; of credit ratings agencies, 37, 192n28; deregulation, 120; economic theory of, 144; of financial industry, 8, 81–82, 132, 156–59; of gambling, viii–ix. See also food and drug regulations
regulatory agencies: capture of, 144–45, 226–27n48; crisis response by, 134–35; failures of, 157–59; financial, 81–82, 119–20, 128, 143, 156–59; heroes in, 144–45, 226–27n48; lobbying of, 83, 144; political pressures on, 81–82; quality standards of, 137–39; underfunding of, 82, 157
Reid, Harry, 181n4
Reinhardt, Carmen M., 183n22

repos (repurchase agreements), 28–29, 36
reputation mining, 23–25, 31–35
Resolution Trust Corporation, 128, 132
restaurants, 67, 114, 167, 201n23
retailers: credit card acceptance by, 68–69; credit card interchange fees, 68, 69–71; marketing promotions at, 49; price markups of, 66–67. See also supermarkets
revealed preferences, 170–71, 232n20
Revlon, 129–30
Reyes, Sonia, 206n41
Richert, Lindley B., 221n6
Ring, Dan, 219n62
Ritalin, 93–94
RJR Nabisco, 124, 222n14
Roberts, John, 160
Roberts, Steven V., 205n24
Robinson, Patrick, 189–90n1
Roche, 89
Rogoff, Kenneth, 183n22
Rolls-Royce, 52, 60
Roman, Kenneth, 197n28, 216n15
Romer, Paul M., 117, 219n1, 220n3, 220nn10–13, 220n15, 220n17, 221n22
Romney, Mitt, 56, 78
Roosevelt, Franklin Delano, 151
Roosevelt, Theodore, 151
Rosenbaum, David E., 227n3
Rosenthal, Frank, 181n4
Rosner, Joshua A., 189–90n1
Ross, Joseph S., 209n30
Rothschild's Department Store, 49
Ru, Hong, 197n38
Ryan, Paul, 156, 228n16

S&Ls. See savings and loan crisis
Samuelson, Paul, 232n20
Santos, Laurie R., 4, 185n13, 185n15
SAT. See Scholastic Aptitude Test
savings, 18, 20, 119, 153–54, 188n6
savings and loan crisis: accounting, 117, 120, 121; bankruptcies, 117, 119–20; beginning of, 118–19;

savings and loan crisis (*continued*)
effects of, 117, 119, 121–22; federal
responses to, 81–82, 119–20; junk
bonds and, 128, 129, 132; looting and, 118, 120–22; phishing in,
81–82, 117–18, 120–22; similarities
to 2008 crisis, 123

Scalia, Antonin, 160

Schank, Roger C., 194n2

Schlink, Frederick J., 137–38, 139,
223–24nn5–6

Schlitz Beer, 49, 50, 53

Schneider, Daniel, 17–18, 188n5

Schoar, Antoinette, 197n38

Scholastic Aptitude Test (SAT),
101–2

Scholz, Susan, 81, 206nn37–38

Schüll, Natasha Dow, ix, 181nn5–6,
181nn8–9

Schultz, Arthur W., 196n8, 196nn10–
13, 196nn19–21, 196nn23–24,
197n26, 215n14

Schwarcz, Daniel, 226–27n48

Searle, 87, 89, 209n27

Seawolf nuclear submarines, 80–81

Securities and Exchange Commission (SEC): failures of, 157–59,
192n28; investigations by, 143, 157;
Madoff case and, 157–59; regulations of, 132; underfunding of,
82, 157

securities industry. *See* financial
industry; investment banks; junk
bonds

securities ratings, 23–25, 27–28, 31,
32–35, 36. *See also* credit ratings
agencies

securities regulation, 132, 156–59

Senate: Appropriations Committee,
206–7n42; Finance Committee,
73; Grassley-Small campaign, xvi,
72–73, 74. *See also* Congress

Sergie, Mohammed Aly, 192n26

Shapiro, Carl, 24, 190n2

shareholder activists, 141

Sherlund, Shane M., 192n29

Shiller, Robert J., 189–90n1, 194n3,
228nn13–15, 230–31n2, 231–32n14

Shin, Hyun Song, 190n3

Shleifer, Andrei, 220n4, 223n29,
223n36, 232n15, 232nn17–18

shopping. *See* consumer spending;
retailers; supermarkets

shrouded attributes, 167–68, 169–70

Sidel, Robin, 201n31, 202n34

Siegel, Jeremy J., 222n11

Siegelman, Peter, 60–62, 198nn3–6

Silverman, Brian, 206–7n42

Simester, Duncan, 68, 70, 201n28

Sinclair, Upton, *The Jungle*, 84, 140,
207nn2–3

Singer, Tania, 194–95n3

Singh, Gurkirpal, 208n12

Skeel, David A., Jr., 225nn22–23

slot machines, viii–ix, x

Small, Art, III, 72

Small, Art, Jr., 72–73, 74

Smith, Adam, 5, 6, 169, 185n16,
186n18

Smith, Gary, 126, 221n8

smoking. *See* tobacco

Snower, Dennis J., 194–95n3

Snyder, James M., 77, 205nn21–22

Social Security, 152, 153–56

Solow, Robert M., 97, 212n6

Solow residual, 97–99

Sorkin, Andrew Ross, 189–90n1

Spiegel, Thomas, 128, 129, 222n18

Stahre, Mindy, 217–18n38

standards, quality, 137–38, 140

Stein, Benjamin, 222n13, 222n17

Stempel, Jonathan, 226n39

Stern, Mark Joseph, 216n26

Stevens, John Paul, 161

Stewart, James B., 222n13, 223n26,
229n26

Stigler, George J., 226nn44–45

Stock, James H., 219n2

stocks: crash of 1929, 134; equity
premium, 127; informed vs. uninformed traders, 168; initial public offerings, 26–27; prices of, xiv,
168. *See also* securities regulation

Storer Communications, 129
stories: in advertising, 46–48, 49–53, 74, 197n34; on drunk drivers, 115–16; in financial bubbles, xiii–xiv; on government roles, 151–53; on health risks of tobacco, 105–6, 109; of house hunters, 64; in human thinking, 10, 45–46, 186–87n26, 194–95n3; on junk bonds, 132–33; mysteries, 58; news, 57–59, 106; New-Story thinking, 152–53, 154–56, 159, 160–62; in phishing, xiii–xiv, 10, 149, 162, 172–73; in politics, 74, 78, 79; in speculative bubbles, 194n3; as variable, 173
story grafting, 10, 46, 53, 74, 105, 149, 172–73
Stowe, Harriet Beecher, 84
Stulz, René M., 193nn50–51
subprime mortgages, xiv, 32–33, 36, 192n30
Sufrin, Carolyn B., 209n30
Suh, Simona, 158, 229n29
Summers, Lawrence H., 223n29, 232n15, 232nn17–18
Sunkist oranges, 51, 53
supermarkets: checkout lanes in, 1, 9; credit card fees paid by, 70; gross margins of, 202n36; product marketing in, 21
Supreme Court: Citizens United decision, 79, 160–62; Eisenhower's appointments to, 151, 227n3; *Laidlaw v. Organ*, 141–42, 225n26; school desegregation, 151
Surgeon General's Report (1964), 106–7, 108, 109
Swagel, Phillip, 76, 204n15
Swaim, William, 84–85
swaps. *See* credit default swaps
Swearingen, Wayne, 122
Swift, Louis, 49
Swift and Company, 49

Tabarrok, Alex, 200n15
TARP. *See* Troubled Asset Relief Program

tastes, monkey-on-the-shoulder, 4–5, 6, 20, 54, 59, 170–71, 172
taxes: on alcohol, 114–15; cuts in, 73, 203n5; on foreign earnings of corporations, 81; uncollected, 82
technical innovation. *See* innovation
television news. *See* news media
Terry, Luther, 107
Tett, Gillian, 189–90n1
Texas Office of Public Insurance Counsel (OPIC), 226–27n48
Texas Strategy, 121
textbooks: economics, 16, 95, 187–88n2; prices of, 95; used, 211n53
Thaler, Richard H., 222n11
theory of mind, 98
Thomas, Clarence, 160
Thomas, Michael M., 191n13
Thorberg, Fred Arne, 218n47
Thoreau, Henry David, xii, 182n15
thrifts. *See* savings and loan crisis
Tillman Act of 1907, 159
TIRC. *See* Tobacco Institute Research Committee
tobacco: advertising, 103, 105, 108, 184n31, 216n27; cigarettes introduced, 103–4; easy availability of, 116; health risks of, xv, 103–8, 109, 217n36; industry-funded research on, 105–6, 109; smoking bans, xv, 108; smoking rates, 104, 108–9, 184n30, 217n35; Surgeon General's Report on, 106–7, 108, 109
Tobacco Institute Research Committee (TIRC), 105–6
Tobias, Ronald B., 58, 198n45
Toobin, Jeffrey, 229–30nn31–33
Topol, Eric J., 90, 209n34, 209n36, 210n39
Torous, Walter, 183n21
Tourré, Fabrice, 143
Touryalai, Halah, 229n18
Tovar Jalles, João, 203n5
Tozzi, John, 202n34
transaction costs, of house purchases, xiii, 64–65, 183n21

Trebbi, Francesco, 205n27
Troise, Frank P., 218n47
Troubled Asset Relief Program (TARP), 76, 204–5n16
Truth in Lending Act of 1968, 68–69
Tufano, Peter, 17–18, 188n5
Tversky, Amos, 182n12
Tyagi, Amelia Warren, 153, 228n7

UL. *See* Underwriters Laboratories
Underhill, Paco, 189n18
Underwriters Laboratories (UL), 138–39
Uniform Commercial Code, 142–43
United Airlines, 35–36, 100–101, 102, 213n10
university earmarks, lobbying for, 206–7n42
University of Pennsylvania Health System, 88–89
university students: Facebook use, 99–100; SAT scores of, 101–2

Vaillant, George E., 110–11, 112, 113, 218nn39–48
van Amsterdam, Jan, xv–xvi, 184n32
van den Brink, Willem, xv–xvi, 184n32
Veblen, Thorstein, 230n1
Velotta, Richard N., 181n4
VIGOR (the Vioxx Gastrointestinal Outcomes Research study), 87–88, 89–90, 91, 92, 208–9n21
Villagra, Teodora, 15
Violante, Giovanni, 188n6
Vioxx, xiv, 87–90, 91, 92, 94, 183n25, 208–9n21, 209–10n37
Virtanen, Michael, t193n38
Vishny, Robert W., 223n36
Visser, Susanna N., 211n50
Volcker, Paul, 118
voters: informed vs. uninformed, xvi, 74–77; median, 74, 75. *See also* politics

Waldmann, Robert J., 232n15, 232nn17–18
Wall Street Journal, 125
Warren, Carolyn, 66, 201n21
Warren, Earl, 151, 227n3
Warren, Elizabeth, 21, 153, 189n19, 228n7
Watkins, John Elfreth, Jr., x, 181n10
Watkins, Julian Lewis, 184n31
Watson, Mark W., 219n2
Waxman, Henry A., 209nn31–33
wedding expenses, xiii, 16, 182n16
Weidner, Justin, 188n6
Weinberg, Sidney, 26–27, 29, 36
Wells, Robin, 185n3
Wells Fargo, 204–5n16
Wenninger, Helena, 212–13n8
Wessel, David, 189–90n1
wheat, grading of, 138
Wheaton, William, 183n21
Where's Waldo, 76
White, Michelle J., 70, 202n37–39
Whitehead, John, 27, 30
Widjaja, Thomas, 212–13n8
Wiley, Harvey Washington, 85, 137, 208nn8–9, 223n4
Willen, Paul, 192n29
Williams, McDonald, 122
Wilson, George H., 48
Wilson, Woodrow, 55
Wilson Ear Drum Company, 47–48
Wolff, Eric D., 131, 222n21, 222n23, 223n24
Wolverson, Roya, 192n26
Woodward, Susan E., 65–66, 200n12, 200n16, 200nn18–19
Wu, Ke Bin, 228nn10–11
Wyatt, Edward, 229n20
Wynder, Ernst L., 104, 105, 106, 215n8, 215n12

Yale University, 99–100
Young, James Harvey, 183n24, 207–8nn4–7